Centennial History of the University of Nebraska

II. The Modern University, 1920–1969

Centennial History of the University of Nebraska

II. The Modern University, 1920–1969

by

R. McLaran Sawyer

CENTENNIAL PRESS · LINCOLN, NEBRASKA

ISBN   0–8220–1605–2

Library of Congress Catalog Card Number: 73–84799

PRINTED IN THE UNITED STATES OF AMERICA

Centennial Press is a division of
Cliff's Notes, Inc., Box 80728, Lincoln, Nebraska, 68501.

To all those who contributed, in whatever capacity, to elevate the University to greatness but who have not been recognized by name in the book, this history is respectfully dedicated.

Contents

Preface

THIS HISTORY of the University of Nebraska covers its second half-century of life. During these years the institution enjoyed its greatest period of growth and development. The task of the educational historian is to explain the development of formal and informal educational institutions to those of the present and future. Consequently, this is an interpretive history of the University of Nebraska. No attempt has been made to chronicle all the myriad events of a half-century.

The chapters have been organized by decades with a separate treatment for administration, academic development, and student life. In keeping with the interpretive nature of this history, facts, names, and occurrences which do not materially contribute to the interpretation have not been included. It is unfortunate that many, within and without the institution, who devoted their energies in support of the University of Nebraska cannot be included by name. However, the support of these thousands was given unselfishly and oftentimes in the spirit of anonymity. To further increase the readability of the book, the title of doctor has not been included in references to members of the faculty or administration. It can be assumed by the reader that nearly all of the faculty and administrators mentioned held the terminal or highest professional degree in their respective disciplines.

To the world outside the academic community, and to a degree even within it, there is often a lack of agreement regarding the purpose of a university in society. While it has often been said that the land-grant university ideal bloomed in the soil of the Midwest, it was not without its periods of drought. While many citizens have regarded the individual academic man as part of a monolithic group, the professorial ranks have been often deeply and fundamentally divided in basic educational philosophy. These philosophical differences combined with the realities of securing public funding and support have produced conflict. During times of economic depression, these conflicts have been especially evident. Occasionally what is stated as educationally based policies are the result of factors unrelated to any educational philosophy, being rather a reflection of economic or political tension. Furthermore, the history of every state-supported university is an inseparable part of the ethos of that state. Popularly accepted concepts of the mass culture as reflected in the action of governors, legislatures, and boards of control set nearly all the parameters for the development of a university. For Nebraska to have produced a Harvard or a University of Wisconsin is as unlikely as for either Massachusetts or Wisconsin to have produced the University of Nebraska.

The author gratefully acknowledges the assistance and criticism of many colleagues. The treatment of the College of Agriculture from 1920 to 1960 benefited from the assistance of Dean Emeritus Marvel L. Baker. The sections

concerning Cornhusker athletics were written by Donald Bryant, sports information director, with editing by the author. George T. Bastian, executive vice
president of the Alumni Association, offered many useful suggestions regarding
student life. The account of academics during the sixties was written with the
advice of Dean Robert D. Gibson, of the College of Pharmacy; Richard G.
Guilford, director of the Graduate School of Social Work; Dean Emeritus
Walter K. Beggs, of the Teachers College; Terry Barton, director of public rela-
tions at the Medical Center; Executive Vice President Merk Hobson; Dean
Charles S. Miller, of the College of Business Administration; Regents Professor
Walter F. Wright, of the College of Arts and Sciences; Emanuel Wishnow,
director of the School of Music; Neal Copple, director of the School of Journalism;
Professor Donald L. Shaneyfelt, of the College of Law; Dean Emeritus Ralph L.
Ireland, of the College of Dentistry; Dean Howard W. Ottoson, of the College of
Agriculture; and C. Bertrand Schultz, Regents Professor and director of the
State Museum.

Joseph G. Svoboda, the University archivist, provided assistance with the
University's historical materials. James E. Potter, archivist at the Nebraska
State Historical Society, and Mrs. Jolene Smith, the society's newspaper librarian,
were helpful in the use of historical materials in their care.

Erwin H. Goldenstein and Royce H. Knapp, my colleagues in the Department
of History and Philosophy of Education, read the entire manuscript and offered
many useful suggestions, as did Assistant Vice Chancellor Gene A. Budig, now
acting president of the university, Illinois State University.

This book would not have been possible without the encouragement and
support of the University administration. The author was given complete access
to all University of Nebraska records in the institutional archives. The interpreta-
tions expressed and the materials selected for inclusion reflect solely the judgments of the author.

The research assistance of my former graduate students, John McSweeney
and Thomas R. Walsh, who performed many hours of tedious work, is acknowledged.

Special gratitude is extended to Mrs. Martha McKelvie for her generous contribution of funds which made possible the publication of this history of the
University's second fifty years, as well as the history of the first fifty years
published earlier. In addition, Mrs. McKelvie's support has enabled the pub-
lisher to make the book available at an unusually attractive price, so that all
those who might like to purchase copies—for themselves or for others—should
easily be able to do so. Everyone who will derive pleasure or benefit from reading
this Centennial History of the University of Nebraska will be endebted to
Mrs. Martha McKelvie.

R. McLaran Sawyer

Lincoln, Nebraska

THE TWENTIES

CHAPTER 1

Administration in a Decade
of Uncertainty

THROUGH THE ZEAL of its faculty, administration, and students, the University of Nebraska at the beginning of its second half-century was firmly established as an institution of higher learning that had won the support of the citizens of the state, many of whom were numbered among its alumni. Writing of its future in the *Semi-Centennial Anniversary Book,* one of its most distinguished professors, Hartley Burr Alexander, declared that the University had "passed from the state of eager hope, which attended its first seasons, to a state of conscious possession, with attainments recognized and promise assured."[1] During the 1920s, however, the full attainment of the University's potential was to be thwarted by a severe decline in farm commodity prices accompanied by rising prices for goods and services. Nebraskans were caught in the price squeeze and, not surprisingly, as farm income dropped, the state legislature and the governor became reluctant to appropriate or recommend the increasingly large sums needed to run the University. Thus, the principal administrative problem of the decade was the familiar one of attempting to operate a growing educational institution with insufficient funds.

In January 1920, the University's academic deans were interviewed about their aspirations for their respective colleges and their ideas about how they might better serve the state. Their comments reveal a good deal both about the University at that stage of its development and its future direction. Dean O. V. P. Stout hoped that the College of Engineering would soon be in a position to train highway engineers as well as to assist farmers with the School of Irrigation at Scottsbluff. Dean E. A. Burnett emphasized the need for additional facilities for the College of Agriculture, which, he said, was entering a period when its work in animal diseases and poultry production would soon benefit Nebraska farmers. Dean Charles Fordyce announced that Teachers College had expanded its programs and was now able to prepare professionally qualified elementary and secondary school teachers as well as school administrators. He further reported that the new Teachers College building, occupied in the fall of 1919, afforded greatly improved facilities for the college's work. J. E. LeRossignol, dean of the College of Business Administration, believed that Nebraska would be recognized as a leader among American universities because it provided for the professional education of business men and women, and Dean W. G. Hastings of the College of Law foresaw that the university-educated lawyer would lead the legal pro-

1. Hartley Burr Alexander, "The Future," *Semi-Centennial Anniversary Book: The University of Nebraska, 1869–1919,* Louise Pound, ed. (Lincoln: University of Nebraska Press, 1919), p. 113.

3

fession toward higher standards. Dean L. A. Sherman, who anticipated considerable growth in graduate enrollment, stated that in his view the goals of the Graduate College were to provide research-oriented study for those who desired to continue beyond the undergraduate level and to enable students to prepare for professions or careers for which advanced degrees were required.[2] Dean Philo M. Buck, of the College of Arts and Sciences, commented on some of the changes which had taken place within the University of Nebraska.

The arts college was once the whole university. From this parent stock there has budded one after another the various colleges which now maintain a separate existence. But the old departments still furnish the main source of instruction in any of the so-called professional colleges. Indications point to the coming of a time when all professional colleges will require the arts degree or its equivalent before they allow the student to begin his professional specialization.[3]

Dean Buck's statement reflects a significant shift in the attitude of the public toward higher education. Following World War I, there was a general feeling that the age of prosperity had arrived at last and that high wages, mass consumption, and mass spending would continue unabated. Tired of wartime deprivations and hardships, the public eagerly sought the good life, and to many in the striving middle class vocational or professional higher education became the means to attain it. Throughout the nation colleges and universities responded to their demand for whatever promised to promote comfort, economic success, and social prestige.

The prosperity of the twenties was much shorter lived in Nebraska than in much of the nation, but in Nebraska as elsewhere, college enrollments grew as young men and women sought the training which would prepare them for a vocation or profession. During the 1920s enrollment at the University of Nebraska increased each year, except in 1921 and 1928, when it was adversely affected by the economic situation, as shown in the following table prepared from University publications.

	Collegiate	Non-Collegiate	Total
1919–20	5,286	1,672	6,958
1920–21	6,724	1,478	7,121
1921–22	6,594	1,602	8,196
1922–23	7,971	1,831	9,802
1923–24	8,654	1,698	10,352
1924–25	9,400	1,538	10,938
1925–26	9,896	1,818	11,714
1926–27	10,053	1,795	11,848
1927–28	10,384	1,491	11,875
1928–29	10,342	1,393	11,735

The trend toward a professional or a vocationally oriented course of study can be seen in the declining registration in the College of Arts and Sciences. In 1919–20, no less than 52 percent of the collegiate enrollment in the University was in the College of Arts and Sciences, but by 1922–23 it had dropped to 36 percent. In 1925–26, it was 31 percent, and in 1928–29 it was down to 28 percent. Although the college continued to teach the majority of their courses to most students in the professional schools, it seemed that nearly three-fourths of the student body preferred an education which prepared them for a specific profession or career. Those who believed that man does not live by bread alone found this a disturbing development.

2. Lincoln, *Nebraska State Journal,* January 4, 1920, p. D-6.
3. Ibid.

In the spring of 1920, the Board of Regents authorized the publication of a handsome booklet entitled *The University of Nebraska—Program of Development 1920 and After*.[4] The board was keenly aware that substantial support would be needed if the University was to meet the rising demand for higher education, and it hoped that an informed public would support the institution in its expanded role. The booklet pointed out that the University was an institution in which the citizens of the state could take pride, "but it cannot rest with past accomplishment . . . it cannot look forward to a growth which will reflect less than the fullest enrichment of the public life of which such an institution is capable." The University was the capstone of public education in the state and its expansion was a natural development, for

. . . the University never becomes less in more fully assuming her natural duties, and it is altogether to the credit of the framers of her charter that even with the setting up of the first college, provision was made for the establishment of the professional schools and the higher forms of graduate instruction.

Alumni and citizens of Nebraska were asked to support future requests for funds to expand the facilities for instruction, buildings, and staff. The original campus, comprising four city blocks lying between R and T, and 10th and 12th Streets, already had been outgrown with the construction of the Temple and an athletic field, and bold steps must be taken if future needs were to be met. The booklet urged that

all the territory adjacent to the present campus that can be procured should be obtained at the earliest possible moment, and plans should at once be laid for its occupation by University buildings and fields. The need is urgent; the opportunity is yearly less favorable; time is money, and, of even more importance, time is state education: every year's delay keeps a percentage of Nebraska's youth from going forward in a training that will benefit not only them and their families, but the whole commonwealth.

To meet the immediate needs of the University a program of eight planks was proposed for the 1921 legislative session:

I. *"An All-University Spirit Throughout All The State."* The public should be aware that "Nebraska is and must always be a school 'of the people, by the people and for the people.'"

II. *Financial Security.* So long as the growing public demands are being met, it should have the necessary increases in public financial support.

III. *Campus Expansion* to meet instructional, dormitory, and athletic needs.

IV. A *Salary Schedule* adequate to hold and secure the best possible faculty. "Let us not forget the great teachers of the past; let us never in the future be content with lesser men."

V. A *Memorial Gymnasium and Stadium* to commemorate those who gave their lives in the war.

VI. A *Library-Museum* for the use of the students and the public.

VII. *Instructional Buildings.* "The University yearly outgrows its facilities."

VIII. An *Extension Program* to bring to all citizens the offerings of the University.

"So that to be a citizen of Nebraska shall mean being an 'N-man,'" the public was invited to "matriculate now in Nebraska's future."

LEGISLATION AND BUDGETS

The state constitutional convention called in 1919 proposed an amendment, approved at the polls in 1920, which provided that the regents should be elected by

4. *The University of Nebraska—Program of Development 1920 and After* (Lincoln: University of Nebraska, 1920).

district instead of from the state at large, as had been the practice since 1875. The merits of elected versus appointed boards had been debated, and there was discussion of the desirability of a single board of control for state institutions of higher learning, but the vote went in favor of maintaining a separate board for the normal schools and of electing the regents by district to insure geographical representation. Most people apparently agreed with a Lincoln paper's editorial comment that "the voters seem to have a sort of sixth sense in detecting men actuated by less than the most worthy motives in seeking the most conspicuous honorary position in the state."[5]

The budget proposed by the Board of Regents for the 1921 legislative session requested $5,644,400 for operations—a sum that included $1,871,100 in federal funds and the University cash fund from student fees. State law required that all money collected by the University be deposited to the state. These funds were then made available to the University by being included in the biennial appropriation. This has always created the false impression that the University received more tax funds than it actually did. Other requests were $215,880 for agricultural extension; $350,000 for construction of a memorial gymnasium and stadium, with matching funds to be raised by subscription; $300,000 for a new nurse's home to replace one destroyed by fire and for a hospital addition in Omaha; and $300,000 for women's dormitories in Lincoln. An additional $29,000 was requested for activities which had been assigned to the University by the legislature: conservation and land survey, land sales checking, and irrigation experiments.

The request for operating funds was supported by Governor Samuel R. McKelvie, but he believed that an appropriation for a Soldiers' Memorial Stadium, as it was then called, should be contingent on the success of a public subscription. The governor's recommendations were accepted by the legislature; in fact, the Senate increased the appropriation for operations and also provided for a memorial gymnasium and a nurses' home. Despite the regent's plea that they be spared additional responsibilities, an appropriation was included for the creation of the University of Nebraska Trades School. This unusual University program was established in 1921 to meet the vocational needs of disabled war veterans. It was subsidized by a federal grant of twenty-five dollars for each student enrolled, and operated for four years, being discontinued in 1924.

Because of the legislature's strong support it seemed for a brief time that the University was entering on a period of prosperity, but by late summer of 1921 the decline in agricultural prices had begun, and optimism disappeared from Nebraska. In August Governor McKelvie announced that under the authority of legislation adopted in 1919 he was requiring all state agencies to establish a special reserve fund comprised of 10 percent of their appropriation, and further that monies from this fund could not be spent without his approval. On August 15, when he met with the Board of Regents to discuss the University's position, Regent George N. Seymour, speaking for the board, denied the governor's right to control funds appropriated for the University subject to the control of the Board of Regents. Since the governor did not agree, it was decided that amicable legal proceedings should be instituted to test the constitutional rights involved.

In a letter to Philip L. Hall, president of the Board of Regents, Governor McKelvie suggested an action in mandamus as the proper legal remedy. He referred to "the amiable manner in which this subject has been discussed," to "the absence of animosity on the part of any of the parties involved," and to the desire he shared with the board that "the legal course to be followed will be

5. Lincoln, *Nebraska State Journal*, October 25, 1922, p. 6.

entirely free from unfriendliness."[6] Litigation was begun, but a compromise was reached and the suit dismissed before it reached the State Supreme Court. The regents agreed in principle to the 10 percent reserve fund under the governor's control, and McKelvie agreed to release to the regents a proportional part of the fund each quarter, provided that a financial emergency at the University had not necessitated the spending of the funds.

By January 1922, the farm commodity recession had worsened and as prices fell public criticism of the 1921 legislative appropriation increased. Democrats accused Republicans of saddling the public with an unbearable tax rate and attributed the high level of state spending to the Civil Administrative Code adopted by the Republican legislature in 1919. The code itself became a political issue, but leaders of both parties urged strict economy in state expenditures, and Governor McKelvie called the legislature into special session to reduce the appropriations made in the 1921 regular session. In the governor's message, which recommended a substantial reduction in the level of state spending, the University's appropriation was cut by a half million dollars; and the legislature not only authorized the governor's recommendation but completely eliminated the funding for a memorial gymnasium.

The editor of the *University Journal,* in its January 1922 issue, observed that in times of emergency

the University is one of the first expending agencies to reduce its budget to the point of real sacrifice and temporary injury. The administration and the alumni feel that they can rely on the sense of justice of the people of the state to recognize this spirit of fair play and, when conditions have changed for the better, reciprocate with funds for a much needed gymnasium and appropriations adequate for a University which will be comparable to those of other states whose superior accomplishments in any other field we are not willing to acknowledge.

Economy in government was the slogan of all candidates in the election campaign of 1922. The public school system was attacked by A. N. Mathers, a banker and politician from Cering, who saw the schools as a great menacing machine whose chauffeur was ex officio the Superintendent of Public Instruction. The machine, Mathers said, was operated "by and for politicians, book sellers, school supply houses, welfare workers, reformers and salary seekers."[7] The Nebraska Taxpayers League advocated a 25 percent cut in all state appropriations and asked for legislation which would permit communities to reduce the cost of education by lowering state school requirements. The league also demanded that the University's accounts be audited and that all its expenditures be investigated by a legislative committee. In the fall of 1922 the Democratic gubernatorial candidate, Charles W. Bryan, defeated his Republican opponent, in part because he had campaigned against increased state expenditures.

When the regents prepared their 1923 budget, in addition to increased operating funds they asked for appropriations to construct a gymnasium and a museum building and to acquire land for campus development. These capital items were eliminated from Governor Bryan's budget proposal. Early in the legislative session an investigation of the University was approved, and action on all University budget matters was postponed until it should be concluded.

For some time a sentiment had been developing among legislators and among some citizens that the University had grown too large, become too complex, and was far too expensive. In January 1923, Representative James Auten of Albion

6. Letter, Samuel R. McKelvie to P. L. Hall, August 16, 1921, MSS, University of Nebraska Archives, Avery Collection.

7. Addison E. Sheldon, *Nebraska, The Land and the People* (Chicago: Lewis Publishing Co., 1931), p. 994.

introduced a resolution calling for a strict accounting from the University for the funds appropriated two years earlier. Despite the accurate records kept by the University administration, the House voted 90 to 10 for a complete legislative investigation of the institution.

The investigation, which began on January 16, 1923, continued for three months. At one of the committee hearings, Speaker A. N. Mathers declared: "Our university is running away with itself. . . . We do not want to cheapen it. But it is becoming a great financial responsibility and we have reached a point where this super-university must be checked." Regent William L. Bates retorted that many University activities had been dictated by politics from the Capitol: "Duplication in the school of agriculture service thru establishment of the school at Curtis, was a political football from the start. The school of irrigation at Scottsbluff is a political football. . . . Thousands of dollars are spent on duplications."[8] And, driving home his point, Bates called attention to three bills introduced at that session which would require that the University perform additional functions but which failed to provide funding.

On March 27, the committee reported that all funds were accounted for and that no financial irregularities had been found. The committee's report, which was accepted by the House, recommended the separation of the Alumni Association from the University, collection of tuition changes for out-of-state students, elimination of duplication in teacher education by reducing the normal school programs to two years, and the stabilization of University of Nebraska enrollments by the establishment of junior colleges. Other recommendations included transferring responsibility for high school accreditation from the University to the state school superintendent, and this proposal was enacted into law in 1927.

The committee report clearly absolved the University and its administration of any wrongdoing, and those who had objected to the rising costs of education were persuaded that "the modern budgets of the University are the result of the natural growth of the institution." A. H. Staley, superintendent of schools at Hastings, was expressing the opinion of many friends of the University when he said: "Some parts of the report would be amusing if it were not so tragic. The whole procedure is to be regretted and I am very sure that the people of the state, 'the so called TAXPAYERS,' are really ashamed of the sort of legislature that we have and [that] is now putting on a vaudeville."[9]

With the investigation concluded, the legislature returned to the matter of the budget. The reduction in the operating budget request recommended by retiring Governor McKelvie was accepted, as was the further reduction proposed by incoming Governor Bryan. To convey their unmistakable interest in economy, the legislators cut the state tax appropriation still more, ending up with a sum $399,580 less than that provided in the 1922 special session.

THE TEN-YEAR PLAN

By 1924 it was apparent that the University, far from moving forward, might be entering a period of decline. Once again, hoping that an informed public would help reverse the trend, the University issued a bulletin, *What Do You Know About Your State University?*, addressed to "the people of the state, the Governor, and members of the Legislature of 1925."[10] The reader was reminded that "the University of Nebraska is primarily a university of the common people

8. Lincoln, *Nebraska State Journal*, March 7, 1923, p. 6.

9. Letter, A. H. Staley to S. Avery, March 28, 1923, MSS, University of Nebraska Archives, Avery Collection.

10. *What Do You Know About Your State University?*, Bulletin 23, Ser. 29, University of Nebraska, October 1924.

and cannot call on fathers of rich students for substantial fortunes as can so many of the privately endowed institutions of the East." It had grown both in the number of students it served and the courses it offered, but "considering the size of the student body, [it] was actually better supplied with buildings twenty years ago." Moreover, "the cost of operation per student today is actually less than twenty years ago, despite the fact that everything costs twice as much as it did then." Economy-minded Nebraskans might be proud of the fact that in 1923 the average cost per student at the University of Nebraska was only $159.32 as compared to $281.44 at twenty-five other state universities, but the economizing had resulted in overcrowded facilities, a lack of proper educational equipment, and large classes. Whereas the average at twenty-three state universities in 1923 was 13.8 students per instructor, at Nebraska the ratio was 18.2. If the University was to progress, the regents requested adequate financial support and the establishment of a one-fifth mill levy for ten years for capital improvements. The bulletin concluded that the institution asked nothing for itself: "The University is an impersonal sort of thing and wants nothing. It is what *you* want. Do *you* want *your* children to have an education? If your children are to have an education, the University must have equipment with which to do the work."

The adoption by the 1925 legislature of a ten-year building program would have provided for orderly, planned growth and would also have constituted a vote of confidence in the University, but retiring Governor Bryan's budget proposed a drastic reduction in operation funds and the ten-year plan was not endorsed. However, the incoming Republican governor, Adam McMullen, '96, approved a one-eighth mill levy for ten years for University development, stating that "it is evident that increased building facilities are required to care adequately for this rapidly growing group of young people."[11] Governor McMullen further approved nearly the full amount requested by the regents for operations.

A bill providing for a one-eighth mill levy for ten years was introduced into the House of Representatives. Because some thought the regents would engage in an "orgy" of construction, the bill was passed by the House with an amendment which limited the amount of construction that could be under contract at one time. The bill was then sent to the Senate. University supporters "thought that the University had finally reached the point where it was no longer necessary to consider the element of politics in the securing of its biennial requirements."[12] The bill was referred to the Senate Finance Committee, where it remained in committee. Finally, by a vote of 17 to 15, the bill was brought to the floor of the Senate for discussion. Senators expressed unwillingness to commit the state to a long-range program, even if future legislatures would have the power to reconsider the commitment. Some senators referred to the proposal as "mortgaging the state for ten years." A conference committee resolved the differences between the House and Senate over University appropriations. The ten-year plan was lost, but $900,000 was appropriated for capital improvements for the biennium. This was more than the one-eighth mill levy would have produced during the biennium, but it left future support again in doubt. As the *Nebraska State Journal* editor commented in its issue of April 20, 1925:

The refusal of the legislature to grant the levy may look like notice that instead of being open to all, the university is to be conducted in the future for the select few. If that is to be the policy of the state, it would be well to declare it officially and ask the

11. *Messages and Proclamations of the Governors of Nebraska, 1854–1941*, Vol. III (Works Progress Administration, 1942), p. 620.
12. *Nebraska Alumnus*, April 1925, p. 148.

Regents to conform to it. If the old policy of the open door is to continue, the case calls for a liberal building appropriation for the next biennium and some declaration of policy that will encourage the Regents to plan confidently for the future.

THE EFFECTS OF HARD TIMES

The salaries offered to the instructional staff at the University had long been low in view of the course loads they carried, and in February 1920, a group of faculty members petitioned the chancellor and the Board of Regents for a more adequate salary schedule. The petition signed by the chairman of the meeting, Guernsey Jones, professor of English history, and Clark E. Mickey, professor of civil engineering, who acted as secretary for the group, stated in part:

We recognize that in the past, owing in part to the professional zeal of members of the faculty, the University curriculum has been expanded beyond the limits justified by the state support; and we ask that hereafter no instructor be appointed in the University for work not now represented in the curriculum until the designed salary schedule shall be in effect.

We ask that as a matter of policy and for the sake of the better morale of the teaching force that when teachers are brought to the University at higher salaries than are paid to the teachers of equal value to the institution; who have long been in service, one or more or the latter be advanced to a salary equal to that granted the newcomer. . . .

We deem it incompatible with the dignity of the University of Nebraska and its value to the state that its salary scale should be less than those of the universities of neighboring states.[13]

At their next meeting, on February 17, 1920, the regents adopted a resolution which recognized that "the first and largest demand on the university's revenues is the fixing, as far as possible under available funds, of adequate salaries in preference to building operations or other activities." The chancellor was directed by the board to prepare "a statement of available resources and schedules of salary increases as will meet present conditions." In March the board increased the salaries of many faculty members, although not to the requested level. In some cases the salaries of individual professors were discussed by the regents and voted on as separate items. But the relief provided by salary adjustment was of brief duration, for the cost of living continued to rise, and by the mid-1920s the University was losing too many faculty members to other institutions. It was reported in the fall of 1926 that one dean and thirty members of the instructional staff had left since the previous year.

Faculty morale declined further as it became necessary to pay competitive salaries to attract faculty replacements, while noncompetitive salaries were paid to many who had given long faithful service to the University. This extreme competition within the University for limited funds, was recalled by John D. Hicks, professor of history, and later dean of the College of Arts and Sciences.

Every department, like every economic interest, was out to get all it could for its own aggrandizement. . . . But the log rolling necessary to get any agreement among the various contenders for spoils would almost put Congress to shame. University professors are terrible in fighters; they operate with no holds or weapons barred.[14]

While serving as chairman of the History Department, Hicks reported that morale was such that, "I had only one department meeting during my four

13. Letter, Guernsey Jones to S. Avery, February 16, 1920, MSS, University of Nebraska Archives, Avery Collection.
14. John D. Hicks, *My Life with History* (Lincoln: University of Nebraska Press, 1968), p. 149.

years as chairman, for the clashing personalities within our group made it completely impossible to transact any business that way."[15] While low faculty salaries were not the sole cause of the declining faculty morale, uncertainty each biennium over general University support made it difficult to face the future confidently. A study made by the chancellor in December 1929 indicated that many faculty members could not live on their salaries. Earlier that same year one full professor was quoted in the student newspaper as saying that his regular University salary had not met annual necessary expenses any year since 1916; he had avoided bankruptcy by teaching in summer and taking temporary employment.

Considering these difficulties one may well ask why there was not a general faculty exodus. For one thing, the mobility of faculties was not as great as it was to be in future years. More significantly, heavy teaching loads, faculty rivalry, and uncertainty about the future were counterbalanced by the presence of bright, eager students. To a dedicated teacher, the stimulus and pleasure of teaching them compensated for innumerable problems outside the classroom. And also Lincoln was a pleasant place to live. Those who left the University frequently did so reluctantly and with regret. John D. Hicks recalled:

It was not easy for me, or for my wife to leave Nebraska. It was almost like leaving home again. . . . We came with few acquaintances; we left with many close friends, the kind one doesn't lose by separation, but for that reason misses all the more. My students . . . were a constant joy, perhaps the most appreciative students I have ever taught. . . . It was hard to leave, and maybe we should have stayed. But one can't have it both ways; we did what we thought we had to do.[16]

Professor E. F. Schramm, who taught geology, explained his continued association with the University in a letter to Chancellor Samuel Avery:

Looking over the salary record . . . you can readily see that if I had not engaged in commercial geological work during the summer months, I would soon have been either in the hands of the undertaker or my creditors. . . . I have remained with the University because I thoroughly enjoy the work and not for the salary that is in it.[17]

Another unfortunate consequence of short rations for the University was the extreme crowding of the available facilities. In 1926, the deans and departmental chairmen reported a serious weakening of the instructional program resulting from a lack of space. The librarian reported that there was not sufficient shelf space for the book collection. "We have been obliged to place some twenty thousand in storage, thereby making them immediately inaccessible. . . ."[18] The College of Dentistry was rated as a class "B" school by the Dental Education Council because of its poor facilities in rented quarters downtown. The Teachers College enrollment had more than trebled since 1921, and it had outgrown its quarters constructed in 1919. The dean of engineering reported that the lack of space was preventing the college from attaining its natural growth, and similar complaints came from other academic leaders at the University. The lack of dormitory space was also a limiting factor on University growth. There was an increasing shortage of suitable off-campus housing, and the older rooming houses in the vicinity of the campus were frequently dilapidated, crowded, and generally charged high rates for the poor accommodations they provided.

15. Ibid., p. 147.
16. Ibid., p. 153.
17. Letter, E. F. Schramm to Samuel Avery, April 17, 1921, MSS, University of Nebraska Archives, Avery Collection.
18. *Nebraska Alumnus,* November 1926, p. 423.

CHANCELLOR AVERY

Samuel Avery had become acting chancellor in 1908 and chancellor in 1909. He served until 1927, remaining in office longer than any of his predecessors. His tenure witnessed an incredible growth in enrollment and an expansion of the instructional program to meet the changing public expectations of land-grant universities. As with all administrative positions, some favored Avery's policies, and others were irritated and offended by them. Those who tended to be reformers were those most frequently critical of the chancellor, while others who shared the basic conservatism of Nebraska recognized the chancellor

Samuel Avery.

as a product of the state. All agreed that Samuel Avery was a shrewd judge of men, and being a conservative, he accepted them as they were rather than as he wished they would be. Dean Hicks of the College of Arts and Sciences,

> . . . early conceived a very genuine admiration for Chancellor Samuel Avery. He was a diamond in the rough who looked more like a farmer uncomfortable in store clothes, than like the head of a great university. He was deeply intent on building up his faculty, and admitted overpaying some recent acquisitions—including me—in order to beat out prospective competitors. . . . He could squeeze a penny hard, especially on minor items—always expected and delivered a tight budget.[19]

John Andrew Rice, a member of the Classics Department during the twenties, who wrote, *I Came Out of the Eighteenth Century*, was extremely critical of Avery.

19. Hicks, op. cit., p. 133.

Every man carries around inside himself two pictures, patterns, ideas, one of the human being as he is, one as he ought to be. I was always getting mine mixed, Avery never, and by the time I knew him he had so long been guided by the is rather than the ought to be, that the is had almost disappeared. But a man has also his own personal is and ought to be, and here again we were different. Whatever of the is of humanity made him uncomfortable, he quietly ignored, or he became suddenly stubborn. He would not join any kind of organization in the town, nor pretend to like football, alumni meetings, "lap suppers,"—the common mode of entertainment in Lincoln—educational conferences; and professional piety froze his face stiff.[20]

An astute academic politician who understood the limits of power inherent in the chancellorship as well as the temper of the state, Avery did nothing to exceed the former or extend the latter. Public controversy or criticism of the University, he believed, inevitably produced a harmful public reaction; hence a controversial person, particularly in a policy role, was detrimental to the best interests of the institution. That he could apply this precept to himself was shown in April 1920, when the University was under attack by some agricultural groups. At that time Avery wrote to Regent H. D. Landis:

I am conscious that if these interests are now affronted in what seems to them a vital issue, I shall be held responsible and my efforts to help them in every possible way during the past eleven years will pass for hypocrisy. It is evident, therefore, from my point of view that if these organizations are disaffected, my usefulness to the University is at an end. In such a case I should have to ask the Regents to relieve me of office and to appoint someone not associated in the minds of these people with the present trouble to stand as the representative of the University before the next Legislature.[21]

In December 1924, Victor B. Smith, a past president of the Alumni Association, wrote a highly critical letter of the Avery administration to the editor of the Omaha *World-Herald*. Of Avery himself, he said:

"The chancellor is, essentially, a man like Henry Clay—a great compromiser. Compromisers have their great moments. Chancellor Avery has had his; there was a time several years ago, perhaps, when the university needed, in its executive office, the qualities which he possesses. But that time is past.

"In the last fourteen years, the university has compromised about every issue of importance that came before it. When the removal of the university campus was a critical issue in 1913, Chancellor Avery did not raise his voice conspicuously "Aye" or "nay." The head of the University—the state's expert on the job—left the decision to the legislature and that body, in a tumult of confusion, left it to a referendum of the people.

"When it became necessary, a few months ago, to relieve a certain university dean from his deanship the chancellor's recommendation to the Regents was that the demoted professor be shorn of his authority but keep his salary—'in order that he won't stir up so much fuss.'

"When football Coach Dawson was charged last year with conduct unbecoming a teacher, the chancellor encouraged the opposition to Dawson when it seemed likely to be dominant and refused to condemn Dawson before the board of regents when it was apparent that Dawson's friends might be in a majority.

"The chancellor should not be blamed too greatly for these compromises—which are merely examples from a host of typical actions. He would be untrue to his philosophy

20. John Andrew Rice, *I Came Out of the Eighteenth Century* (New York: Harpers, 1942), p. 276.

21. Letter, Samuel Avery to H. D. Landis, April 10, 1920, MSS, University of Nebraska Archives, Avery Collection.

if he did otherwise. His policy is to find out what is wanted and swing into line with the majority. An ideal public servant."[22]

The *World-Herald* editorially supported the position that the University needed more positive leadership than Avery was prepared to give. On December 15, three days after the publication of Smith's letter, the chancellor was tendered an expression of confidence by his deans. It was their opinion "that there is no executive charged with like responsibilities with whose work they are familiar that could have served the interests of the University, under the conditions which have surrounded it, more successfully."[23]

On May 8, 1925, Avery asked the regents to be relieved of office on August 31, 1928, more than three years distant. Charles H. Morrill, former regent and University benefactor approved the strategy and wrote the chancellor:

Allow me to congratulate you on your tactics in resigning in *1928*. This was a shrude [sic] move and absolutely unhorses the opposition to your policy as Chancellor and leaves you free and independent to act in accordance with your views for the best interest of the University."[24]

In addition to the public criticism, some faculty members had been restive for some time. Professor Hartley Burr Alexander of the Department of Philosophy, had earlier complained "of a 'kitchen cabinet' government, which attached to Chancellor Andrews and attaches to Chancellor Avery—the 'kitchen' counselors referred to being minor employees of the administration building."[25] The pressure of the office was beginning to have its effect. In October 1926, Avery complained to a friend, regarding his part in a campaign to close the movie houses on Sunday, "I do not think that the good people should expect me to lead a division of shock troops in every fight, especially when they do not hesitate to turn their guns on my interests whenever they see fit."[26]

By January 1927, Samuel Avery's health had broken, and he requested an immediate leave of absence from the regents. The leave was granted and August 31, 1927, set as the date for Avery's retirement as chancellor. Following his retirement as chancellor, he returned to the chemical research that he had abandoned in 1908, and served as chancellor emeritus and professor of research in chemistry until his death in 1936. For some Samuel Avery had been a good chancellor because of his willingness to compromise; to others this was the great fault in his administration. His most severe critics credited the chancellorship with more power than it possessed. The University could not control, nor direct, many of the forces which affected its fate. It is doubtful that a different chancellor could have overcome the economic forces which caused this to be an era of uncertainty.

THE SEARCH FOR NEW LEADERSHIP

In January 1927, Dean Edgar A. Burnett, of the College of Agriculture, was appointed acting chancellor. A committee composed of Regents William P. Warner, Frank J. Taylor, and Earl Cline was formed to search for a successor to Chancellor Avery. Numerous leading university presidents were consulted

22. Omaha *World-Herald*, December 12, 1924, p. 4.

23. MSS, December 15, 1924, University of Nebraska Archives, Avery Collection.

24. Letter, C. H. Morrill to Samuel Avery, May 11, 1925, MSS, University of Nebraska Archives, Avery Collection.

25. MSS, undated, University of Nebraska Archives, Avery Collection.

26. Letter, Samuel Avery to W. A. Luke, October 4, 1926, MSS, University of Nebraska Archives, Avery Collection.

for possible candidates. The faculty of the University were asked for recommendations. Professor E. H. Barbour wrote: "It seems to me that it would meet the sentiment of most of us if we could get a qualified man from the outside, however, this seems doubtful. Our salaries do not tempt people from outside our own ranks."[27]

In June the regents invited A. G. Crane, president of the University of Wyoming, to meet with them concerning the chancellorship. Crane was offered the chancellorship of the University of Nebraska, but declined the appoint-

Edgar Albert Burnett.

ment. By this time, the regents were being advised by residents of western Nebraska of their preference for someone who was a resident of the state for the chancellorship. The Chadron Chamber of Commerce was specific and recommended the appointment of Professor George E. Condra, of the Department of Geology. On December 3, 1927, the regents discussed the matter of the chancellorship. Regent Stanley D. Long moved that George E. Condra be elected as chancellor of the University for two years. Regents Long and Landis voted for the motion; Regents Cline, Taylor, Warner, and Webster opposed it. Regent Landis then proposed that Condra be elected as chancellor for one year. This was defeated by the same vote as the previous proposal. At their meeting on March 3, 1928, the Board of Regents voted unanimously to appoint Edgar A. Burnett the University's chancellor from March 1, 1928, to June 30, 1929, thus removing Burnett's administration from an acting status during the 1929 legislative session. Subsequently, at a meeting on September

27. Letter, Ervin H. Barbour to William P. Warner, April 11, 1927, MSS, University of Nebraska Archives, Avery Collection.

6, 1928, by a unanimous vote, the board elected Burnett chancellor without limit of tenure.

Edgar Albert Burnett was born on a farm near Harland, Michigan, in 1865. He studied animal husbandry at Michigan State Agricultural College and was awarded the Bachelor of Science degree in 1887 and an honorary Doctor of Science in 1917. He taught at Michigan State from 1889 to 1893. For several years he managed the Hiram Walker farms in Canada. In 1896, he was named professor of animal husbandry at South Dakota State College. He joined the faculty of the University of Nebraska as professor of animal husbandry in 1899. In 1901, he was made director of the Nebraska Agricultural Experiment Station, and from 1901 to 1907, was associate dean in charge of agricultural instruction. When the Industrial College was divided in 1909 and the Engineering College moved to the city campus, he was appointed dean of the College of Agriculture.

Burnett had been named acting chancellor partially because he was the senior University dean. He also enjoyed faculty support for the temporary appointment because few faculty members considered him a likely prospect for the permanent appointment. His appointment as chancellor resulted from the inability of the regents to agree upon an outsider who would accept the post and from their approval of his temporary leadership. The appointment also ended the speculation and uncertainty prevalent since Chancellor Avery's leave had begun more than a year and a half before.

THE LAST OF THE DECADE

The budget submitted by the regents for the 1927–29 biennium was substantially reduced by Governor McMullen. Operating funds were increased by less than $400,000 over the 1925–27 appropriation, and the request for building funds was cut almost in half. From an article which appeared in the *Nebraska Alumnus*, May 1927, it is clear that Burnett was not surprised. He wrote that in view of "our urgent need for new buildings this seems a backward step, but taken in connection with the financial condition of the State, the cost of the new Capitol, and a State deficit to be met . . . it should give a measure of satisfaction."

In 1929 the regents asked for a substantial increase in appropriations for operations and construction. They explained that more operating funds were necessary because "richer universities are continually taking our well known professors at decided increases in salary. Unless we can meet some of these opportunities by larger salaries here we shall continue to lose such professors at an alarming rate."[28] Recognizing that past appropriations for the University had not kept up with its growth, the incoming governor, Arthur J. Weaver, '95, increased the operating request by a half million dollars but reduced the amount of construction funds in his proposed budget. As usual, the legislature cut the governor's budget, and Weaver, having second thoughts about state expenses, vetoed a $100,000 addition to the University's appropriation voted by the Senate.

The true level of University support by the legislature during the twenties is shown in the following table. The appropriation figure is the actual cost to Nebraska taxpayers; it does not include money from student fees, athletic tickets, federal funds, or any other revenue generated within the University. The enrollment figures are for fiscal rather than the academic year and include students in all University programs, as well as some double counting.

28. *Daily Nebraskan*, October 7, 1928.

	Appropriations by State	Students Enrolled
1919–21	$3,527,985	13,557
1921–23	$3,669,104	16,652
1923–25	$3,258,670	21,290
1925–27	$4,541,500	23,562
1927–29	$4,148,230	23,610
1929–31	$4,852,000	23,037[29]

Chancellor Edgar A. Burnett summarized the financial dilemma for the alumni in this way at the Round-Up luncheon in 1928.

As you progressed toward graduation, you came to know that the University itself had problems,—problems of finance almost as difficult as your own in student days,—problems which for it have increased with the years as our student family has multiplied, which were never more serious than they are today.

As we look about for a remedy we turn instinctively to the alumni for support. Nebraska is young as universities go, but not too young to build up traditions which bind the alumni to their alma mater even as at Yale, Harvard, and Princeton alumni furnish a strong arm of defense in endowments and material resources.[30]

Despite the economic situation in the state during the 1920s, some additions to University facilities were secured. The most acute need was for academic buildings. In 1925, after architects declared that University Hall, built in 1870, was unsafe for further use, the tower and the top three stories were removed, but the basement and first floor of the building continued to house classes. For many alumni the campus would never be the same again with U Hall stripped of its majesty. What the building symbolized was suggested in a poem written in 1925 by M. C. Thomas, a student in English 109:

UNIVERSITY HALL

There is no one to understand this place,
Destroy it quickly, tear the powdered walls;
Stop not to see the yellow fragments fall,
Rebound in dust and quiver in the sun!
Here is a body with the spirit fled,
Hollow, forgotten. Don't pretend to grieve,
You headlong and impious ones who swarm
About it now! You're of another race.

Where is the spirit of this barren place,
This loyal, ruined, ill-made house of ours?

—Wherever keep the heroes of the plains,
—Wherever wait the hopes of driven years,
—Wherever rest the souls of pioneers.[31]

Also in 1925 the walls of Nebraska Hall began to crumble and one story was removed. Constructed in 1887–88 and remodeled in 1908, it was the fourth of the original University buildings; only University Hall, the Chemical Laboratory, and Grant Memorial Hall were older.

Two classroom buildings were added to the city campus during the twenties: Morrill Hall in 1927 and Andrews Hall in 1928; while on the College of Agriculture campus the College Activities Building was completed and oc-

29. *Financial Report* of the University of Nebraska for the Year Ending June 30, 1931, p. 64.
30. *Nebraska Alumnus,* June 1928, p. 273.
31. *Daily Nebraskan,* November 19, 1925.

cupied in 1927. New buildings at the College of Medicine in Omaha were Conkling Hall (1922) and Unit II of the University Hospital (1927); and at Curtis additions were made to the girls' dormitory in 1929. Morrill Hall, which was dedicated in 1927, was financed by tax funds prompted by a generous donation from Charles H. Morrill, one of many he had made. A successful Stromsburg farmer, Morrill was a regent from 1890 to 1902. In a letter of April 4, 1926, accompanying a large gift he wrote to Chancellor Avery: "I'm now nearing eighty-five years of age. As I look backward viewing my past life and my varied experiences, I consider the 12 years I acted as Regent and as President of the Board of Regents of the University of Nebraska the brightest and most interesting period of my life."

Perhaps the most spectacular additions to the University plant during the decade were Memorial Stadium and the Coliseum. In 1919, immediately after World War I, Vincent C. Hascall, a former Nebraska quarterback who was active in the Omaha N-Club, proposed the erection of a stadium as a memorial to the young men of Nebraska who had died in the service of their country. However, no action was taken at that time. In 1921 the proposal was revived by Harold F. Holtz, the secretary of the Alumni Association, and Marcus Poteet, a law student who worked part-time in the chancellor's office. At a convocation in the spring of 1922 launching the proposal, faculty, students, alumni, and friends of the University pledged financial support. Financing was to be arranged by a private group, the University of Nebraska Athletic Building Association, which would borrow the construction money. At this period in Nebraska it was hard to borrow money for such a project; the University had pledged a portion of the athletic receipts to retire the debt, but there was no tangible security. Finally, when it seemed the project might die, George W. Holmes, president of the First Trust Company of Lincoln, offered to guarantee the $300,000 loan. His confidence in the University and its supporters was fully warranted; although the financial debacle of the late twenties and the thirties resulted in many defaults, the stadium pledges and bonds were paid on schedule.

Ground-breaking for Memorial Stadium was held on April 26, 1923, and it was dedicated at Homecoming on October 20 at the Kansas-Nebraska football game, the third game of the 1923 season. Later, when the University needed accommodations for the Printing Division and the Repair Department, the space under the west wing was adapted to that purpose, and at the same time windows and plumbing were added. A hundred thousand dollars was needed to carry out the work, and this was the only money from tax funds used in the construction of Memorial Stadium.

In 1924, John K. Selleck, University business manager of athletics and a member of both the Athletic Board and the Athletic Building Association, approached the latter with a new proposal. He suggested the construction of a large multi-purpose building to be used for basketball games and other University functions. As before, the building would be financed with money borrowed by the Building Association, for which the University and the state would not be responsible, and the debt would be paid out of athletic receipts. Once again George Holmes came to the rescue, loaning the money when no bank was willing to do so. The decision of the Board of Regents to add a stage increased the utility of the building, and this addition was funded with tax money. Several names were considered for the new building, which was opened for use in the fall of 1925. The most popular were Cornhusker Hall, Nebraska Auditorium, and the one selected by the regents—the Coliseum.

The decade of the twenties had been a time of uncertainty at the University. The anticipated prosperity and good times had vanished with the decline in agricultural prosperity. The leadership capabilities of Chancellor Avery were questioned from both within and without the institution. Serious disagreements regarding the rapidly expanding scope of the University's educational curricula produced visible disharmony within the academic community and even among its strongest supporters. To make matters still worse, while enrollments steadily expanded, the budget became increasingly inadequate. During the twenties, many plans, hopes, and dreams had gone awry.

CHAPTER 2

A Decade of Academic Change and Expansion

DURING THE DECADE of the twenties the instructional programs offered by the colleges of the University of Nebraska expanded in both scope and depth. Public support for educational programs designed to prepare students for a specific profession was partially responsible for the reorganization of the University in 1919. In this reorganization, the Colleges of Business Administration and Dentistry were established as separate professional colleges within the University. This same sentiment stimulated research affecting problems of Nebraska business and agriculture.

The consequences of this increased vocationalism unleashed hostilities throughout American higher education during the twenties. At the University of Nebraska enrollments were shifting to those programs which prepared students for a specific vocation. Nearly all agreed, however, that a balance between the traditional liberal arts and vocational curricula was essential. Regent John E. Miller expressed a popular belief when he praised the leadership of Chancellor Avery because "he never permitted himself to forget that Nebraska is first an agricultural state, and that a reasonable balance between strictly cultural and industrial or practical work must be maintained."[1]

The achievement of this balance between the professional schools and the College of Arts and Sciences became the burning issue of the twenties. For some, University growth in the area of vocational and professional programs compromised the intellectual integrity of the University. The issue was one on which honest men could disagree. The point at issue was, should the professional colleges be equal in all matters with the nonprofessional colleges. Educational conservatives regarded themselves as the guardians of traditional truth and wisdom, while the progressives considered their position in harmony with the needs of a changing society. These issues were debated not only at the University of Nebraska, but throughout the land, within and without academic circles.

In the fall of 1923, Willa Cather, one of the University's most distinguished alumnae, published in the *Nation* a commentary on her native state. The University had changed, as had the state, and perhaps not for the better.

In this time of prosperity, any farmer boy who wishes to study at the state university can do so. A New York lawyer who went out to Lincoln to assist in training the university students for military service in war time exclaimed when he came back: "What splendid young men! I would not have believed that any school in the world could get together so many boys physically fit, and so few unfit."

1. *Nebraska Alumnus,* October 1927, p. 387.

Of course there is the other side of the medal, stamped with the ugly crest of materialism, which has set its seal upon all of our most productive commonwealths. Too much prosperity, too many moving-picture shows, too much gaudy fiction have colored the taste and manners of so many of these Nebraskans of the future. There, as elsewhere, one finds the frenzy to be showy: farmer boys who wish to be spenders before they are earners, girls who try to look like heroines of the cinema screen, a coming generation which tries to cheat its aesthetic sense by buying things instead of making anything. There is even danger that that fine institution, the University of Nebraska, may become a gigantic trade school. The classics, the humanities, are having their dark hour. They are in eclipse. But the "classics" have a way of revenging themselves. One may venture to hope that the children, or the grandchildren, of a generation that goes to a university to select only the most utilitarian subjects in the course of study—among them, salesmanship and dressmaking—will revolt against all the

Registration in the Coliseum.

heaped-up, machine-made materialism about them. They will go back to the old sources of culture and wisdom—not as a duty, but with burning desire.[2]

Mass culture with its materialism, equalitarianism, and relative values had appeared. What was the proper function of a state university? Should it confine its efforts largely to that limited number who seek truth and mental discipline through a study of the liberal arts? Or should it offer instruction in all areas of knowledge for which there is a reasonable public demand? Could these two points of view be reconciled?

These questions were being asked on all American campuses, especially on those of the Midwestern land-grant universities. At the University of Nebraska, these questions were focused on the relationship of the Teachers College to the College of Arts and Sciences.

THE TEACHERS COLLEGE

The Teachers College was not provided for in the original University charter. For some, the creation of an autonomous Teachers College represented the sur-

2. Willa Cather, "Nebraska: The End of the First Cycle," *The Nation*, September 5, 1923, quoted in Virginia Faulkner, *Round-Up: A Nebraska Reader* (Lincoln: University of Nebraska Press, 1957), p. 7.

render of higher education to vocationalism. The independent Teachers College became the symbol of change; those who objected to the changes which had been taking place in higher education now had something tangible to oppose.

The champion of the conservative view at the University of Nebraska was Hartley Burr Alexander, professor and chairman of the Department of Philosophy. A native of Lincoln and an 1887 graduate of the University, he joined the faculty in 1908. Alexander had received the Doctor of Philosophy from Columbia University and had published widely. He was recognized as an outstanding scholar and as a popular instructor. His opposition to the idea of an autonomous Teachers College was definite. Alexander's statement made a few years earlier clearly explained a widely held belief.

The College of Arts and Sciences, The Teachers' College, and the Graduate School, form an intimately related group (the first-named being the parent of the others), the teachers in any one of these serving as the teachers of one or more of the others, the degrees given being directly related, and the courses required being largely identical. There is every reason, therefore, why these colleges should be organized in close co-operation. This can only be by subordination, to some extent; and the proper subordination is of the Teachers' College (for which all but 15 hours of the required work is Arts College work) and the Graduate School (resting upon Arts College requirements) to the Arts College. Indeed, the Teachers' College ought to be no more than a department (or at most a "school," like commerce and fine arts) of the Arts College. . . .

But in any case, if the Teachers' College is to be preserved in its present form, the health (and indeed the very existence) of the Arts College depends upon its release from Teachers' College requirements (which now continually hamper and interfere with its work). This can best be brought about by securing through the legislature, the enactment of a law (once, I believe, in the statutes), granting state teachers' certificates to all graduates from any four-year course of study offered by the University. Such a law would take the Teachers College work out of its position of special privilege and put it upon its own merits along with other branches of study.[3]

The movement for an independent Teachers College began with a speech by Harry H. Reimund before the high school section of the Nebraska State Teachers' Association in 1920. Reimund was superintendent of schools at Tekamah. His address was entitled "The Value to the High Schools of Nebraska of an Autonomous Teachers College in the State University." He was troubled about the teaching ability of university graduates. "Our young men and women have been graduated from the regular four-year course in the Art and Science College and have been turned loose on the High Schools of the state to get their training at the expense of the High School students."[4] As many schoolmen saw the problem, "the devotee of the humanities has been prone to cling to the idea that special preparation for teaching is not necessary. That is to say he believes that if one has a high degree of scholarship the teaching will somehow take care of itself. . . ."[5] Control by the College of Arts and Sciences of the degree requirements, the number and content of teaching methods classes, as well as supervision of practice teaching by academic departments of the Arts College was considered fatal to the development of teaching as a profession by many schoolmen.

Under the leadership of Superintendent Reimund, a group of leading Nebraska educators met with Chancellor Avery, in January 1921, regarding teacher education. It was made clear that continued support of the University of Nebraska

---

3. MSS, University of Nebraska Archives, Avery Collection, Hartley Burr Alexander File, undated memo.
4. Harry H. Reimund, *The Value to the High Schools of Nebraska of an Autonomous Teachers College in the State University* (Tekamah: Tekamah Journal Print, 1920), p. 1.
5. Ibid.

by the state's public school leaders was dependent upon the reorganization of teacher education. Following this meeting with Nebraska educators, Chancellor Avery sought the advice of national leaders in higher education. He was advised that independent teachers colleges were now common in state universities and that their establishment was a desirable move. President Coffman, of the University of Minnesota, wrote: "The Teachers' College should grant its own degrees, if other colleges of the university grant their degree. It should be entitled to the same rights and privileges that other professional schools are entitled to."[6]

At the meeting of the Board of Regents on February 4, 1921, the chancellor was instructed by the board to define more clearly the Teachers College as a professional college. On March 29, 1921, the regents adopted, on the motion of Regent Landis, a new policy regarding the Teachers College. The college was recognized as an autonomous professional college such as those of agriculture, engineering, business administration, and pharmacy.

The faculty of the teachers college shall exercise the usual faculty control over its students, curricula and degrees. The degree to be announced in the next catalog shall be "Bachelor of Science in Education." If the Progress of education in the country at large and the development of teachers colleges generally in state universities warrant it, the degree of Bachelor of Arts in Education may be authorized at any time.[7]

In April 1922, the Bachelor of Arts degree was authorized for Teachers College by the Board of Regents.

The policies of the regents for the establishment of an independent Teachers College were resisted by some faculty members. Despite the consultation with faculty members and with Dean Philo M. Buck, Jr., of the College of Arts and Sciences, prior to the policy change, the change was forcefully opposed by some of the Arts faculty. The chancellor wrote one school superintendent: "I understand that a few people in the Arts College insist that they are going 'to fight' in regard to putting into effect the new regulations in regard to the Teachers' College."[8] Chancellor Avery and Regent Harry D. Landis corresponded regarding the matter and concluded that Dean Philo M. Buck, Jr., was responsible for much of the obstructionism. In an unusually candid letter, Regent Landis wrote the chancellor:

Would think that Dean Buck would spend his time deaning in his college and leave the teachers of the State alone as this contact belongs to the Teachers College from now on and is not a problem of Dean Buck's. I am gradually becoming convinced that Buck is not a fit man for Dean, his actions have aroused my suspicions that he is superficial, and a narrow man seeking only self advancement and not keeping the University's interests in mind. You may register me as determined that Dean Buck shall have a thorough investigation.[9]

At the next meeting of the Board of Regents following the Landis letter, on April 20, 1922, Dean Buck was granted a leave of absence beginning in the fall to accept an exchange professorship in India. During Buck's absence, Chancellor Avery accepted the additional responsibilities of dean of Arts and Sciences.

By the spring of 1924, Dean Buck had returned to his University duties. However, it appeared that his relationship with some members of the Board of

6. MSS, University of Nebraska Archives, Avery Collection, "Summary of Questionnaire to College Deans and Presidents," Teachers College File.

7. *Minutes,* University of Nebraska Board of Regents, March 29, 1921.

8. Letter, Samuel Avery to R. D. Moritz, April 4, 1921, MSS, University of Nebraska Archives, Avery Collection.

9. Letter, H. D. Landis to Samuel Avery, April 15, 1921, MSS, University of Nebraska Archives, Avery Collection.

Regents, which had become strained earlier over the Teachers College's independence, had not improved. On April 11, 1924, the regents requested Chancellor Avery to prepare a report on the effectiveness of Dean Buck's leadership of the Arts College. At their next meeting the report was made, and a Department of Comparative Literature established with Dean Buck as its chairman. While other factors in addition to the conflict between the College of Arts and Sciences and the Teachers College were undoubtedly involved in the removal of Buck from his deanship, this was the main factor in the regents' action. The handling of this personnel change was one of the examples cited by Victor B. Smith in his letter of criticism of Chancellor Avery which appeared in the *World-Herald* on December 12, 1924. Also, at this meeting, the Board

Students being trained to teach commercial subjects in high school.

of Regents adopted a resolution, "That under existing conditions no one connected with the university at present, should be considered with the permanent deanship of the college of arts and sciences."[10]

Despite the difficulties of winning its independence, the Teachers College enjoyed rapid growth during its first decade of independent life. In the academic year of 1919–20, the enrollment in Teachers College was 417; by 1929–30, it had increased to 3,280. At the beginning of the decade, the professional work in education was carried by three departments. By 1924, the professional work of the college was conducted by eight departments: Educational Psychology and Measurements, Charles Fordyce, chairman; Elementary and Rural Education, Lida B. Earhart, chairman; History and Principles of Education, Dean William E. Sealock, chairman; Kindergarten-Primary Education, Clara O. Wilson, chairman; School Administration, Frank E. Henzlik, chairman; Secondary Education, Herbert Brownell, chairman; Techniques of Instruction in English, Frederick A.

10. *Minutes,* University of Nebraska Board of Regents, April 18, 1924.

Stuff, chairman; and Vocational Education, Harry E. Bradford, chairman. In January 1925, the Teachers College High School was separated from the Department of School Administration and organized as a separate department within the college with Charles W. Taylor as principal and director of teacher training. The Department of English (professional), formerly the Department of Techniques of Instruction in English, was abolished by the regents in 1926, and Professor Stuff returned to the faculty of the College of Arts and Sciences.

Closely related to the growth of the Teachers College was the expansion of the University summer sessions. With the establishment of a professional college in education, large numbers of teachers sought additional university work during the summer. The development of the Extension Division was stimulated by the expanded program in professional education. Professor Albert A. Reed, the director of the Extension Division, was also a member of the faculty of the Teachers College.

THE COLLEGE OF ARTS AND SCIENCES

During the decade of the twenties, the College of Arts and Sciences continued to provide the majority of University students with most of their classroom instruction. Accompanying the expansion of pre-professional and professional courses of study, the faculty of the college functioned as a service unit to the entire University. Although the number of students enrolled in the College of Arts and Sciences decreased as a percentage of the total student body, the instructional work of the college grew. This change in the role of the College of Arts and Sciences was a reflection of changes taking place in American higher education as the public came to regard universities as institutions for professional or career preparation.

With the appointment of Herman G. James, as dean of the College of Arts and Sciences in 1925, the work of the college became more harmonious. The new dean held degrees from the University of Illinois, University of Chicago, and the Doctor of Philosophy from Columbia University in political science. Prior to coming to the University of Nebraska, he had been professor of government at the University of Texas. James was an excellent dean for the college, but resigned in 1929 to accept the presidency of the University of South Dakota. He was succeeded by John D. Hicks, who was chairman of the Department of History.

Shortly after Dean James assumed his position, a graduate of the class of 1925 complained in the *Nebraska Alumnus*: ". . . my University has failed me. It taught me idealism and I needed realism. It taught me theory and I needed practice. It drew me in, a freshman, did not advise, let me learn when it was too late and then turned me out—four years behind the man did not go."[11] As a result of this and other criticism, a group of students petitioned Dean James for permission to form an undergraduate committee to examine and criticize the college. With the cooperation of the faculty and University administration, the study was made and recommendations offered. The findings of the committee were summarized for the alumni:

The kernel of the student's criticism is that the Arts College has no sense of a definite purpose, such as the professional schools have, and that consequently it has become a dumping-ground for students who do not fit into any of the other colleges. . . . In general, the report asks for more stringent entrance and scholarship requirements; freer reign to the individual capable of doing better than average work; loosening of purely administrative bonds; and a more friendly attitude from the faculty.[12]

11. *Nebraska Alumnus*, February 1926, p. 74.
12. *Nebraska Alumnus*, November 1926, p. 444.

The regents, in the fall of 1927, authorized the College of Arts and Sciences to offer a program leading to the degree of Bachelor of Arts with Distinction. Professor Charles H. Oldfather hoped that "out of the congeries of courses now offered in our universities a small group may be formed which will follow the tradition of a genuine 'Arts College' curriculum."[13]

The academic departments of the College of Arts and Sciences during the twenties greatly expanded their course offerings on the graduate level. In the 1920–21 academic year, the Department of English offered 12 graduate classes, chemistry 13, history 17, and French 6. By the 1929–30 academic year, the number of graduate classes had been expanded to 22 in English, 19 in chemistry, 23 in history, and 12 in French.

Because of the increased emphasis on graduate-level work, higher academic standards were required of new faculty members. In 1926, under the leadership of Dean James, the departmental chairman adopted a policy that in the future:

. . . no person should be appointed to the rank of assistant professor or above in the College of Arts and Sciences who does not have the equivalent of a doctor's degree; and that instructors should be appointed with the understanding that in no case would they be reappointed for a fourth year as instructor. If at the end of three years it is not possible or desirable to advance them to the rank of assistant professor the chairmen felt that it would be better for them and for the institution that they should go elsewhere and be replaced by a new crop of younger instructors.[14]

The adoption of this policy indicates the desire of the departmental chairmen, the dean, and the University administration to keep pace with rising academic standards. The policy reflected practices adopted earlier by most leading American universities.

The faculty of the College of Arts and Sciences, during the twenties, included in its membership many of the University of Nebraska's best known professors. Among them were: Joseph E. A. Alexis, professor of Romance languages; Albert L. Candy, professor of mathematics; John E. Almy, professor of experimental physics; Edgar L. Hinman, professor of logic and metaphysics; Carrie A. Barbour, assistant curator of the museum and assistant professor of paleontology; Sherlock Bronson Gass, professor of English; Erwin H. Barbour, professor of geology; John R. Pool, professor of botany; Nels A. Bengston, professor of geography; Prosser H. Frye, professor of English; William C. Brenke, professor of mathematics; Fred Morrow Fling, professor of history; Goodwin D. Swezey, professor of astronomy; Harriett Alice Howell, associate professor of elocution and dramatic art; Frederick A. Stuff, professor of English; Eck Frank Schramm, professor of geology; Louise Pound, professor of the English language; Laura B. Pfeiffer, associate professor of history; Lawrence Fossler, professor of Germanic languages; Paul H. Grumann, director of the School of Fine Arts and professor of dramatic literature; Charles H. Oldfather, professor of ancient history; Robert D. Scott, professor of modern English drama; Clarence A. Forbes, assistant professor of the classics; and Carrie B. Raymond, director of music.

SCHOOL OF JOURNALISM

Journalism began at the University in the English Department as a news writing course in the mid-nineties. It was expanded in 1915 and a certificate program announced in 1917. By the early twenties, there was a growing demand for a School of Journalism within the College of Arts and Sciences. The proposal

13. *Nebraska Alumnus,* September 1927, p. 340.
14. Letter, Herman G. James to Samuel Avery, March 26, 1926, MSS, University of Nebraska Archives, Avery Collection.

for an expanded journalism curriculum received considerable support from the rural newspaper publishers of the state. In 1923, the Board of Regents authorized the establishment of the School of Journalism. Students from the school dominated the staff of the *Daily Nebraskan,* which achieved new heights of excellence in reporting campus life. Additional practical experience was gained through the publication of the *Cornhusker* annual and *Awgwan,* a humor magazine published monthly by Sigma Delta Chi, the professional journalism fraternity.

The first director of the School of Journalism was Miller Moore Fogg. Few faculty members matched his service to the University. He joined the faculty in 1901 as an instructor and soon organized the University debate program around the "Nebraska System" for training in argumentative composition. Professor Fogg's "Think Shop" was an important part of his training scheme for debaters. He organized the Nebraska High School Debating League in 1908. Prior to his death in 1926, Fogg served as chairman of the Student Publication Board,

Daily Nebraskan staff at work.

supervised the University News Service, and coached the intercollegiate debaters. From a beginning in 1923 with 92 students, the School of Journalism grew to an enrollment of 223 by 1929.

THE COLLEGE OF LAW

In January 1920, the Board of Regents discussed the desirability of reorganizing the College of Law. A special committee of Regents, Landis, Brown, and Judson, was formed to study the advantages of such a reorganization. In May 1920, the committee of regents recommended to the board the appointment of a full-time faculty and new dean. The current dean, Judge William G. Hastings, it was suggested, should be named dean emeritus and professor of law. The Board of Regents was influenced in forming this policy by former Dean Roscoe Pound, who advised from his position as dean of law at Harvard.

I am indeed rejoiced to know that you intend to put the Law School of the University of Nebraska on the map. . . . this cannot be done by putting the school in charge of a retired practitioner who has expended his best energies in the practice, and filling the faculty up with half-time men, whose main interests are in client care-taking. . . .

I hope the Regents will find it possible to put a thoroughly trained man in charge, give him a well-trained faculty on full time, and I am confident that if they do so they will find presently that the School stands where it ought to, not only in the estimation of the bench and bar of the state, but in the legally educated world in general.[15]

Largely on the recommendation of Dean Pound, the University regents appointed Warren A. Seavey as dean of law. He had received the Bachelor of Arts and Bachelor of Laws degrees from Harvard University and had taught at the law schools at Harvard, the University of Oklahoma, and Tulane University. Immediately before coming to the University of Nebraska, Seavey was a member of the faculty at the Law College of the University of Indiana.

After consulting with leading members of the Nebraska bar, Dean Seavey recommended a number of reforms to Chancellor Avery. These included faculty improvement by appointing professional law school teachers to the faculty, the strengthening of instruction in the basic law courses, and the elimination of those courses beyond the scope of the three-year law program. Finally, he stressed the importance of the Law College faculty taking a leading part in the activities of the State Bar Association.

Besides the dean the Law College had three full-time faculty members, in addition to its part-time faculty, in the fall of 1920. The faculty was composed of Professors Henry H. Foster, William G. Hastings, and Charles A. Robbins and Assistant Professors George N. Foster, John J. Ledwith, and Ralph P. Wilson. The standards of the College of Law were rising. In January 1921, the entrance requirements were increased to 60 semester hours of college credit for regular admission to the college. The Nebraska Bar Association supported this increase. Sixty semester hours had already been required by the law colleges in the state universities of the adjoining states of Iowa, Kansas, Colorado, and South Dakota. In 1926, Dean Seavey resigned to accept a professorship at the University of Pennsylvania. The regents appointed Professor Henry H. Foster, who had been a member of the faculty since 1920, as the new dean.

THE COLLEGE OF ENGINEERING

Throughout this decade the College of Engineering offered four-year degree programs in the fields of agricultural, architectural, chemical, civil, electrical, and mechanical engineering. A fifth-year program in cooperation with the College of Business Administration could be added to any of the regular four-year programs which led to the degree of Bachelor of Science in Commercial Engineering. Although the number of students enrolled in the College of Engineering increased during the decade, the relative enrollment declined. In 1919–20, 10 percent of the University's students were enrolled in engineering; in 1924–25, it was 7 percent, and in 1929–30, 8 percent.

Dean O. V. P. Stout retired as dean of the college of Engineering in the spring of 1920 and was succeeded by Olin J. Ferguson, a member of the faculty since 1912. A native son, Ferguson had graduated from the University of Nebraska in 1903 and had industrial and teaching experience in the field of electrical engineering. At his request, the regents authorized the employment of a radio operator for the department of electrical engineering in June 1922. By March 1923, radio station WFAV was broadcasting to the state, and if conditions were favorable, to the nation. The station was operated jointly by the College of Engineering and the Extension Division. The broadcasts featured such educational fare as: Wednesday night concerts from students in the School of Fine

15. Letter, Roscoe Pound to Samuel Avery, June 25, 1920, MSS, University of Nebraska Archives, Avery Collection.

Arts, dramatic readings by members of Miss Howell's classes, and talks by members of the University faculty. It was reported in the *Daily Nebraskan* that:

University people are refusing to indulge the 'jazz craze' . . . the University community has presented a worthy example to those throughout the country who are engaged in the business of supplying food for public thought. We hope that the Nebraska station will not step down an inch from this standard; let us remember that popularity is much more agreeable than essential.[16]

In June 1925, the regents faced the problem of either purchasing new equipment for WFAV or using part-time, at no cost, the facilities of KFAB, the Nebraska-Buick broadcasting station. Lacking the needed funds for the modernization of the station, the regents accepted the offer of KFAB. It is unfortunate that the University of Nebraska, a pioneer in the establishment of public broadcasting, was forced to withdraw for lack of funds.

THE COLLEGE OF BUSINESS ADMINISTRATION

During the twenties, the College of Business Administration was under the administration of Dean James E. LeRossignol. Steady growth characterized this college, then housed on the third floor of the social science building. The work of the college was not only concerned with instruction, but also with the improvement of business in Nebraska. In 1921, a Committee on Business Research was organized to analyze and make recommendations to the businessmen of the state. This effort was expanded in 1927 with the creation of the Department of Business Research, with T. Bruce Robb as chairman. By 1929, twenty-four studies of business activity had been published in the *Nebraska Studies in Business* series. Among the areas investigated were: "The Influence of Automobiles and Good Roads on Retail Trade Centers," "Some Aspects of Grocery Store Failures," and "Retail Purchasing Power in Lincoln."

The college grew from 607 students in 1919–20 to 908 in 1925. In March 1925, the regents approved the division of the college into two departments, the Department of Business Organization and Management under the chairmanship of Oscar R. Martin and the Department of Economics with George O. Virtue as chairman. The course offerings of the college were expanded to include additional work in accounting, business statistics, business finance, banking, and agricultural credit.

DENTISTRY, PHARMACY, MEDICINE, AND NURSING

The College of Dentistry was established in 1904 as the private Lincoln Dental College. In 1918 by action of the regents, it became the School of Dentistry of the University of Nebraska. By act of the legislature in 1919, the school became the College of Dentistry. Throughout most of this decade, the college struggled to improve its facilities and to raise its standards. By the end of the decade, it had accomplished both.

At the beginning of the decade, entrance requirements for the dental course were the same as those for the College of Arts and Sciences. In 1921, the requirements were raised to 30 hours of acceptable college work. In 1923, the regents approved a cooperative program between the College of Arts and Sciences and the Dental College which enabled the student to receive both the Bachelor of Science and Doctor of Dental Surgery degrees in a six-year program. A seven-year program was later adopted, leading to the Bachelor of Arts and Doctor of Dental Surgery degrees.

16. *Daily Nebraskan*, February 6, 1924.

The College of Dentistry, in 1927, moved to Andrews Hall. This enabled it to provide more adequate facilities for its instructional program. As late as 1906, it was possible to enter the practice of dentistry by the apprenticeship route. The University of Nebraska Dental College was a major factor in the rising level of professional dental care available to Nebraskans. Wallace Clyde Davis was dean from the time of the school's affiliation with the University of Nebraska until late 1922. He was succeeded by George Albert Grubb, dean through the period of great change during the twenties.

During the short four-year life of the University of Nebraska Trades School, the College of Dentistry offered a two-year non-collegiate course in mechanical dentistry. This program trained a number of urgently needed qualified dental technicians. With the termination of the Trades School program in 1925, this course was discontinued.

The College of Pharmacy under the administration of Dean Rufus A. Lyman pioneered in the establishment of pharmacy as a profession. In 1920 the college offered a two-year program of studies leading to the Graduate in Pharmacy certificate, a three-year program leading to the degree of Pharmaceutical Chemist, and a four-year program leading to the Bachelor of Science in Pharmacy. By mid-decade the requirements for the Graduate in Pharmacy had been changed from two to three years and the two-year program eliminated. In 1927, the three-year program was discontinued, and only the four-year course leading to the Bachelor of Science remained. Professors Joseph B. Burt, Fred S. Bukey, and Charles L. Wible assisted Dean Lyman in the development of the professional program.

Although separated from the principal site of the University of Nebraska, the College of Medicine and the School of Nursing, both located in Omaha, shared in the developments affecting the health-related fields. During the first half of the decade, Irving S. Cutter served as dean of medicine.

In February 1921, the legislature undertook an examination of the University Medical School curriculum. Senator Henry Pickett, a contractor from Wahoo, introduced a bill which would require the establishment of professorships in eclectic and homeopathic medicine in the College of Medicine. In the House of Representatives a similar bill was introduced by S. J. Franklin, a farmer from Beaver City, and was narrowly defeated by a 37 to 38 vote. In a letter to the legislature, the Board of Regents firmly opposed the bill.

For the University of Nebraska to establish and maintain departments of eclectic and homeopathic medicine would be (a) a step backward in medical education (b) opening the door for the establishment of additional departments of medical cults (c) the present high standard of the College of Medicine would be injured incalculably (d) expense.[17]

Some considered the proposed bill as a move, planned by a group from Lincoln, to destroy the college. It is much more likely that the passage of the legislation was sought by those who wanted to open the door of the Medical College to eventual instruction in osteopathy and chiropractic.

Dean Cutter resigned in 1925 as dean of the College of Medicine to accept a similar appointment at Northwestern University. J. Jay Keegan was appointed to fill the vacancy. Under Dean Keegan's leadership, the second unit of the University of Nebraska Hospital was opened in 1927. This doubled the capacity of the hospital and substantially improved the facilities for clinical instruction. Dean Keegan resigned as dean in 1929 to return to teaching and private medical

17. Letter, F. W. Judson to Members of the Legislature, March 1, 1921, MSS, University of Nebraska Archives, Avery Collection.

practice. Professor C. W. M. Poynter, who had been chairman of the Department of Anatomy since 1918, was named acting dean. The regents later made his appointment permanent.

The School of Nursing, affiliated with the College of Medicine, enjoyed substantial growth during this decade. In 1919–20, the school enrolled 38 students. The three-year program led to a Diploma of Nursing, while those desiring a degree could follow a five-year cooperative program between the College of Arts and Sciences and the School of Nursing. By the end of the twenties, enrollment of the School of Nursing had passed the 100 mark. Charlotte Burgess was director of the school during the twenties.

COLLEGE OF AGRICULTURE

Few University programs had a greater impact on the daily lives of Nebraskans than those of the College of Agriculture. It was estimated in the mid-twenties that as a direct result of the University's agricultural work the value of farm production in Nebraska had been increased $26,205,000 annually.[18] This was the result of research carried out in Lincoln and at the various experiment stations over a period of years. In addition to collegiate-level instruction, the college provided educational programs on the secondary school level in the Nebraska School of Agriculture at Curtis and in the School of Agriculture at Lincoln, until its closing in 1928. While in operation, the University of Nebraska Trades School in cooperation with the College of Agriculture provided work in agriculturally related skills. Other "short course" offerings further expanded the instructional services of the college.

From the beginning of the decade until the time of his appointment as chancellor, Edgar A. Burnett served as dean of the College of Agriculture and director of the Agricultural Experiment Station. After Burnett's appointment as chancellor, William W. Burr was appointed to the post of dean and director, which he held until the fifties. On the collegiate level, enrollments in the College of Agriculture expanded over 300 percent in the decade of the twenties, numbering 751 students by 1929–30. The instructional program reflected the growth of agriculture as an academic discipline as well as the rising public support for the college. Academic growth was evidenced by the establishment of the Department of Poultry Husbandry as a separate department from that of animal husbandry in 1922. The offering of a professional degree in home economics, in 1924, further documents the academic maturity taking place in the curriculum of the college. Burgeoning enrollment in the instructional programs at both the collegiate and noncollegiate levels demonstrated public support and confidence.

Economic benefits for the farmers and ranchers of Nebraska increased as the faculty of the College of Agriculture focused its attention on agricultural problems of the state. These investigations were primarily related to the improvement of agricultural production and to the most effective use of available resources. The solution of these problems of immediate concern not only helped the agriculturalist to improve his production, but laid the foundation for future research.

In the Department of Agricultural Chemistry, under the chairmanship of Morris J. Blish, work was done by Clifton W. Ackerson on poultry metabolism. Blish and Rudolph M. Sandstedt studied the chemistry of baking and increased the marketability of Nebraska wheat. The Agronomy Department was concerned with Nebraska soils and crop production. An outstanding member of the department was Theodore A. Kiesselbach, whose broad interests touched many

18. *What Do You Know About Your State University?*, Bulletin 23, Ser. XXIX, University of Nebraska, October 1924, p. 34.

aspects of plant science and crop production. His influence in the college stimulated both the quantity and the quality of research. For example, with the help of his research associates, Kiesselbach's work contributed directly to increasing corn production. Professors Howard J. Gramlich and William J. Loeffel, as members of the Department of Animal Husbandry, demonstrated more effective use of livestock feeds.

Another prominent member of the College of Agriculture faculty was Leunis Van Es. A native of the Netherlands, he held degrees in both medicine and veterinary medicine. He joined the faculty in 1918 and was named chairman of the Department of Animal Pathology and Hygiene in 1919. As a scholar, Van Es made valuable contributions to the understanding and prevention of cattle,

"Cow and Hen Special" at Wayne, Nebraska, on April 17, 1926. Courtesy of the Nebraska State Historical Society.

sheep, swine, and poultry diseases. He recognized the responsibilities of the University to the people of that state and many of his publications dealt with the everyday problems of the farmer, stockman, and farm wife.

During this decade the Department of Dairy Husbandry maintained dairy herds at Lincoln, North Platte, Scottsbluff, and Valentine. The emphasis of this work was to demonstrate the high level of production possible with improved breeding and proper herd management. Publications by Professor Lawrence K. Crowe emphasized quality control for dairy products and their use in the manufacture of sherberts and ice cream.

Under the leadership of Margaret S. Fedde, chairman of the Department of Home Economics, the degree program in professional home economics was begun. Publications by Majorie R. Clark analyzed the contributions made by farm women as well as facilities on the farm available to them.

In the Department of Horticulture, the work of Professor Harvey O. Werner was outstanding. His research had great impact upon potato culture practices as well as the improvement, production, storage, and marketing of the potato in Nebraska. George L. Peltier and Robert W. Goss, of the Department of Plant Pathology, influenced production of wheat and potatoes by developing methods of preventing and controlling diseases which affected these crops in Nebraska. The publications of Professor Horace C. Filley and the staff of the Department of Rural Economics explained the economics of agriculture to the farmer and rancher.

The experiment stations at North Platte, Scottsbluff, and Valentine provided the staff of the College of Agriculture with valuable laboratory facilities. William P. Snyder was superintendent of the North Platte Station during the twenties. Under his direction, studies were made on the use of alfalfa hay in its various forms. Snyder's work with cattle was much less extensive but was also of basic importance. At the station improved management practices for dairying were developed and quality breeding stock was provided for the area. The livestock at this station was also used for instructional purposes by local high school classes and by 4-H Club members. In cooperation with the Dry Land Office of the United States Department of Agriculture, an extensive program in dry-land farming was conducted at North Platte. These studies involved different tillage methods, different times of tillage, and the relation of these to the storage and use of soil moisture.

The Scottsbluff Station, near Mitchell, was operated in close cooperation with the Office of Western Irrigation Agriculture of the United States Department of Agriculture. Some of the research done by Werner, Goss, Peltier, and others of the staff based at Lincoln was conducted at Scottsbluff. The Valentine Station, established as the result of a law passed by the 1909 legislature, was primarily engaged in livestock production. The superintendent of the station was Edgar M. Brouse. As ranching replaced farming in this area, the work of the station shifted to meet the new demands. The early work at Valentine was of great service to the settlers of the Sand Hills, but the most significant contribution from the station resulted from a long series of studies on the effects of various feeding programs.

Related but separate from work of the College of Agriculture in raising the standard of living of Nebraskans, was the Conservation and Survey Division. Led by George E. Condra, the division contributed to the wise development of the natural resources of Nebraska. During this decade, bulletins appeared which began a systematic inventory of the state's natural resources. Not only did Condra and his staff emphasize the exploitation of resources, but also they devoted equal attention to the spread of good conservation practices, including planting of trees.

Academically the University of Nebraska was a different place in 1930 from what it had been in 1920. Not only had it grown in number of students, but of greater importance, it had expanded its vision to meet the needs of the people of Nebraska. The University was participating in changes common to all institutions of higher education in the nation. Here, as elsewhere, expansion was accompanied by growing pains. The severity of these symptoms was greatest, perhaps, in the land-grant universities of America's heartland. However, by 1930, after a decade of change and expansion, the University of Nebraska had become an institution of service for the people of the state to an extent unknown in its past.

CHAPTER 3

Student Life in the Jazz Age

THE SEMI-CENTENNIAL of the University of Nebraska was celebrated in May 1919. For students the event was a milestone. "It marked the end of a period of growth from one lonely school house, bordering on a more lonely stretch of dreary prairie, to a varied array of college buildings set on a campus teeming with the busy life of thousands of young students."[1] The principal event of the occasion was "pageant of freedom, tracing the march of freedom from the earliest days until the death of militarism with the defeat of the Germans. . . . in a series of military tableaux made effective by elaborate scenery and artistic dancing."[2] The pageant was written by Hartley Burr Alexander and staged by Professor R. D. Scott.

With this act of purification, the University washed itself of the charges of disloyalty raised during the World War and prepared for a return to "normalcy." However postwar inflation and declining farm commodity prices hampered students in their enjoyment of the Jazz Age. As the campus population grew to over ten thousand, a figure not again reached until after World War II, housing too became a serious problem. This shortage stimulated the growth of fraternities and sororities and increased the traditional rivalry between Greek and "Barbarian." Student social life underwent changes with the beginning of prohibition, the increased availability of automobiles, and the arrival of "big time" football.

In anticipation of the changes resulting from a rapidly growing student body, Professor Grummann announced in the fall of 1920 that weekly all-student convocations were being discontinued. In the future, special convocations would be called when speakers of national importance or special interest visited the campus. As the number of University-sponsored functions declined, the number of events scheduled by student groups increased. This was especially true of social events. Advertisements urged student organizations to engage the "Original Southern Rag-A-Jazz Band," which had just returned from its summer tour on the west coast. Those who preferred less jazz were urged to hire Leo Beck's "Syncopated Symphony." Student groups eagerly sought to return their social life to "normalcy" and if possible to improve upon it. Imagination produced sorority rushing parties described as a "La Belle Vanitie" dinner dance, a "Vanity Fair" luncheon, a "moon winks romp," and a "daisy" breakfast.

By December 1920, the social season was in full swing. The parties and dances were bigger and better than ever, but so was their cost. A meeting was held at the Temple at which all the fraternities and sororities agreed to temporarily withhold their patronage from hotels, dance halls, and amusement places until prices were reduced. A short time later, the Inter-Fraternity Council

1. *Cornhusker,* 1920, p. 42.
2. Ibid.

adopted a resolution canceling all fraternity formals from January 15, 1921, until the end of the school year. However, students were not seemingly hampered in their social activities by the brief ban on formal dances. As students devoted more time to pleasure, scholarship declined. Dean Carl C. Engberg thought that students were affected by the current labor unrest. "People cannot get anybody to do anything. The same is true of the schools. Students don't get down to business. Another reason is the tremendous craze for entertainment. People are just wild over the movies, dancing and other forms of entertainment."[3] Fortunately, the dean noted, "The girls don't do so many fool stunts and don't chase around on the streets like the boys. . . ."[4]

There were complaints by citizens that more students now smoked and that many girls at the University wore rouge. Students did, however, have their defenders in the public press. A Lincoln paper defended the student body: "Because a girl uses rouge it is not a sign that she is a 'wicked vamp' nor is the young man who smokes when in the presence of his girl friends any worse than the able bodied man in the street car who lets a lady stand for ten or twelve blocks without offering her his seat."[5]

Another characteristic of student life during the Jazz Age was the identification many students sought with the University through affiliation with the growing number and variety of campus organizations. Readers of the State Journal were undoubtedly amused when they learned that some groups of men students could be identified by their characteristic appearance. "A recent example was observed last week when a young man, one day after he had pledged a certain fraternity started parting his hair in that distinctive style by which 'ye shall know them.' "[6]

At the beginning of the decade, University authorities attempted to meet the growing housing crisis by furnishing six old houses, purchased earlier, in the 12th and R Street area for use by women students. These "cottage" rooms were rented for $36 to $58 per semester, and the number of applicants greatly exceeded the available spaces. The problem of housing was becoming increasingly desperate. The situation received study by the regents, administration, faculty committee, and the alumni. Always, the lack of funds prevented adequate University action. However, the opening of Ellen Smith Hall at 14th and R Streets in the fall of 1920 provided a center for campus activities and housed the office of Amanda Heppner, the dean of women. The building was named in memory of Ellen Smith, the first woman teacher in the University and its first registrar.

The Student Council, which had been founded in 1917, was nearly abolished in 1921. Lawrence W. Metzger, '21, who was president of the Student Council, proposed to a mass meeting of the student body that the organization be abolished. A Daily Nebraskan editorial agreed, "Personally we believe that it will be a wise move if the students of this school decide to do away with the Student Council."[7] Its critics asserted that matters brought to the council for consideration had already been decided upon by other student organizations, and that action by the Student Council was superficial. By a student vote of 177 to 159 the Student Council was retained. The issue generated little student concern because the real but limited power of student government resided in the class societies which were dominated by the fraternities and sororities. The strengthening of the Student Council was the "Barb" answer to "Greek" dominance of

3. Lincoln, *Nebraska State Journal*, May 28, 1920, p. 7.
4. Ibid.
5. Lincoln, *Nebraska State Journal*, April 18, 1920, p. B-3.
6. Lincoln, *Nebraska State Journal*, April 25, 1920, p. B-3.
7. *Daily Nebraskan*, March 3, 1921.

student life. The student annual of 1921 described the workings of campus politics.

This society [Student Council] is a real democratic organization and should be given more power. It has suffered during its existence because of the jealousy of other students' societies, such as class organizations, which have feared that it might tread on their toes and take away some of their power. The Student Council should be permitted to "tread on the toes" of some of the class societies for one paramount reason—it is a body selected by the students at a general election, while class societies which hold the power, with the exception of some of the more democratic girls' organizations and a very few others, are chosen merely by the members of that organization for the year before and in many respects are not at all representative of the student body.[8]

In February 1928, the faculty Committee on Student Affairs investigated the undergraduate class societies at the request of the Student Council. The faculty

Amanda Heppner, dean of women, with a group of girls on the steps of Ellen Smith Hall in 1922. Courtesy of the Nebraska State Historical Society.

committee dissolved a number of the class societies because "they rendered no particular service to the School. . . ."[9] The abolished class honor societies were Mystic Fish for freshman girls, Green Goblins for freshman men, Xi Delta for sophomore girls, Iron Sphinx for sophomore men, Silver Serpents for junior women, Vikings for junior men, and the Valkyrie for senior women. In all these organizations the membership was dominated by those affiliated with fraternities or sororities. Membership, for instance, in the Mystic Fish was limited to one representative from each sorority and only two from the remainder of the student body. Because the faculty committee believed that the Innocents and Mortar Board contributed useful services to the University they were retained. Mortar Board was established on the Nebraska campus in 1921 when Black Masque, a local organization founded in 1905 affiliated with the national organization and became the Black Masque Chapter of Mortar Board.

During the early years of the twenties students discussed the latest fashion

8. *Cornhusker,* 1921, p. 387.
9. Lincoln, *Nebraska State Journal,* February 7, 1928, p. 1.

and not all favored the new styles. Gale Grubb, '21, the editor of the *Awgwan* was critical of female fashion. "Modesty has given way to daring, beauty to undisguised attempts to exhibit charms, and form has been supplemented by shape."[10] Story Harding, '22, editor of the *Daily Nebraskan*, agreed, "kneelength dresses of the modern girl have cast modesty from the dictionary."[11]

While accepted standards of proper dress were changing the accepted norms of good taste in student publications had not changed. In the 1921 *Cornhusker*, the section on student life produced a torrent of criticism. Forty-two students were severely ridiculed by name. It was written about one student that "she has never had friendly relations with 'Pepsodent' or 'Woodburys.' "[12] There was criticism by the student body, faculty, regents, and the public against this breach of good taste. Attempts were made to require students to return their annuals to have the offensive pages removed, but this could only be partially successful. Under the increasingly watchful eye of the Student Publication Board, the editors of the 1922 *Cornhusker* promised,

. . . that it may through its pages give a true reflection of the activities and life of the University. . . . It is further hoped that this may be done in such a manner that every member of the faculty, every alumnus, and every student may take genuine pride in this, his year book, and in turn have a higher regard for the noble ideals of our University.[13]

A feature of the annual that year was a section of the "best looking" girls at the University by the noted illustrator and artist, James Montgomery Flagg. Those chosen were Isabelle Evans, Vivian Hanson, Helen Kummer, Mildred Taylor, Mildred Hullinger, and Esther Crider.

During these years students maintained many old traditions and initiated some new ones. Ivy Day continued to be celebrated in May and was expanded to include Round-Up in 1922. Homecoming and the Olympics remained the important events of the fall season. In the Olympics remained the important events of the fall season. In the Olympics the freshmen battled the sophomores for the right to discard their green caps. If they were defeated by the sophomores they were required to wear these caps for another semester. University Night was still the "largest fun fest of the year," until the last years of the decade. The distribution of *Shun*, the Sigma Delta Chi scandal sheet, was an eagerly anticipated part of the University Night program. The contents of *Shun* in 1923 resulted in the temporary suspension of Sigma Delta Chi, the professional journalism fraternity.

Other traditional student activities were the Farmer's Fair, the Kosmet Klub production, the Cornhusker Banquet, the Girls Cornhusker Party, and the Girls Cornhusker Luncheon. Compet, the wild celebration and parade after the annual inspection of the ROTC cadets, concluded with the students swarming by all means of conveyance to the amusement park at Capital Beach. New student events of the early twenties were the Freshman Barbecue and Dad's Day, first held in 1922.

The Ambassadors Club, formed in 1922, was "an organization created for the purpose of 'putting across' the University in the home town and home community," of the student.[14] Considering the fate of the University in the special legislative session of 1922, it needed all the local support a student group could generate. Students in the College of Arts and Sciences founded two new organi-

10. *Daily Nebraskan,* May 15, 1921.
11. Ibid.
12. *Cornhusker,* 1921, p. 480.
13. *Cornhusker,* 1922, Foreword.
14. Ibid., p. 310.

zations. The Centurians was for men and the Vestals of the Lamp was for women. The purpose of these two groups was "to raise and perpetuate the ideals of the College, to stimulate interest in its traditions, and to guide the student opinion of the thousands of Arts College registrants."[15] The initiation ritual was written by Professor Hartley Burr Alexander, the champion of the Arts and Sciences.

Among the less serious organizations was the Order of the Golden Fleece. It had been founded in 1917, discontinued in 1918, and reactivated in 1920. Membership was limited to women students with red hair. In 1922, there were twenty-seven eligible natural hair tints. They varied from "reddest of the red" to "near-brown." Students in the twenties had a wide variety of organizations with which they might affiliate. Most students were joiners, some belonged to as many as ten or twelve student groups.

Many memorable events occurred during these years. The Palladian Society celebrated its Semi-Centennial in 1921. That same year the *Cornhusker Song-book* was published. It sold for $1.75 and included such future favorites as the "Marching Song," "Hail to Thee," and forty-eight other songs. In the spring of 1922, the iron fence around the campus was removed. With the removal of the fence, the traditional tobacco barrier, the regulation of smoking became more difficult. The fence was later erected around Wyuka Cemetery in Lincoln, and stands there today.

Students, faculty, and alumni were saddened by the death of Jack Best in 1923. For thirty-four years he had been the trainer for Cornhusker teams. Chancellor Avery expressed the general feeling:

The grand old man of the University has left us. The sadness among students and instructors has never been greater. Of all who have been in the University's service, he was probably the best beloved. I remember his great popularity with the students even in my own student days. . . . He was always kindly, devoted, faithful. His real sympathy and affection for those who came under his care was most remarkable. He leaves behind him an enduring monument in the memories that cluster about his name. His memory will be cherished long after many who have held a more exalted position are forgotten.[16]

Early in 1924, the Board of Regents assigned Dean Carl C. Engberg the additional responsibilities of dean of men. He was specifically charged by the regents "to enforce stringent rules against liquor drinking among students."[17] Many University students apparently did not comply with the provisions of prohibition. One student group favored a campus referendum on the subject of national prohibition. The idea was copied from some eastern colleges. Chancellor Avery ruled against the idea of a student vote on prohibition.

It is possible that some other schools have permitted a referendum among their students as to whether or not they favor upholding the Constitution of the United States and the enforcement of the law. Such a proposal, however, in the University of Nebraska is preposterous.[18]

Dean Engberg reported to the regents that after his investigation of campus drinking, when "it became my duty to inquire into the moral conditions in the University, many sad things came to light."[19] Although the dean did not describe

15. *Ibid.*, p. 399.
16. *Daily Nebraskan,* January 21, 1923.
17. *Minutes,* University of Nebraska Board of Regents, January 22, 1924.
18. *Daily Nebraskan,* January 30, 1924.
19. Report from Dean Carl C. Engberg to the Chancellor and Board of Regents, undated, MSS, University of Nebraska Archives, Avery Collection.

what "sad things" he discovered, he believed that "only through the earnest co-operation and wise leadership of such a group [the fraternity alumni] can the evils of drinking at home-coming time, improper amusements at parties, foolish probation and initiation stunts, etc. be controlled."[20]

Because of the very large number of campus organizations the role of the extracurriculum was even questioned by the student body. In February 1924, a student vote was taken on a plan which would limit the number of organizations to which a student could belong. The election was held under the auspices of the Student Council while Clifford M. Hicks, '24, was president. The system for limiting membership in student organizations proposed by Mortar Board was adopted for women students, while the all-University proposal was narrowly defeated.

Student publications improved during the middle years of the decade as a result of the establishment of the School of Journalism. Among the publications, the *Awgwan* had the most uncertain life. It was suspended in 1923 and reinstated in 1924. The humor magazine was plagued with financial problems and was found guilty of exercising poor judgment in the selection of its material. Constantly under the watch of the Student Publication Board, the *Awgwan* was again suppressed for publishing offensive material in 1929.

Most students at the University of Nebraska were, at least partially, self-supporting. A survey in 1925 revealed 41 percent of the men and 19 percent of the women students were wholly self-supporting; 35 percent of the men and 19 percent of the women were partially self-supporting. The male student who worked averaged ten hours a week on an outside job compared to three hours for the female student. Students reported that their average expense for the school year was $714.66 for men and $729.85 for women. With nearly 80 percent of the student body employed, University of Nebraska students were not affluent. The myth of Jazz Age prosperity found little substantiation in Nebraska—on or off campus. To assist students to remain in school, in 1921, the YMCA and the Lincoln Lions Club instituted a cooperative program in the operation of a student employment office.

By mid-decade, the Board of Regents increased its concern for, and supervision of, student life. In January 1925, the regents amended their by-laws to create a committee on student relations within the board. During the summer of 1925, the regents with the cooperation of the city of Lincoln established the "University Zone." No student organization was permitted to acquire or use property within the zone without the permission of the Board of Regents. The plan envisioned the east side of 16th Street as a "co-ed" avenue. By the fall of 1926, Alpha Omicron Pi, Alpha Delta Theta, Pi Beta Phi, Kappa Delta, Delta Delta Delta, Alpha Chi Omega, and Delta Gamma occupied new sorority houses and Delta Tau Delta and Beta Theta Pi new fraternity houses.

During this time of growth by social fraternities and sororities, a majority of the student body were not members of "Greek" organizations. Nevertheless, the popularity of University-sponsored parties was in a state of decline, as recognized in an article in the *Daily Nebraskan*. "It is a by-word on the campus that few students other than freshmen, (usually very rustic freshmen) attend the parties. Whether it is because the parties are dull, or merely because the students are out of the habit, we do not know."[21] Greek-letter student organizations despite their minority position clearly dominated the University social scene.

The University Players presented the drama, "The Red Cockatoo," which

20. Ibid.
21. *Daily Nebraskan*, October 21, 1925.

was highly critical of sororities, in the spring of 1926. By the fall, disapproval of the "Greek" system had increased. Professor John Andrew Rice, chairman of the Classics Department, was a leading critic. He charged that the "Greeks" dominated the social life of the University, were essentially aristocratic and undemocratic, and that they fostered an un-American sense of values among their membership. These charges were not new, nor was this the last time that they would be voiced during the University's second half century. The development of the fraternity and sorority system at the University of Nebraska had resulted largely from the inability of the University to provide housing for students. Guy Kiddoo, '14, properly assessed the situation:

Fraternities represent the present trend in general. . . . Lowering of standards is no more in evidence among fraternities than in colleges as a whole, and in all social groups. . . . There is a real need for some device for bringing the students together in social groups. Fraternities are practically the only means for accomplishing this. The dormitory system would be better, but would involve a great deal of expense.[22]

During the decade of the sixties, the construction of a large University dormitory complex contributed to the weakening of the Greek system.

The greatest controversy to involve the University community during the mid-twenties concerned the ROTC program. In March 1926, at a convention of seventy-five Baptist pastors held in Lincoln, a resolution was unanimously adopted calling for an end to compulsory military training at the University of Nebraska. Representatives of the Methodist church passed a similar resolution. Rev. Harry Huntington, the Methodist student pastor at the University, organized a statewide citizens committee to oppose military training. The clergyman expressed the group's opposition to the military requirement. "It [compulsory military training] looks like an attempt to militarize the nation. Having put down militarism we are in danger of it from this source."[23] The Board of Regents took exception to Rev. Huntington's remarks and officially recorded their protest:

The Board disapproves the attitude of certain religious and welfare workers assigned to the University who do not seem to realize the gross impropriety of accepting the good will and hospitality of the institution and conducting from offices given them by the Regents a campaign against the traditional policies of the institution and against the authority of the governing board.[24]

The regents acknowledged that the board was not legally required to make two years of military training a mandatory requirement. However, the regents believed that there was a moral commitment to continue compulsory ROTC for all physically fit male freshmen and sophomore students. The policy of the Board of Regents was supported by many social fraternities, alumni, and the American Legion. However, Rosalind M. Griffin, '01, the first woman to run for the office of University regent disagreed, stating "that military training belongs with other trade and vocational subjects and, like them, it should be elective."[25]

On February 1, 1927, Frank S. Wells, a farmer from Fairbury, introduced into the Nebraska House of Representatives a bill which would prohibit mandatory ROTC participation. Representative Wells's proposal was sent to the House Committee on Education for a hearing. The bill stated simply, "Military training in the University of Nebraska shall be optional with the students and not a compulsory requirement for graduation."[26] At the hearing, Representative Wells

22. Lincoln, *Nebraska State Journal*, November 23, 1926, p. 7.
23. *Daily Nebraskan*, March 12, 1926.
24. *Minutes*, University of Nebraska Board of Regents, March 20, 1926.
25. Lincoln, *Nebraska State Journal*, July 7, 1926, p. 8.
26. Ibid., February 19, 1927, p. 1.

was the leading spokesman for his bill, while Major Marcus F. Poteet, a Lincoln attorney, led those who were opposed to the bill. The Wells bill died in committee, and insufficient public interest prevented its supporters from bringing the issue to a public vote by the means of a referendum.

Early in 1927, the College Activities Hall on the Agricultural Campus was opened for student use. This provided a long needed meeting place for students on the East Campus. During these years, the lack of University facilities for student housing and recreation was direct stimulation to the growth of social fraternities and sororities. As was true earlier in the decade, public criticism of the "Greek" system again surfaced. Harvey Newbranch, '96, editor of the Omaha *World-Herald,* argued in 1927 for "at least one year when all students would be on parity and there would be no 'barbarian.' He deplores the prema-

University of Nebraska Pershing Rifles in 1923. Courtesy of the Nebraska State Historical Society.

ture grouping of students into cliques 'in which friendships are narrowed, rather than broadened, and in which a false sense of values is acquired.' "[27] The solution proposed was the establishment of a system of University dormitories for all freshmen students. Pledging would be deferred until the second year of college when "they might acquire a balanced judgment that would prevent their heads being turned by the almost sensual equipment and designs of the costly houses that are built by the aid of wealthy alumni and required to make easier the securing of the necessary new members each year."[28]

Although the Alumni Association, University administration, and faculty favored the creation of a dormitory system, it was impossible to secure the necessary financing. Inducements to private investors failed to improve the situation and with the rising enrollment the housing problem was becoming critical. The regents were particularly concerned about the living conditions of women students. In September 1928, they adopted new rules for women students requiring them to live only in approved rooming houses, sorority houses, University dormitories, and in private homes where they were employed as domestic help. Amanda H. Heppner, as dean of women, was given general supervision of

27. *Daily Nebraskan,* March 1, 1927.
28. Ibid.

women's housing. In 1927, Theos Jefferson Thompson, a member of the Chemistry Department since 1918, was appointed dean of students with general responsibility for all student activities. The editors of the *Cornhusker* commented, in 1928, that Dean Thompson, "has won the hearts of the students."[29]

Finally, in 1929, the efforts of the regents and University administration to improve housing conditions were rewarded. The legislature authorized the regents to lease to a private corporation University land for the construction of fireproof dormitories. A $200,000 appropriation was made to purchase land and to provide partial funding of a dormitory. Following the pattern established in the construction of the Stadium and Coliseum, a Women's Dormitory and Dining Room Corporation was created. This private corporation contracted with the Board of Regents to furnish a dormitory, which would become University property when it had been paid for out of its revenues and the dormitory corporation dissolved. Consequently, the credit of the state of Nebraska was not involved. The dormitory was named after Carrie Belle Raymond when it was opened in the thirties.

The YMCA and YWCA, centers of student activity during much of the twenties, suffered definite reversals near the end of the decade. Public criticism of University Night, the major fund raising activity of the YMCA, resulted in the banning of that traditional event in 1927. A *Daily Nebraskan* editorial stated that "Feeling against continuance of University Night has been growing for several years as the various acts seemed to be degenerating more and more from year to year without any effective preventive measures by the Y.M.C.A. under whose auspices and for whose benefit the show was staged."[30] Although the skits were presented by various campus groups, the YMCA was held responsible for their content. The expectation of student-imposed censorship was unrealistic.

After the banning of most of the undergraduate class honor societies in 1928, the Black Masque chapter of Mortar Board and the Innocents continued the tradition of the honor societies. Selection by one of these organizations was perhaps even more prestigious than before. A new University of Nebraska tradition was begun by the Innocents in 1928. This was the awarding of a unique trophy bell at the annual Missouri-Nebraska football game. This bell, which is still awarded to the winner of this traditional rivalry for a year's keeping, has a long history. According to one account, the bell was removed by four student cadets from the belfry of a "colored" church in Seward, Nebraska, in 1898. The cadets were members of the Delta Tau Delta and Phi Delta Theta fraternities. The Delts outnumbered the Phi Delts, and so the bell was taken to their house as a trophy. Later, the Phi Delts pilfered the bell and enshrined the trophy in their house. For the next thirty years, the bell remained in the possession of one or the other fraternity, its fate being determined by the vigilance of one and the cunning of the other. The Delta Tau Delta–Phi Delta Theta bell feud ended when the fraternities agreed to donate the bell as a trophy for a greater rivalry—that of Nebraska-Missouri football.

The traditional campus rivalry between students in the College of Engineering and the College of Law erupted again in the spring of 1927. Rudolph Umland, x'29, remembered the altercation:

The engineers had constructed a dirigible balloon and mounted it on a pole on the campus to advertise the annual "Engineers' Week." Some law students partly wrecked the balloon one night and the engineers considered it a direct attack upon the college honor. Names were called and threats exchanged. On the night of the riot the engi-

29. *Cornhusker*, 1928, p. 18.
30. *Daily Nebraskan*, May 4, 1927.

neers were giving a public demonstration of the work of their college. I was assisting in the testing of concrete in one of the laboratories. Suddenly there were four blasts of a steam whistle—a signal that the lawyers had again attacked our balloon. We dropped our work and rushed from the building.

The lawyers had succeeded in entirely wrecking the balloon this time. We saw a large party of them fleeing up one street so we set off in pursuit. The miscreants reached the Phi Alpha Delta fraternity house, crowded in, and locked the doors. We milled around the house and shouted to them to come out and fight like men. They replied by hooting at us from the windows and throwing ripe eggs.

"Let's break in the doors!" some one shouted.

The doors readily gave way under our impact and we swarmed into the house. Several fledgling lawyers were caught and made captive; the others retreated up the stairway to the third floor. Pressing after them, we were halted near the upper landing

Engineers' advertisement for E Week partially burned by law students.

by a shower of blows from milk bottles, chairs and clubs. More than one skull was bruised in the melée that followed. I remember feeling the trickle of warm blood down my own face when a chair leg hurtled through the air and struck me. The police had meanwhile arrived and were trying to break up the mob outside. We made captives of all the men in the house and led them to the campus pool where we ducked them, one by one. It was only after several fire trucks had arrived, and the firemen had put their hoses into play, that the mob was finally dispersed. The fraternity house presented a sorry spectacle.[31]

Student conduct during the "Jazz Age" was greatly influenced by the automobile. By the late twenties, many cars appeared on the campus. The used model T Ford was exceptionally popular with students. The establishment of a policy of regulating the use of cars by students was announced in the fall of 1927. William P. Warner, president of the Board of Regents, explained, "There is too much diversion from the real purpose of attending the university. . . . We can't hardly get around the campus because there are so many autos. . . . Whether all are here for a legitimate purpose is questionable."[32] Regulation of student

31. *Nebraska Alumnus*, April 1940, p. 8.
32. *Daily Nebraskan*, October 23, 1927.

cars had already started at the Universities of Missouri, Oklahoma, Illinois, Purdue, and Indiana.

During the last year of the decade, the dominance of social fraternities and sororities again became a matter of intense controversy. Many Nebraskans objected to the alleged exclusiveness of fraternities and sororities. Victor M. Hovis, a clergyman and politician from Lexington, introduced a bill into the Nebraska House of Representatives in 1929 which would

. . . prohibit students in the state university, state normal schools or other institutions of higher education supported in whole or in part by public funds or public taxation, to join or pledge themselves to join any college fraternity, sorority or any other secret society of any kind whose active membership is composed of college students before they have completed at least one college year in said institution.[33]

The bill was reported out by committee and received favorable consideration by the House on its first and second readings. Just days before the bill was

Parking jam at the Coliseum in 1926. Courtesy of the Lincoln *Journal-Star*.

to be considered by the House for its final reading, the University of Nebraska Inter-Fraternity Council abolished the traditional probation period for fraternity pledges. Dean T. J. Thompson approved because "whatever innocent or rough treatment has been accorded the neophyte the general public, quite unfamiliar with fraternity life, has regarded probation with suspicion; and I believe university administrators and faculty members usually have viewed the practice with some apprehension."[34]

On its third reading the Hovis bill received 36 affirmative votes, 49 negative votes, and 15 not voting. Fifty-one votes were required for passage. Representative Vernon D. Andrews, a banker from College View, opposed the bill. "This is equivalent to abolishment of fraternities and sororities by knocking one leg at a time from under them. Students need this semi-dormitory control, especially freshmen."[35] Representative Marion J. Cushing, a farmer from Ord, favored passage of the Hovis bill. "Probation, Rough house, Pre-initiation stunts abolished.

33. *House Journal of the Legislature of the State of Nebraska, Forty-Fifth Session* (Lincoln, 1929), p. 828.
34. *Daily Nebraskan*, February 24, 1929.
35. *House Journal 1929*, p. 828.

Hell week a thing of the past by vote of the inter-fraternity council University of Nebraska. Taken from newspaper the day after this bill passed committee of the whole. Not merely a coincidence. I vote aye."[36]

Despite the criticism and attempted legislative regulation during the twenties, "Greeks" still dominated student activities. In the student election of May 1929, the "barbs" were organized under the leadership of Alan G. Williams, '31 and Ruth Hatfield, '31. These leaders, the editor of the *Daily Nebraskan* reported, were able, "to wield the 'iron hand' in the barb bloc."[37] With about 65 percent of the women students not members of a sorority and 55 percent of the men not fraternity members, a "barb" victory was not impossible. On election day, slightly over one-third of the student body voted. This was a record student vote. Because of their greater interest, the "Greeks" were again able to win all

University of Nebraska Band in 1922. Courtesy of the Nebraska State Historical Society.

twenty seats on the Student Council, as well as the vacancies on the Publication Board. Fraternities and sororities dominated the student life of the University because of their wide involvement in all student activities. The more numerous independent students simply did not participate in University affairs to the extent necessary to influence events in proportion to their numbers.

VARSITY ATHLETICS

Although varsity football dominated the sports scene during the twenties, many students were active participants in other athletics. Names like Roland Locke, a sprinter supreme, Ed Weir, and Paul Zimmerman brought Nebraska national track and field attention. Basketball developed such stars as Mutt Volz, Phil Gerelick, Elmer Holm, and A. J. Lewandowski. George F. Branigan and Max R. Karrer were members of the wrestling team. Other sports for men were boxing, swimming, tennis, and baseball. Women, too, had an athletic program. Under the leadership of Mabel Lee, the director of physical education for

36. Ibid.
37. *Daily Nebraskan,* May 7, 1929.

women, the tradition of women's sports at the University was expanded. The Women's Athletic Association sponsored a rifle, basketball, Nebraska ball (a combination of volley ball and cage ball), hockey, and soccer teams. Orchesis was the honorary interpretive dance group.

While athletics had long been a part of campus life at the University of Nebraska, it was the decade of the twenties that has often been called the "Golden Era of Sports." Of the major sports, none could compete for popularity with king football.

Nebraska's football began drawing national attention during the "King" Cole and "Jumbo" Stiehm regimes. With the successful launching of the Notre Dame series in 1915, the Cornhuskers established a base from which to spring into the big time. Nebraska football had already gained such stature and acceptance in the hearts of Nebraska fans by the twenties that coaches were subject to cheers and jeers that hazard the occupation. Monday quarterbacks were as enthusiastic in 1920 as they are today.

Henry F. Schulte, who was to become perhaps the most beloved of all Nebraska coaches and was to have the Field House named in his honor, became Nebraska's football and track coach in 1919. However, he stepped down as football coach after the 5–3–1 season of 1920. Fred Ware, who with Gregg McBride—both of Omaha *World-Herald* fame—wrote *Fifty Years of Football* in 1940, wrote that Schulte

. . . was a patient, painstaking, persevering, highly gifted instructor of individuals. This explains his unparalleled success during 20 years of labor with runners and jumpers and weight men. It explains his awe-striking football lines. His tackles and guards and centers worked together with 20-jewelled precision, but he couldn't co-ordinate his backs with one another, nor his backfield with his lines.[38]

Nebraska returned to the Missouri Valley Conference in 1921, and an eloquent, emotional, and daring coach named Fred T. Dawson arrived in Lincoln to coach the Cornhuskers. Dawson united Schulte's linemen with some powerful, well drilled backs, and for the next four years Nebraska fans were to have some potent thrills.

Dawson's first Nebraska team, inspired by his locker-room and practice field oratory which often moved the Cornhusker players to tears, won seven and lost only one game, a 7–0 loss to rival Notre Dame. This misfortune was to ignite Nebraska toward history-making successes in 1922 and 1923. The top prize of the 1921 season, aside from the Missouri Valley title, was the 10–0 victory over the mighty Panthers of the east, Pittsburgh.

Recitation of the 1921 squad roster sounds like a Whos' Who of Nebraska Football—Leo Scherer, Adolph Wenke, Raymond (Bud) Weller, John Pucelik, Captain Clarence Swanson, Roy (Link) Lyman, Harold Hartley, Joy Berquist, Verne Lewellen, Dave Noble, Bob Russell, Andy Schoeppel, Floyd Wright, and many more. Swanson's pass-catching marks still stand in the Cornhusker record book. Many of these same stars were on hand for the 1922 season, which saw a repeat 7–1–0 record. Again, the only loss was to an eastern power, this time Syracuse, 9–6. The Huskers retained the conference crown.

The year 1922 to this day remains a crucial one in Nebraska football history, from standpoints of prominence, practicality, and nostalgia. On November 30, 1922, the Cornhuskers achieved distinction that would remain theirs forever, supremacy over the Four Horsemen of Notre Dame. True, Grantland Rice was not to compare Stuhldreher, Miller, Crowley, and Layden to Famine, Pestilence,

38. Frederick Ware with Gregg McBride, *Fifty Years of Football* (Omaha: World Publishing Co., 1940), pp. 30–31.

Destruction, and Death until October 18, 1924, but Nebraska football fans have always gained smug satisfaction from the knowledge that their Cornhuskers beat "The Four Horsemen" two out of three years.

The Omaha *World-Herald* sports editor described the big day of the 1922 Notre Dame game this way:

Fifteen thousand paid, another six thousand looked on from roofs, coal piles, poles and trees as Dawson's literally thundering horde vanquished Notre Dame. . . . As significant as the foe and the score of 14 to 6 was the setting. It was the last game on the old wooden-stand flanked field.[39]

Undefeated in nine games and tied only by Army, was the Notre Dame team that Knute Rockne brought to Lincoln, confident that no blemish would result from this, the season's final contest. It was the final contest for the Cornhuskers, too, and also a farewell to old Nebraska field. Fifteen thousand paid their way within the fence. They saw the Huskers strike twice in the second quarter, with an unstoppable backfield of Noble, Hartley, Lewellen, and Russell behind a crushing line that made no mistakes. Hartley plunged across for the first touchdown. Noble fielded a pass from Hartley and with sprint speed threw his big body into three challengers, knocked them rolling and scored the second touchdown. In the third period Layden passed to Miller for the losers' only points. Yards for Nebraska 357, for Notre Dame 270. Downs for Nebraska 19, for Notre Dame 10.

Nebraska's fortunes dipped in 1923 to a 4–2–2 record, but the events of November 10 rewarded the Cornhusker faithful with a second straight victory over Notre Dame to ruin Irish dreams of an unbeaten season. This time the count was 14–7, with Noble scoring twice. First, he ran 24 yards, and later took an 18-yard pass from Rufe Dewitz to insure his place in Nebraska football legend, three touchdowns in two successful games against Rockne's mighty Irish.

The year 1924 was to signal the end of the Dawson era, colorful and constructive to the Cornhusker legend as it was. Dawson was ill, and the team which featured All-American tackle Ed Weir and many sophomores was inconsistent. Notre Dame gained revenge (34–6), and the Huskers wound up 5–3–0, not an impressive enough mark to spare Dawson.

During the next four seasons, 1925–28, Nebraska won twenty-three games, lost only seven and tied three. However, this would not suffice for the rabid Cornhusker fans, and Ernie Bearg left under criticism when this 1928 club failed to beat Army and lost a Rose Bowl bid. Bearg, by all accounts, was a football fundamentalist who apprenticed under Bob Zuppke of Illinois and believed only in power. Critics claimed he scorned deception. No one could fault Bearg's opener, though. Blessed with Weir and some fine products of the Swanson era, the 1925 Cornhuskers opened against mighty Illinois and the incomparable Gallopin' Ghost, Red Grange. Late in the final quarter, Grange stumbled to the bench in tears after Joe and Ed Weir, Lonnie Stiner, and Harold Hutchinson combined to throw the ghost for minus 40 yards rushing. That was not all that frustrated Grange. Frank Dailey intercepted one of his passes and got the first Nebraska touchdown with a 40-yard return. A second interception by guard Walter Scholz set the stage for "Choppy Rhodes's score and a 14–0 Nebraska victory, one of the most brilliant moments in Cornhusker history.

Bearg's 1925 team also closed on a high note, a 17–0 win over Notre Dame in what was to be the series final game. Nebraska scored fourteen points in the first quarter on a run by Rhodes and a pass from Jay Brown to Avard Mandary

39. Ibid., p. 33.

that covered thirty yards. However, the loss did not sting Irish officials as much as some reported hassles with Nebraska fans. Whether or not incidents did occur or whether Rockne wanted out of the Husker series that had cost him dearly continues to be debated to this day. Nevertheless, a few days after the game Notre Dame charged Nebraska with ill treatment and disrespectful conduct by Nebraska fans toward the Irish players and fans. The series did not resume until 1947. Through 1925, the series record was 5–5–1, testifying to some gallant warfare.

The 1925 season ended 4–2–2 with a loss to Missouri, a tie with Kansas State, and a surprise defeat by Drake. Demands for more deception were being heard.

Bearg put together 6–2–0 seasons in 1926 and 1927, but the Cornhuskers could not dislodge Missouri from the Missouri Valley championship. Bearg had to defend power over deception after the 1927 season, promising that his type of football would gain the first Big Six title in 1928.

All of the state-supported schools in the Missouri Valley Conference except Oklahoma A & M had pulled out the previous year to form the Missouri Valley Intercollegiate Association. That name never caught on, however, and the league that included Nebraska, Kansas, Missouri, Oklahoma, Iowa State, and Kansas State became the Big Six. After World War II, Colorado joined to make it the Big Seven, and in 1960, Oklahoma State, the old Aggies, returned to the fold to complete the present-day Big Eight lineup.

Bearg made good on his promise as Missouri was routed 34–0 before 35,000 fans, after wins over Iowa State, Montana State, and eastern power, Syracuse. Kansas fell 20–0, and Oklahoma was stunned 44–6. Nebraska was spearheaded by a hard running heavyweight named Lafayette Russell, and only a scoreless tie with Pittsburgh marred the Husker record after seven games.

For the Nebraska-Army game, Nebraska chartered a special train, and the Cornhuskers headed east, confident of victory. Experts, players, and Bearg made a fatal mistake. They underestimated Army coach Captain Laurence McC. Jones, who twelve years later was to lead the Cornhuskers to that cherished Rose Bowl spot. Nebraska morale dipped when Bearg benched Russell for disciplinary action and gave the signal-calling job to senior "Blue" Howell, who had never quarterbacked before. Nebraska was defeated, 13–3.

Not even an 8–0 win over Kansas State in the final game could erase the hurt that accompanied the dashing of Rose Bowl hopes in Nebraska. Bearg, the man who chose power over quickness and deception, had been deceived one too many times. He resigned.

As the 1920s drew to a close, a depression was descending on the land, but a little man with a bald head and a dignified bearing was to provide hope, inspiration, and thrills to dust-blown, impoverished Nebraskans in the 1930s. Dana Xenophon Bible, who would be known and loved as "D.X." or the "Little Colonel," came to Nebraska in 1929. He launched an era that was to accomplish more victories than Nebraska had ever known, or would know, until the arrival of Bob Devaney in the 1960s.

Bible's 1929 team felt the pinch of graduation and won only four games, while losing one and tying three. The four wins and one tie were in Big Six action, and "D.X." had the first of many championships.

It would take another year of building before Nebraska could achieve greatness again. However, with the foundation of the 1920s on which to build and with a master technician in the "Little Colonel," Nebraska's Cornhuskers would throw off the shackles of the depression and march gallantly into the next decade.

THE THIRTIES

CHAPTER 4

Administration During the Great Depression

DESPITE THE ECONOMIC difficulties of the early twenties, that decade ended with farm income higher than any year since the end of the World War. Economists, businessmen, and farm leaders were confident that the period of postwar economic adjustment was past. In 1929, the stock market crash foreshadowed a decade of depression in which unemployment, low farm prices, and general economic collapse swept the nation and world. Nebraska felt the impact of this economic catastrophe. It was to face a rapid decline in farm commodity prices, reaching the lowest point in the state's history in December 1932. Economic historians agree that at this time, the economy of Nebraska, as well as that of the nation, was nearer total collapse than it had ever been, even during the hard times of the middle nineties. Although farm commodity prices increased slowly during the thirties and federal programs assisted farmers, recovery during the decade was to be an elusive goal for Nebraskans. In fact, only the economic stimulation of World War II finally brought a prosperous agriculture. Farm commodity prices declined faster and farther than those of manufactured products and did not recover as well—even with federal assistance. Compounding the hardship, a drought, which greatly decreased crop yield, swept across America's heartland. From 1931 to 1937, rainfall was below normal for every year except 1935. In 1934, it was the lowest since 1864.

Rapidly the economic crisis exacted its price in the state. According to James C. Olson, Nebraska historian:

The condition of the farmers affected Nebraska merchants, lumber dealers, realtors, school teachers, laborers, and artisans. Housewives stocked their pantry shelves with the simplest essentials; construction lagged; school administrators curtailed their programs as tax receipts went down. . . .[1]

The University of Nebraska administration and Board of Regents, like the citizens of the state, faced critical financial difficulties. How could the University continue to play its role in providing educational opportunities to all those young people of Nebraska who sought to better themselves through higher education? Paradoxically, while state tax revenues declined, the number of those who sought self-improvement through state-financed higher education generally increased. Many agreed with Chancellor Edgar A. Burnett: "I recall the advice given by Chancellor Canfield of this university in the panic times of the 90s. If you can not earn, you can at least learn."[2] This spirit seemed to be a principal motivation for students, faculty, and citizens.

1. *Nebraska: A Guide to the Cornhusker State,* quoted in James C. Olson, *History of Nebraska* (Lincoln, University of Nebraska Press, 1966), p. 292.
2. *Daily Nebraskan,* February 1, 1932.

The administrative crisis of the thirties was that of maintaining a University of acceptable quality, open to all graduates of accredited high schools during a time of declining state revenue. Most Nebraskans were not opposed to the state University and its programs. However, it soon became clear that most citizens supported and elected economy-minded political leaders who voted for sharp reductions in state expenditures to meet depression conditions. Senator Charles D. Green, a farmer from Sidney, stated what came to be a widely held belief that the state University must adjust its programs and finances to the realities of the depression. "The taxpayers," he said, "cannot maintain such an aristocracy as the University of Nebraska. We do not want to cripple the University but it can be maintained at its present standard at a lower cost."[3]

Through these trying years, Edgar A. Burnett provided courageous leadership. His administration was characterized by the firmly held conviction that the hard times were not permanent, and that the University should maintain its variety of programs and services to the state. He believed that there were better times ahead and that the people of Nebraska would then need and demand a fully developed land-grant university. When economic conditions worsened, Chancellor Burnett maintained his faith in the future, although some concessions were demanded by greatly reduced budgets. However, as the decade closed it was quite clear that Chancellor Chauncey S. Boucher, did not share Burnett's optimistic vision of the future of the University.

During the thirties, the growth of the professional programs of the University continued. Just as they had during the twenties, the students regarded higher education as the best means for attaining economic security. Their chief aim came to be that of becoming qualified, licensed, or certificated for a profession. In 1932–33, the Graduate College enrolled more students than at any other time during the decade. The College of Agriculture, after a temporary drop in enrollment, finished the period with substantial growth. A similar pattern was evident in the College of Business Administration. There was a slight decline in attendance at the College of Dentistry. The student population at the College of Medicine remained stable, but the number of pre-med students increased considerably. The School of Nursing made notable growth. The Teachers College suffered a steady decline in undergraduate enrollment which reflected the scarcity of teaching positions. However, the development of graduate work in Teachers College was responsible for much of the growth in the Graduate College enrollment. Enrollments in the College of Arts and Sciences remained relatively stable throughout the decade.

The total registrations for the thirties, according to the University's yearly catalogs, including summer sessions and extension registration were:

	In Colleges	In Schools	Total
1929–30	10,021	1,292	11,313
1930–31	10,052	1,672	11,724
1931–32	9,533	1,640	11,173
1932–33	8,761	1,515	10,276
1933–34	7,880	2,858	10,738
1934–35	8,254	2,251	10,505
1935–36	8,859	2,099	10,958
1936–37	9,025	2,723	11,748
1937–38	9,073	2,452	11,525
1938–39	9,462	2,874	12,336

In a letter to the alumni Chancellor Burnett in February 1930 expressed his optimism for the future. To those who believed that the "Golden Age" of the

3. Omaha *World-Herald*, March 24, 1933, p. 7.

University of Nebraska was achieved during the 1890s and the decade which followed, he stated, "The golden age of the University lies not in the past, but just upon the horizon where the sun breaks through the passing cloud in promise of the coming day."[4] Although some outstanding faculty members had been lost to other institutions, the chancellor in the same letter expressed his faith in the quality of the faculty.

Today we have a notable faculty, with virility, character, and scholarship never excelled in our history. We also have a large group of young men on our faculty, who have not yet come to their full maturity and reputation. They represent the finest product of other universities and need only time, experience, and productive scholarship to give them recognition and prominence in their respective fields.[5]

In the spring of 1930, the Board of Regents approved a system of sabbatical leaves for the faculty. The plan provided for a year's leave at half pay or a semester's leave on full pay for advanced study or travel. The adoption of this plan indicated clearly the recognition by the University administration and the Board of Regents of their role in providing opportunities for faculty development. Burnett gave his strong support to the program by stating: "Through this plan our older professors will be refreshed by new contacts, while the younger staff will secure wider recognition."[6] Between 1930 and 1932, eight faculty members were granted sabbatical leaves. Facing a difficult financial situation in 1932, however, the regents discontinued the sabbatical leave program. In addition to the establishment of a sabbatical leave program, the broad vision of the Board of Regents was also in evidence by the purchase of a private school of music and the establishment of a course in architectural engineering at the beginning of the decade. Certainly, these actions would not have been considered unless the regents shared some of the optimism and hopes of Chancellor Burnett.

While the chancellor and regents prepared their first budget proposal of the decade for submission to the governor, confidence in the strength of the economy prevailed. Chancellor Burnett believed "the promise of better conditions is just ahead. This is no time for pessimism and gloom. . . . Faith and courage will make the year 1931 a year of substantial achievements."[7] To many citizens of Nebraska, courage in the face of economic adversity meant strict economy in state expenditures. In 1931, Charles W. Bryan defeated incumbent Governor Arthur J. Weaver on the issue of economy in state government.

In his final budget message to the legislature, retiring Governor Weaver had recommended a cut of $945,000 below the request of the Board of Regents. The regents had requested $55,000 less than had been provided by the state in 1929. Incoming Governor Bryan endorsed the University budget recommended by his predecessor. Early in the legislative session, a resolution was introduced to require the chancellor to appear before the House and answer charges of financial irregularities in University funds. The charges were made by Anton Jensen, a former faculty member. Jensen had been a member of the Department of Romance Languages during the twenties and was discharged by the Board of Regents on a formal charge of insubordination. He considered himself the victim of an unjust University policy, that of requiring the doctorate or equivalent for a permanent appointment in the College of Arts and Sciences. The resolution

4. MSS, Alumni Letter, February 1930, University of Nebraska Archives, Burnett Collection.
5. Ibid.
6. MSS, "Our Educational Equipment," October 1930, University of Nebraska Archives, Burnett Collection.
7. MSS, "A New Year's Letter," December 30, 1930, University of Nebraska Archives, Burnett Collection.

requiring the appearance of Chancellor Burnett and Anton Jensen before the House committee was defeated.

However, the next day another resolution was offered to investigate the state University by six representatives. The chief sponsor of the resolution was Dr. Claire Owens, an osteopath from Exeter, who asked: "What I want to know is why the University of Nebraska is running the state government."[8] Her resolution too was defeated, but by only five votes.

Although the University was spared the ordeal of a hostile investigation, its budget request was far from secure. To be sure, a bill authorizing the Board of Educational Lands and Funds to lend money to the University for dormitory construction was approved, but this did not provide funds for operations. Legislators were undecided about appropriations and wanted to consult with their constituents. On May 2, 1931, the legislature adjourned without adopting an appropriation bill to fund the expenses of the state. Governor Bryan quickly called for a special session of the legislature to convene on June 9, 1931. In his message to this legislature, Governor Bryan recommended lower appropriations for all state institutions, including the University of Nebraska. The regents responded to Bryan's request and accordingly, the budget for the biennium 1931–33 ultimately totaled $4,378,600. This amount was a reduction of $407,000 from the sum recommended by Governors Weaver and Bryan in January.[9] In the budget that was adopted, the University cash fund and federal funds amounted to $3,076,061.

Frequently, rural legislators objected to what they considered excessive salaries at the state University. Representative E. T. Peck, a farmer from Falls City, saw the issue in simple terms. "I am not in favor of putting schools and good roads above our homes."[10] It was much less painful and surely better politics to reduce property taxes at the state level than at the county or municipal level. This attitude was the source of much of the legislative resistance to the budget requests of the state University.

In February 1932, a raid was conducted by federal prohibition officers at the Coliseum. The federal agents reported finding "a number of paper cups filled with beer, a bucket filled with ice and two bottles of beer and a number of empties, a pint of colored moonshine whiskey, this bottle was partly full, two bottles containing wine, and a syphon with extra cartridges."[11] The raid occurred some time after the conclusion of a student party and the students had left the building; only the chaperones remained. Many faculty members believed that the federal agents had been encouraged to stage the raid by an unnamed University authority. The incident produced a strong faculty protest. Dean Charles H. Oldfather wrote the chancellor:

. . . the officers, previous to the raid, had discussed it with someone, not yourself, who was presumed by them to have authority to speak for the administration of the university, and that this individual had conveyed the impression to them that the university would welcome such a raid. Consequently, the officials felt that they could descend upon a university building in the manner that they would invade a speak-easy, with the approval of the administration. . . . anyone on our campus who displays such a total lack of understanding of the ordinary affairs of life is utterly unfit to be in a position by virtue of which outsiders may feel that he is speaking for the administration of the

8. *Daily Nebraskan*, February 6, 1931.

9. *Financial Report of the University of Nebraska for the Year Ending June 30, 1933*, p. 64.

10. Lincoln, *State Journal*, June 13, 1931, p. 1.

11. MSS, Sworn statement of Harry A. Pound and Harold D. Wilson, February 20, 1932, University of Nebraska Archives, Burnett Collection.

university, and that steps should be taken whereby it may never be possible for such a person to again compromise the university in the eyes of the citizens of our state.[12]

The public reaction was hostile. G. S. Christy, president of the Tax Payers League of Nemaha County, warned: "If we can not run the State University without a lot of drunks on the teaching staff, I will come back to the Legislature and see to it that all the good work I have done for the Uni, shall be put in reverse motion."[13]

The Board of Regents conducted a hearing on the matter. A motion was made, and a vote taken, to demand the resignation of the faculty members involved. The motion failed. Although no federal or state charges were filed against them, Professors Lowry C. Wimberly and Norman E. Eliason were suspended from their posts, without pay, until September 1933.

It became apparent to the Board of Regents, in mid-1932 that a decline in University cash receipts had developed. These funds were from student fees and the sale of agricultural products. Some adjustment in the 1933 budget was required. Chancellor Burnett wrote a number of prominent citizens regarding the desirability of a faculty salary cut as a means to "put the University in the best possible position to meet the legislature next winter."[14] The majority of replies favored a salary cut. William P. Warner from Dakota City advised, "I think a reduction of the salary schedules would be very popular."[15] University benefactor George W. Holmes believed "a reduction in salaries would be the soundest course of procedure. I say this just a little reluctantly because I appreciate that none of the salaries on the campus are high."[16] Frank A. Anderson, an attorney from Holdrege, opposed the idea.

A voluntary reduction would merely whet the appetite of the public and agitate the legislators to enforce an additional reduction. . . . your teaching staff should not in any wise be offered as a voluntary sacrifice upon the altar of what may appear at the moment to be public policy and expediency.[17]

On April 5, 1932, the Board of Regents cut all salaries of $1,000 or more per year by 10 percent. Chancellor Burnett, whose salary had been criticized in some newspaper editorials, requested the regents to reduce his salary 20 percent. Regent Fred A. Marsh believed that there was little choice in the proper decision to be made. "A great emergency exists. We should not need the Governor or a Legislature to point our duty. Hundreds of hard working people are daily giving up all that they have and in many cases with deficiency judgments that will keep them in bondage throughout all the years to come."[18]

Despite the economic difficulties, the Board of Regents took steps to insure that the lack of money for tuition would not prevent Nebraska's most academically talented young people from attending the University. In January 1932,

12. Letter from C. H. Oldfather to E. A. Burnett, February 18, 1932, MSS, University of Nebraska Archives, Burnett Collection.

13. Letter from G. S. Christy to E. A. Burnett, March 2, 1932, MSS, University of Nebraska Archives, Burnett Collection.

14. Letter from E. A. Burnett to A. J. Weaver, March 25, 1932, MSS, University of Nebraska Archives, Burnett Collection.

15. Letter from Wm. P. Warner to E. A. Burnett, March 23, 1932, MSS, University of Nebraska Archives, Burnett Collection.

16. Letter from George W. Holmes to E. A. Burnett, March 18, 1932, MSS, University of Nebraska Archives, Burnett Collection.

17. Letter from Frank A. Anderson to E. A. Burnett, March 26, 1932, MSS, University of Nebraska Archives, Burnett Collection.

18. Letter from Fred A. Marsh to E. A. Burnett, March 2, 1932, MSS, University of Nebraska Archives, Burnett Collection.

Regent Arthur C. Stokes proposed that tuition scholarships be awarded by the Board of Regents to a limited number of outstanding high school graduates. A special committee composed of Regent Fred A. Marsh; A. A. Reed, director of the University Extension Division; Professor R. D. Moritz, director of the summer session; and L. E. Gunderson, finance secretary of the board, was appointed to develop the idea. On March 19, 1932, the Board of Regents adopted a plan for a system of Regents Scholarships. Although other types of scholarships were discontinued by the regents during the depression, they were able to maintain the Regents Scholarship program.

THE CRISIS OF 1933

The nation elected Franklin D. Roosevelt in the fall of 1932, on the promise of securing a "New Deal." In Nebraska, too, the electorate favored the "New Deal" and voted a Democratic sweep. Roosevelt carried every county except Keya Paha and Lancaster, and the Democrats, for the first time since 1916, elected their entire state ticket. The Democrats won overwhelming control of the legislature. The election was the most substantial protest vote in the history of the state. The people wanted real change.

It was evident as the Board of Regents prepared their budget request that the University was entering a period of retrenchment. The budget submitted to Governor Bryan was 10 percent less than had been appropriated by the previous legislature. Governor Bryan recommended additional cuts of $800,000 from the sum appropriated the previous biennium.

On the eleventh day of the legislative session, a resolution was introduced by Senator E. M. Neubauer, a farmer and stockman from Orleans, calling for an investigation of the state University. Two days later, a similar resolution was introduced in the House by Robert C. Vance, a farmer from Milford. A joint committee of ten was created to conduct the investigation. All members of the committee were economy-minded Democrats. The only professional man on the committee was Jackson Chase, an Omaha attorney. Five committee members were farmers, one was a newspaper editor, one a contractor, one a farm implement dealer, and one was an automobile dealer. The Investigative Committee determined at the beginning that its task was not to discover mismanagement at the University. They did not believe it existed. Their responsibility was to determine where expenses should be cut and where duplication of services should be eliminated at the state University.

While the committee was making its study, legislators were introducing bills providing for a reduction of expenditures at the state University. Representative Trenmore Cone, a sand and gravel dealer from Valley, introduced two bills affecting the University. H.R. 424 required the state auditor to examine the accounts pertaining to student activities, athletic associations, field houses, and stadiums connected with the University of Nebraska. H.R. 517 proposed that the schools of architecture and fine arts be abolished, that salary limits be imposed on the chancellor, deans, and professors, and that all nonacademic salaries be reduced 20 percent.

Senator H. E. Sanden, a specialty salesman from Omaha, introduced two bills affecting the University which he thought would produce tax relief. S.F. 381 would require the state University and the normal schools to withdraw from membership in the North Central Association of Colleges and Secondary Schools. Some believed that this accrediting association was responsible for the high costs of education because of the standards it maintained. To be sure, an unaccredited University could probably be operated more cheaply than an accredited institution. Senator Sanden's other proposal, S.F. 382, provided for the discontinuance of the Teachers College and all programs of teacher education at the state University. Teacher education was to be offered only by the normal schools. Although none of these bills were adopted, they were given serious consideration by legislative committees and, in some cases, they were advanced to final reading.

As the weeks passed, apprehension over the recommendations of the Legislative Committee investigating the University grew. In early March, Superintendent W. P. Snyder and Marvel L. Baker from the Experiment Station at North Platte were asked by the chancellor to meet with Representative P. M. LaVelle from North Platte regarding the legislative attitude toward the state University. LaVelle, a member of the Finance Committee, thought that the appropriation would likely be below that recommended in the Bryan budget. "He was of the opinion that the money *now* appropriated for North Platte was not too large and inquired how he might protect the North Platte budget against an unreasonable cut."[19]

But even the self-interest of senators and representatives could not protect the University from a fatal cut in legislative support. On March 18, 1933, the long awaited report of the joint legislative investigating committee was made public. The committee recommended that the appropriation for the University of Nebraska be cut at least $385,000 below the budget request of economy-minded Governor Bryan. In a clear usurpation of the powers of the Board of Regents the Legislative Committee made specific salary recommendations for each faculty member. "These salaries have been considered individually by the Committee and it is only after very careful consideration that the Committee has concluded that the salaries be reduced to the figures suggested in the schedule and that these revised salaries should be adhered to and remain in force during the coming biennium."[20]

The salary cuts proposed by the committee were not uniform, but varied considerably among colleges of the University. The cuts recommended were: the College of Arts and Sciences 27.4 percent, School of Journalism 24.4 percent, Law College 26.5 percent, Graduate College 21 percent, College of Engineering 19.7 percent, College of Pharmacy 19.5 percent, College of Business Administration 16.2 percent, Teachers College 14.3 percent, College of Dentistry 12.7 percent, Medical College 9.8 percent, School of Fine Arts and Music 9.2 percent, and the College of Agriculture 7.6 percent. All other University activities suffered cuts which ranged up to 100 percent. The report concluded:

The Committee is satisfied that the University of Nebraska is being operated and managed in an efficient manner and that this institution reflects credit on the State of Nebraska and is a University of which every Nebraska citizen may well be proud. The Committee has approached and carried on its task of studying the affairs of this institution with the sole desire of rendering a constructive service to both the tax payers of the State and to the institution.[21]

The committee's report immediately drew fire from supporters of the University. Eight prominent clergymen from Lincoln opposed the report. "We feel that the proposed reduction in the University budget is unfairly applied to departments and that such drastic reductions are destructive to the policy of free education in Nebraska."[22] The salary schedule proposed by the Legislative Com-

19. Letter from E. A. Burnett to Regent M. A. Shaw, March 16, 1933, MSS, University of Nebraska Archives, Burnett Collection.

20. *House Journal of the Legislature of the State of Nebraska, Forty-Ninth Session* (Lincoln, 1933), p. 1026.

21. Ibid., p. 1032.

22. Handbill, "The Ministers of Lincoln Back the University of Nebraska," March 1933, University of Nebraska Archives, Burnett Collection.

mittee was regarded by many as a most serious threat to the integrity of the University of Nebraska. The Board of Regents stated:

It is only a step from fixing individual salaries to appointing janitors, professors, and administrative officers. Determination of salaries by the legislature would place a premium on the political activities of professors and would prove embarassing to members of the legislature.[23]

The editor of the Omaha *World-Herald* questioned the wisdom of the Legislative Committee recommendation limiting the salaries of University administrators and faculty to less than that of elected state officials. "Positions for which one may qualify only by years of study and preparation are not on a par with those gained by political luck. Nothing would undermine the usefulness and value of the state university more than to drive its best professors into other schools."[24]

The effect of the Legislative Committee's recommendations on the research activities of the University could be just as crippling as it would be to the instructional program. Superintendent W. P. Snyder, at the North Platte Station, reported that a 30 percent cut in his budget would mean "turning out at least three men with families, two of them over-seas men, one of them with four small children, and none of them with any savings laid by or any possible employment in sight, and no wife's folks to live with."[25] A 50 percent cut in the station's budget, the recommendation of the Legislative Committee, Snyder reported, "might be more easily met. That would practically mean, at least in so far as experimental work is concerned—*The Closing of the Gates*."[26] There could be no doubt; the University of Nebraska was fighting for its life as an institution of higher education.

THE COMPROMISE OF 1933

The academic community and University of Nebraska supporters prepared for battle. A mass student meeting, attended by over one thousand, condemned the Legislative Committee's report as destructive of the state University. The legislature accepted the student's resolution and thanked them for their concern.

The legislative debate began. In the House of Representatives attempts to restore University funds to the level recommended by Governor Bryan failed. A rider was proposed to the House's appropriation bill requiring the state University to withdraw from the North Central Association of Colleges and Secondary Schools. Legislators had surely been impressed by the march on the capital, earlier in the session, by agitated farmers demanding tax relief from the legislature. Representative John Havekost, a farmer from Hooper, saw no justification to restore the budget to the Bryan proposal. "I want to call your attention to the taxpayers' condition to pay. Many of the producers of this state are operating below zero. We want to conserve the schools, but over and above all, we should conserve the homes."[27] However, those who favored additional cuts in the University budget by abolishing the Teachers College could not muster sufficient support to amend the House appropriation bill.

During the time between the House's passage of the University appropriation and Senate consideration of the budget, serious charges were made against the

23. Letter from Board of Regents to Hon. Walter Jurgensen, Lieutenant Governor of the State of Nebraska and George W. O'Mally, Speaker of the House of Representatives, undated, MSS, University of Nebraska Archives, Burnett Collection.

24. Omaha *World-Herald*, March 20, 1933, p. 12.

25. Report, W. P. Snyder to E. A. Burnett, March 26, 1933, MSS, University of Nebraska Archives, Burnett Collection.

26. Ibid.

27. Omaha *World-Herald*, March 28, 1933, p. 6.

University of Nebraska by the State Sheriff. He complained that the University was a seed bed of Communist activity. "We've got enough on them to show they were trying to set up a communist organization within the university. . . . They were holding meetings and organizing."[28] Many people thought, as was reported in the Omaha *World-Herald*, that the sheriff had more to fear from criminals and gangsters than University students.

There may be a half dozen ardent youths in the university, there may even be a dozen, who are theoretical rebels against the existing order. It would be strange if they were not. For youth is the age of daring dreams, of radicalism, of opposition to what is, of an earnest desire to make the world over again.[29]

Chancellor Edgar A. Burnett answered the challenge to free discussion at the University. In a public statement he "stressed the fact that the University is a place where political, religious and economic questions should be discussed without prejudice or bias, that out of this type of discussion comes a more enlightened public consciousness."[30] Fortunately, the charges were given little consideration by the state Senate. However, after the conclusion of the legislative session, Chancellor Burnett received some correspondence from senators indicating that unless campus dissent was kept under control, it could result in a legislative investigation the next legislative session.

The state Senate began its debate on the University appropriation. The cuts made by the House were restored and the Senate approved the Bryan budget. Ultimately, after a legislative compromise, the Board of Regents were able to adopt a biennial budget of $3,352,180. This was over a million dollars less than the budget of the 1931–33 biennium.

CONSEQUENCES OF THE CUT

The University of Nebraska Board of Regents adopted an economy budget in June 1933. All salaries over $1,500 were reduced 22 percent, in addition to the 10 percent cut ordered the previous year. While university faculties in other states took similar salary reductions in 1933, most had not been subjected to a cut in 1932. The School of Fine Arts was closed. The new School of Music was retained, and the regents hoped that it would be able to produce sufficient income to retire the debt incurred in its purchase. Forty-two major and twenty minor faculty positions were eliminated from the budget. All tuition scholarships, except for the one hundred fifty Regents Scholarships, were eliminated. The budgets of the experiment stations were cut 25 percent. Part of the University Hospital in Omaha was closed, and the facilities for out-patient care reduced. Other economies included the postponement of all construction and most building maintenance.

Although the faculty took their salary cuts in stride, many real hardships resulted. The elimination of the School of Fine Arts was unfortunate. The drastic reduction of scholarships deprived the faculty and student body of capable students and intellectual stimulation. The deletion of more than fifty courses from the instructional offerings in the colleges produced confusion for students and faculty. Class size was increased to lower instructional costs. The library suffered also, and it prompted faculty reaction. In December 1933, Professors Nels A. Bengtson, William C. Brenke, Joyce O. Hertzler, Norman L. Hill, John E. Kirshman, James L. Sellers, Dean A. Worcester, and Harry J. Kesner petitioned the chancellor:

28. Omaha *World-Herald*, April 6, 1933, p. 3.
29. Omaha *World-Herald*, April 11, 1933, p. 10.
30. *Daily Nebraskan*, April 11, 1933.

The discovery that our *library* is now unable to make any new book purchases has produced a deep and common concern upon the part of the members of the faculty. Incidental exchanges of opinion revealed the general belief that the welfare of the University was so seriously involved as to warrant a general discussion of ways and means to meet the emergency.[31]

A critical problem of faculty morale developed in the relationship between those on the faculty at the College of Agriculture and those on the faculty at the city campus. In June 1933, thirty-one members of the College of Agriculture faculty petitioned the chancellor and Board of Regents for redress of their economic grievance. Specifically the complaint was: "We are expected to give 11 months' service each year at a remuneration no greater than that received by other Faculty workers for 9 months' service."[32] The complaint proved the point that hard times are usually destructive of faculty harmony. Chancellor Burnett expressed his concern and disappointment to W. P. Snyder at North Platte:

Unfortunately the question of extra compensation for the summer months seems to have become acute at the Agricultural College at a time when it cannot be settled because there are no funds available. Their proposal for the solution of the question, namely, that we cut all instructors in the summer school to 10 per cent of their annual salary and include all persons marked on the agricultural payroll eleven months service in the list to receive the extra 10 per cent does not seem feasible either, since it is not the practice of leading universities and it would drive away men of distinction who are able to command a great deal more money for summer session work elsewhere and who unfortunately have not come up under the theory that when a man is employed by the state they have a right to his full and unlimited service at any time they may require it.

I have proposed to [Dean William W.] Burr and [Professor Horace C.] Filley that we place all Experiment Station men on a nine months basis as is being done in Ames, but this does not seem to satisfy them either so that the matter is still a source of irritation to them and I suppose they believe I do not sympathize with their point of view.

One of the most unfortunate phases of the situation is that they have developed an inferiority complex over the question and seem to feel that if we do not recognize their extra services in the same way that we recognize the summer school we are discriminating against them and saying in effect that they are less important to the University than are the people on this campus. Nothing could be so injurious to them and to the University as to have them generally feel that they are being discriminated against.[33]

Paradoxically while the faculty at the College of Agriculture believed themselves to be innocent victims of economic discrimination, there were those on the city campus who thought that the agriculture faculty was favored. In truth, all faculty members were victimized by the hard times and all subsidized the instructional program by personal economic sacrifice, large classes, and a reduction in the amount of graduate student assistance.

HARD TIMES CONTINUE

In the remaining legislative sessions of the decade, 1935, 1937, and 1939, financial support for the University of Nebraska remained nearly constant. A serious economic squeeze developed from the nearly static financial support and

31. Letter from Nels A. Bengtson *et al.* to E. A. Burnett, December 1, 1933, MSS, University of Nebraska Archives, Burnett Collection.

32. Petition, College of Agriculture faculty, June 6, 1933, MSS, University of Nebraska Archives, Burnett Collection.

33. Letter from E. A. Burnett to W. P. Snyder, June 12, 1933, MSS, University of Nebraska Archives, Burnett Collection.

a slowly rising enrollment. The rising costs of goods and services during these years further compounded the problem. The University of Nebraska budget for the 1939–41 biennium was still $890,000 less than it had been in the 1931–33 biennium.

In their quest for funds, the University Board of Regents sought federal support for campus construction through the State Planning Board. Some money was obtained for maintenance purposes, but little could be obtained for new construction because the legislature failed to provide state matching funds. The Student Union was built with federal money and the receipts from a special student fee. In 1936, the Board of Regents requested Governor Roy L. Cochran to support their request for a ten-year building program. The construction was to be financed from an annual .2 mill state tax levy. This special tax would provide for the construction of a new library, classroom building, engineering classroom and laboratory facility, Teachers College High School building, and an auditorium on the city campus. It would also provide for a home economics building on the agricultural campus and an additional dormitory at Curtis. For the medical campus in Omaha, a new dispensary building was proposed.

University supporters were hopeful that the new unicameral legislature might be more generous in its support of the University than the bicameral legislature had been. Chancellor Burnett expressed this hope:

The University is today confronted by a serious question: Is it to go forward or turn backward? It has been repressed by one legislature after another. It has been allotted only the barest running expenses. Will the new legislature, in organizing a great new system of state government, show its wisdom in taking the situation in hand and in giving the University a square deal?[34]

Governor Cochran recognized the need for additional facilities at the state University. However, because of the drought he did not believe that he should recommend the ten-year building program. A bill was, nevertheless, introduced in the Unicameral to provide a ten-year building program for the state University and state normal schools. The measure was introduced by Senator Leland R. Hall, a banker from Roseland. The bill survived until its third and final reading, at which time it failed to pass by one vote. Had the emergency clause not been necessary, the program would probably have been adopted. Without the emergency clause, the bill would have been of little value, since it would not have gone into effect until after the State Board of Equalization had set the state tax levy.

The near realization of the needed building program and the circumstances of its defeat produced a feeling of despair for many at the University. The instructional program had taken terrible cuts. Optimism and faith in the coming of a better day was more difficult than ever to maintain. The instructional costs per student continued downward:

Biennium	Instructional Costs, Per Student, Per Year
1929–31	$210
1931–33	204
1933–35	153
1935–37	149[35]

In an address to an alumni group, Chancellor Burnett recognized the growing problem of faculty morale. The principal cause, he believed, was economic. A

34. MSS, "The University Asks Two Things—Will It Get Them?" December 1936, University of Nebraska Archives, Burnett Collection.
35. *Daily Nebraskan*, February 26, 1937.

comparison of the average salary at the University of Nebraska for 1934 to 1935 with those at fifty-one land-grant universities showed professors at Nebraska receiving $352 below the average, associate professors $265 below the average, and assistant professors $230 below the average. The Nebraska faculty carried a heavier teaching load than those at universities of comparable size. This resulted in less faculty time for scholarly research and professional improvement. About half of the University of Nebraska faculty had less than fifteen years of professional experience. A relatively young faculty with declining morale, the chancellor explained, made the University of Nebraska a most favorable place from which other universities might recruit able, proven faculty.

They naturally look for young men with Ph.D. degrees with from three to ten years teaching experience, with published papers in their special field, and with good personality and initiative. Our greatest losses are from this group. These young teachers naturally marry as soon as they feel they have a position which promises permanence. The increasing cost of a young family, together with the rising cost of living, places them under economic pressure to which they are likely to yield when invited at a larger salary to some other university having a good reputation.[36]

Unfortunately for Nebraska, the University of Nebraska was becoming a good place for a young faculty member to begin an academic career that would bloom at another institution.

The economic difficulties which beset the University of Nebraska also troubled the other segments of public education in the state. Economic hardship caused the public school leaders of Nebraska to ask the state University to change its entrance requirements. In 1936, members of the Nebraska State Teachers' Association were critical of the mathematics and foreign language entrance requirement. These educators favored more recognition for vocationally oriented school subjects. With only 20 percent of the state's high school graduates attending a college or university, they argued, the curriculum should give more concern to the educational needs of the majority. Most small Nebraska high schools simply could not afford to offer both a college preparatory course and a program of practical terminal education, and school boards dared not operate a high school which would not admit students to the state University.

In May 1937, the Board of Regents approved a modification in University entrance requirements. The change recognized high school units in the natural and social sciences for meeting entrance requirements. Prior to the change, majors and minors from high school were recognized only from the fields of English, foreign languages, and mathematics. These substitutions in entrance requirements resulted as much from the economic plight of Nebraska high schools, as the desire of public school leaders to advance a more utilitarian curriculum.

CHANCELLOR EDGAR A. BURNETT RETIRES

On July 5, 1938, Chancellor Burnett requested the Board of Regents that he be granted a leave of absence and then be retired as chancellor emeritus. The regents granted both requests and in addition named Burnett as university historian. Dean Henry H. Foster, of the College of Law, was appointed acting chancellor until September 1938, when Dr. Chauncey S. Boucher assumed the chancellorship.

In recognition of Chancellor Burnett's leadership, the Board of Regents adopted a resolution which:

36. MSS, Burnett Speech, May 1937, University of Nebraska Archives, Burnett Collection.

. . . expresses its deep sense of gratitude and obligation for the distinctive service he has rendered the institution during one of the most trying periods in its history. His unfailing courtesy, excellent judgement and other fine traits of character gained the respect and confidence of every member of this Board.

His retirement has brought to each of us a distinct feeling of personal loss. We know that the members of the faculty, the friends of the University and the people of the state of Nebraska share with us the same sentiments we here express.[37]

Edgar A. Burnett had given long service to the University of Nebraska. He was professor of animal husbandry from 1899 to 1907, associate dean of the College of Agriculture 1901 to 1909, and dean from 1909 to 1928. In 1928 he was named chancellor. He had provided steady leadership when it was essential for the survival of the University of Nebraska. When many within and without the University lost their faith in the future, Chancellor Burnett rallied confidence in the future of the state and nation.

There is no investment comparable to the investing of time and money in one's self. Stocks and bonds may depreciate, real estate become hard to sell, commodities go for next to nothing, and yet time and money invested in education pay dividends all thru life. . . . Hard times should always be times of preparation for something better in the future.[38]

Guided by this philosophy, he resisted the abolition of University programs and services. If, as he believed, a better day would eventually follow the period of economic hardship, a multi-purpose university could more effectively meet the future needs of the state than one which had been dismantled during the years of depression. Burnett underestimated the severity and length of the great depression, but so did most Americans.

To the faculty and student body, Chancellor Burnett was accessible, encouraging, and a friend in time of need. Many students were financially aided by his personal loans. Burnett wrote a coed:

You may depend upon me to take care of the fee for you at the beginning of the next semester. Should you feel that you prefer to repay this later, you may do so after you have earned the money. There is no necessity for you to give me any memorandum, and should circumstances be such that it is a hardship for you to repay this later you need not feel it to be necessary.[39]

Three years later, when the loan was repaid, Chancellor Burnett wrote, "I had altogether forgotten the payment which I made for you back in '31, but am glad you are in a position to repay it and shall try to pass it on to some other needy and deserving student who may now be in the University."[40] Many former students recall loans they received from the chancellor which enabled them to continue their education.

Despite his confidence in the future, Chancellor Burnett recognized the difficulty of securing adequate financial support for the University. He asked in 1932, whether the University of Nebraska

. . . can maintain its rightful place in the field of education unless it had more than purely legislative appropriations. For years the people of Nebraska through taxation have appropriated funds for the most necessary development of the institution but have seldom been able to go much beyond that.[41]

37. *Minutes,* University of Nebraska Board of Regents, July 5, 1938.
38. *Daily Nebraskan,* February 1, 1932.
39. Letter from E. A. Burnett to Maxine Myers, September 29, 1931, MSS, University of Nebraska Archives, Burnett Collection.
40. Letter from E. A. Burnett to Maxine Myers, February 19, 1934, MSS, University of Nebraska Archives, Burnett Collection.
41. E. A. Burnett, "A University Foundation," *Nebraska Alumnus,* January, 1932, p. 2.

Chancellor Burnett's solution was the establishment of a University of Nebraska Foundation. Funds from the foundation could support programs in the arts, research, faculty development as well as the construction of needed facilities that could not be realized from state funds. The University of Nebraska Foundation was created on June 3, 1936. It was a major achievement in the administration of Chancellor Edgar A. Burnett, and one which was to grow in importance to the University of Nebraska in the next three decades.

Except for the construction of the Student Union, the Burnett administration created no building program. Burnett's greatest achievement was in preventing the destruction of the University of Nebraska in the interest of economy. Although the School of Fine Arts was a casualty of the times, the Graduate School of Social Work was the child of the depression. Regardless of the hardships, the University of Nebraska was preserved virtually intact for a better day. This was a tremendous achievement for an educational leader in a state devastated by depression and drought. Chancellor Edgar A. Burnett died at Lincoln on June 28, 1941.

CHANCELLOR CHAUNCEY SAMUEL BOUCHER

At the meeting of the University Board of Regents on July 5, 1938, Regent Robert W. Devoe introduced a motion to name Dr. C. S. Boucher, then president of the University of West Virginia, as chancellor of the University of Nebraska, effective September 1, 1938. The motion was adopted. This appointment was made at the same meeting of the Board of Regents at which Chancellor Burnett was granted a leave of absence and Dean Foster appointed acting chancellor. Also at this meeting, the regents purchased an official residence for the new chancellor at 21st and A Streets. Chancellor Boucher was selected without faculty consultation or the benefit of a special committee of the Board of Regents to evaluate prospective candidates for this vital position.

Chauncey S. Boucher was not a stranger to the University of Nebraska. In April 1935, he spoke at a Phi Beta Kappa convocation in Lincoln. The future chancellor recommended the "Chicago Plan" as the best hope for university reform. This plan called for, in part, student freedom in class attendance, organization of a junior and senior college division, and promotion from one division to the other by comprehensive examination. The Nebraska faculty reaction, as reported by the *Daily Nebraskan,* to the "Chicago Plan" was that it "calls for a higher type of student than that which is found generally in a state university, which by its very nature must admit all those who possess a high school diploma."[42] Remedying this situation became a major goal of the new University administration.

Chauncey Samuel Boucher was born in Chicago, Illinois, in 1886. He received his collegiate education at the University of Michigan, where he was awarded the A.B. in 1909, the M.A. in 1910, and the Ph.D. in history in 1914. In 1936, he received an honorary L.L.D. from Washington and Jefferson College. As a historian, he distinguished himself as a specialist in pre–Civil War Southern history. Boucher was president of the Mississippi Valley Historical Association in 1921 and associate editor of its journal from 1921 to 1924. He held academic appointments in history at Washington University in St. Louis, Ohio State University, University of Texas, University of Wisconsin, and the University of Chicago. From 1926 to 1935, Boucher was dean of the College of Arts, Literature and Science at the University of Chicago. Prior to his appointment as chancellor of the University of Nebraska, Boucher was president of the University of West

42. *Daily Nebraskan,* April 5, 1935.

Virginia, where his leadership was questioned by the American Association of University Professors. His appointment was in part due to the insistence of some on the city campus faculty that the new chancellor not be from agriculture and preferably be from outside the University. Dean Oldfather wrote the new chancellor, "You can be assured of my most hearty support, and I am bold enough to assure you as well of the backing of the College of Arts and Sciences."[43]

In his first address to the faculty at the University of Nebraska, the new chancellor suggested that a thoroughgoing reevaluation of higher education was past due. "This merely means that what is right and what is wrong, educationally, changes periodically in the light of changing conditions and new developments."[44] The basic administrative problem at the University of Nebraska

Chauncey Samuel Boucher.

was still that of maintaining "the best possible educational program at the university level that can be conducted for the state of Nebraska with the resources of men, money, and equipment placed at our disposal."[45] Boucher's concept of the role of the chancellor in securing legislative support for the University was to submit a well prepared budget request: "It is not the business of the chancellor or the board to argue. . . . It is their business to give information to the governor, the legislative council and the legislature. Then it is up to the institution to fit itself in the program decided upon."[46] If the chancellor and the Board of Regents did not champion the financial needs of the University, the necessary

43. Letter from C. H. Oldfather to C. S. Boucher, July 7, 1938, MSS, University of Nebraska Archives, Boucher Collection.

44. C. S. Boucher, "Address to the Faculty," *Nebraska Alumnus,* October 1938, p. 3.

45. Ibid.

46. Omaha *World-Herald,* December 13, 1938.

appropriations would not be granted. In the quest for state financial support, the other state institutions would have those who would forcefully request funds, whether or not the University of Nebraska entered the contest. A good chancellor or board ought not be too proud to fight.

Chancellor Boucher did not believe that great harm would come to the University of Nebraska from a reduced budget. The public land-grant universities of the Midwest enrolled too many students who were intellectually "unfitted for the work, undecided as to the course to follow."[47] Perhaps during a period of reduced financial support, the University could be purged of much of its unnecessary academic retinue.

To initiate this new policy, Chancellor Boucher proposed the establishment of two-year terminal programs, the creation of state junior colleges, and the encouragement of vocational programs in the public high schools. Obviously, the result would be that many small high schools could not prepare students to enter the state University, but highly motivated students could make up this deficiency through the home study program offered through the University Extension Division. The rural or small town high school graduate would likely have to make a much greater effort to qualify for University admission under this scheme. Since many rural and small town people opposed taxes for the University, this plan, if it had been accepted, would have discriminated against these small town high school graduates.

Those who had long opposed the cost of education welcomed the views of the University chancellor. Many citizens agreed with the report of the legislatively established State Educational Survey, published in 1939, that many of Nebraska's young people had been over-educated. "Most college graduates hope to become lawyers, doctors, teachers, technicians, administrative or supervisory workers; yet only 19 percent of the job opportunities lie in this classification."[48]

The establishment of more vocational programs and the reduction of purely academic offerings in the public high schools and in the state University was popular with many prominent citizens. For example, Ed S. Miller, a prominent Omaha businessman, wrote the chancellor supporting the change:

By lessening the scope of the work to be done at the University, by readjustment and proper co-ordination of the educational work done above the grade school you have outlined a sensible plan whereby we can preserve the quality of the higher educational work of our State. And after all it is quality not quantity, that we need and want.[49]

Within the University, as well as without, there was some support for this major policy shift initiated by the chancellor. Professor A. L. Lugn, a geologist, wrote:

I believe firmly in maintaining high standards all along the line in the real 'University' part of the institution. I am also firmly convinced that State education is on the right track when we make plans for the kind of 'Vocational Completion' courses you have proposed.[50]

The first budget request of the Boucher administration was submitted to the governor for the 1939–41 biennium. It was the lowest request since 1925. The Unicameral reduced the amount further. The budget finally adopted by the Board of Regents for the biennium was $3,488,600. This was $283,840 less than

47. *Daily Nebraskan,* February 3, 1939.

48. Omaha *World-Herald,* November 26, 1939, p. 5-c.

49. Letter from Ed S. Miller to C. S. Boucher, February 2, 1939, MSS, University of Nebraska Archives, Boucher Collection.

50. Letter from A. L. Lugn to C. S. Boucher, April 28, 1939, MSS, University of Nebraska Archives, Boucher Collection.

the previous biennium. At this level of financial support, the chancellor warned, the University of Nebraska might lose its accreditation. This could be prevented, Boucher suggested, and the institution improved if the Unicameral would adopt legislation authorizing the Board of Regents to limit the enrollment at the University of Nebraska. The bill to grant this power to the regents was adopted on a 34 to 4 vote and signed into law.

The approval of a Junior Division at the University by the faculty Senate and its adoption by the Board of Regents was the first phase of the chancellor's plan. Boucher outlined his goal to a fellow university administrator:

All freshmen will be admitted to the Junior Division and will be admitted to the college of their choice as rapidly as they can qualify. We contemplate that many will not qualify for admission to a college and will be given a junior college general education program, perhaps with some vocational flavor and will be eased out of the institution in good standing, if possible, with some kind of a certificate for one or possibly two years of junior college work. After a few years we will be able to inaugurate a gradual program of selective admission even to the Junior Division.[51]

This new policy ultimately meant that the University of Nebraska would adjust its enrollment to the funds available and graduate only those with above-average academic ability or those who could reasonably expect to find immediate employment in their profession. "Why should engineering colleges spend money turning out bond salesmen?" the chancellor asked.[52]

BEAT BY THE DEPRESSION?

The long financial starvation of the University of Nebraska produced a major shift in its policy by the end of the decade. Legislatively this change meant that the University would take what funds it could get and, rather than fight for more, make the best of it by adjusting the enrollment. To those schoolmen and school board members who believed that the young people of the state were being over-educated, it meant a shift to vocationalism and away from academics, with the blessing of the chancellor. To the young people of the state, the policy meant that fewer could go to the state University and that those from rural areas and small towns would be at a competitive disadvantage with those from the cities of the state.

Chancellor Boucher had surrendered to the depression! Whereas Chancellor Edgar A. Burnett had kept faith in the future and preserved the University for a better day, the new chancellor had lost his faith in the inevitability of that better day. The new leadership proposed pruning the University of Nebraska back to the "real University" and a group of two-year vocationally oriented programs. The success or failure of this policy ultimately depended on faculty acceptance. Chancellor Boucher recognized this in his first address to the faculty. "No educational program can be successfully administered in any institution until and unless the group most vitally concerned with instruction—the faculty—is, in clear majority, in sympathy with the program as a result of a conviction of its soundness. . . ."[53]

A majority of the faculty did not accept this new direction of University policy. The administrative crisis of the next few years was to become one of leadership more than one of economics.

51. Letter from C. S. Boucher to President Robert E. Doherty, Carnegie Institute of Technology, March 28, 1940, MSS, University of Nebraska Archives, Boucher Collection.
52. *Daily Nebraskan*, February 3, 1939.
53. C. S. Boucher, "Address to the Faculty," op. cit., p. 22.

CHAPTER 5

Academics and Hard Times

THE DECADE OF THE thirties was a time of questioning by many Americans. They began to question the economic system. What portion of the nation's resources should be allocated for public use through taxation, who should pay the tax, and which programs should be supported? As the national economic situation worsened, the budgets of all public colleges and universities were cut by concerned state legislatures. In a time of retrenchment requiring perhaps the discontinuance of educational programs, what should be sacrificed on the altar of economy?

During the administration of Chancellor Edgar A. Burnett, decisions which would result in the termination of instructional programs at the University of Nebraska, with the exception of the School of Fine Arts, were avoided. This policy was not the result of timidity, but rather of the firmly held conviction that a state land-grant university should meet the varied needs of the public for both cultural and vocational programs. If reductions were required, they should be spread throughout the institution rather than sacrificing any program for which there was a public demand. Chancellor Burnett believed that the balance between the cultural and vocational programs should be maintained in the University.

This was a time of considerable discussion and innovation in higher education, such as the beginning of the General College at the University of Minnesota, the establishment of the Great Books–based curriculum at St. Johns College, and the reorganization at the University of Chicago. The Nebraska faculty was well aware of these movements toward academic reorganization. In 1936, the University Senate discussed the creation of a lower division for entering freshmen. The proposal was patterned after one used at Louisiana State University. This scheme differed from the Minnesota General College in that it was a one-year, rather than a two-year program. Some faculty members favored curricular reform which would provide a year of general education. A Senate committee was established to consider this type of curricular reform.

In the spring of 1937, the report of the faculty committee was presented to the Senate. A majority of the members of the committee did not favor the establishment of a lower division for entering students. However, nine of the twenty members of the committee submitted a minority report which favored the creation of a separate lower division. The faculty vote was nearly equally divided on the issue. The greatest objection to the proposal came from the faculty of the College of Engineering, who believed it vital for the college to advise freshmen students. For the remaining years of the Burnett administration the issue rested.

Within days after assuming the chancellorship, C. S. Boucher recommended the formation of a faculty committee to consider curricular reorganization. As dean of the College of Arts, Literature and Science at the University of Chicago, the new chancellor had participated in one of the most widely discussed curriculum reorganzations of the century. Although he recognized that the University of Nebraska differed greatly from the University of Chicago, he clearly indicated his belief that the times demanded a reorganization of instructional programs.

Like Hutchins at Chicago, the chancellor of the University of Nebraska denounced those who sought a college degree for economic or social reasons. Half-humorously, Chancellor Boucher told members of the Omaha Rotary Club that one solution to the demand for college degrees would be to award them with the birth certificate. "Then we can get down to the serious business of education immediately, with emphasis on mental training rather than on routine fulfillment of courses and hour requirements."[1] Enrollment figures show, however, that most students at the University of Nebraska considered their program of studies to be vocational. Few endured the hardships of being a student during depression times to seek eternal truth.

A committee was organized under the chairmanship of Dean C. H. Oldfather, of the College of Arts and Sciences, to evaluate University instructional policies and practices. A subcommittee led by Henry H. Marvin, professor of physics, proposed to the University Senate, in the fall of 1939, that a Junior Division be established at the University of Nebraska. Students would remain in the division for one or two years and would be divided into five classifications: Group A for those who were qualified to enter the college of their choice, Group B for those who exhibited deficiencies which must be removed before they could qualify for entrance in a college, Group C for those students taking a terminal program, Group D for special students, and Group E for those who were undecided about vocation or college. Professor Marvin urged the adoption of this plan.

With rare exceptions the university does not now provide opportunities for general or vocational education if students fail in their attempt to qualify in the liberal arts, scientific or professional courses. It also seems advisable that such terminal courses should be developed in order to salvage many students by developing occupational and civic efficiency. These courses may appropriately be developed by the university if the need is not met elsewhere.[2]

The adoption of this proposal certainly contained the promise of the University of Nebraska expanding its offerings in vocational education. Not only would the traditional programs be maintained and improved but new vocational programs could be developed to meet the needs of young people. However, any expansion in program required either additional funds or the elimination of existing programs. The potential for vocational programs at the University of Nebraska was not realized because of the economic situation and an unwillingness to discontinue established conventional academic work.

THE COLLEGE OF AGRICULUTURE

During the thirties, William W. Burr was dean of the College of Agriculture and director of the Experiment Station. Except for a slump in enrollment during the worst years of the depression, the college experienced a steady growth. At the end of the period, student enrollment was 43 percent higher than at the beginning of the decade. In addition to providing the instructional program for its growing numbers, the faculty contributed substantially to the improvement of agricultural efficiency, and thereby improved the quality of life for rural Nebraskans.

Professors Leunis Van Es and Jesse F. Olney, of the Department of Animal

1. Omaha *World-Herald,* February 15, 1939, p. 1.
2. Lincoln, *State Journal,* October 14, 1939, p. 1.

Pathology and Hygiene, published important papers on animal diseases which had cost Nebraska farmers much needed income. Research on the control of poultry diseases attracted the attention of the United States Livestock Sanitary Association and the American Veterinary Association. This work greatly increased the use of good poultry management practices. Van Es and Charles B. McGrath contributed to the understanding of swine erysipelas, a disease which was becoming a serious problem and was little understood by veterinarians. As a service to the farmers, stockmen, and veterinarians of Nebraska, nearly seventy thousand specimens from diseased animals were examined during these years by the Department of Animal Pathology and Hygiene. These examinations required considerable staff time, but afforded the department a survey of the animal disease situation in the state.

The Agronomy Department, chaired by Theodore A. Kiesselbach, despite the drought, hot winds, and grasshoppers, developed several new types of hybrid corn adapted to Nebraska. Through University publications and participation in meetings of the Nebraska Crop Growers Association, information regarding the improved varieties of corn, wheat, and other small grains was made available to farmers. The research in small grain production was extensive, and much of it was conducted in cooperation with agencies of the United States Department of Agriculture. Studies were also made in the production of forage crops. A continuing search for, and the development of, varieties adapted to Nebraska conditions was made throughout the period. Hewitt M. Tysdal was a leading investigator in the production of alfalfa. Other forage crops studied included sweet clover, sudan grass, lespedeza, and sorghums. The Agronomy Department, in cooperation with the Conservation and Survey Division, undertook a long-term study of the succession of abandoned land in Kimball County in 1935.

Substantial growth took place in the Department of Home Economics under the chairmanship of Margaret S. Fedde. The number of courses offered by the department expanded to meet the rising public demand. The addition of Ruth M. Leverton to the staff marked the beginning of serious work in human nutrition. Many of the other publications by members of the department were valuable contributions to the evaluation and use of consumer goods.

The work of the Department of Animal Husbandry proved to be of great value to the stockman of Nebraska. During the depression the practice of contract feeding of livestock became common. R. R. Thalman investigated this feeding method and various management systems in growing and fattening cattle. His findings enabled many producers to operate at a profit, when such an operation was extremely difficult. Similar work in swine production was carried on by William J. Loeffel, who also cooperated with Arthur D. Weber and Martin A. Alexander on the improvement of feeding programs for sheep.

The efforts of Professors Morris J. Blish and Rudolph M. Sandstedt, in the Department of Agricultural Chemistry, emphasized studies of the characteristics of wheat and the milling and baking qualities of flour. Their research resulted in some thirty-five publications during the decade. In 1936, Blish was awarded the Thomas Burr Osborne medal by the American Association of Cereal Chemists in recognition of his research contributions. The Department of Agricultural Chemistry worked closely with Frank E. Mussehl and Clifton W. Ackerson of the Department of Poultry Husbandry in studies of poultry feeds.

The Department of Plant Pathology stressed study of plant diseases which affected crops produced in Nebraska. George L. Peltier was chairman of the department until 1937, at which time he was succeeded by Robert W. Goss.

The work conducted at the agricultural experimental substations was a major part of the program of the College of Agriculture to improve the quality of rural life in Nebraska. The locations of the substations enabled their staffs to study problems peculiar to that region of the state. The largest of the substations was at North Platte. The superintendent, until his untimely death in 1934, was William P. Snyder. He was succeeded by Leslie L. Zook. The principal investigator at the station was Marvel L. Baker. A native of Kansas and a graduate of Kansas State Agricultural College, Baker first became connected with the University as a member of the faculty at the School of Agriculture at Curtis. After a short period as cashier in a bank at Curtis, Baker rejoined the University staff as Animal Husbandryman at North Platte in 1930. His wide acquaintance in western Nebraska and friendship with many livestock producers made him a valuable communication link between agricultural leaders and the University. His work enjoyed the support and confidence of Superintendents Snyder and Zook, as well as that of Dean Burr and Chancellor Burnett.

Under Marvel L. Baker's direction a comprehensive program of beef cattle research was initiated. This program had a great economic impact on western Nebraska. Through the medium of "Feeders' Days" and various publications, information gained in the program of beef cattle research was made available to producers. The knowledge gained not only solved immediate problems but also served as the basis for future research. Studies on the feeding of rye and wheat to cattle had an immediate and beneficial effect for the dry-land farmer who suffered from a glutted rye market. The research at the station also showed producers that production practices popular in other parts of the nation were not suitable for western Nebraska. After a three-year research program, it was determined that the popular practice of creep feeding calves was not suitable for the North Platte region.

Animal research at the station, under Baker's direction, was also concerned with swine production. This effort was affiliated with the Regional Swine Breeding Laboratory directed from Iowa State College at Ames, Iowa. The United States Bureau of Animal Industry and the agricultural departments of the participating states sponsored this extensive research. Other activities at the North Platte station included the maintenance of a registered Holstein herd, research on production of sheep and lamb feeding, and a poultry flock testing program.

At the experimental substation at Valentine, studies were made in the adaptation of forage and grain crops to that area of the state. Until 1935, the station maintained an excellent herd of Holsteins and Milking Shorthorns. Edgar M. Brouse, station superintendent, continued his work on winter rations for growing calves and the effect of winter gains on the following summer. This research was of incalculable value not only to Nebraska producers, but also to all cattlemen interested in growing calves.

The substation at Scottsbluff emphasized primarily crop production. Cultivation under conditions in the North Platte Valley required high operating costs which in turn required high returns. This could be realized only by superior cultural methods, good crop production practice, and the wise use of water and fertilizers. The station staff did much to assist the people of western Nebraska in the solution of their production problems. In 1931, a program was begun in the production of vegetables and small fruits in the hope of promoting processing industries in the area.

At the beginning of this decade, an experimental farm was established near Alliance. This was a cooperative effort of the University and the county commissioners of Box Butte County. The work here also emphasized finding solutions to the agricultural problems peculiar to a specific part of Nebraska. The staff at the experimental station at Lincoln and the out-state substations made significant contributions to the economic survival of Nebraskans during the terrible depression and drought years of the thirties.

THE COLLEGE OF ARTS AND SCIENCES

Few colleges of the University of Nebraska were affected by the financial cuts of the decade more severely than the College of Arts and Sciences. Although the enrollment of students who majored in the college declined slightly, the enormous service function of the college remained constant because the college granted more hours of student credit than any other college. It accounted for between 55 and 57 percent of the credit hours earned at the University each year during this decade. Deans Hicks and Oldfather constantly complained to the chancellor that the college was not receiving adequate financial support. They questioned the allocation of funds on the basis of college enrollment. The number of students enrolled in a college, Dean Hicks protested, neither reflected the teaching load of the college's faculty nor the value of the college to the University.

Any one or two or three of our professional or vocational schools could be abolished, and the University of Nebraska would still be a leading educational institution. But the elimination of the Arts College, without full provision having been made for carrying on the work that it does, would wreck us in the eyes of the whole educational world.[3]

While no serious scholar could doubt the value and service of the College of Arts and Sciences, there was fierce competition among the colleges for student enrollment. A proposal favored by the faculty of the College of Arts and Sciences would require all entering freshmen to be enrolled in a junior division of the Arts College. The proposal to require attendance by these students in a series of general lectures caused considerable apprehension among the faculty in the other colleges. Dean Hicks wrote the chancellor that the "pretense that the Freshman Lecture course is an 'orientation' course in the broader sense of that term is definitely abandoned. We are trying merely to show our freshmen what the Arts College curriculum has to offer."[4] Most of the other college faculties were not willing to place all entering students into the hands of the rival faculty. Dean John D. Hicks believed that the competition for students had produced a

. . . cheapening of curriculums as a means of competing for student affiliations. Under the present system each college is tempted to do whatever it can to show a large number of student enrollments, and the elimination of difficult required courses is a temptation. Several of the colleges have eliminated a laboratory science; Business Administration has lately done away with the language requirement. . . .[5]

The dean further warned that unless "the present tendency to undercut its requirements is not checked, it [the College of Arts and Sciences] may as a matter of self-preservation find it necessary to join with the rest in debasing its curriculum."[6] The competition of the market place had entered the University. Departmental budgets, faculty positions, and even the retention of junior faculty members were at stake.

The instructional load of the College of Arts and Sciences and the financial problems of the depression resulted in real hardship and harm to the instructional program. Large classes necessitated the use of unsound educational practices.

3. Report, Dean of the College of Arts and Sciences—J. D. Hicks to Chancellor E. A. Burnett, July 2, 1930, p. 6, MSS, University of Nebraska Archives, Burnett Collection.
4. Report, Dean of the College of Arts and Sciences—J. D. Hicks to Chancellor E. A. Burnett, July 8, 1931, MSS, University of Nebraska Archives, Burnett Collection.
5. Report, Dean of the College of Arts and Sciences—J. D. Hicks to Chancellor E. A. Burnett, July 2, 1930, p. 8, MSS, University of Nebraska Archives, Burnett Collection.
6. Ibid.

For example the practice of hiring undergraduate students to grade the papers of other undergraduates was unfortunate. Dean Hicks found it "leads to the gravest abuses."[7] Too many undergraduate paper graders were influenced by maintaining fraternity scholarship standings or by engaging in politics. "If he is politically prominent he may repay his supporters and punish his adversaries."[8]

A far more serious instructional crisis was caused by the death and retirement of many of the College of Arts and Sciences' most experienced and recognized scholars. Funds were generally not available to replace them by professors of equal fame. The deaths of Harold H. Waite, chairman of the Department of Bacteriology and Pathology; Robert II. Wolcott, chairman of the Department of Zoology; Lawrence Fossler, chairman of the Department of Germanic Languages; Prosser H. Frye, professor of English; and Fred Morrow Fling, professor of European history, eliminated scholars with national reputations from the University. The retirements of Laura B. Pfeiffer, associate professor of European history; Albert L. Candy, chairman of the Department of Mathematics; Erwin H. Barbour, chairman of the Department of Geology; and Professor Goodwin D. Swezey, professor of astronomy, also created vacancies which were difficult to fill. The salary level at the University of Nebraska was too low to attract senior professors from other institutions.

These faculty changes marked the end of the days of the "old-time professor" at the University of Nebraska. The new style professor would be better prepared academically, more dedicated to his profession than to any institution, and far more mobile. Professor Goodwin DeLoss Swezey, *the* Department of Astronomy at the University for forty years, symbolized for many the old-time professor, dedicated to his students. Despite repeated disappointments, he never lost faith that the University would provide an adequate observatory. On the event of his retirement, the editor of the Omaha *World-Herald,* wrote:

Prof. Swezey was long beloved among faculty men at Lincoln. His years of communion with the skies had dimmed his eyes a bit and wrinkled his face but he never lost his enthusiasm for the study of the stars. . . . He never lost that enthusiasm although his hopes for a decent observatory were doomed to be annually disappointed. . . .

If there are any compensations Prof. Swezey will find them in the fact that his students, although few, were earnest; that his equipment, although inadequate, was yet sufficient to stir the imagination of those who, with him, gazed at the illimitable universe and wondered at the insignificance of man.[9]

Not only did Swezey fail to get his observatory, but with his retirement, the Department of Astronomy perished and was absorbed by the Department of Mathematics. The editor of the *Daily Nebraskan* lamented: "And now his very department is sacrificed in an attempt to balance a heartless budget. College editors are supposed to be cynical and cruel, but the spectacle of Professor Swezey's exit from Nebraska annals leaves an empty spot."[10] To many, the Department of Astronomy had symbolized the search for truth in a world devoted to materialism.

In the spring of 1932, Dean John D. Hicks accepted an invitation to join the Department of History at the University of Wisconsin. "Professionally it was a long step forward, and I didn't want to be dean anyway."[11] Chancellor Burnett

7. Letter from John D. Hicks to E. A. Burnett, December 10, 1930, MSS, University of Nebraska Archives, Burnett Collection.

8. Ibid.

9. Omaha *World-Herald,* April 5, 1932.

10. *Daily Nebraskan,* April 5, 1932.

11. John D. Hicks, *My Life with History* (Lincoln: University of Nebraska Press, 1969), p. 153.

wrote the regents informing them that the loss of Dean Hicks "is proof of the fact that our greatest danger lies in losing men at the top rather than at the bottom of the faculty schedule."[12]

The choice of the faculty and administration for the deanship was Charles Henry Oldfather. He had joined the Nebraska faculty as professor of ancient history in 1926. Besides holding the Ph.D. from the University of Wisconsin, he had been awarded the D.D. from McCormick Theological Seminary. During a temporary absence of Dean Hicks, Oldfather had been appointed acting dean of the college. In a letter to the chancellor the future dean revealed his understanding of academic power. "After all, I suppose that the main task of an 'acting' anything is to see to it—but with proper show of dignity—that nothing serious be done. At least that much you may properly expect of me in the five months of my incumbency."[13]

As dean of the College of Arts and Sciences, Oldfather enjoyed the confidence of the University administration and the support of his faculty. At the time of his appointment as dean after the resignation of Hicks, Chancellor Burnett found him "a man of fine education, a popular teacher, and has a rather more judicial temperament, I think, than has Dean Hicks."[14] Dean Oldfather saw the goal of the College of Arts and Sciences as "the molding of citizens who will have an understanding of the world as it is and an appreciation of what the past and present have to offer. In short, it is the purpose of this college to turn out intelligent and useful members of society."[15] Certainly, the contributions to society by University of Nebraska alumni bear eloquent testimony to the success of the college in reaching this goal.

By this time, the *Prairie Schooner,* which had begun publication in 1927, had won national recognition. The magazine was founded by members of Sigma Upsilon, the literary fraternity, and was called "Prairie Schooner" to honor the pioneers who settled Nebraska. Under the editorship of Lowry C. Wimberly, it gained the attention of recognized literary critics by 1931. Among the authors who launched their careers by publishing in the *Prairie Schooner* were Mari Sandoz, Helen Margaret, Albert Halper, David Cornet De Jong, Dorothy Thomas, William March, and Jesse Stuart.

Despite the large classes and heavy teaching load, productive faculty scholarship continued. A book on economic geography by Professors Nels A. Bengtson and Willem Van Royen won national awards. Professors Joy P. Guilford, of the Department of Psychology, and Rudolph A. Winnacker, of the Department of History, brought recognition to the College of Arts and Sciences by being awarded substantial research grants by the Social Science Research Council. Few faculty members could match the amount of public service contributed by John P. Senning, professor of political science, who helped to design the unicameral legislature of Nebraska.

The largest departments in the College of Arts and Sciences during the thirties were those of English, history, romance languages, chemistry, and mathematics. The fastest growing department was that of political science.

During these years, a significant change was taking place in the activities of the University of Nebraska Museum. With the vast improvement in facilities resulting from the construction of Morrill Hall, during the twenties, and the

12. Letter from E. A. Burnett to Regent Stanley D. Long, May 17, 1932, MSS, University of Nebraska Archives, Burnett Collection.

13. Letter from C. H. Oldfather to E. A. Burnett, March 20, 1931, MSS, University of Nebraska Archives, Burnett Collection.

14. Letter from E. A. Burnett to Regent Stanley D. Long, May 17, 1932, MSS, University of Nebraska Archives, Burnett Collection.

15. *Daily Nebraskan,* November 27, 1934.

development of a young enthusiastic staff, the work done at the museum soon attracted national attention. The existence of great fossil beds in Nebraska influenced the museum staff to undertake important paleontological research. The program of field work was greatly expanded with private funds. Money for this research came from the bequest of Charles Morrill and from Childs Frick, a son of the famous industrialist Henry C. Frick of United States Steel. Frick was a curator at the American Museum of Natural History. Support for research was also made by Hector Maiben, a successful Nebraska farmer. The field work was under the direction of C. Bertrand Schultz, who was appointed assistant director of the museum in 1938. Erwin H. Barbour, a faculty member since 1891, was director of the museum. Among the displays added to the museum collection during this decade were the August Eiche bird collection and the Adam Breede collection of African big-game animals.

THE COLLEGE OF BUSINESS ADMINISTRATION

Throughout the depression decade, James E. LeRossignol was the dean of the College of Business Administration. In 1932–33, the enrollment in the college was at the low point of the decade. By 1937, enrollment was nearly 57 percent higher than in 1932. This rapid recovery and growth in enrollment was in large measure the result of increased public interest in improving business methods and management. Changes in the curriculum of the college reflected the business problems of the time. In 1930, courses were added in money and banking and in the study of the Federal Reserve System. By 1933, a course was added which considered economic planning in the United States. Course offerings were later expanded to include work in marketing analysis and cooperative marketing agencies. In 1933, a combined program was established by the Colleges of Business Administration and Law. Under this plan, students in their junior year in the College of Business Administration who had completed all required courses could enter the College of Law, and the first year of law would complete the requirements for a degree from the College of Business Administration.

The faculty of the college was active in publication and service to the people of the state. Professors John D. Clark and Karl M. Arndt conducted numerous public lectures throughout Nebraska. The publications of Professors George M. Darlington, Dana F. Cole, Clifford M. Hicks, Cleon O. Swayzee, and Clarence E. McNeill also brought recognition to the College of Business Administration.

In a report to the chancellor, Dean LeRossignol summarized the activities of the College of Business Administration:

The demand for our graduates is increasing in a most gratifying way. . . . we have now a College faculty comparable to that of any school of business administration in the United States, except the very largest, and I hope we may be able to keep it up to the present standard and make improvement from time to time.[16]

THE COLLEGES OF MEDICINE, DENTISTRY, AND PHARMACY

Enrollment at the College of Medicine, in Omaha, was very stable throughout the decade. The number of pre-med students on the Lincoln campus increased dramatically as the profession became more attractive to students. This increasing interest was very noticeable after 1934.

The budget cuts of 1932 caused a reduction in the number of patients served by the Medical College dispensary in Omaha. It was unfortunate that during a

16. Letter from J. E. LeRossignol to E. A. Burnett, June 20, 1937, MSS, University of Nebraska Archives, Burnett Collection.

time of economic hardship, the regents were forced to curtail the level of medical services available to the poor at the Medical College. The economic consequences of the depression affected educational policy in many ways. In the College of Medicine, this was strikingly evident in the School of Nursing. Did the School of Nursing have a responsibility to protect the economic interests of the profession? Should educational policies be adopted to restrict entry into the profession? In 1934, Dean C. W. M. Poynter, of the College of Medicine, considered these questions in a letter to the chancellor:

As you know there has been a movement on to reduce the number of Nursing Schools and with this the number of young women taking nursing. This has been on account of the large amount of unemployment and the feeling that there had already been an excess number of people thrown into this vocation.

It seems desirable, in conjunction with raise of standards that the University should advance the requirements for entrance to the Nursing School.[17]

The University *Bulletin* for 1934–35 added, "Beginning in September 1935, applicants for admission to the three-year course leading to the degree of Graduate Nurse must present not less than thirty acceptable credit hours, representing an attendance at an approved college for one year."[18] By the fall of 1937, the requirement for 30 hours credit was made optional, but "preference is given to applicants who present thirty or more acceptable college semester hours."[19]

Although no college was more seriously affected by the economic decline than the College of Dentistry, the college made real progress in the development of its curriculum and the spreading fame of its faculty. The Dental Educational Council of America advanced the college's rating to "A" in 1933. In general the profession of dentistry was not prosperous during the depression. Enrollment in the College of Dentistry fell from a high of 128 in 1929–30 to 63 students in 1938–39.

In 1933, a group of forty-five practicing dentists from southeast Nebraska protested to the Board of Regents the competition from the Dental College Clinic. This complaint was the direct result of the depression. The grievance was expressed to the president of the Board of Regents by one practitioner:

The College of Dentistry is in direct competition with the dentists of Lincoln and Nebraska, and in times when there was plenty for all the situation was different, but in these times of depression, it does not seem fair that the dentists should be saddled with competition from the State University. . . .

From the standpoint of most of the dentists that I have contacted, the protest is in the fact that there are too many people found at the University clinic for dental services, that should be employing a private dentist.[20]

The complaints continued and charges were made against the professional conduct of the dean and some members of the dental faculty. In October 1935, the Board of Regents conducted a formal public hearing on the management of the Dental College and its clinic. The board found that the charges made against Dean Grubb and some faculty members of unprofessional practices were not supported by fact. The regents also approved the management of the Dental Clinic and determined that its operation was consistent with University policy and legislative appropriation. The competition between the private dentist and the University Dental Clinic was unavoidable. Since the clinic was required to

17. Letter from C. W. M. Poynter to E. A. Burnett, April 14, 1934, MSS, University of Nebraska Archives, Burnett Collection.

18. *Bulletin* of the University of Nebraska, Catalog Issue, 1934–35, p. 213.

19. *Bulletin* of the University of Nebraska, Catalog Issue, 1937–38, p. 255.

20. Letter from Dr. M. C. Pedersen to Earl Cline, August 14, 1933, MSS, University of Nebraska Archives, Burnett Collection.

operate on a self-sustaining basis, it could not limit its services to charity patients.

To conform with the rising entrance standards required by the Dental Educational Council of America, the pre-dental requirements were extended from one to two years work in 1935. Dean Grubb reported to the Board of Regents that the new requirements "will result not only in turning out a product (graduates) better fitted to render the health service that dentistry is, but this product will be a higher type of cultured citizen."[21]

Dean George A. Grubb retired as dean of the College of Dentistry in 1939. Bert L. Hooper, professor of prosthetic dentistry, was then appointed dean. He had been a member of the faculty since 1923. Hooper continued to serve as dean until 1958.

During this decade, the College of Pharmacy remained under the able leadership of Dean Rufus A. Lyman. In 1937, the first issue of the *American Journal of Pharmaceutical Education* was published under the editorship of Dean Lyman. Through this journal and the work of the faculty, the College of Pharmacy became well established. This enabled the college to attract and hold an excellent faculty. Harald G. O. Holck, from the University of Chicago, joined the Nebraska faculty in 1936. His interest in research and publication was a valuable asset to the College of Pharmacy.

THE COLLEGE OF ENGINEERING

Enrollment in the College of Engineering was remarkably steady during the depression. Although there was a decline in 1932 and 1933, the number of students at the end of the decade was slightly larger than at the beginning of the depression. At the beginning of the decade, the Department of Architectural Engineering was changed to the Department of Architecture by the Board of Regents. In 1931, the degrees of Bachelor of Architecture, Bachelor of the Arts of Architecture, and Master of Architecture were authorized by the regents. The degree of Master of Science in Architectural Engineering was authorized in 1939. Between 1930 and 1934, the chairman of the Department of Architecture was Harry F. Cunningham. He was succeeded by Linus B. Smith. The dean of the College of Engineering throughout the depression decade was Olin J. Ferguson, who had been appointed dean in 1920.

During the thirties, there was great interest in the creation of public power districts. As public corporations were formed to undertake these developments, the faculty of the College of Engineering became a source of expert advice. Considerable opposition developed to some of these projects, and those faculty members who served as professional consultants were drawn into the controversy. This was particularly true with the Tri-County Project, organized in 1933, as the Central Nebraska Public Power and Irrigation District. Opponents of the project denounced it as "an engineering monstrosity." The chief engineer for this project was Professor Clark E. Mickey, chairman of the Department of Civil Engineering at the University of Nebraska. Although his work for the Central Nebraska Power and Irrigation District was accomplished while on a leave of absence granted by the Board of Regents, critics held the University responsible. The intensity of the controversy caused Regent Stanley D. Long to complain bitterly about Professor Mickey:

You will note that this man is still causing trouble, and as I see it, he can cause more trouble in a few weeks than six regents can straighten out in a life time. If I understand things properly, Professor Mickey is supposed to teach Civil Engineering at the En-

21. Memo, Dean of the College of Dentistry to the Board of Regents, December 13, 1935, MSS, University of Nebraska Archives, Burnett Collection.

gineer's College in Lincoln, and I don't know where he gets the authority to go out over the State and antagonize the people by telling one group that they should take water from another group.

I have been living in the Republican Valley most of my life, but the Platte Valley is also in my district and he puts me in between two fires.

If this man can not quit this, I am going to ask for his resignation at the next Board Meeting.[22]

Many opponents of the plan referred to it as "Mickey's Project." After considerable difficulty, the Public Works Administration approved the proposal and contracts were awarded for the construction of Kingsley Dam, near Ogallala,

Engineering students acquiring foundry experience.

which forms Lake C. W. McConaughy. Professor Clark E. Mickey survived the controversy and retired as emeritus professor of civil engineering in 1947.

THE TEACHERS COLLEGE AND THE EXTENSION DIVISION

The dean of the Teachers College for most of this decade was Frank E. Henzlik. He first joined the University faculty in 1924 as professor and chairman of the Department of School Administration. In 1931, when Dean William E. Sealock accepted the appointment of president of Omaha's municipal university, Henzlik was named dean of Teachers College. The new dean was a graduate of Central Missouri State Teachers College in 1916, and was awarded the Bachelor of Laws from the University of Missouri in 1921. Becoming more interested in teaching than in the practice of law, he entered public school work. After several years experience as a school superintendent, Henzlik enrolled in the Teachers College at Columbia University, where he earned the A.M. and Ph.D. During his long tenure as dean of the Teachers College, lasting until 1958,

22. Letter from Stanley D. Long to E. A. Burnett, August 3, 1933, MSS, University of Nebraska Archives, Burnett Collection.

Henzlik shaped the development of professional education at the University of Nebraska. His vision of the role of the teacher in society was noble.

If the intellectual level of Nebraska citizens is to be raised, this development will depend largely upon placing in our communities teachers of culture, character, and ability. Just as a stream never rises above its source, likewise, people can never rise above the level of the teachers of their children. If teachers are to serve properly, they must realize that the training and education received in the university is not wholly for what it may mean to them personally, but that they may return to the communities of the state and share with the children and people the benefits received from university training.

It is, then, one of the missions of the college to foster, in those preparing to teach, right professional attitudes and personal ideals, professional honesty, and the ideal that schools are maintained for children and not for teachers.[23]

During the depression years there was a decline in the undergraduate enrollment in the Teachers College. This resulted from the scarcity of teaching positions. However, the enrollment of the Graduate College was greatly stimulated by teachers returning for advanced degrees during the summer sessions. With this increased interest in graduate work by teachers and administrators, the influence of the Teachers College increased in the public schools of Nebraska. During the school year 1933–34, it was reported that over 38 percent of the city and village elementary teachers, 40 percent of the high school teachers, and 60 percent of the school superintendents in Nebraska had received all or a part of their professional education in the Teachers College of the University of Nebraska.[24] Consequently, those who favored extensive cuts in expenditures for public education considered the Teachers College as a major obstacle in the path of drastic retrenchment. Specifically, the Teachers College was accused of: forcing unreasonably high educational standards upon the public schools, cooperating with school superintendents to prevent cuts in teachers' salaries, and recommending to various communities the erection of expensive school buildings and costly educational programs.[25]

The depression made it very difficult for many communities to maintain their public schools. The main thrust of the Teachers College, in addition to the preparation of teachers and administrators, was to assist the struggling local boards to maintain a reasonably good school system with very limited funds. This task was a cooperative venture of the Teachers College and the Extension Division.

In late 1931, a grant was made by the Carnegie Foundation for the Advancement of Teaching to support the development and the use of correspondence study to supplement the restricted curriculum of small high schools. Under the direction of Knute O. Broady and Professor A. A. Reed, director of the University Extension Division, the program developed rapidly. This effort to enrich the curriculum of small high schools attracted national recognition. In 1933, Broady and Reed were sent by Chancellor Burnett to report their work at the Citizens Conference on the Crisis in Education called by President Franklin D. Roosevelt.

The experiment consists in supplying from the State University Extension Department Correspondence courses in whatever subjects any student in a small high school may desire to study. The student attends high school regularly and devotes a portion of the regular school time to the correspondence study under the supervision of the

23. *Daily Nebraskan,* December 11, 1934.
24. Report, Dean F. E. Henzlik to E. A. Burnett, July 5, 1934, MSS, University of Nebraska Archives, Burnett Collection.
25. Letter from E. A. Burnett to Professor A. A. Reed, February 17, 1933, MSS, University of Nebraska Archives, Burnett Collection.

high school teacher. The written lessons are sent to the State University for correction and grading.[26]

This program enabled the small high school to meet the needs of students at a time of real crisis. The significance of this service is apparent in a letter to Chancellor Burnett from the school board at Chester, Nebraska.

Anyone familiar with the situation knows that the services being rendered by this high school would be impossible were we to be dependent upon our own resources in this small community without the services of these outside agencies. The point of the whole matter is that alone we can only be narrow, inefficient and uneconomical in our educational program.[27]

Although educators would question the soundness of the small school in the future, Dean Henzlik firmly believed that "Nebraska's small school systems are potentially one of the state's greatest assets. The people of the small communities and cities believe in these institutions."[28]

The elementary schools were also benefited through the program of assistance to local school systems. In cooperation with the Department of Elementary Education, the Extension Division distributed instructional materials to teachers. Many members of the Teachers College faculty taught extension classes throughout Nebraska to help raise the professional competence of in-service teachers. The extension effort of the Teachers College faculty was exceeded only by that of the College of Agriculture.

The chief limiting factor on the influence of the Teachers College to raise the quality of public education in Nebraska was a lack of funds. The Superintendents and Principals Association requested "that a way might be found whereby the excellent services of the people's Teachers College might be made available . . ." to more communities.[29] Chancellor Burnett replied regretfully "that the appropriation for the next biennium will permit little, if any, expansion in the University program. . . . I sympathize thoroughly with your program, and perhaps sometime we may work it out more fully."[30]

In 1937, legislation was adopted which raised teacher certification standards and centralized the certification procedure in the state Department of Public Instruction. Colleges and school superintendents were no longer permitted to issue their own certificates. This was a significant step in raising professional standards for teachers. Dean Frank E. Henzlik was a major force in the adoption of this legislation.

THE GRADUATE COLLEGE

At the end of the thirties, the Graduate College enrollment was 24 percent larger than at the beginning of the decade. Dean Fred W. Upson optimistically reported in 1934:

There has been a definite elevation of standards through general adoption of the comprehensive examinations for the Ph.D. degree, and the entrance and final written examinations for Master's degree candidates. The formation of a graduate faculty with

26. Report, A. A. Reed and K. O. Broady to E. A. Burnett, April 1933, MSS, University of Nebraska Archives, Burnett Collection.

27. Letter from School Board of Chester, Nebraska to E. A. Burnett, January 22, 1935, MSS, University of Nebraska Archives, Burnett Collection.

28. Letter from F. E. Henzlik to E. A. Burnett, November 25, 1931, MSS, University of Nebraska Archives, Burnett Collection.

29. Letter from E. L. Novotny to E. A. Burnett, April 6, 1935, MSS, University of Nebraska Archives, Burnett Collection.

30. Letter from E. A. Burnett to E. L. Novotny, April 9, 1935, MSS, University of Nebraska Archives, Burnett Collection.

definite standards of admission has stimulated research activity and in a number of cases, further training on the part of the faculty.[31]

However, the same year, a survey made by the American Council on Education of institutions which offered the doctor's degree found satisfactory only the University of Nebraska's programs in botany, chemistry, education, English, plant pathology, and plant physiology. The Graduate dean was disappointed with the report.

This is not enough for a university of Nebraska's standing. We can remedy this situation only by means of an enlarged program for the Graduate College and better support of research, for this report is primarily a reflection of the productive scholarship of the Universities of the country.[32]

There was little doubt, among the faculty, that the small number of programs approved by the council was the result of a lack of financial support for research.

By the end of the decade, the new Graduate dean, Harold W. Stoke, reported to Chancellor C. S. Boucher that an examination of the list of recent faculty publications "reveals the interesting fact that the scholarly output of this faculty compares very favorably in quantity and I dare say in quality, with Universities which have achieved a greater degree of prestige in the popular mind."[33] To encourage research activity at the University of Nebraska and to focus attention on faculty scholarship, the University Research Committee was established in the fall of 1939. The specific responsibility of this important committee was to be:

1. The development and coordination of research projects, particularly cooperative projects involving several departments or even Colleges.
2. Serving as an advisory editorial Committee for the publication of University Research Notes.
3. Canvassing sources of support among foundations and research agencies, and supplying appropriate information to the faculty and to the adminstrative staff.
4. Serving as a liaison agency to assist faculty and students with grants-in-aid committees, research organizations, foundations, etc.
5. Administering a revolving research fund which can be turned to the support of research projects in any department or school on the campus.[34]

These objectives clearly indicate the dependence of growth in faculty research on increased funds. It is also clear that the University of Nebraska had not received much state support for research activity.

During the thirties, the largest number of Ph.D. degrees were awarded in the fields of chemistry, botany, educational psychology, geography, history, and agronomy. At the master's level, the Departments of School Administration, English, History, Chemistry, Secondary Education, and Educational Psychology led in recommending candidates for degrees.

THE SCHOOL OF MUSIC

In the fall of 1930, the University of Nebraska Board of Regents purchased the private University School of Music, located at 11th and R streets. The

31. Report, Fred W. Upson to E. A. Burnett, June 30, 1934, MSS, University of Nebraska Archives, Burnett Collection.

32. Ibid.

33. Letter from Harold W. Stoke to C. S. Boucher, October 5, 1939, MSS, University of Nebraska Archives, Boucher Collection.

34. Letter from C. S. Boucher to members of the University Research Committee, October 27, 1939, MSS, University of Nebraska Archives, Boucher Collection.

private institution was established in 1894 as a music conservatory by Willard Kimball. The school continued in private hands until the time of its purchase by the regents from Adrian M. Newens and George P. Kimball. The purchase price was $100,000, of which $10,000 was paid in cash. Chancellor Burnett and the Board of Regents anticipated "that the earnings of the School of Music will be sufficient to take care of the rest of the obligations as they come due."[35] It is unlikely that the regents would have taken this action if they had forseen the future financial difficulties of the decade.

It was imperative after the depression legislative sessions of 1931 and 1933 that the School of Music operate at a profit. This was not easy because of a decided drop in student enrollment at mid-decade. The faculty members who taught the work in applied music were paid on a fee commission basis. In April

The School of Music Building. Courtesy of the Nebraska State Historical Society.

1932, the Board of Regents reduced the amount paid to instructors of applied music from 40 percent to 30 percent of the cost of lessons. The continuance of instruction in applied music on this basis quickly brought the competition of the market-place into the school. Some instructors waged a price war against others; imaginative teachers developed techniques for giving private lessons to small groups. The situation worsened. By 1937, a group of senior faculty members from the School of Music petitioned the chancellor, "We are in actual distress about the welfare of our families and some even stand to lose their homes unless something can be done to place us on a substantial basis."[36]

On April 1, 1937, the Board of Regents reorganized the School of Music. In all but special cases the practice of paying the faculty on a commission basis was discontinued. A permanent faculty of a director and thirteen full-time instructors was authorized. With this action, the School of Music was given real equality with the other schools and colleges of the University and the

35. *Daily Nebraskan,* September 21, 1930.
36. Petition, Faculty of School of Music to Chancellor E. A. Burnett, February 4, 1937, MSS, University of Nebraska Archives, Burnett Collection.

financial security necessary for its development. Through most of these difficult years, Howard Kirkpatrick was director of the School of Music. In 1939, Arthur E. Westbrook was appointed director. Under his leadership the University of Nebraska School of Music was established as a leader in its field.

THE GRADUATE SCHOOL OF SOCIAL WORK

The establishment of the Graduate School of Social Work resulted from the increasing need for professional social workers and the rising standards required for accreditation by the American Association of Schools of Social Work. The creation of this new school did not indicate the beginning of a new program. As early as 1908, an undergraduate curriculum was established in the Department of Sociology to prepare social workers. By 1924, a four-year sequence of course work had been organized. These courses were accredited, in 1933, by the American Association of Social Workers, and undergraduate students in the program were admitted to junior membership in the association. The Graduate School of Social Work at the University was established by the Board of Regents in 1937, following action by the American Association of Schools of Social Work and the American Association of Social Workers, which limited recognition to those professional programs conducted on the graduate level.

Ernest F. Witte was appointed the first director of the school. He had an excellent academic background and brought a real understanding of Nebraska problems to the position. As state administrator for the Nebraska Emergency Relief Administration and as regional representative for the Social Security Board, Witte had gained real insight into the state's needs. Those who opposed him were politicians who objected to his methods. "Mr. Witte insisted on businesslike methods and the employment of trained workers as far as possible, whereas, the county commissioners seemed to be prejudiced against trained workers and, of course, desired to use their friends or political acquaintances."[37]

More serious opposition to the establishment of the Graduate School of Social Work came from those who favored strict economy. What the University needed, many thought, was pruning rather than growth. "Let's quit adding and start doing some substracting. Let's eliminate the school of social service before it is started. Let's cull regents—let's cull."[38] The school was retained, but the personal attacks against its director increased.

The School was established by the Board of Regents without them telling the legislature that they were going to establish the School. The legislature, therefore, feels that they were tricked by the Board of Regents, and in seeking an outlet for expression of this resentment they centered on Witte.[39]

In September 1939, Frank Z. Glick assumed the directorship of the Graduate School of Social Work. Dr. Witte had resigned to accept a position at the University of Washington.

The educational program of the University of Nebraska had survived the worst of the great depression without major dismemberment. This accomplishment was made possible by the optimistic and determined leadership of Chancellor Edgar A. Burnett and major economic sacrifices of the faculty. Considering the depth of the financial crisis in Nebraska, the work of the colleges

37. Letter from Fred W. Upson to C. S. Boucher, November 1, 1938, MSS, University of Nebraska Archives, Boucher Collection.

38. Kearney, Nebraska, *Hub*, October 16, 1937.

39. Letter from C. S. Boucher to Dean Edward H. Laner, University of Washington, May 12, 1939, MSS, University of Nebraska Archives, Boucher Collection.

and schools at the University of Nebraska showed great powers of survival. This can rightly be interpreted as a tribute to the character of those who comprised the University community.

The research work of the faculty in the College of Agriculture and Business Administration sought solutions to problems affecting the daily lives of many Nebraskans. Their success in research activities greatly benefited the state. The establishment of the Graduate School of Social Work and the efforts of the College of Engineering faculty to assist in the development of public projects also reflected the desire of the regents to provide those services needed during the depression. Through the combined efforts of the Extension Division and the Teachers College, local school systems were assisted in providing educational opportunities during a difficult period. In all its academic programs, the University of Nebraska sought to fulfill its promise of teaching, research, and service despite the depression.

CHAPTER 6

A New Deal in Student Life

STUDENT LIFE AT the University of Nebraska, like that on all American campuses, was deeply affected by the depression. During the first years of this difficult decade, few realized the long period of hardship ahead. Many believed at first, that the economic problems would be of short duration and that the relative prosperity of the late twenties would soon return. The student body retained much of its optimism until nearly mid-decade. During the last half of the period, students joined the majority of society in believing that hard times were here to stay.

Despite economic difficulties, many qualities of student life remained unchanged. Idealism, long a quality of young people, continued and was even sharpened by the times. Opposition to militarism reasserted itself. University students opposed paternalism. As always, however, students sought lasting friendships and good times, despite the hardships of the Great Depression.

Still this generation of Americans, both on and off college campuses, was profoundly affected by economic privation. The effect of this on student behavior at the University of Nebraska was noticed by the faculty. Students were different in the late thirties from those in the late twenties. Horace Clyde Filley, professor of rural economics, thought that students "are working harder and are somewhat more serious-minded than the students ten years ago."[1] James L. Sellers, professor of history, said, "They look as young as ever but seem more mature. The cockiness and self-assurance of ten years ago, in considerable measure, have disappeared. This is a more likeable and a more teachable student body than we had ten years ago."[2] Professor of English, Sherlock B. Gass, did not think students had changed too much. "To be sure, the illusion that hard cash is the chief value of education has been a little tarnished by hard experience, but it still shines bravely for lack of other gleans on our horizon."[3] Lowry C. Wimberly, professor of English and editor of the *Prairie Schooner,* incisively reflected on student change:

Ten years ago the round, beaming type of countenance predominated. It was the type of face that one associates with childishness, smugness, and blissful ignorance. But since 1929 faces have grown appreciably longer and sadder and more thoughtful. The eye has taken on a melancholy cast, cheeks are somewhat more sunken, and lines of care and deliberation mark the brow. This is all to the good. I have made no investigation of the physiognomy of genius and common sense, but my guess is that the great benefactors of the human race were long-faced. And I believe that we are now entering upon what may be called a long-faced and more thoughtful era.[4]

1. "The Thin Thirties," *Nebraska Alumnus,* February 1939, p. 8.
2. Ibid.
3. Ibid.
4. Ibid., p. 9.

As the economic plight of the nation worsened by 1932, public concern about student behavior lessened as the citizenry became absorbed in their own problems. Students had little time or inclination for many of the high jinx of the past. Judge Polk, the Lincoln municipal judge, found the University student body law-abiding. "If it were not that students are always in a hurry trying to keep up with this so-called fast age, we would hardly know they were around, at least from a judicial standpoint. . . ."[5]

Much discussion developed within the student body, during the early thirties, over the issue of student housing. While many students lived on fraternity or sorority row, the majority of the University's students were housed in private boarding and rooming houses. The quality of much of this housing was low. In 1930, the editor of the *Daily Nebraskan* described many student rooming houses. "All too frequently some penny snatching woman rents the space under her eaves, which can be called a room only by the greatest stretch of imagination, for $6 to $8 to some poor student working his way through school and too poor to pay $10 for a decent place to stay."[6] These rooms were described as being cold in the winter and nearly unbearable when the sun shone brightly in the spring. The accommodations were spartan.

Usually it is customary that hot water for bathing purposes be supplied on Wednesday and Saturday night. Frequently these nights pass with the landlady forgetting to turn on the heater. The occupants of such a woman's house can choose between climbing into a tub of icy water or going dirty.[7]

The condition of men's rooming houses was conceded to be generally worse than that of women's rooming houses. To remedy the situation in women's housing, the Board of Regents adopted a plan during the twenties which called for the construction of Carrie Bell Raymond Hall. After some delays, the residence hall was opened in the fall of 1932.

Despite the improvement in living conditions resulting from the construction of the new dormitory, some women students objected to the construction of University dormitories. Aartze Potts, '31, a graduate student, was opposed to dormitories. "They herd you around like a bunch of cattle . . . and treat you like a bunch of half wits."[8] Johanna J. Kollmorgen, '33, did not think students should be compelled to live in dormitories. "I wouldn't like to be hurdled into a big mob of girls and be obligated to do what they tell you to. Students wouldn't be satisfied with their conditions if they were compelled against their will, and, besides, many students could not afford it. . . ."[9]

Nonfraternity men were strongly opposed to living in University housing. John Sullivan, '32, was emphatic: "I'm decidedly against any plan which might limit the present liberties of barbs."[10] Many men students conceded, however, that dormitories were suitable for women students. Coeds were not considered able to take care of themselves and frequently needed protection.

At the time of the opening of Carrie Bell Raymond Hall, Chancellor Burnett outlined the regents' policy of paternalism. "Many girls come to the University of Nebraska direct from their own homes without much experience in making their way among strangers. A dormitory or residence hall provides a congenial group of young women living in a community organized and operated wholly

5. *Daily Nebraskan,* January 8, 1932.
6. *Daily Nebraskan,* February 25, 1930.
7. Ibid.
8. *Daily Nebraskan,* December 10, 1930.
9. Ibid.
10. Ibid., December 9, 1930.

in their interest."[11] The regents' policy was in apparent agreement with the wishes of most parents who sent their daughters to the University of Nebraska.

All women students were not required to live in a dormitory; there was not sufficient capacity. However, it was anticipated that in the future the University of Nebraska could provide housing accommodations for all freshmen women. With this commitment to provide housing for large numbers of students, the Board of Regents and the University administration embarked on a policy which would require much of their attention during the coming years.

Student politics during the thirties became much more than the traditional contest between the Blue Shirt and Yellow Jacket factions. As the decade began, David Fellman, '30, proposed a plan for proportional representation on the Student Council, giving a greater voice to non-Greeks. The plan was adopted

Carrie Bell Raymond Hall. Courtesy of the Lincoln *Journal-Star*.

and resulted in increased political activity by the Barbs. By the fall of 1931, the traditional two-party system was threatened when only the Blue Shirts filed candidates for some class offices. The Yellow Jacket and Barb groups declared the minor class offices superficial.

At the request of the senior men's honorary society, the Innocents, the Student Council, during the presidency of Edwin J. Faulkner, '32, was asked to appoint a committee to realign student political parties. The solution recommended by the committee called for increasing the political activity of the majority of the student body—the Barbs. At the spring election in 1932, the success of this effort was apparent. The Blue Shirt faction which had long enjoyed power was overthrown by an alliance of Yellow Jackets and Barbs. This fraternity-barbarian coalition was, however, of short duration.

By 1933, a "new deal" also came to campus politics at the University of Nebraska. Two new student political parties were formed. The Green Togas party was established by twenty Greek organizations, which had formerly been affiliated with either the Yellow Jacket or Blue Shirt factions. The Progressive

11. Edgar A. Burnett, "Why We Build Residence Halls," *Nebraska Alumnus*, September 1932, p. 7.

party was formed with membership from fifteen Greek organizations and with Barb support. In the first clash between these rival groups, the Progressive party was the victor. The Student Council was a major factor during this time in revitalizing campus political activity.

The controversy of the national political scene was reflected in campus life. In September 1932, a chapter of the Young Democratic Club of America was organized on the University of Nebraska campus. The next month, some thirty students formed a Socialist Club. Later a campus student Republican Club was established. A mock election was held on the campus in October 1932; Herbert Hoover won, nearly two to one.[12] The campus was a poor reflection of both state and national political sentiment. Franklin D. Roosevelt carried Nebraska with 359,082 votes to 201,177 for Herbert Hoover.

Opposition to compulsory ROTC training surfaced again during the early thirties. As earlier, the opposition to required military training came from students, concerned citizens, clergymen, and even from within the Board of Regents. Regent Fred A. Marsh wrote Governor-Elect Charles Bryan in 1930: "It is time, I think, that Nebraska should call the hand of this military clique which has been running this gigantic bluff on our people. I have reason to believe that our Board of Regents, as at present constituted, is strongly militaristic."[13] By early 1931, the student movement in opposition to compulsory military training was in full swing. The Student Council voted 17 to 3 to favor the optional substitution of physical education for military drill.

The controversy was heightened when Colonel William H. Oury, professor of military science and tactics, charged that those who opposed compulsory military drill "are all operating under the direct influence of the soviet government at Moscow."[14] The colonel was a graduate of the University of Nebraska, class of 1897, and had entered the army as a captain in the Nebraska National Guard in 1898. He had a successful military career and held the Distinguished Service Medal and other decorations.

Opposition to required military training was not confined to the campus. The Nebraska Farmer's Union took the position that "a farm boy in Nebraska has a right to an education . . . without being drafted into the army."[15] The Omaha *World-Herald* editorialized that "Colonel Oury, as a valiant soldier of the United States, should turn his attention from the study of military tactics and strategy long enough to familiarize himself with the ideals of his country and the rules of debate as they prevail among gentlemen."[16]

The conflicting opinions on the subject of required military drill were heard at a meeting of the Board of Regents in May 1931. Robert J. Kelly, '31, president of the Student Council, questioned the leadership training given in military classes. "The leadership developed by yelling commands at students and having them obeyed is not the type of leadership needed in a democracy. . . ."[17] Fred V. Grau, '31, "presented the argument that military drill impresses the inevitability of war as a means of settling disputes on the minds of those students forced to participate."[18] After hearing the arguments, the Board of Regents announced they would consider the issue.

By the next year, the question of military drill attracted little interest on the

12. *Daily Nebraskan*, October 27, 1932.

13. Letter from Fred A. Marsh to Charles W. Bryan, March 12, 1930, MSS, University of Nebraska Archives, Burnett Collection.

14. Omaha *World-Herald*, February 17, 1931, p. 14.

15. Ibid., February 4, 1931, p. 12.

16. Ibid., February 17, 1931, p. 14.

17. *Daily Nebraskan* May 10, 1931.

18. Ibid.

University of Nebraska campus. The Board of Regents continued their policy of requiring military drill for able-bodied students. The sociability of the military programs was responsible for much student acceptance and some students were planning military careers. The annual Military Ball and the election of an Honorary Colonel added social excitement to student life.

Student conduct and morality was an issue for some citizens during the early years of the depression. Dean R. Leland, Presbyterian student pastor, stated in Omaha that "Hollywood notions of love, marriage, romance, happiness and a good time pervade the student body at the University of Nebraska."[19] However, most people did not agree with the chaplain, except on the issue of smoking.

Few objections were raised about men students smoking, but smoking by women students was considered in a different light. University regulations prohibited smoking in sorority houses and dormitories. Many women students

Conscientious objectors excused from military training taking required physical exercise.

openly favored a policy change. Frances K. Holyoke, '31, thought, "The idea that coed smoking rooms would shock the people of the state and raise violent opposition is a big mistake. Nebraskans are not hicks. They are not long whiskered, countrified, narrow minded folk. They know what the score is."[20] Dean Amanda Heppner ruled, "The state is not ready for such a move. If, eventually, a majority should approve, or at least not condemn coed smoking, then it might be permitted. That is another question."[21]

In the 1931 session of the Nebraska legislature, Senators C. W. Johnson, a farmer-stockman from Potter, and J. A. Axtell, an insurance man from Fairbury, introduced bills to prohibit smoking in the state University and normal schools. Senator Henry Behrens, a farmer from Beemer, supported the bill. "I don't think it proper for the young to come to the university to learn to smoke or drink whisky. The people have a right to say what they do at the university."[22] Senator William H. Pitzler, an attorney from Nebraska City, stated in opposition:

The bill may increase what it seeks to prohibit . . . just as a keep off the grass sign seems to tempt one to trample upon it. Children are not taught by prohibitions and

19. Ibid., October 10, 1930.
20. Ibid., October 29, 1930.
21. Ibid.
22. Ibid., March 12, 1931.

don'ts. That instinct to do what they are forbidden stays with them a long time, sometimes until they get into the state senate.[23]

Nevertheless, the state Senate approved the bill by a 24 to 7 vote. The proposed legislation remained in a House committee and was indefinitely postponed on the last day of the legislative session.

In July 1933, the Board of Regents abandoned its long-standing ban against tobacco advertisements in the *Daily Nebraskan*. This resulted not from an approval of tobacco, but from a desperate need for revenue to keep the publication alive. With the revival of *Awgwan* in 1931, student publications attracted much interest.

In addition to the authorized student publications, a radical student paper, *With Fire and Sword*, appeared in 1930 and 1931. This clandestine sheet's purpose was "to cast light upon the many rank weeds that grow in the garden called the University of Nebraska."[24] It was published by a group calling themselves the "Gadflies," and appeared in mimeograph form. The publication was highly critical of the University administration and faculty. The administration was accused "of being a paternalistic, reactionary and buck-passing body, hidebound and viciously arbitrary in spirit, and grossly inefficient in operation."[25] One dean was described as "an out-and-out enemy of liberal education—a ranting vocationalist, utterly lacking in culture and totally ignorant of the fundamental instincts of a gentleman."[26] With the appearance of *With Fire and Sword*, in 1931, Chancellor Burnett issued the statement:

An anonymous publication is always a cowardly thing. The statements in this publication are libelous, both as to members of the university faculty and to members of the legislature. The university will undertake to discover the author or authors of this publication, and when discovered will turn them over to the proper authorities for prosecution.[27]

With the issuance of this statement, the publication of *With Fire and Sword* ended as mysteriously as it had begun.

The long-standing rivalry between the students in the Colleges of Law and Engineering was somewhat restrained by the depression. Disputes over possession of the Law College's "brown derby" did not produce the near riots of an earlier day. In March 1932, students from the Colleges of Law and Engineering held a meeting at the Cornhusker Hotel at which the feud was ended. The "peace conference" was arranged by a committee of six students, three from each college: Willard J. Dann, '32; Gerald F. Briggs, '36; and Lyle W. Mabbott, '32, from the College of Engineering; Glen McKinney, '32; Thomas Dowd, '33; and Robert W. Young, '34, from the College of Law.

Among the Greeks, the hard times were not at first evident. In 1931, Sigma Chi and Delta Upsilon both moved into new houses. However, in 1932, house decorations for Homecoming were discontinued in the interest of economy. The disapproval of Greek organizations, frequently seen in Nebraska newspapers, especially the Omaha *World-Herald*, during better times, was reversed during the hard times. The *World-Herald* said in 1933:

Sororities and fraternities, with their mysteriously secret names, grips, passwords and mottoes, seem an anomaly in a democratic commonwealth. . . .
    But when one realizes that the numbers of these somewhat sophomoric bodies are

23. Ibid.
24. Ibid., March 30, 1930.
25. *With Fire and Sword*, March 28, 1930.
26. Ibid., April 21, 1930.
27. *Daily Nebraskan,* March 19, 1931.

the sons and daughters of Nebraska farmers and bankers and merchants and lawyers, the fear of snobbery disappears. It is ridiculous to talk of class distinction in a state like Nebraska. And then it is true that for many years, and even now, the fraternities and the sororities have assumed the major burden of providing rooming and boarding houses for the students, under proper supervision—a duty that the state for years refused to acknowledge, and it does not, today satisfy. . . . They are useful and not dangerous.[28]

Apparently, the depression had a real leveling effect to some editorial writers.

Many future faculty members of the University of Nebraska attended the University during the early thirties. The class of 1930 was especially prolific in future faculty—James Blackman, Jr., Raymond C. Dein, Elvin F. Frolick, and Edward W. Janike were all classmates. Emanuel Wishnow was a member of the class of 1932.

During the middle years of the decade, financial crises appeared in many of the Greek houses on the University of Nebraska campus. Fraternities and sororities had long played a major role in student life at the University and had provided desperately needed student housing. By 1934, many fraternities were on the verge of insolvency. To meet this emergency, the executive committee of the Alumni Council, composed of Claude S. Wilson, '01; Clarence Hinds, '18; Dr. Carl A. Bumstead, x'12; and C. Vance Traphagen, x'17, recommended to the Board of Regents the establishment of an Inter-Fraternity Board of Control. Claude S. Wilson told the regents that they should establish financial supervision of the fraternities, "unless we clean them up, someone else will."[29] The regents agreed and approved the creation of the Board of Control, requiring all fraternities to be under its financial supervision. C. Vance Traphagen promised that "if the fraternities cannot help themselves, the board stands ready to step in and take a hand in the proceedings."[30] Despite this alumni help, some fraternities' financial plight was beyond redemption. Sigma Phi Epsilon and Delta Chi merged to reduce expenses; as did Phi Sigma Kappa and Sigma Phi Sigma. Delta Theta Phi, a law fraternity, Delta Sigma Phi, and Phi Kappa closed their houses.

However, by the spring of 1935, Dean T. J. Thompson could report, "Bills are being paid, and the fraternities are working toward a permanently healthy condition."[31] In addition to alumni interest, the faculty advisers and student members of the Inter-Fraternity Council devoted much effort to save the Greek system on the University of Nebraska campus. Dan Charles Easterday, '34; Otto Kotouc, Jr., '34; Byron W. Goolding, '34; Charles L. Bursik, '35; and Burr O. Ross, '36 were undergraduate members of the council. Professors Eck F. Schramm and Clarence J. Frankforter were the faculty advisers during the critical time.

Women students showed increasing interest in campus political reforms. Mortar Board adopted a resolution, in 1934, calling for a "clean-up" of women's campus politics. The resolution stipulated that:

1. Present alliances will be abolished and formation of new agreements will be forbidden.
2. Women officers will be elected on merit only and not as the result of alliances.
3. Organized groups will be forbidden to draw up slates and prohibited from 'forcing' girls to support certain candidates.[32]

28. Omaha *World-Herald*, September 17, 1933, p. 10-E.
29. Lincoln, *State Journal*, February 16, 1934, p. 3.
30. *Daily Nebraskan*, February 16, 1934, p. 3.
31. Lincoln, *State Journal*, March 24, 1934, p. CD-2.
32. Omaha *World-Herald*, October 24, 1934, p. 2.

This call for reform was signed by Alaire Barkes, Mary Edith Hendricks, Anna Pickett, Gladys Klopp, Lois Rathburn, Virginia Selleck, Faith Arnold, Elizabeth Bushee, Phyllis Jean Humphrey, Elizabeth Moomaw, Elizabeth Schearer, and Lorraine Hitchcock, who were almost all members of the class of 1936.

A revision of the point system for women's activities, originally adopted during the twenties, was accomplished by the Associated Women Students, during the presidency of Mary Edith Hendricks, '36. The scheme limited the number of activities in which a coed could participate. Elizabeth Bushee, '36, president of the Women's Athletic Association, praised the reform proposal. "Personally, I feel this change will mean a great deal to all university women, as it will give many more girls a chance to participate in activities. . . ."[33] This movement to increase student participation in campus activities and to reduce the impact of student politics was also apparent in men's activities. In 1934, the Innocents were reorganized to reduce the influence of campus politics in selecting the membership.

Campus elections, during these middle years of the decade, reflected the politics and problems of the depression. The victorious Green Togas campaigned in 1934 for the establishment of a student-operated secondhand book store. The economic issue assumed a major role in student consideration. The vote was reported in the *Daily Nebraskan* as one of the largest ever recorded. The losing Progressive party had emphasized "honesty in student government." The student voter of 1934 voted his pocketbook. By 1936, student political party realignment produced the Progressive and Greek Council parties as the contenders for support. Not only did these organizations seek the presidency of the junior and senior classes, but also control of the Student Council.

Campus opinion on national political issues was measured in a poll conducted by the *Daily Nebraskan* in early 1936. Students favored the presidency of Franklin D. Roosevelt over Herbert Hoover, three to one. The Republican candidate for President of the United States, Alfred M. Landon, was less popular with students than ex-President Hoover. Students at the University of Nebraska favored much of the New Deal legislation. The Agricultural Adjustment Administration, Tennessee Valley Authority, Civilian Conservation Corps, Federal Housing Administration, Home Owners Loan Corporation, Reconstruction Finance Corporation, Securities and Exchange Commission, Works Progress Administration, and Public Works Administration all received student endorsement. The National Recovery Act, Social Security Act, Wagner Labor Act, the soldier's bonus, and the Townsend Plan were not approved by a majority of students at the University of Nebraska.

As the European political situation worsened and war clouds began to form, student opposition to military training was slightly lessened. When the National Student League and the League for Industrial Democracy called for a national student strike on April 12, 1935, against military preparedness, the Lincoln campus was quiet. The students had seriously considered participation, but had decided against it.

Strikes are well known in the United States. The news columns of the nation's press have been crowded with stories of strikes in various industries. They have passed, but leaving behind them a distinctly bad taste in the country's mouth. A student protest strike can have nothing but a similar effect.

In addition, such a move would leave the college wide open to the charge of radicalism, which many are all too ready to hurl at the educational institutions. Someone has said that there is nothing worse than a young conservative, but he forgot to mention a young radical. Somewhere between the two there is a liberal middle course, that

33. *Daily Nebraskan,* February 21, 1936.

should prove attractive to an intelligent student body. Surely there can be better ways to combat fascism and war than absurd exhibitions of force.[34]

However, in late 1935, students at the University of Nebraska voted 1,392 to 796 their belief that a program of national military preparedness would result in "an end to peace."[35]

Despite the substantial student fear that military preparedness would lead to war, the Board of Regents maintained its policy requiring ROTC training. The formation of Phalanx, a national military honorary society on the campus in 1934, indicated that not all feared military preparedness. The goal of this organization was to encourage "training and the fostering of a spirit of military preparedness."[36] In 1936, programs in engineering and field artillery were added to the existing infantry courses in the ROTC curriculum at the University of Nebraska.

The law-engineer feud became a battle of words, rather than deeds, during the mid-thirties. The *Awgwan* of March 1936 featured articles entitled "What the Engineers Think of Law Students" and "The Lawyers Say 'Nertz' to the Engineers." A major campus event of the academic year was the production of the Kosmet Klub. The original student productions during these years were: 1934, "The Campus Cop," 1935, "Kiss Columbo," and 1936, "Southern Exposure." These shows were a distinctive part of student life at the University of Nebraska.

The most significant accomplishment affecting student life at the University of Nebraska in the depression decade was the construction of the Student Union building. During the first years of the decade, many student leaders urged the construction of a Student Union building. Financing the project seemed to be an insurmountable task. The Board of Regents were not, at first, very interested in the project. With President Roosevelt's New Deal, especially the Public Works Administration, the problem of finance was solved. After a period of doubt about becoming involved with a federal agency, the University of Nebraska Board of Regents, submitted an application to the PWA for assistance to build a Student Union. With the construction of this facility and the opportunities for social activities which it provided, student life at the University was greatly enriched.

Most students at the University of Nebraska worked during the depression, in order to be able to afford their education. Student employment made possible by grants to the University from the Federal Emergency Relief Administration helped both undergraduate and graduate students. The merchants and residents of Lincoln provided numerous job opportunities for deserving students. Dean T. J. Thompson reported that students spent on the average $440 for all expenditures during the 1933–34 school year. Some spent as little as $200 cash for a year's schooling.

Despite the hard times, most alumni recall the difficult middle years of the thirties with happy memories and a real feeling of accomplishment. The spirit of these years was summarized by Lee P. Young, Jr., president of the Class of 1934.

Perhaps the most difficult times of modern education have been weathered by the class of 1934. Our graduation will see the fulfillment of an education against great financial odds.

Commencement will not be the swan-song of the senior class; rather the prologue to greater accomplishments. The class' achievements in school during the past four

34. Ibid., March 5, 1935.
35. Ibid., December 18, 1935, January 22, 1936.
36. *Cornhusker*, 1935, p. 144.

years will be merely a background for future attainments. We hope that we have contributed materially to our alma mater; many changes have been instituted—worn out traditions abolished; worthy ones strengthened—sincere attempts have been made to clean up campus politics. We believe that this will prove to be an incentive to students in the future toward taking an increased interest in university affairs. May our class be remembered as having been a benefit to the University of Nebraska.

It is our sincere hope that the class of 1934 will retain its Esprit de Corps through the years—may the spirit and courage that has lasted through school continue and bring with it success![37]

During the last years of the decade, although the nation's economy was not much improved, student life lost much of the drabness of the difficult middle period. In the enthusiasm and buoyancy of youth, Nebraska students had survived the worst of the depression and would now make the best of hard times. The *Cornhusker,* of 1937, emphasized student activities and humor to an extent unknown during the middle thirties. Student publications again carried advertisements for local orchestras, recalling from better days that "after all. . . It's the Orchestra that Makes the Affair." Typical of the return of "good times" was the Corn Cob-Tassel Halloween party of 1937. For only thirty-five cents students were treated to a carnival, dance, and "Big Apple" dance contest. For most students the dollar date was a major event. Students were usually paid between fifteen and thirty cents per hour for part-time work. A dollar was a lot to spend.

The opening of the completed Student Union building in May 1938, was a major event of the last years of the thirties. The first Student Union Board was composed of faculty, alumni, and student members. The faculty members were Professors Earl W. Lantz, Eldred O. Morton, Mabel Lee, Martha Ann Park, Karl M. Arndt, and Eck Frank Schramm. Milton Anderson, '26, Ray Ramsey, '28, and Lucile Reilly, '34, were the alumni members. The student members were Genevieve Bennett, '38, Al Moseman, '38, Jane Wolcott, '38, Morris Lipp, '39, Bob Simmons, '39, Jean Morgan, '40, and Lucille Green, '39.

Corn-Cobs, the men's pep club, was reorganized in the spring of 1938 on a nonfraternity basis. This was an indication of the lessening of Greek influence on the campus. Fraternity-sorority power in student politics was further weakened by the dissolution of the Green Toga party in the fall of 1937, and its replacement by the Liberal party. This new party's platform proclaimed: "The Liberal political party was formed at the beginning of this school year because of the wide dissatisfaction with the manner in which student government has been managed during the past two years."[38] The rival Progressive party's platform stated that its purpose was to "work for the welfare of the entire university. The name progressive means just what it implies: Progress and not politics."[39] Student politics had changed greatly during the depression decade. Partly platforms were now much different from those of the Yellow Jacket and Blue Shirt parties of an earlier time. Barb support had become the swing vote in campus elections. The use of student identification cards was regarded as a significant electoral reform. "The dream of every Student Council became a reality when the 1938–39 members put on a general election entirely free from double voting and other unfair practices."[40]

In these closing years of the depression decade, students at the University of Nebraska adjusted to the economic hardships of the times and survived them.

37. Ibid., 1934, Preface.
38. *Daily Nebraskan,* May 11, 1937.
39. Ibid.
40. *Cornhusker,* 1939, p. 35.

They became increasingly fearful of the coming conflict in international politics and opposed the involvement of the United States in an overseas war.

We must reaffirm our faith in democracy, the last stronghold of tolerance and liberty and freedom to prove that the "Unknown Soldier" and the thousands he exemplifies did not fight and die in vain. . . . How shall we perpetuate our democratic institutions? War is the breeding ground for dictatorships. Peace is democracy's salvation.[41]

This hope became increasingly difficult to maintain with the beginning of the European war in 1939. When the territory of the United States was attacked, in the next decade, the students, faculty, and administration of the University of Nebraska rallied to the support of their nation.

VARSITY ATHLETICS

Red clay from Oklahoma swept over Nebraska in rolling blankets during the depression-racked 1930s as drought and hard times brought misery to the midlands. The University of Nebraska football team, as it has done so many times, provided the citizens of Nebraska an escape. Money and water were scarce, but the Cornhuskers gave the people a common bond and helped make the perilous decade tolerable.

Chief architect of Nebraska's dominance over the Big Six Conference was Dana X. Bible, the "Little Colonel," who arrived in 1929 and steered the Cornhuskers through the darkest part of the Great Depression. During the seven years Bible coached the Cornhuskers, Nebraska teams achieved victory totals unmatched before or again until the advent of the Bob Devaney era in the 1960s.

Although he was a master of his profession, Bible was more than a football coach. Soft-spoken, persuasive, inspiring, understanding, meticulous, and demanding of excellence are all words that describe Bible. He had a spell-binding charm and a deep insight into what makes a young man love football.

Bible attacked his new job at Nebraska with unequaled vigor. He toured dust-blown Nebraska, visiting towns large and small, in search of promising football players for his Cornhusker teams. The "Colonel" enjoyed and recognized the public relations value of stopping along the road to visit with a heat-seared farmer. The farmer probably was a Nebraska fan to begin with, but he certainly would be after a chat with D.X. Also, perhaps, he was the father, uncle, or cousin of a strapping young man who just might make a winning Cornhusker. So Bible recruited, organized, and inspired, and the Nebraska team won.

The D. X. Bible record is remarkable, considering the times and the obstacles associated with the era. In eight years, Bible's teams won the Big Six title six times, finished second once, and fourth once, his second year at Nebraska, 1930. He never had a losing season, nor a losing conference record. All together, Bible's Cornhuskers piled up a record in Big Six plays of 33 victories, only 3 losses, and 2 ties. Overall, his record was 50 wins, 15 defeats, and 7 ties.

With this foundation, Bible's successor, Major Lawrence M. (Biff) Jones, was able to continue the tradition of excellence. The Nebraska record for the 1930s was phenomenal: 62 victories, 21 defeats, and 8 ties, overall, with 39 victories, 7 defeats, and 4 ties in the Big Six. Only against Pittsburgh and Minnesota did Bible's magic fail. He was able to tie the mighty Panthers twice, but he could never achieve victory over them or the powerful Golden Gophers. Ironically, though, it was Bible who created the schedules which were to bring Nebraska fame.

41. *Daily Nebraskan*, November 11, 1938.

Fred Ware and Gregg McBride in their *Fifty Years of Football* salute Bible this way: "He gave Nebraska a stabilized schedule—the five conference contests, plus Pitt, Minnesota, Iowa and Indiana. He gave Nebraska prestige among the so-called socially prominent schools. . . . He brought Minnesota back—seemingly to stay."[42]

The "Little Colonel," Dana Xenophon Bible (center), with W. H. Browne (left) and Henry (Indian) Schulte (right). Courtesy of the Nebraska State Historical Society.

What kind of a coach was Bible and what problems did he face? Ware and McBride give this impression:

As [Ernie] Bearg scorned strategy, Bible scorned unadulterated, unrelieved power. Power was necessary, of a certainty, but power alone wouldn't get you far. In the beginning, Bible lacked the requisites for power production, and he lacked the essentials for speed and deception. Material slumped to the lowest point in years. Bearg's last season (1928) was also the last for many of his finest players. There were no replacements. As many boys as ever sought places on the varsity, but their talent was meager, and often the sort of competitive urge necessary for football was lacking.

It was indeed remarkable that the little bald master did as well as the record shows.[43]

Bible received little criticism for failing to beat Pitt and Minnesota, chiefly because of all his other victories. However, because he recommended Jones as

42. Frederick Ware with Gregg McBride, *Fifty Years of Football* (Omaha: World Publishing Co., 1940), p. 36.
43. Ibid.

his successor after Texas wooed him away, Bible was forgiven. Jones was to beat both Pitt and Minnesota and to bring the nation's football spotlight blazing on the Cornhuskers during the latter years of the decade.

Ware and McBride offer a solid testimonial to the affection Nebraskans had for D. X. Bible:

> No coach ever served a university more faithfully and generously and ably than Dana Bible served Nebraska. His was a rebuilding job whose cause is still mysterious. It was a difficult one. But steadily, every year, he made progress. He used to smack his lips and drawl: "We're comin' along. We're getting' a little bit stronger. I just think we'll be puttin' Minnesota and Pitt on the short end one of these days."
>
> This no Bible-coached team was ever to do. That glorious task was left for the man Dana Bible recommended as his successor. Dana Bible's last service to Nebraska was one of his greatest. . . [recommending Biff Jones].[44]

Nebraska's Cornhuskers did not open the decade in a fashion to signal the greatness that was to come. In fact, 1930 was the low point of Bible's tenure, a fourth-place finish in the Big Six with a 2–2–1 record and a season record of 4–3–2. Nebraska did battle Pitt to a scoreless tie, but it was a disappointing start. There were flashes of fine play from All-American Hugh Rhea and from All—Big Six players, End Steve Hokuf, Guard Elmer Greenberg, and Halfback Harold Frahm. However, the 1930 season was to be the only lackluster campaign of the Bible era.

Starting in 1931, a rampaging fullback named George Sauer moved cross-town from Lincoln High to the University of Nebraska, and Bible's team improved. Nebraska ripped through the Big Six undefeated, scoring 58 points to a mere 10 for the opposition. During Sauer's tenure, the Cornhuskers were 23–4–1 overall and 15–0–0 in Big Six play. By 1933, Sauer was known nationwide, earning All-American honors.

But George Sauer was not the only Cornhusker with first-rate credentials. Lawrence Ely was tabbed All-America at center in 1932. All-Conference teams were dominated by Nebraskans, George Koster, Everett Kreizinger, Corwin Hulbert, Chris Mathis, Lee Penney, Bruce Kilbourne, Gail O'Brien, Warren DeBus, Frank Meier, Bernie Masterson, Hubert Boswell.

With Sauer's graduation, Bible shifted the spotlight to halfback Lloyd Cardwell in 1934. Ware and McBride saluted Cardwell with the ultimate tribute: "the only Cornhusker of whom oldtimers have said, 'He's like Chamberlin.' "[45]

While the 1934 Cornhuskers dipped to second in the Big Six with a 4–1 record and were 6–3–0 overall, "Cardie" and a new fullback got the Bible-men back on top in 1935 with a 4–0–1 record in the league and a season mark of 6–2–1. Sam Francis was the fullback that had the fans comparing his rushes to those of Sauer, and in 1936, Francis combined an Olympic shot-putting trip to Germany with an All-American football campaign. Nebraska was 7–2–0 for the year and 5–0–0 in the Big Six. While the Huskers could not beat Minnesota or Pittsburgh because of depth problems, they were the toast of the prairies. This team was labeled by many as "one of the finest lineups ever to play for Nebraska"[46] and included Les McDonald, Elmer Dohrmann, Fred Shirey, Ted Doyle, Charley Brock, Johnny Howell, Ronnie Douglas, Cardwell, and Francis. Truly, it was a magnificent Cornhusker eleven.

Bible had achieved notable success at Nebraska and the Cornhuskers were nationally known and respected. So it was inevitable that another school would

44. Ibid., p. 38.
45. Ibid.
46. Ibid.

come recruiting. After the 1936 season the University of Texas beckoned, Bible accepted and advised Nebraska officials that the best possible successor would be Major Jones of Army and Oklahoma fame. Thus closed one dramatic chapter in Nebraska football history, while another and even more exciting chapter opened.

Biff Jones became athletic director and football coach in the winter of 1937 and brought with him a philosophy of "a little more ruggedness, a little more primitive power. . . . But the insistence upon acuteness and deception and speed remained."[47] Nebraska fans mourned the loss of Bible. However, on October 2, 1937, Major Jones sent the Bible holdovers into their opening game, against age-old nemesis, Minnesota. When the game was concluded, Jones had done what Bible could not do, deliver a 14–9 victory over Minnesota, the first win over the Gophers in twenty-four frustrating years. Jones's team went on to win the Big Six and post a 6–1–2 season, with help from conference players Dohrmann, Shirey, Brock, Howell, and Mehring.

Graduation losses riddled the Nebraska team in 1938. However, Jones sowed the seeds of greatness by playing a multitude of sophomores during the long 3–5–1 season. This netted a fourth place Big Six finish—lowest since 1930. Jones had recognized undeveloped talent, and the sophomores of 1938 were the Big Six runners-up in 1939. That was only the real beginning of the Biff Jones story as the 1930s closed. Nebraska in 1940 was to scale the national heights and become the first and only conference team ever to play in the Rose Bowl. Missouri, with Paul Christman at quarterback, won the Big Six in 1939, but runner-up Nebraska was the conference comer.

Nineteen hundred thirty-nine was a year to remember. After an opening 7–7 tie with Indiana, the Cornhuskers turned Bob Defruiter loose against Minnesota and took a 6–0 decision at Memorial Stadium. Twice in three years Biff whipped Bernie Bierman's giants, and the faithful danced in the streets. Everyone but Missouri fell in Big Six play, but the most savory treat of all was Nebraska 14, Pittsburgh 13. Biff and his Boys had whipped both the Untouchables, Minnesota and Pittsburgh, in a 7–1–1 season.

So the 1930s came to a dramatic and colorful close, with high hopes for the 1940s. World War II was to tear down years of progress for the Nebraska team, but not before the season still cherished by generations of Nebraskans, the Rose Bowl year.

Throughout the 1930s, athletes in all other sports gained fame and victories for the Cornhuskers. While the basketball teams, coached by Charles Black, 1929–32, and W. H. Browne for the remainder of the decade, could not win a Big Six title, they did provide action and a number of stars like Don Maclay, Steve Hokuf, George Wahlquist, and Bob Parsons. Overall, the Husker cagers had a record of 81–107 and a Big Six record of 47–51, finishing second three times.

Nebraska's track team, under the immortal Henry F. Schulte and later Ed Weir, dominated the Big Six, winning five outdoor titles and finishing second four times. Indoors, the Cornhuskers won seven titles and produced great stars such as Cobe Thomson, Don Gray, Harold Jacobson, Sam Francis, Lloyd Cardwell, Wilson Andrews, and Bob Simmons, one of Nebraska's finest middle-distance and hurdle stars.

Nebraska wrestlers failed to land a championship during the decade, but the Husker swimmers ruled the Big Six in the same fashion as their track and football brethren. Coaching of the wrestlers was handled by John Kellog and Jerry Adam. Nebraska swimming teams won four titles and finished second five times with help from athletes like Harry Kuklin, Bernie Masterson, Dick Hagelin,

47. Ibid.

C. Fletcher Spicer, and Ralph Ludwick. Hagelin became the Husker coach, succeeding Jack Minor and Rudy Vogeler.

Tennis also drew attention, coached by sportswriter Gregg McBride.

The 1930s had seen the University of Nebraska stabilize and develop the intercollegiate athletic program from the 1920s. Looming ahead, however, was the period of World War II, in which Nebraska's hard-won athletic fame was to become a war casualty. However, that was to be seen in the next decade.

University students during the thirties adjusted well to the realities of the depression. The hard times reduced the traditional Creek-Barb differences as all sought to prepare for an uncertain future. The influence of the times was also apparent in the construction of the Student Union, symbolizing the greater unity of the student body. The increased interest in the Student Council as a major factor in campus life also marked the growth of a more democratic campus atmosphere. By the end of the decade the international situation was becoming a major campus concern.

THE FORTIES

CHAPTER 7

Administration During the
Turbulent Forties

THE DECADE OF THE forties was a time of crises and unforseen problems for the nation, state, and the University of Nebraska. As the period opened, many Nebraskans feared that the economic hardship of the thirties would continue. However, during the spring and summer of 1941, the ruinous ten-year drought was broken, World War II was raging in Europe and Asia, and by the end of the year, the United States was at war with the Axis powers. The times were demanding of all Americans, and like most colleges and universities, the University of Nebraska was to meet the wartime challenge and contributed substantially to the national victory.

Rising agricultural production in Nebraska, made possible in part by the efforts of the College of Agriculture, raised farm income to new highs—over a billion dollars in 1947. The agricultural prosperity, from 1940 to 1950, was not the result of speculation which had characterized the apparent good times during and following World War I. Farm debt was substantially reduced during this decade. "Taken as a percentage of total farm value, mortgage debt decreased from 27.2 percent in 1940 to 5.9 percent in 1950."[1] During these same years, farm population declined while the state's urban population increased. This growing urban population became increasingly interested in higher education. The G.I. Bill after the war enabled more Nebraskans than ever before to consider attending the University.

The administrative problems confronting the chancellor and Board of Regents during this period of great public expectancy centered on the questions: Would the University of Nebraska be permitted to share in the improvement of the state's economy? How could the institution contribute to the improvement of Nebraska in a time of war and peace? Could the University maintain the quality of its educational program and perhaps even regain the more prestigious position it formerly held?

For more than half the decade, the chief administrative official of the University was Chancellor Chauncey Samuel Boucher. He not only believed that a plateau had been reached in the level of tax support which would be made available to public universities, but he also believed that the University had enrolled the maximum number of students who could profit from a traditional education beyond the high school. In 1939, Boucher had expressed his feelings at a meeting of the North Central Association of Colleges and Secondary Schools by saying that:

---

1. James C. Olson, *History of Nebraska* (Lincoln: University of Nebraska Press, 1966), p. 330.

. . . though it can not be shown that too much money has been spent on education, it can readily be demonstrated that too much has been spent unwisely. The educators are not alone to blame, though many of them may justly be charged with a share of the blame. The major responsibility lies with the public who insisted that the highest levels of educational advantages in all fields be made available to all comers, without regard to individual differences in aptitudes, capacities, and needs educationally. Too many college and university administrators, who should have known better, gave this public interest unwarranted encouragement merely to get more students in order to get more buildings, equipment, and staff members, without sufficient regard for the quality of educational results. Too many of these higher educational leaders have been guilty of intellectual dishonesty.[2]

Chancellor Boucher, at the University of Nebraska, had resisted this popular trend. However, the citizens of the state continued to seek the advantages of higher education in growing numbers, particularly after the war. Boucher's failure to resolve the problem of increasing demand for education and university services and inadequate state tax funds caused the faculty to lose confidence in him as their spokesman and academic leader.

In 1946, Reuben G. Gustavson, assumed the chancellorship. He, unlike his predecessor, quickly won the confidence and support of the faculty. During his administration, real progress was achieved at the University of Nebraska. The level of state support was substantially increased, the problem of the enrollment explosion was solved, an improved faculty morale was achieved, and major steps were taken to raise the academic stature of the University of Nebraska.

The enrollment figures for this decade dramatically portray one of the major changes which took place during this decade.

	Collegiate	Non-Collegiate and Special Programs	Total
1939–40	9,284	2,984	12,268
1940–41	8,986	3,143	12,129
1941–42	8,252	4,056	12,308
1942–43	7,426	4,901	12,327
1943–44	5,364	5,860	11,224
1944–45	5,865	8,544	14,409
1945–46	8,668	7,946	16,614
1946–47	12,998	8,665	21,663
1947–48	13,521	9,094	22,615
1948–49	13,649	8,946	22,595

There was no doubt, as the decade began, that the University of Nebraska was reaping the fruits of long economic starvation. Chancellor C. S. Boucher reported to the alumni that "the University of Nebraska ranked higher in 1909 than it does today."[3] Regent Robert W. Devoe, in 1941, frankly told the legislators, "We've scraped the bottom of the barrel. . . and now the legislature either must appropriate the necessary funds or the university will become a second rate school."[4]

The long period of financial starvation also produced a reaction within the individual colleges that could ultimately destroy the University. The chancellor identified this divisive force as "a tendency for the colleges of the University to

2. C. S. Boucher, "Some Current Educational Problems and Some Possible Adjustments . . . ," MSS of speech delivered at meeting of the North Central Association of Colleges and Secondary Schools, Chicago, Illinois, March 31, 1939, University of Nebraska Archives, Boucher Collection.

3. C. S. Boucher, "A Report of Stewardship," *Nebraska Alumnus,* February 1940, p. 5.

4. *Daily Nebraskan,* April 2, 1941.

become too self-sufficient: to think too much in terms of individual college interests and not enough in terms of University interests and welfare."[5] Much of this feeling among the college faculties was the result of Boucher's conviction that college enrollments should be adjusted to fit the level of legislative tax support. In April 1940, he stated, "Our appropriation at present would probably adequately run a school of 5,000 students. . . ."[6] The college faculties believed that their programs were in danger. Many even wondered what departments or colleges might be sacrificed in any adjustment of enrollment to appropriation.

The low investment by the state in the University began to draw unfavorable comment. It was reported that investment per student at the University of Nebraska in building and teaching equipment was a modest $1,282. It was $1,476 at the University of Missouri, $1,685 at the University of Kansas, and $2,853 at the University of Iowa. Average faculty salaries at all ranks were lower at the University of Nebraska than at the Universities of California, Illinois, Minnesota, Michigan, Wisconsin, Indiana, Iowa, Ohio State, Purdue, and Iowa State. Dean A. J. Brumbaugh from the University of Chicago, who was secretary of the North Central Association of Colleges and Secondary Schools, questioned the ability of the University of Nebraska to offer work leading to the doctor's degree. Chancellor Boucher reassured him:

The point you raise in your letter is a valid one, and all we can say is that we regret that our educational expenditure per student is lower than is characteristic of most institutions offering graduate programs leading to the doctor's degree. I can say this, however, that our Graduate Council guards jealously and rigorously our standards for the doctor's degree; only those departments are permitted to offer the degree that have thoroughly adequate staff and equipment; and our doctor's degrees are awarded sparingly and never on a wholesale basis.[7]

Charles Y. Thompson, president of the Board of Regents, reported to Governor Cochran his fear that,

If we should continue below the minimum [expenditure] for any length of time, we may expect to have our credits questioned: and such a development would immediately place unsurmountable difficulties in the paths of our present students and would drive out future students elsewhere.[8]

Even the Omaha *World-Herald,* long a supporter of small state budgets, recognized the financial crisis at the state University.

This academic deterioration is a direct result of stringent economics enforced upon the university, along with all other public functions by drouth and depression. The economies were necessary. It was proper that the university should share in the common tightening of the belt. But there is a limit to the length of time one can survive on starvation rations. A first class university cannot operate indefinitely on a third class budget. Some time the people must face the question: Shall we maintain an excellent university or a poor one?[9]

The need was clear; the decision rested with the governor and with the legislature.

The regents requested Governor Cochran to approve a University budget calling for an increase from $3,488,600 to $3,931,300 in state tax funds. The gover-

5. *Nebraska Alumnus,* February 1940, p. 5.
6. *Daily Nebraskan,* April 21, 1940.
7. Letter from C. S. Boucher to A. J. Brumbaugh, May 31, 1941, MSS, University of Nebraska Archives, Boucher Collection.
8. Letter from Charles Y. Thompson to Governor R. L. Cochran, November 27, 1940, MSS, University of Nebraska Archives, Boucher Collection.
9. Omaha *World-Herald,* December 8, 1940, p. 8-c.

nor cut the regents' budget request by 16.9 percent. The recommended amount was less than that which had been provided by the legislature for the 1939–41 biennium. Governor Cochran stated, "In preparing this budget I have found it necessary to depart from my knowledge of needs and have been guided rather by my knowledge of the reduced ability of the taxpayers to pay."[10] The incoming governor, Dwight Griswold, recommended a slightly higher University budget and the legislative appropriations committee raised the figure to the same amount as appropriated for the 1939–41 biennium. Ultimately, a University budget was adopted which provided for a slight increase. However, because of the designation of funds for the construction of a Foods and Nutrition building on the East Campus, the construction of a boy's dormitory at Curtis, the purchase of Bancroft School from the Lincoln Board of Education, and the establishment of the Chemurgy project, the actual operating funds available to the Board of Regents were reduced about $90,000 for the biennium.

Several months after the experience of this legislative session, Chancellor Boucher expressed interest in leaving the University of Nebraska. He wrote somewhat despairingly to a friend who was secretary to the University of Wyoming Board of Trustees:

My main interest is education, and I do not want to be in an institution where my thoughts and energies will have to be devoted to fighting political intrigue to enable the institution to function at all. Of course I do not mind temporary flurries that are likely to develop in the life of any University, but I do not have the stomach for a long battle conducted over a period of time by a demagogue or a group of political tricksters who do not hesitate to injure a University without cause or reason other than to serve selfish political interests. This seems to be what is threatened at Nebraska.[11]

The chancellor, however, was not offered the presidency of the University of Wyoming and remained at the University of Nebraska.

However, during these years, an important administrative change was made by the Board of Regents. George W. Rosenlof, who had been professor of secondary education since 1934, was appointed University registrar. He replaced Florence I. McGahey, the registrar since 1917. A policy decision affecting the faculty was the adoption of faculty tenure regulations by the Board of Regents on February 1, 1941.

Despite the bleakness of University finances, there were some accomplishments which offered hope for the future. In 1940, the Nebraska Memorial Association was dissolved when the last outstanding bonds were paid. Memorial Stadium was free of debt. The gifts of Don L. Love, former Lincoln mayor, also came at a crucial time. In 1938, Mr. Love provided for the construction of Julia L. Love Hall on the city campus. In 1940, he endowed the construction of Love Memorial Cooperative Hall on the East Campus. However, the greatest contribution of Don L. Love was made at the time of his death—funds for the construction of a long-needed library building. This private gift enabled the University to meet a need which had been acute for nearly a decade.

When the international situation worsened, the Board of Regents sought to make the position of the University of Nebraska clear in the event of American involvement in the European war. The regents wished to avoid the difficulties which had plagued the University of Nebraska at the time of World War I. On October 12, 1940, the Board of Regents stated their position.

10. *Daily Nebraskan,* January 9, 1941.
11. Letter from C. S. Boucher to Faye E. Smith, August 17, 1941, MSS, University of Nebraska Archives, Boucher Collection.

The Board wishes it to be known that if any student or employee of the University of Nebraska should be so misguided as to violate any Federal or State law regarding subversive activities he will thereby give cause for severance of his connection with the University. We prefer to make such a statement before, rather than after, any specific reason for it may have arisen.[12]

By the late spring of 1941, the question of giving "All Out Aid to Britain not necessarily short of war" was being discussed by faculty and students. A *Daily Nebraskan* survey indicated that 114 of 207 faculty members favored aid to Britain. In May, 186 faculty members expressed their position in a Memorial to the President of the United States.

We the undersigned citizens of the Republic and members of the various faculties of the University of Nebraska, do for ourselves in our individual capacities affirm with the utmost seriousness that the present months are critical in the world conflict between the Axis powers and those peoples who would remain free. We believe that the cost in blood and sacrifice of every kind entailed by securing an Axis defeat in Europe and Asia will be many times less than the cost we shall be compelled to pay after an Axis victory in the Old World, in order to defend ourselves in the New.[13]

This faculty statement drew immediate criticism from Nebraska State Senator Don Hanna, a rancher from Brownlee, who introduced a resolution in the legislature which stated in part:

The signatories on said petition represent merely the conclusion reached by a few academic minds and fine-spun theorists who are not the spokesmen or the leaders of the state of Nebraska and whose views on most public questions are visionary and impracticable, by reason of the rarefied atmosphere in which these signing professors live and have their being. . . .[14]

With the unanimous consent of the legislature, Senator Hanna was permitted to withdraw his resolution the day following its introduction.

As the year 1941 closed, the Japanese attacked Pearl Harbor, and the United States was at war with the Axis powers. At a University convocation, held days after President Roosevelt's war message to Congress, Chancellor Boucher accepted the new challenge given the University community.

We have no misgivings on the score of loyalty: we all stand ready and anxious to comply fully and at once with any suggestion or request that may come from any agency of the Federal Government. . . . Whenever the Government may want volunteers from college and university men and women for any special types of military, technical or industrial service, the word will be passed to you immediately and recruiting agents will be given all possible assistance in the enlistment of student or staff volunteers.[15]

THE UNIVERSITY AT WAR

In response to the requests of the federal government, the Board of Regents, University administration, and faculty acted promptly. As early as October 1939, the regents had approved a civilian pilot training course in the College of Engineering. Also prior to Pearl Harbor, a group of special engineering, science and management defense training courses were begun under the supervision of the Engineering College. In April 1943, the Board of Regents approved contracts with the federal government providing for the training of an air crew group for

12. *Minutes,* University of Nebraska Board of Regents, October 12, 1940.
13. *Daily Nebraskan,* May 18, 1941.
14. *Legislative Journal of the State of Nebraska, Fifty-Fifth Session,* p. 1460.
15. C. S. Boucher, "Speech to Students, Faculty, and Administrative Staff," December 17, 1941, MSS, University of Nebraska Archives, Boucher Collection.

the Army Air Corps, an expanded Reserve Officers Training Corps, and the Army Specialized Training Program. The Colleges of Medicine and Dentistry operated at capacity, with all prospective graduates being assigned to the army or navy by the Federal Procurement and Assignment Commission. A Special Training and Reassignment School (STARS) unit was established on the East Campus. These special programs enrolled 7,750 servicemen in 1943–44, and 822 in 1944–45.

In January 1942, the Board of Regents approved a policy of granting faculty leaves of absence for the "Duration of the War." Earlier these leaves had been granted for only one year. During the period of war mobilization, 151 members of the instructional and administrative staff were granted leaves to enter the armed forces or to serve in federal civilian administrative or war research agencies.

The admission of Japanese-Americans as students in the University of Nebraska was considered by the regents in the spring of 1942. The regents' policy required that all students of Japanese extraction be cleared by the Federal Bureau of Investigation before they could enter the University. It was further agreed that a quota of twenty-five native-born Japanese-American students be established. The number was later increased to fifty. Although the majority of Nebraskans accepted this policy, there was some opposition to it. Arthur E. Rogers protested the University policy in a letter to Governor Griswold.

Are we going to allow them to go to our University next year? . . . I am just guessing if the public knew and with the feeling towards the Japs, there would be very few of the present regents re-elected. I don't feel this should get into the political scrap, but with the terrible feeling against the Japs, there should be some way of eliminating them from our University.[16]

With the support of many community organizations, the Board of Regents continued to permit a limited number of Nisei to attend the University of Nebraska throughout the war. In regard to students who as conscientious objectors had refused participation in ROTC, the board approved their admittance as students in May 1942.

The decrease in University enrollment, during the war years, was the source of real budget problems for the University administration because 44 percent of the University budget was derived from the cash fund which included student tuition. A decrease in the amount collected in student fees could easily upset the established budget. On January 31, 1942, the Board of Regents took steps to reduce the University operating expenses. Among the economies was the reduction of night use of buildings to reduce heating and lighting costs, and a nearly 50 percent reduction in the number of campus telephones. By May, Chancellor Boucher was cautioning the deans against recommending faculty members for tenure if a "one year only" appointment could be used. On November 7, 1942, the Board of Regents appointed John K. Selleck as comptroller of the University of Nebraska. Selleck, a graduate of the University, had long been business manager of the Athletic Department, and his careful management of its funds had enabled the Nebraska Memorial Association to retire its bonds despite hard times and depression. This same careful financial administration, the regents believed, was needed by the University.

The budget request for 1943–45 was almost identical to that of the previous biennium. The legislative appropriation was identical to that of the previous legislature. The appropriation was the largest possible under the circumstances of the war. Senator Tony Asimus, a businessman from O'Neill, proposed to the

16. Letter from Arthur E. Rogers to Governor Dwight Griswold, June 4, 1943, MSS, University of Nebraska Archives, Boucher Collection.

legislative education committee that the cost of educating University students should be borne by the counties from which they came on a per capita cost basis, but the suggestion was not accepted by the committee.

Although the legislatively approved budget did not increase, the cost of all goods and services used by the University rose sharply. Faculty salaries were the only exception to this increase. The University was greatly aided by the federal contracts for the training of military and nonmilitary personnel in meeting its fixed costs. In January 1945, the Board of Regents reported to the legislature that they had earned a profit of $100,000 by educating army and navy students.

Mid-war, in 1943, Chancellor Boucher consulted his deans on the state of their colleges. The University administration sought to evaluate the condition of the University as a necessary preliminary for postwar planning. Engineering Dean Ferguson's reply exhibits the feeling of depression about the University's future common among the faculty.

Frankly, the principal reason why we haven't lost more good men is because we didn't have them,—couldn't attract them to us originally at what we could afford [to pay] them in salaries and in research opportunities. . . . we are so restricted in our opportunities, because of bare cupboards, and heavy duties that we have anesthetized much of the interest that our men have in research. I trust that it isn't devitalized and I believe that with encouragement at least a few of our present staff could become notable producers.[17]

The other deans were not as outspoken as was Dean Ferguson.

Shortly after consulting his deans, Chancellor Boucher sent a working paper to the deans, Faculty Advisory Committee, and the regents. The chancellor was responding to the writers and speakers who

are daily urging our people and our leaders to give thought to, and prepare for, the necessary readjustments to the peace that will follow the war. Similarly, those concerned with the future welfare of the University of Nebraska should now give thought to, and prepare for, any and all eventualities with which the University may be confronted after the clash of arms has ceased. One of these eventualities seems more likely to be University appropriations no larger, or possibly even smaller, in the period following the war than in the period before the war.[18]

The chancellor believed that the University of Nebraska had slowly declined in its relative position as an institution of higher education for thirty years. Its present status, Boucher believed, was not enviable. He then issued his widely quoted statement: "Some universities today are in what may be called the aeroplane class, others are in the Cadillac class, some in the Buick class, some in the Plymouth class, while the University of Nebraska, due to poverty, might justly be said to be in the Model T class."[19]

To raise the University of Nebraska to its earlier position of distinction, the chancellor believed that it would require at least an increase of 25 percent in the level of state tax support. This possibility he dismissed as "unlikely." Without this substantial increase in state support, other alternatives should be considered. Chancellor Boucher outlined a solution to the problem. To improve the quality of the faculty, he opposed all blanket salary increases for the faculty, even though the blanket cuts of the thirties had never been fully restored. Faculty salary raises could be made on a selective basis by a "reduction of the salaries

17. Letter from O. J. Ferguson to C. S. Boucher, February 11, 1943, MSS, University of Nebraska Archives, Boucher Collection.
18. C. S. Boucher, "Some Current Questions of University Policy," February 1943, MSS, University of Nebraska Archives, Boucher Collection.
19. Ibid.

of the necessary number of the least efficient staff members."[20] The number of appointments to full professorships, at attractive salaries, should be very restricted. This would result in frequent resignations by the faculty at the lower academic ranks. The chancellor defended this practice. "A department that is unbalanced in rank distributions by having a few at the top and many at the bottom ranks, but all of high quality, will be a better functioning department than one that has a more normal distribution through all ranks characterized throughout by mediocrity."[21]

Chancellor C. S. Boucher further recommended a policy which would deliberately seek "to strengthen some colleges, schools or departments at the expense of others by allocating funds generously to the budgets of some colleges, schools, or departments and niggardly to others."[22] The result of these suggested alternatives to the crisis at the University of Nebraska was the complete loss of Chancellor Boucher's potential for faculty leadership. To many it symbolized an unconditional surrender by the University administration to all those individuals and forces who had opposed the University. Obviously it was also threatening to those of mediocre research production.

THE END OF THE BOUCHER CHANCELLORSHIP

In January 1945, Chancellor Chauncey Samuel Boucher decided to ask the Board of Regents for his early retirement. He said he was in poor health, was losing his hearing, and wished "to avoid becoming an embarassment to the University and a burden to my family as a result of a serious breakdown physically and nervously that is foreshadowed."[23] The Board of Regents was presented with the chancellor's request at their meeting on March 3, 1945. It was agreed to keep the chancellor's request in strict confidence and to postpone any action on the request in the hope that his health would improve and the request could be withdrawn. The secret was well kept, and no action was taken on the request for nearly a year.

In February 1945, a faculty revolt against the chancellor's leadership began. A faculty assembly was suggested at a meeting of the University of Nebraska Chapter of the American Association of University Professors to discuss the University financial crisis. At this meeting a committee stated to the regents that their action was required by the failure of the University administration to present the faculty position to the governing board. Specifically the committee protested that:

It became clear at once that the faculty was greatly perturbed by the failure of the University to provide a blanket adjustment of salaries for all members of the staff. There was evident a deep and powerful conviction that this adjustment should have been made several years ago and certainly two years ago, when the Legislature was in session. The faculty clearly felt that it had been overlooked when there was no restoration of the cut in salaries as conditions improved. The faculty discussed this matter in the light of a promise to restore salaries which, as it understood, was made before Chancellor Boucher's incumbency. Furthermore, the faculty expressed the fear that representations to the Legislature now in session would again turn out to be inadequate, because many persons do not fully appreciate the faculty's deteriorating financial situation. The faculty instructed the Committee to seek an interview with

20. Ibid.
21. Ibid.
22. Ibid.
23. Letter from C. S. Boucher to Board of Regents, January 18, 1945, MSS, University of Nebraska Archives, Boucher Collection.

the Chancellor and the Board of Regents at an early date so that a rehearing before the Appropriations Committee would be possible.

Moreover, the faculty showed itself to be profoundly disturbed by the University's difficulty in retaining good men. The faculty feels that in the past we have lost more than our share of good men, they know that men we desperately need have recently gone from us or have promised to go, and they are convinced that we are sure to lose many more excellent men in the near future. These men often leave us not because they dislike Lincoln or the State or the University but because they see no future for themselves here. Their sense of discouragement can be laid to several causes. Some of these are the low level of faculty pay in general, the seeming lack of university funds to provide a sufficient increase in salary to retain good men, and the inadequate pension allowance on retirement. We know whereof we speak because men who have left us or are leaving have told us frankly why they were not reluctant to leave and have described the situation in the terms just mentioned. . . .

But while the immediate occasion of our appearance before you has to do with financial conditions, we believe that you should be aware of a further feeling within the faculty which we know is of great importance in the minds of our better men and our younger men when they consider offers from other institutions. This, in brief, is a general question respecting the future of the University itself. It may not be known to all of you that the University enjoys a higher reputation outside the State than it appears to enjoy within the State. We know that young men have been led to come to us partly because of the University's high reputation and have been greatly surprised to discover the present atmosphere of gloom. We have no solution for this situation, but we know that it exists. It is of the greatest concern to departmental and college administrators who see the necessity of recruiting staffs on a large scale in the immediate future.

The committee wishes to thank you for this opportunity of appearing before you. It desires, also, to re-emphasize its sincere belief that such a meeting as this should turn out to be to the advantage of our institution.
Signed by the Committee:

> J. L. Sellers, Chairman
>   Professor of History
> M. A. Basoco
>   Professor of Mathematics
> W. L. DeBaufre
>   Professor of Engineering Mechanics
> H. C. Filley
>   Professor of Rural Economics
> C. A. Forbes
>   Professor of the Classics
> R. W. Frantz
>   Professor of English
> C. M. Hicks
>   Associate Professor of Business Organization
> C. W. Scott
>   Professor of School Administration[24]

The faculty committee also met with Governor Dwight Griswold and members of the legislature. Senator Ladd J. Hubka, a lawyer from Beatrice, wrote: "Gentlemen, as far as I am personally concerned, the only thing that I do not understand is why the devil they didn't do it a long time ago."[25] This faculty action resulted in a substantial increase in the amount of state tax support for the University. The legislative appropriation included funds for blanket salary increases and the construction of Burnett Hall, the Military and Naval Science Building,

24. *Minutes,* University of Nebraska Board of Regents, March 3, 1945.
25. Letter from Ladd J. Hubka to C. S. Boucher and John K. Selleck, March 6, 1945, MSS, University of Nebraska Archives, Boucher Collection.

an addition to Avery Laboratory, and improved facilities at the North Platte Experiment Substation. At last there was some prospect that the University of Nebraska might be permitted by the legislature to share in the state's improving economic condition.

In January 1946, the University administration sought to improve faculty participation in University policy determination. This was done by reemphasizing the role of the Chancellor's Faculty Advisory Committee. This committee was established in 1940, but had never achieved its potential function as a bridge between the University administration, regents, and the faculty.

On February 28, 1946, Robert W. Devoe, president of the Board of Regents, announced the acceptance of Chancellor Boucher's resignation. It would take effect on September 1, 1946. A regent's committee, composed of Robert W. Devoe, Marion A. Shaw, and Frank M. Johnson, was formed to consider possible candidates for the chancellorship. An initial favorite of the Board of Regents for the appointment was Milton Eisenhower, then president of Kansas State College at Manhattan. Apparently he was not attracted to the Nebraska appointment.

The Board of Regents requested that a faculty committee be formed to advise them on the selection of a new chancellor. At a faculty Senate meeting, a list of five names was submitted by the executive nominating committee, and they were approved by the faculty. The committee consisted of H. C. Filley, professor and chairman of the Department of Rural Economics; Theos J. Thompson, dean of student affairs; Robert W. Goss, dean of the Graduate College; Harvey O. Werner, professor of horticulture; and James M. Reinhardt, professor of sociology.

In addition to this official faculty committee, another faculty group also petitioned the Board of Regents to be consulted in the selection of the chancellor. This group called itself the Executive Committee of the Faculties of the University. Its chairman was Clarence E. McNeill, professor of economics. The committee, popularly known as the "commando committee" also attempted unsuccessfully to win administrative control of the summer session from Dean Moritz. The committee was regarded with suspicion by a majority of the faculty and determined opposition by the University administration. Chancellor Boucher reported to the regents:

I am told that the commando leaders are saying all over the campus to other faculty people, 'We got the blanket increase in salary for you at the meeting of the last Legislature. If you will stick with us now, we can get anything we want in administration and salary increases.'[26]

The existence of this group indicated the degree of estrangement between the University administration and the faculty.

As the discussion of filling the chancellorship became more widespread, the Student Council wrote the Board of Regents expressing the qualifications they thought desirable for a university chancellor. The students sought a candidate who would be concerned with student welfare, unite the University as an intellectual community, and be a man who would meet socially with students.

After consultation with the faculty committee composed of Professors Reinhardt, Werner, and Filley and Deans Goss and Thompson, the Board of Regents announced May 8, 1946, the appointment of Reuben Gilbert Gustavson as the chancellor of the University of Nebraska. He was unanimously endorsed by the faculty committee and would assume the position on September 1, 1946. Chancellor Chauncey S. Boucher subsequently taught at Knox College from 1947 to 1952. He died in 1955.

26. Letter from C. S. Boucher to Members of the Board of Regents, April 12, 1946, MSS, University of Nebraska Archives, Boucher Collection.

CHANCELLOR REUBEN G. GUSTAVSON

The new chancellor was born in Denver, Colorado, on April 6, 1892. He received the A.B. and M.A. degrees from the University of Denver in 1916 and 1917. Gustavson was awarded the Ph.D. by the University of Chicago in 1925. He was an instructor in chemistry during 1917–18, assistant professor 1918–19, and associate professor of the Colorado Agricultural College, Fort Collins; assistant professor of chemistry 1920–21, associate professor 1921–27, and professor 1927–37 at the University of Denver; professor and chairman of the Department of Chemistry, 1937–43 at the University of Colorado; dean of the Graduate

Reuben G. Gustavson.

College 1942–43, and president of the University of Colorado 1943–45; executive vice president and dean of the faculties at the University of Chicago from 1945 until his acceptance of the chancellorship at the University of Nebraska.

Gustavson was an internationally recognized research scientist and had contributed to the war effort through research. He served as liaison officer between the University of Chicago atomic bomb project group and the United States Army and was director of one of the high altitude physiological research projects for the Office of Research and Development. Robert W. Devoe, president of the Board of Regents, believed that Gustavson "is exactly the type of man we feel is needed for the future development and progress of the University of Nebraska."[27]

It was soon apparent that the new chancellor conceived of the University of Nebraska in broad terms of learning and service to the state. "The university in

27. "Dr. R. G. Gustavson New Chancellor," *Nebraska Alumnus*, June 1946, p. 23.

the last analysis is not a group of buildings although buildings are important. It is not the laboratories, important as they are. . . . In a very real sense it is a comradship between the people of the state, the faculty and staff of the university, and the students."[28] This relationship "means that your university through scientific research and through public services will extend its campus to accept the problems . . . of Nebraska."[29]

Within a short time, Chancellor Gustavson outlined his views of the problems facing the nation and the University of Nebraska. Less than three weeks after settling in Lincoln, he told members of the legislature that the issue of war and peace was the central issue of the time. The development of the atomic bomb required an intelligent quest for world peace. The University of Nebraska should contribute to the solution of this basic world problem.

Specific University problems discussed by Chancellor Gustavson during his first months in office were those of a lack of research, problems concerning the Colleges of Medicine and Agriculture, and the place of athletics in a university. The chancellor urged that a much greater emphasis should be placed on research at the University of Nebraska. He hoped that the people of the state would recognize that quality research would bring real benefits to the people of the state and nation.

The College of Medicine, the chancellor emphasized, could perform a vital service for the state. He stressed the importance of medical research and the necessity of a research-oriented faculty in a quality medical school. This type of faculty would be a full-time rather than part-time faculty. To those who believed that the College of Medicine had been neglected by the University administration in recent years, he stated: "I can pledge to you as Chancellor of the University of Nebraska that I shall always have a very real and active and ever-present interest in the welfare of the medical school."[30]

The faculty and supporters of the College of Agriculture were reassured by the new chancellor that "the University of Nebraska recognizes as one of its fundamental responsibilities the development of a sound, agricultural program for the state, and, in turn, for the nation."[31] The College of Agriculture, many believed, had not received the level of support which it deserved during the Boucher administration. In the legislature, this attitude was responsible for some senators favoring a separate appropriation for the College of Agriculture. Chancellor Gustavson restored the necessary feeling of unity within the academic community.

One of the chancellor's most controversial policies was that concerning varsity athletics. Gustavson declared, in the spring of 1946, that the Nebraska football team should be kept on an amateur basis. He deplored the rising tide of professionalism in college athletics. The Nebraska enthusiasm for football caused the editor of the Omaha *World-Herald* to speculate:

In the old days, Nebraska had enough football material to get along pretty well with little or no professionalism. Time will tell whether these days are gone forever. If they are, and the University makes a not very exciting record just playing students, there may be a good deal of sniping, with Dr. Gustavson as the target. The so-called downtown [Lincoln] alumni may be expected to be especially vocal. It will be interesting to see what happens.

28. Lincoln, *State-Journal*, November 5, 1946, p. 1.
29. Ibid.
30. "Remarks of Dr. R. G. Gustavson at Public Affairs Luncheon in Omaha, September 13, 1946," MSS, University of Nebraska Archives, Gustavson Collection.
31. R. G. Gustavson, "Address to Nebraska Livestock Feeders Association, Fremont, September 19, 1946," MSS, University of Nebraska Archives, Gustavson Collection.

Alumni who agree with Dr. Gustavson that athletics ought to be amateur had better be ready to do battle for him.[32]

During the football seasons from 1946 to 1949, the University of Nebraska football team won eleven and lost twenty-six games. In 1946, the Board of Regents approved the establishment of the Cornhusker Achievement Fund to provide scholarships for athletes. Chancellor Gustavson reasoned that universities should be honest with themselves in the matter of football. "If we are going to have intercollegiate athletics as merely part of our physical education program, then there must be one set of rules. But if we are going to have athletics as sort of a pageantry with emphasis on a gate from $3 to $5 from the public, then that is another matter."[33]

In the reform of college football, Chancellor Gustavson played a losing game. During the last four football seasons of this decade, the University of Nebraska football team had three coaches. They were George "Potsy" Clark, B. E. "Bernie" Masterson, and J. William Glassford. The resignation of Bernie Masterson as head football coach in 1948, was a clear indication of the alumni influence in football. There was considerable speculation prior to the resignation that Coach Masterson's contract might be "bought up." Apparently it was.

With the construction of Memorial Stadium during the twenties, football at the University of Nebraska had become more than a regular University activity. To many citizens, the University football team had come to be a symbol for the entire state. A Nebraska alumnus, Merlin R. Garey, wrote to the chancellor:

It seems to me that Nebraska is in a peculiar position, and that the Nebraska football team means as much or perhaps even more to Nebraskans generally than to the student body. The reason for this is that the Nebraska football team has come to represent Nebraska. It is the one thing around which all Nebraskans can rally. It is the one thing which holds Nebraska spirit high.

During the bad years when Nebraska suffered from floods and drouth, heat and grasshoppers, no crops and low prices, farm foreclosures and migration of its people to other states, dust storms and everything tragic, there was one thing of which Nebraskans could always be proud, that was the winning Nebraska football team, known and respected everywhere.[34]

With a substantial segment of the state's population sharing this sentiment, Chancellor Gustavson had little real opportunity to reform college athletics at the University of Nebraska. The public wanted a winning team and a good show.

POSTWAR UNIVERSITY ADMINISTRATION

Chancellor Gustavson recognized that a major problem facing the University of Nebraska was that of rebuilding the faculty. It was obvious from the older age of those at the rank of professor, that the University had not been able to retain many of its bright young faculty members. It was also evident that another cause of this undesirable faculty condition was the low level of financial support given the University. To win popular support for the University of Nebraska, Chancellor Gustavson instituted a series of talks to interested groups throughout the state. During his first year as chancellor, he delivered over 400 talks to citizen groups. He easily established good rapport with his audience, and could communicate with any group in a highly effective way. This enabled Chancellor Gustavson to draw upon a vast amount of latent University support,

32. Omaha *World-Herald,* June 3, 1946, p. 10.
33. Omaha *World-Herald,* January 15, 1947, p. 9.
34. Letter from Merlin R. Garey to R. G. Gustavson, December 21, 1948, MSS, University of Nebraska Archives, Gustavson Collection.

which existed throughout the state. This asset had not been effectively employed by the University administration since the time of Chancellor Burnett.

The chancellor soon realized that his office would require considerable absence from Lincoln. In 1947, Carl W. Borgmann, formerly associated with Gustavson at the University of Colorado, was appointed by the regents as dean of the faculty. Gustavson and his principal dean launched a plan whereby they could better understand the University and its problems, as well as assist the faculty to evaluate itself. One day each week, for a period of three years, they met with a department to discuss its problems and goals. This was also a highly effective way of establishing good lines of informal communication between the faculty and University administration. The expansion of membership in the Faculty Senate to include assistant professors was also an important step to increase faculty participation in University affairs. The effect of these policies was to raise the morale of the faculty and to increase the administration's opportunity for improving the quality of the faculty.

The rapidly expanding enrollment at the University was a continual problem following the war. Although the Board of Regents had the authority to limit enrollment under a law passed in 1939, it was during this period that such action was first taken. Restrictions were placed by the Board of Regents on attendance in the College of Engineering, the music program in the School of Fine Arts, and the College of Pharmacy.

At the time the University of Nebraska faced its greatest enrollment pressure, the state colleges were operating below capacity. This prompted some to suggest that the state colleges and the University of Nebraska should be combined under a single administration. Both the Board of Regents and the State Normal Board opposed a merger. The decision to grant degrees in the liberal arts at the state colleges was made to increase their attractiveness to potential students. By 1949, the enrollment bulge was over at the University of Nebraska and student enrollment fell for the first time since the war.

During World War II and its aftermath, Americans became increasingly aware of minority groups and racial discrimination. At the University of Nebraska, the problem of racial discrimination centered in women's housing. In June 1944, the Board of Regents adopted a policy requiring that University women's dormitories be operated on a racially segregated basis. However, if at least sixteen women students would request nonsegregated housing, an "international" house could be operated by the University for their use. The Board of Regents justified this policy, "since it is advisable to avoid agitation of interracial questions whenever possible."[35] The regents hoped that their adopted policy "in regard to the housing of women students . . . may meet with the approval of a majority of the citizens of the State. . . ."[36] The International House opened in the fall of 1944 with four Nisei, three Negro, and one Puerto Rican student out of a total of twenty-four residents. By 1947, there were student complaints to the University administration about the regents' racial segregation policy. In a letter to the editor of the *Daily Nebraskan* two coeds complained: "Doesn't it stand to reason that the very fact that this restriction exists brands the university as an institution which professes democratic qualities but whose democracy is less democratic than it has the potentialities to be?"[37] A similar protest was made by the Student Council on the issue of racial discrimination in the Big Six Conference.

In the matter of human dignity and equal opportunity for all, regardless of

35. *Minutes,* University of Nebraska Board of Regents, June 17, 1944.
36. Ibid.
37. *Daily Nebraskan,* March 23, 1947.

race, those advocating change found strong support in Chancellor Gustavson. In a letter to Regent George Liggett and the other regents, he objected to the regents' policy on racially segregated housing.

I wish to state that I find my own position with the University growing more and more untenable because of the segregation practices which we have in the University. I so sincerely believe in equal rights for all our citizens that I find the administration of the segregation rule most obnoxious. The practice is completely contrary to basic religious convictions which I hold and which I am sure all of you subscribe to. . . .

If you as a Board feel that you can act in accordance with my recommendation, I assure you that no incident giving rise to just criticism of our University will occur.[38]

In October 1949, the Board of Regents revoked their policy requiring racial segregation.

THE LEGISLATURE

If the University of Nebraska was to meet successfully the crisis placed upon it by a large enrollment, years of inadequate state financial support, and a slowly declining position as an American university, its treatment by the legislature was of major importance.

In the first budget request of the Gustavson administration, the Board of Regents sought a two million dollar increase. In addition, a substantial request was made for building construction. The regents' request received strong public support. Chancellor Gustavson told the public that 6,000 students enrolled at the University were ex-servicemen. "The University recognizes its responsibility and is doing everything within its powers to meet this obligation. The University recognizes that these young people must receive their education now, not ten years from now."[39] The campus veterans' organization adopted a resolution making its position clear to the people of Nebraska.

We believe that the returned veteran, seeking an education is entitled to receive the same unhesitating support from those who he loyally defended. . . . it it imperative for the State Legislature to appropriate a sufficient sum of money now, to make it possible for the University to meet the demands of its enrollment. To delay this appropriation is to ask the veterans to accept either an inferior education or no education.[40]

The eventual University appropriation for the 1947–49 biennium from state taxation was $6,596,000. This was an increase of slightly more than $1,800,000 from the previous biennium.

In addition, the regents' request for building funds produced a major victory. The legislature adopted a bill introduced by Senator C. Petrus Peterson, a Lincoln lawyer, providing for a ten-year 1.1 mill state levy to provide funds for construction at state institutions. The University of Nebraska's share of these funds was to be 40 percent. The final legislative vote on the special tax levy was 37 for the bill, 2 opposed, and 4 not voting. This long-term commitment was vital to the University. Not since 1928, had the legislature been willing to assure the Board of Regents of long-term financial support for capital improvements. The razing of University Hall began a new era of construction at the University of Nebraska.

38. Letters from R. G. Gustavson to George Liggett, October 17, 1949, MSS, University of Nebraska Archives, Gustavson Collection.

39. R. G. Gustavson, "To Build One of the Best . . . ," *Nebraska Alumnus*, January 1947, p. 4.

40. Omaha *World-Herald*, November 28, 1946, p. 28.

By 1948, it was apparent to Chancellor Gustavson that the University's future was dependent on an antiquated state tax structure. He boldly wrote the regents:

I should very much like to have your personal reaction to my supporting a sales tax/ or an income tax in the various speeches that I am making throughout the state and, of course, I could write a series of articles for the newspapers. . . . It seems to me that our chances of getting our budget are very much dependent on finding a' broader tax base for the state income.[41]

Regent George Liggett wrote to Gustavson and presented the following warning and advice: "Should you come out on a tax matter you are bound to draw the fire of the opposition. My observations are that people generally hate to pay taxes, any taxes. It seems to me that it would be better for you to keep strictly to school matters."[42] The advice was followed.

The budget request of the regents for the biennium beginning July 1, 1949, was $10,000,000 from tax funds—a 20 percent increase. The request was cut by Governor Val Peterson to $7,800,000 and the legislative appropriations committee recommended a further reduction of $400,000. Chancellor Gustavson called upon those who supported the University cause to rally to its support. The public response was great. The Nebraska Council of Church Women replied to the call for support. "As Christian women, we are concerned with the importance of opportunities for our children and young people, and are disturbed by indifference shown toward values as revealed by the present Legislature's attitude toward appropriations for our state University."[43] Support for the University grew rapidly. Finally, a compromise agreement was reached by Governor Val Peterson, Senator John Callan, chairman of the Budget Committee, Chancellor Gustavson, and Regent Robert Devoe that an appropriation of $8,000,000 from state tax funds would be made for the University. The final legislative vote on the budget was 25 to 6.

During this legislative session, L.B. 514 was introduced by Senators Cliff N. Ogden, Omaha; William Hern, Valentine; and W. J. Williams, Ravenna, which would require a loyalty oath from the faculties at the state University and the normal schools. At a hearing on the proposed legislation, Chancellor R. G. Gustavson, Dean Frederick K. Beutel of the Law College, and Professor John P. Senning of the Department of Political Science all testified in opposition to the proposal. Dean Beutel expressed the opinion that the law would be unconstitutional. Furthermore, he stated, "I wouldn't sign it and wouldn't have to."[44] The dean's judgment on the constitutionality of the issue was later proven correct. In early May, the bill was withdrawn at the request of Senator Williams. However, during the first legislative session of the next decade such legislation was approved.

The issue of possible disloyalty was, however, raised. In late May 1949, the Board of Regents adopted a resolution endorsing an earlier policy statement of the Association of Governing Boards of State Universities on campus subversion. The statement opposed the use of textbooks which subscribed to subversive doctrines of government, condemned the use of the classroom for indoctrination, and disapproved of the employment of those who advocated the violent overthrow of the government. The regents' resolution urged faculty support. The University faculty responded to the request with the following statement:

41. Letter from R. G. Gustavson to Robert W. Devoe, December 23, 1948, MSS, University of Nebraska Archives, Gustavson Collection.
42. Letter from George Liggett to R. G. Gustavson, January 1, 1949, MSS, University of Nebraska Archives, Gustavson Collection.
43. Omaha *World-Herald,* May 4, 1949, p. 8.
44. Lincoln, *State Journal,* March 24, 1949, p. 1.

In view of the resolution adopted by the Board of Regents of the University of Nebraska on May 28, 1949, reiterating its long established principles in support of instructional practices in the University which are consistent with the best interests of our democratic form of government, the faculty of the University takes satisfaction in presenting the following statement:

1. We believe that there are no individuals now identified with either the instructional, research, or administrative staffs of the University whose loyalty to the government of the United States is questionable. Moreover, we believe that the faculty and administrative staff of the University are composed, without exception, of persons who are sincerely devoted to the democratic principles upon which our form of government institutions are founded.

2. We support the policy of the Board of Regents that any person who advocates the overthrow by violence of our present democratic form of government should not be permitted to remain as an employee of the University.

3. We believe, further, that those basic principles of academic freedom which permit and encourage the free, honest, and impartial discussion and analysis of the various forms of government are essential to the development of competent, inquiring minds without which democracy cannot prosper. We believe that such principles of academic freedom can be adhered to in teaching at the university level without involving practices inimical to our own democratic principles. We further believe that these principles of academic freedom are being adhered to in the University of Nebraska.[45]

On June 20, 1949, Chancellor Gustavson wrote the Federal Bureau of Investigation. "If you are now, or in the future should be, in possession of information as to the presence of communistic activities or Communists at the University I shall appreciate it if you would so advise this office."[46] In response to a similar inquiry from United States Senator Hugh Butler, J. Edgar Hoover replied:

I received your letter of September 2, 1949, inquiring if the FBI had occasion to make any study of the University of Nebraska with reference to its teaching force from a standpoint of possible un-American activities. Although I would very much like to be of service, no investigation of that type has been conducted by this Bureau.[47]

When the decade of the forties had closed, the University of Nebraska had met the challenge of war and had begun to resolve the problems of postwar readjustment. The level of financial support from the State of Nebraska had been increased which enabled the institution better to meet the rising public demand for instruction, research, and service. The decade began with the University "scraping the bottom of the barrel" and ended on a wave of optimism. Clearly, the University of Nebraska was a better educational institution at the end of the forties than at the beginning. The University was again on the move.

45. *Minutes,* University of Nebraska Board of Regents, May 28, 1949.

46. Letter from R. G. Gustavson to Federal Bureau of Investigation, June 20, 1949, MSS, University of Nebraska Archives, Gustavson Collection.

47. Letter from J. Edgar Hoover to Hugh Butler, September 9, 1949, MSS, University of Nebraska Archives, Gustavson Collection.

CHAPTER 8

Academic Progress in an
Era of Crisis

THE DECADE OF THE forties brought both challenge and progress to the instructional, research, and public service programs of the University of Nebraska. As the decade began, it appeared that some regarded the University as of limited usefulness to the state. With the nation's entrance into World War II, however, the University of Nebraska demonstrated its capacity for meeting the needs of society in a time of crisis. The small group who had sought to cast doubt on the utility of the University, in the interest of economy, lost most of its support during the forties.

Through the war years, special instructional programs were established to meet military and civilian requirements. The University staff provided increased public service and consultation to support the state and nation in wartime. These efforts ranged from helping farmers to meet the exceptional demands for their products to a lecture series instituted by members of the College of Arts and Sciences to discuss the nation's war goals.

After V-E and V-J days, the University of Nebraska faced an enrollment boom which was unparalleled in its history. This caused numerous problems for the faculty and administration of the various schools and colleges of the University. Among these problems were the revising of the curriculum to meet the needs of the students, recruiting a quality faculty, building high faculty morale, and the raising of the level of faculty scholarship.

In the first year of the decade, the Educational Committee of the State Planning Board made recommendations for the reform of state-supported educational institutions. The proposed reform was dictated by a sense of false economy and would have resulted in restriction of educational opportunity. The restriction would have affected most those rural youths who had been denied the opportunity of a quality high school education. State Engineer A. C. Tilley, chairman of the State Planning Board, believed that the academic failure rate at the state University proved that higher education was sought by too many students who were unsuited for it. "The student mortality is founded on the fact that heretofore the state has not provided the typical high school graduate the opporunity of getting an education along the lines which are best fitted for his needs."[1] For the majority of high school graduates, he believed a vocational or trade school education was desirable.

The Junior Division at the University of Nebraska was Chancellor Boucher's answer to the problem of poor academic preparation. The idea of the Junior Division contained the suggestion of reform, implying that a vocational program

1. *Daily Nebraskan,* April 30, 1940.

could be established for some students unprepared for college, and that this type of technical education could be offered at the state university. However, at the University of Nebraska, the possibilities inherent in the plan were not realized. Chancellor Boucher, in fact, regarded this division as a screening agency for University students. On the other hand, Dean Nels A. Bengtson sought to achieve the stated goals of the Junior Division. Terminal curricula were proposed in the areas of engineering, agriculture, architectural drafting, business, and home economics. However, these two-year programs did not attract the student registrations that were predicted.

By the fall of 1945, the Junior Division offered noncredit courses for those students who were academically deficient. Rather than serving as a means of eliminating students, the division now helped the poorly prepared student to make up his deficiencies. With the arrival of Chancellor Gustavson, the Junior Division was extensively reorganized. In October 1949, the Board of Regents discontinued the two-year degrees offered through the Junior Division. This marked the abandonment of this division as conceived by Chancellor C. S. Boucher. By the fifties, its title was changed to the University Junior Division and Counseling Service.

Low faculty morale was another major problem affecting the work of the colleges during the first half of the decade. In addition to the faculty salary situation, the seeming lack of a uniform criterion for faculty promotion was the source of much concern. During the years of the Boucher administration, many faculty members believed that academic promotions were not made objectively. As early as 1941, a faculty committee had recommended that academic titles should not be given in lieu of salary increases. The matter of academic rank was also a factor in the faculty protest to the Board of Regents in 1945.

The solution of this morale problem was a major goal of Chancellor Gustavson. He appointed a special faculty committee to study promotion policies at the University of Nebraska. In April 1948, the committee reported its findings on the promotion policies of the colleges. Very substantial differences were found in the criteria employed by the colleges in determining those qualified for academic promotion. The College of Agriculture listed its requirements in order of importance as, "personal fitness, effectiveness of service, whether teaching, research or extension, general training, publications if in research."[2] The College of Arts and Sciences defined its criteria as "research and publication, attendance upon meetings of learned societies, qualities of teaching."[3] The Teachers College enumerated its requirements as "teaching ability, professional training, personal qualities, scholarly production, high standing in professional organizations."[4] The faculty committee summarized its findings on the requirements for academic promotion:

All of the Colleges except Dentistry mention teaching and all except Engineering refer to research or publications. These two criteria appear to be regarded as of primary importance. It is significant that no recognition seems to be given for public services. It might be in order for the faculties to reconsider the relationship of their services to the welfare of the people.[5]

The faculty committee recognized that the work of the colleges differed, and that consequently differences should exist in their promotion policies. However, it was strongly recommended that each college clearly state its performance

2. MSS, "Report of Special Committee on Policies of Promotion in Rank," April 28, 1948, University of Nebraska Archives, Gustavson Collection.
3. Ibid.
4. Ibid.
5. Ibid.

criteria for faculty advancement and make such a policy statement available to all faculty members. This was an important report, and it received the support of Chancellor Gustavson, who, like others, believed that faculty morale is partially dependent upon a promotion policy which is clearly stated, objective, and lacking in political considerations.

Although the enrollment at the University showed a marked rise during the year 1945–46, it increased dramatically in the fall of 1946. The Board of Regents consequently adopted regulations to restrict University admissions in the fall of 1947. The policy required entering freshmen or sophomore students to apply before the first of August for the fall semester. Nebraska residents entering the freshman or sophomore classes were required to have graduated in the upper half of their high school class, while nonresidents were required to have graduated in the upper one-tenth of their high school graduating class. Freshman registration in the College of Engineering was limited to 500 students. The Department of Music of the School of Fine Arts limited its freshmen to 65. A year later, similar restrictions were established by the Board of Regents for the College of Pharmacy, where entering students were required to have graduated in the upper quarter of their high school class. It is not surprising that during these years the general level of student scholarship at the University of Nebraska was high.

The dedication of Love Memorial Library, in October 1947, was an important milestone in the academic history of the University. Although the building had been completed earlier, it was used as a military barracks during the war years. The availability of the building for library use was a long-awaited improvement in academic facilities. At the dedication ceremony, Chancellor Gustavson said, "To me the library is the very citadel of democracy"; and Library Director Frank A. Lundy added, "The gauge of a university of the first rank is its library."[6] The new library provided the University of Nebraska with one of the best library facilities in the Midwest. Unfortunately, by the late sixties, the library situation at the University was nearly as bad as it had been before the move into Love Memorial Library in 1947.

The endowment of the Montgomery Lectureship on Contemporary Civilization by Ora C. Montgomery was another significant contribution to the intellectual life of the University. The University Research Council approved the establishment of a lectureship which would bring to the campus eminent scholars who would discuss topics of current interest with the faculty, students, and the general public. The Board of Regents approved the establishment of the lectureship series in 1946.

During this decade, as always, the academic work of the University of Nebraska was accomplished by the separate schools and colleges. Here the problems of war and peace, enrollment pressure, curriculum change, and a host of other challenges were met and conquered by the faculty and administration.

THE MILITARY COLLEGE

Although it was not a regularly constituted college, the action of the Board of Regents in contracting with the federal government to train military units created a quasi military college at the University of Nebraska. In command of these instructional units was Colonel James P. Murphy, who was appointed professor of military science and tactics in June 1942.

By March 1943, the Air Crew Training Detachment was established at the University. The curriculum for this group included mathematics, physics, Eng-

6. *Daily Nebraskan,* October 7, 1947.

lish, history, geography, physical education, medical aid, civil air regulations, and flight training. The courses were taught by the regular University faculty, with the exception of the flight training, which was given by the Lincoln Flying School. The academic program for the Air Crew group was under the direction of Dean Charles H. Oldfather. Harold E. Wise, associate professor of secondary education, served as coordinator for the program. The athletic program was under the direction of Raymond G. Clapp, professor of physical education for men.

A Special Training and Reassignment School (STARS) was established in 1943. The University of Nebraska STARS unit was one of the largest in the nation. During the period of its existence from April 16, 1943, to March 20, 1944, over 8,000 servicemen were tested, classified, and assigned. Professors Jules P. Colbert and James S. Blackman, from the College of Engineering, were assigned full-time duties with the STARS unit.

The Army Specialized Training Program (ASTP) was installed during the summer of 1943. This military program closely resembled a civilian educational program. Curricula were established in engineering, pre-medicine, pre-dentistry, and foreign area and language study. The civilian director of the ASTP program was Dean Olin J. Ferguson. C. Bertrand Schultz served as its educational supervisor. Dean Oldfather managed the area studies and Joseph E. A. Alexis the language work.

The Air Crew and ASTP students were housed on the city campus in Love Library and in the Athletic Field House. The STARS unit was housed in the Foods and Nutrition Building on the East Campus. The cafeteria in the Activities Building on the agricultural campus and the Student Union on the city campus were used as mess halls.

At the College of Medicine, in Omaha, army and navy students comprised nearly the entire student body. The situation was the same at the Dental College in Lincoln. These students were also under Colonel Murphy's command.

The unofficial military college was of short duration, but it made a substantial contribution to the war effort. The instructional work in those programs was carried out by the regular University of Nebraska faculty, with only a few exceptions. The success of these programs resulted from the fine spirit of cooperation between the faculty, administration, and the military. Colonel Murphy remarked in 1945 that "the boys liked the atmosphere here. . . . Many of them were easterners and believed we were backwoodsmen when they first arrived. They later changed their minds. They like the way the faculty conducted their classes and we look with pride on the accomplishments at the University of Nebraska."[7] It was a job well done!

THE COLLEGE OF ARTS AND SCIENCES

Throughout the forties, the College of Arts and Sciences continued under the direction of Dean Charles H. Oldfather. The enrollment of those who majored in some departments of the college declined during the war years, but it still maintained the largest student body of any college in the University.

Some significant administrative changes were made in the College of Arts and Sciences in the early forties. Before American entry into the war, the Department of Germanic Languages and Literature was transformed into the Department of Modern Languages. In June 1940, the Board of Regents separated the Department of Psychology from the Department of Philosophy. Professor Arthur F. Jeness was appointed the first chairman of the Department of Psychol-

7. Ibid., April 22, 1945.

ogy. Ray William Frantz succeeded Thomas M. Raysor as chairman of the Department of English in 1940. Also, at this time, C. Bertrand Schultz was appointed director of the State Museum. Schultz, who succeeded Erwin H. Barbour, received his undergraduate degree from the University of Nebraska in 1931, his master's degree two years later, and the Ph.D. degree in 1941. He had been in charge of field parties since 1928 and was named assistant director of the museum in 1938. In the summer of 1947, museum field parties made a significant discovery of man's early existence in the western hemisphere. This discovery, made near Cambridge, Nebraska, was a major scientific discovery of the decade.

After American entry into World War II, the College of Arts and Sciences faculty contributed not only to the training of servicemen, but also made additional contributions to the war effort in general. Joyce O. Hertzler, chairman of the Sociology Department, organized a war lecture committee to make available to the people of Nebraska a series of lectures on subjects related to the war and its impact upon society. A list of twenty-seven lectures was prepared, including such topics as: "America's Objectives," "American War Economics," "The Role of Physics in the War," and "Agriculture after the Second World War." The lecturers for the series were drawn from the faculties of all the colleges; some twenty-four professors participated. Many faculty members used their academic specialization to support the war effort. Professor E. F. Schramm instituted a special course in map-reading for military students. George L. Peltier, chairman of the Department of Bacteriology, produced penicillin for experimental use in the Lincoln hospitals.

In the years following the war, as in the other colleges, the College of Arts and Sciences was challenged by an enrollment boom. Between the academic years 1944 and 1945 and 1948 and 1949, the number of students enrolled in the college more than doubled. This required a substantial increase in the size of the teaching staff, as well as heavy teaching loads. At the beginning of the second semester in 1947, Professor Kenneth Forward, who directed the freshman English program, reported that over 3,000 students were enrolled in beginning English classes. He added that, "Instructors have been drawn from all parts of the country to meet the emergency, and some are Nebraska graduates. A few instructors are veterans' wives, whose husbands are undergraduates."[8]

The move of the College of Arts and Sciences into the newly completed Burnett Hall did much to relieve the crowded teaching conditions. Despite the hardships associated with the heavy enrollment, the scholarship of the students was high and the instructional program was effectively organized and conducted.

Faculty scholarship too was again winning national recognition. James M. Reinhardt, professor of sociology, received national recognition for his work on the sociological aspects of crime and law enforcement. In the Department of Chemistry, important research findings were published by Norman H. Cromwell, Cliff S. Hamilton, and Walter E. Militzer. Benjamin Boyce, Lowry C. Wimberly, and Walter F. Wright from the Department of English received recognition for their scholarship. In the Department of Philosophy, Oets K. Bouwsma, Charles H. Patterson, and William H. Werkmeister were active scholars. Publications in the field of political science were made by Norman L. Hill and Lane W. Lancaster. Other members of the faculty from the College of Arts and Sciences who published widely in scholarly journals during the forties for their research were Alvin L. Lugn, professor of geology; Earl E. Lackey, associate professor of geography; Carl E. Georgi, professor of bacteriology; Theodore Jorgensen, Jr., associate professor of physics; Boyd G. Carter, associate professor of romance

8. Ibid., February 18, 1947.

languages; and Donald W. Dysinger and Theodore T. Smith, professors of physics.

An important administrative change also was made during the forties in the two schools which were attached to the College of Arts and Sciences. In January 1940, the University of Nebraska Board of Regents established the School of Journalism and the School of Fine Arts as collegiate schools. Although they remained a part of the Arts College, they became largely autonomous. At their meeting on January 6, 1940, the regents adopted a policy providing that:

The regulation of all internal affairs of such a school, including courses of study and credits, shall be in the faculty thereof, subject, however to all rules regarding prescribed work for degrees which the faculty or faculties of the college or colleges within such schools exist have adopted. The administrative head of a collegiate school shall be called a director. He shall be responsible, as are deans, directly to the Board through the Chancellor's Office except in matters of budget and apportionments and in reference to such matters shall confer with the dean of his respective college.[9]

At the School of Journalism, Harold Hamil replaced Gayle C. Walker as director in 1941. The popular Professor Walker resigned the directorship, which he had held since 1936, because of poor health. He continued on the faculty until his death. During the war years, the enrollment of the School of Journalism was very small, usually fewer than a hundred students. In 1944, Harold Hamil resigned the directorship to accept a newspaper position, and Forrest C. Blood was appointed acting director. After the war, in 1946, William F. Swindler was appointed director of the School of Journalism. He had taught journalism at the University of Missouri and had been director of the School of Journalism at the University of Idaho. Under his direction, and with the support of the Nebraska Press · Association, the University of Nebraska School of Journalism made notable progress in its facilities, curriculum, and faculty.

Throughout this decade, the director of the School of Fine Arts was Arthur E. Westbrook. He stated the goal of his Department of Music as "Music for the Masses." After the war, the school's enrollment increased dramatically, especially in music. This enrollment pressure ultimately required the Board of Regents to set a quota on freshman enrollment in the Music Department.

The Board of Regents reorganized the Art Department after the war at the suggestion of Director Westbrook. Duard W. Laging was named chairman of the department, succeeding Professor Dwight Kirsch. Faculty members of the School of Fine Arts who received recognition for their creative work during this decade were Kathrine B. Faulkner, Elizabeth M. Tierney, and Emanuel Wishnow.

THE COLLEGE OF AGRICULTURE

Except for the war years, the College of Agriculture made steady growth in the forties in its enrollment. Moreover, the college faculty and staff had helped increase agricultural production in the state and nation.

Leadership of the college during most of this decade was ably provided by Dean William W. Burr. He first joined the University staff in 1906, at the North Platte Experimental Substation. Here he became a national authority on dry-land farming. In 1913, he was granted leave by the regents to direct a dry-land experiment station for the United States Department of Agriculture. Burr was appointed chairman of the Agronomy Department in 1916 and assistant director of the Agricultural Experiment Station in 1919. He succeeded Chancellor Edgar A. Burnett as dean of the College of Agriculture and director of the Ex-

9. *Minutes,* University of Nebraska Board of Regents, January 6, 1940.

periment Station. Although he was eligible for retirement during the early years of the Gustavson administration, the chancellor requested his continuance as dean beyond the normal retirement age. Chancellor Gustavson said of his dean of agriculture, "Dean Burr has been one of my closest friends and most efficient advisors. . . . His loyalty to the University was shown in his willingness to serve an additional year with me while I became acquainted with the problems of the Agriculture College."[10] Dean Burr, famous for his modesty in accepting personal praise, remarked at the time of his retirement, "I have enjoyed working with students here at Ag College because of their spirit of cooperation. No one man can insure the success of a campus program. It is up to the individual student to reflect the entire policy of the college."[11]

Left to right: College of Agriculture Dean Burr, Secretary of Agriculture Anderson, and Professor Marvel L. Baker.

In May 1948, after consulting with a faculty committee, the Board of Regents appointed William Vincent Lambert as dean of the College of Agriculture. He was a native Nebraskan and a 1921 graduate of the College of Agriculture. His master's degree was awarded by Kansas State College, and the Ph.D. degree by the University of California. Lambert had been associate director of the Purdue Agriculture Experiment Station and was administrator for agricultural research at the United States Department of Agriculture immediately prior to accepting the appointment at the University of Nebraska. Chancellor Gustavson said of his new dean, "Dr. Lambert is one of the Nation's top-flight research men. . . . He knows the Midwest and will bring a wealth of experience to the State and University."[12]

10. Omaha *World-Herald,* November 1, 1947, p. 2.
11. *Daily Nebraskan,* November 2, 1947.
12. Omaha *World-Herald,* June 17, 1947, p. 1.

Other major administrative changes in the College of Agriculture during the forties were the appointments of Professor Marvel L. Baker as associate director of the Agricultural Experiment Station and acting dean of the college in the absence of Dean Burr and Harry G. Gould as acting director of the Agricultural Extension Service.

Although the faculty of the College of Agriculture and the staff of the Agricultural Experiment Station had long been engaged in seeking solutions to the problems of agriculture, the amount of research during the forties greatly exceeded that of the earlier years. This was possible because of better financial support from the state and more cooperation between the Agricultural Experiment Station and the United States Department of Agriculture. This improvement was reflected in the work in all the departments of the College of Agriculture.

In the Department of Agricultural Chemistry, publications by Rudolph M. Sandstedt, Eric Kneen, and others reflected their continuing interest in the factors affecting the milling and baking qualities of wheat as well as the nutritional value of poultry feeds. The program of tractor-testing, conducted by the Department of Agricultural Engineering, had substantial impact on the rapid technological evolution of farm tractors and other agricultural equipment. Other areas of interest also investigated by the department were the use of electrical equipment on the farm, corn and alfalfa drying equipment, and mechanical corn pickers and other harvesting machines.

The Department of Agronomy staff, one of the strongest in the college, was concerned with a broad field of research activity dealing with plants and soils. The members of the department conducted their research at the various outlying experimental substations and initiated the "Outstate Testing Project" during his decade. This project enabled studies of crop production to be made throughout Nebraska. In cooperation with the Department of Animal Husbandry, the effect of time of cutting on the feeding value of prairie hay was studied. The agronomy staff investigated other crops considered to have possible value under Nebraska conditions, including flax, sesame, castor beans, annual rapes, and sunflowers. The principal researchers in the department were Theodore A. Kiesselbach, Frank C. Duley, Thomas M. McCalla, and Elvin F. Frolik.

The Department of Animal Husbandry was under the chairmanship of William J. Loeffel. In the summer of 1941, Marvel L. Baker transferred from the North Platte Experiment Substation to Lincoln in order to strengthen the statewide coordination in animal husbandry activities. Dean Burr supported this by calling the first statewide conference for experiment station workers. This meeting, which has been held annually, was an important step in the development of close cooperation and coordination of the efforts of the College of Agriculture and the Experiment Station to improve agriculture in Nebraska.

The research conducted by the staff in the Department of Animal Husbandry was concerned with beef cattle, dual-purpose cattle, swine, and sheep. After the resignation of R. R. Thalman in 1941, Marvel L. Baker was given the responsibility for continuing beef cattle research. The staff also evaluated feeding grain sorghums and other proteins. Baker and Edgar M. Brouse, superintendent of the Valentine station, continued with their cooperative research on cattle production in the Nebraska Sandhills. This research had begun in the 1920s and during this decade yielded important results covering a wide range of feeding supplements with prairie hay. The work was interrupted by an outbreak of the dreaded X-disease. The cause of the disease was discovered by Baker, Brouse, and Carl Olson, Jr., chairman of the Department of Animal Pathology and Hygiene. Additional research was concerned with problems of Vitamin A deficiency in feed-lot cattle and with feeds for pigs and lambs.

There was also considerable activity in the other departments of the college. The Department of Animal Pathology and Hygiene continued to be under the chairmanship of Leunis Van Es until his retirement in 1945. He was succeeded by Carl Olson, Jr. In 1949 the chemurgy research program, which had begun as a separate entity, was assigned to the Experiment Station. Some of the crops studied for possible chemurgic uses were safflower, castor beans, sesame, flax, mustard, and sunflowers. The Dairy Department staff undertook extensive research in the artificial breeding and feeding of dairy cattle. The leading investigators in the department were Herbert P. Davis and Irwin L. Hathaway. The Department of Entomology had three departmental chairmen during this decade, Myron H. Swenk, Herman D. Tate, and Ephraim Hixon. Some twenty-seven publications were issued concerning the control of insect pests.

The Curtis Boys' Ranch of the College of Agriculture.

Margaret S. Fedde was chairman of the Department of Home Economics. Ruth M. Leverton continued to carry out her valuable research in human nutrition, which was closely related to the war effort. In the Department of Horticulture, John E. Weaver worked on his studies of potatoes and native grasses. At the end of the decade, he was selected as an honorary president of the International Botanical Congress held in Stockholm, Sweden, in 1950.

In 1949, the Department of Rural Economics became the Department of Agricultural Economics. The title change reflected the broadened scope of the departmental interest. Publications by members of the department considered such economic issues as farm tenancy, farm size, farm income, and marketing practices.

During this decade the work carried out at the experimental substations was increasingly important to Nebraska agriculture. The University established Box Butte Experimental Substation. The land and buildings were owned by Box Butte County and were assigned to the University of Nebraska for research purposes by the county commissioners.

At the North Platte Substation, the staff examined the place of pastures in dairy production and rotation of grazing pastures. The work done with cattle, swine, sheep, and poultry was directed by the staff of the Department of Animal Husbandry. Also at the North Platte Substation, as well as at those near

Valentine and Scottsbluff, considerable effort was devoted to the cultivation of trees and shrubs.

The staff at the Scottsbluff Substation conducted an impressive research program related to the problems of agriculture in the North Platte Valley. Its livestock work was with the use of crops produced under the intensive agriculture of the valley. Beet by-products were studied. At the Valentine Substation, Superintendent Brouse worked with cattle and studied the factors affecting production in the sub-irrigated meadows of the region.

This decade witnessed a great advance in the quantity and quality of the work done by the staff of the Experiment Station. This was accompanied by a heightened spirit of cooperation among the members of the staff throughout Nebraska. Furthermore the Nebraska Experiment Station staff expanded cooperative research with experiment stations in other states and various research agencies of the United States Department of Agriculture. This benefited not only Nebraska but also the nation.

THE TEACHERS COLLEGE AND UNIVERSITY EXTENSION

Except for a slump during the war years, the undergraduate enrollment in the Teachers College was nearly stable throughout the forties. However, the relative position of the college's enrollment declined. In 1939–40, 23 percent of the University students were enrolled in the Teachers College; in 1949–50, it was 21 percent.

The problem of inadequate facilities continued to hamper the work of the Teachers College. The Committee of the Superintendents and Principals Association of Nebraska, established in 1935, again urged the University administration to assign a higher priority to teacher education. This committee under the chairmanship of E. L. Novotny, school superintendent at Beatrice, asked the regents to make enlarged facilities available to the Teachers College in 1941. However, the college faculty continued to be housed in the Teachers College building, and the Teachers College High School with an enrollment of over 300 students shared the building with them.

Despite the crowded conditions, the mission of the college expanded. In 1942, the Board of Regents authorized the establishment of the Department of Music Education in the Teachers College under the chairmanship of Professor Westbrook. The regents endorsed the recommendation of the Graduate College faculty that the Master of Education degree be awarded in May 1945. The Teachers College faculty hoped that this degree would "make professional training more effective, allow for specialization in a particular area of professional education and offer training to meet requirements for the Nebraska professional administration and supervisory certificate."[13]

However, the request of the Teachers College faculty for approval of work leading to the Doctor of Education degree did not get the support of the Graduate College faculty. This group contained a few members of the Teachers College faculty during the forties, and the price for the Graduate faculty's support was high. An amendment to the proposal of the Teachers College faculty was offered authorizing the Doctor of Education degree to require that, "The total amount of work in courses other than in Education shall be at least one-half of the total of the undergraduate and graduate seven-year program, exclusive of thesis."[14] The amendment was unacceptable to the Teacher College faculty, and Dean Henzlik

13. Ibid., May 17, 1945, p. 2.
14. Letter R. W. Goss to C. S. Boucher, December 20, 1945, MSS, University of Nebraska Archives, Boucher Collection.

asked that the proposal be tabled. Hostility toward work in professional education was very much in evidence.

The Teachers College did, however, continue to have a real impact upon the public schools of the state. In 1948, it was reported that "more than 40 percent of the elementary and high school teachers with college degrees and approximately 50 percent of the administrators now serving in the accredited public schools of Nebraska have had part or all of their professional training in the University Teachers College."[15]

Frank E. Henzlik, dean since the twenties, continued to exercise firm leadership in the college during the decade. To those who favored the development of professional education as an academic discipline, Henzlik was the undisputed champion of the cause; for those opposed, he was a fierce opponent. To Henzlik, the teacher was much more than an academician.

Teaching is not confined to the imparting of knowledge, nor even to stimulation of learning. . . . At its best, it is never a one-way affair but a sharing process, a two-direction communication. It is a way of life by which we help others as well as ourselves to discover and fully realize a happy and good life.[16]

To increase the dialog between the faculty and students enrolled in the Teachers College was a goal of the dean. In 1944, he appointed a faculty committee composed of Professors Earl W. Lantz, Luvicy M. Hill, and Hazel Davis to develop a plan for greater student participation in policy matters. The Student Advisory Committee to the Dean of Teachers College was formed to implement the faculty committee's report.

During the postwar years, the faculty of the Teachers College took an active part in scholarly publication and other educational work. Frank E. Sorenson became a pioneer in the development of air-age education in the public schools of the state and nation. Royce H. Knapp contributed significantly to research in social science and citizenship education through his publications and consultation with major public school systems. Galen Saylor wrote important college textbooks and became a leader in the National Association for Supervision and Curriculum Development. Dean A. Worchester in educational psychology became a national leader in intelligence testing.

The University Extension Division, long closely associated with the Teachers College, reached new heights of service to the people of Nebraska, the nation, and the world. In 1941, Knute O. Broady was appointed director of the Extension Division. He succeeded A. A. Reed, who retired after having been director since 1912. During World War II, the Extension Division provided correspondence courses, under federal contract, to thousands of service personnel. Services to the civilian community included evening and off-campus classes, high school correspondence study, operation of rural traveling art galleries, rental of audio-visual aids, sponsorship of the "Forum of the Air" and "Book Nook News" on radio station KFAB, and numerous lecture institutes and short courses.

The influence of the University of Nebraska became worldwide, in part, because of the work of the University Extension Division. In 1948, Norman F. Thorpe, assistant director of the division, visited the schools of the Panama Canal Zone in response to a request "to help improve the standard of teaching in the public schools there."[17] The instructional program of the University of Nebraska Extension Division was also visible in Japan, Germany, Argentina, Ecuador, and Peru.

15. *Daily Nebraskan*, February 27, 1948.
16. Ibid., April 9, 1948.
17. Omaha *World-Herald*, July 10, 1948, p. 2.

THE COLLEGE OF LAW

The College of Law, during the forties, underwent a temporary closing, a change of deans, a major curriculum reorganization, and a postwar reopening with heavy enrollment pressures. The enrollment slowly declined during the first years of the decade, and after American entry into the war, the students nearly disappeared. At the end of the academic year in 1943, Dean Henry H. Foster advised Chancellor Boucher, "Without regard to what other law schools are doing or to rules of the law school association, it is possible to justify a temporary discontinuance of law school instruction at Nebraska."[18] The chancellor recommended to the Board of Regents that the College of Law be closed for the duration of the war. The board followed this recommendation; the college was not reopened until January 3, 1946.

During the war years, while the College of Law was closed, Dean Henry Hubbard Foster reached the mandatory retirement age. He had been a member of the college faculty since 1920 and dean since 1926. He had given long service to the University and had been a close adviser to Chancellors Avery and Burnett. However, Dean Foster was best known for his classroom teaching and his interest in the students of the College of Law. He maintained a voluminous correspondence with graduates of the College of Law. A feature written for the *Daily Nebraskan* reported that as a teacher he was unforgettable:

His former students also recall with amusement Dean Foster's passion for illustrating his lectures. One instance was a picture on the lecture hall wall showing a series of gravestones bearing inscriptions relating to old English law which the dean emphatically wished his students to remember as obsolete. The drawing soon became another tradition of the College—"Dean Foster's Graveyard."[19]

In anticipation of reopening the College of Law, Chancellor Boucher wrote to the deans of major law schools requesting recommendations for the deanship at the University of Nebraska College of Law. In September 1945, the Board of Regents appointed Frederick K. Beutel as dean of the College of Law. Roscoe Pound had advised concerning the Beutel appointment, "He is a man of excellent training, and first rate ability both as a law teacher and as an administrator. He is energetic and resourceful, and I should feel he is quite equal to the position you suggest."[20]

Frederick Beutel, at the time of his appointment at the University of Nebraska, was assistant solicitor for the United States Department of the Interior. However, he was not new to university teaching, having been a faculty member in the law schools at the University of Pennsylvania, William and Mary College, Northwestern University, and dean at Louisiana State University. Influenced by his experiences in the federal bureaucracy, Dean Beutel instituted major curricular changes in the Law College. He believed that lawyers should be trained for roles in the administrative and legislative branches of government in addition to their traditional participation in the judicial. Dean Beutel explained his concept of modern legal education. "Fifty years ago when law school curricula were established . . . government was a necessary nuisance, which had very little part in our every day life or in the practice of law. . . ."[21]

18. Letter Henry H. Foster to C. S. Boucher, June 23, 1943, MSS, University of Nebraska Archives, Boucher Collection.

19. *Daily Nebraskan,* October 7, 1945.

20. Letter Roscoe Pound to C. S. Boucher, July 17, 1945, MSS, University of Nebraska Archives, Boucher Collection.

21. *Daily Nebraskan,* April 23, 1948.

In the postwar era he argued that, since "government interferes with everything we do, so public law has risen to tremendous importance in the practice of every lawyer. . . ."[22] Furthermore, the new curriculum would give the law student the experience necessary to practice before administrative boards and tribunals which were not courts.

The new curriculum required a minimum of at least six years of collegiate work, two years of general college work and four years of law school. However, those entering the College of Law with a bachelor's degree from an approved institution could still earn the LL.B degree in three years.

In 1949, Beutel resigned the deanship, but remained as a professor of law until his retirement in 1963. Edmund O. Belsheim, a member of the Law College faculty since 1946, was named dean by the Board of Regents. Other changes in the college during the postwar years were the adoption of the honor system for examinations and participation by the faculty and students with the Lincoln Bar Association and the Lincoln Barrister's Club in the formation of the Lincoln Legal Aid Bureau.

THE COLLEGES OF MEDICINE, DENTISTRY, AND PHARMACY

The enrollments in the Colleges of Medicine and Dentistry, because of the attendance of military personnel, reached new heights during World War II. The College of Medicine attained its peak enrollment of the decade with 434 students in 1943–44. The College of Dentistry began the forties with only 57 students and ended the period with 142. The College of Pharmacy grew from 93 to 280 students in the same period, although it experienced an enrollment decline from 1941 to 1945.

The war years brought unexpected demands upon medical education. To meet the increased national requirements for physicians, class sizes were increased and the curriculum was shortened to three years of continuous medical study. Also, because of war conditions, the College of Medicine first awarded its degree in Omaha rather than Lincoln in March 1943.

The unusual demand for medical personnel caused by the war had the effect of focusing the public's attention on the needs of the University of Nebraska Medical College to a degree unknown in the past. The regents responded by providing several major improvements in clinical facilities. In 1943, the Board of Regents leased land to the Omaha Children's Memorial Hospital for construction of a new hospital. A similar arrangement was made in 1945 with the Lutheran Hospital Association of Omaha. An agreement with Douglas County in 1947 provided for clinical work in psychiatry for medical students at the Nebraska Psychiatric Unit located at the Douglas County Hospital. By 1948, Bishop Clarkson Memorial, Nebraska Methodist, and Immanuel Deaconess hospitals were added to the list of extramural hospital clinics.

C. W. M. Poynter was appointed dean emeritus of the College of Medicine by the Board of Regents in 1946. He had served as dean since 1929. Harold C. Lueth, an associate professor of medicine at the University of Illinois, was named as his successor. Curricular changes in the College of Medicine during the postwar years included the addition of a degree program in medical technology in 1946 and programs of specialization in surgery, obstetrics, neuropsychiatry, and orthopedic surgery for physicians.

The School of Nursing, like the Medical College to which it was attached, reached a new peak in enrollment during World War II. In 1946, Irma Maurine Kyle replaced the retiring Charlotte Burgess as director of the School of Nursing.

22. Ibid.

The College of Dentistry, in Lincoln, showed nearly a 300 percent increase in enrollment during the forties. Bert L. Hooper was dean throughout this period of dynamic growth. Before the war the Department of Children's Dentistry was established under the chairmanship of Ralph L. Ireland. In 1943, the title of the department was changed to that of Pedodontics and Orthodontics. By 1946 the specialization had developed to the point where separate departments of Pedodontics and Orthodontics were formed. The University Board of Regents approved the recommendation, in 1948, that the Department of Pedodontics offer work leading to the degree of Master of Science in Dentistry. These developments in the College of Dentistry reflected the advancements of the profession and the growth of its technology.

Class in the School of Nursing.

Throughout these years, the College of Pharmacy remained the smallest of the health-related colleges. In June 1946, Rufus Ashley Lyman retired as dean of the College of Pharmacy, having been a Nebraska faculty member for forty-two years. He had joined the faculty in 1904, became director of the School of Pharmacy in 1908, and the first dean of the College of Pharmacy in 1915. The development of the pharmacy profession was, in large part, the story of Lyman's life. He had been awarded his first degree by the University of Nebraska in 1897, and was deeply influenced by his teachers. "Four men were my inspiration in those days . . . only Dr. Barbour is left. The others were Dr. Ward, later dean of the medical college, Dr. Bessey, and Dr. Lees who taught Greek. I never learned much Greek but I got much inspiration from that man."[23] One lesson Lyman recalled learning from the careers of his teachers was that, "This university has been built by the men who stayed by it—not by those who have gone away."[24] Rufus A. Lyman could be counted in that company. Joseph B.

23. Ibid., May 26, 1940.
24. Ibid.

Burt, a member of the College of Pharmacy faculty since 1920, was appointed by the regents to succeed Lyman.

In September 1947, the College of Pharmacy instituted a major curricular change in the undergraduate program. Two different curricula were offered students, the Practical Course in Pharmacy, and the Scientific Course in Pharmacy. The first was designed for those who expected to enter the practice of retail pharmacy and the second for those who intended to continue with advanced study in the pharmaceutical sciences. The intent of this change was to prepare the way for additional graduate programs in the College of Pharmacy. But, just as in the case of professional education, the College of Pharmacy had difficulty in obtaining approval of doctorate-level work. Dean Robert W. Goss of the Graduate College expressed his doubts to Chancellor Gustavson on this issue. "The Pharmacy College requested permission to offer work for the Ph.D.

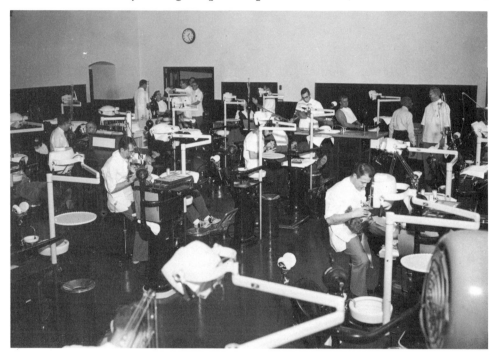

Students gaining clinical experience in the College of Dentistry.

Degree several years ago and the Graduate Council refused to approve on the grounds that the undergraduate program in Pharmacy was too narrow and vocational to serve as a foundation for a Ph.D. program."[25]

The issue of Ph.D. work in pharmacy was not settled during this decade. However, the matter generated considerable faculty discontent, resulting in the resignation of two outstanding faculty members, Arthur E. Schwarting and Paul J. Jannke. The low state of faculty morale in the College of Pharmacy was evident in Jannke's somewhat bitter, but forthright letter of resignation.

We have never enjoyed the support of the Administration in our proposed graduate program. Dean Goss has never endorsed openly the very curriculum which he, personally, suggested we adopt. At a later date, Chancellor Gustavson recommended that we plan a curriculum on the basis of interdepartmental areas. Even though the general idea and the areas were accepted by the University Senate, the chairman of only one department agreed to cooperate with us; all of the others refused, and despite

25. Letter R. W. Goss to R. G. Gustavson, April 15, 1947, MSS, University of Nebraska Archives, Gustavson Collection.

our pleas, neither the Graduate Dean nor the Chancellor stepped forward to lend assistance. It is obvious to me that there are those persons who prefer to limit the College of Pharmacy to an undergraduate status.[26]

Personality differences and misunderstandings obviously contributed their share to the complexity of the issue. Ultimately, despite the opposition, an inter-departmental Ph.D. program was approved.

Important research findings were published, in the forties, by Paul J. Jannke, Donald M. Pace, Harald G. O. Holck, and Arthur E. Schwarting, all of the College of Pharmacy.

THE GRADUATE COLLEGE

Except during the war years, enrollment in the University of Nebraska Graduate College showed substantial growth. At the end of the decade, there were nearly 600 more graduate students on the campus than in 1940.

In 1940, the long-standing requirement that Doctor of Philosophy dissertations be published was abolished and published abstracts substituted. Cliff S. Hamilton, chairman of the Department of Chemistry and Chemical Engineering, was appointed by the Board of Regents in 1940 as acting dean of the Graduate College. He replaced Harold W. Stoke. The next year, Robert Whitmore Goss, chairman of the Department of Plant Pathology, was named Graduate dean.

A most significant advance in graduate education and scholarship at the University of Nebraska was the creation of the University of Nebraska Press. Not only did it provide an outlet for scholarly work, but it also served to stimulate research. The University Press was part of the Publication Department under the direction of Emily Schossberger. Two of the press's early publications were James S. Olson's *J. Sterling Morton* and *Peace Without Hate* by George W. Norris.

THE COLLEGE OF ENGINEERING

No college of the University of Nebraska contributed more to the war effort or experienced more postwar growth than the College of Engineering.

The Civilian Pilot Training Program, authorized by the Board of Regents before American entry into the war, was under the direction of Professor Jiles W. Haney of the Department of Mechanical Engineering. In early 1941, Chancellor Boucher appointed Dean O. J. Ferguson as special defense liaison officer to develop those special training programs requested by the federal government. During the war years about 5,000 students were enrolled in programs to supply technically trained men for national defense industries. Courses were offered in such subjects as ultra-high-frequency technique, drafting and shop mechanics, aircraft assembly inspection, and time and motion study. These courses were taught in Lincoln, Omaha, and several other locations. Toward the end of the war, the federal regional administrator of the program wrote the chancellor, "It is the personal opinion of the undersigned that the production record of your area could not have been attained without the program carried on by your institution. . . ."[27]

In May 1945, the Board of Regents appointed Roy M. Green as professor of civil engineering and assistant dean of the College of Engineering with the

26. Letter Paul J. Jannke to Joseph B. Burt, June 4, 1948, MSS, University of Nebraska Archives, Gustavson Collection.

27. Letter Huber O. Croft to C. S. Boucher, August 6, 1945, MSS, University of Nebraska Archives, Boucher Collection.

understanding that he would become dean upon the retirement of O. J. Ferguson. The retiring dean, Olin Jerome Ferguson, had served in that capacity since 1920. Few administrators or professors could match his good rapport with students and faculty. At the time of his retirement from teaching, several years after his administrative retirement, he expressed what the College of Engineering had meant to him.

Perhaps you can apprehend what this expanding square of dedicated land means to me, when you think of the thousands of "boys" whom I have watched go through it from freshman-entrance to senior-exit, to enter upon professional life in the wide, wide world. Perhaps you can comprehend my chief concern—success for our alumni. Perhaps you can understand my gratification in the records you have been making of good citizenship, self-reliance, productive employment. Perhaps you can believe that I count you all my close friends, no matter of what vintage you are; no matter whether our personal contacts have been many or few. (And I know you will understand me when I say that one of the best ways to make friends is to have a warm-hearted secretary in the outer office!)[28]

Maud Melick was this person. She was secretary to Deans O. V. Stout, O. J. Ferguson, and Roy M. Green. In 1912, Miss Melick published the first engineering alumni letter and in the ensuing years remembered and recognized nearly all the graduates of the college. Through her efforts, the College of Engineering maintained a personal relationship with its graduates unsurpassed by any other college of the University.

During the postwar period, the College of Engineering enrollment dramatically increased. It was 1,076 students in 1945–46 and 1,909 in 1948–49. This produced staffing problems for the dean and heavy teaching loads for the faculty. Furthermore, the changing role of the engineer in society now demanded more than just a "high top boot and woolen shirt" engineer. Under Dean Green's leadership, curricular revision was begun in an attempt to prepare engineering students for their expanding professional role. Dean Green defined the challenge:

Today's engineers must not only be a technician, but an able administrator. He must also possess a working knowledge of the society in which he lives because his work now is reflected to so many social and economic phases of our society. He must be a useful, informed citizen to perform his job competently. We hope to achieve this end by giving students a broader base upon which to pyramid their professional experiment.[29]

In conformity with the changing status of the engineer in society, there was an accompanying upgrading of professional competency for engineers. In 1947, the Board of Regents authorized the College of Engineering to grant the professional degrees of Agricultural Engineer, Electrical Engineer, Chemical Engineer, Civil Engineer, and Mechanical Engineer. Later, the additional professional degree of Architectural Engineer was also approved by the regents.

In June 1947, the name of the college was changed from the College of Engineering to the College of Engineering and Architecture. At this same meeting, the Board of Regents approved the faculty recommendation establishing a five-year curriculum in architecture.

The College of Engineering and Architecture faculty and curriculum were greatly improved during the decade of the forties. Its facilities were expanded by the purchase of the Bancroft school property and the construction of Ferguson Hall. The heavy teaching load, after the war, produced some faculty dis-

28. Letter Olin Jerome Ferguson to "Dear Fellows," July 13, 1949, MSS, University of Nebraska Archives, Gustavson Collection.
29. *Daily Nebraskan,* January 13, 1946.

content, but the majority of the faculty uncomplainingly met the challenges of the decade.

THE COLLEGE OF BUSINESS ADMINISTRATION

Enrollment in the College of Business Administration, like that of the Colleges of Engineering and Law, reflected the interest of veterans in a higher education that would prepare them for a specific career. In 1943–44, the college enrolled only 457 students; in 1947–48, with the veteran enrollment at flood tide, it had 2,104 students. Classes were large, teaching loads heavy, but the instructional program was effectively organized.

In 1941, James Edward LeRossignol retired as dean of the College of Business Administration. He had been director of the School of Commerce, the parent of this college. When the legislature created the College of Business Administration in 1919, LeRossignol became its first dean. Under his able leadership, the college nearly quadrupled its enrollment and provided a growing number of trained business leaders to the state and nation.

John Davidson Clark assumed the responsibility of the deanship in September 1941. A native of Wyoming, he was graduated from the University of Nebraska in 1905 and received the LL.B. degree from Columbia University in 1907. He then practiced law in Cheyenne and went into the oil business. He became president of the Midwest Refining Company, and a vice president of Standard Oil of Indiana. Clark gave up this successful career to enter the academic world. In 1931, he was awarded the Ph.D. in economics from Johns Hopkins University. At the time of his appointment as dean at the University of Nebraska, Clark was practicing law in Cheyenne. However, he had taught at the University of Denver and the University of Nebraska. Clark led the college in preparing for the postwar period. A significant economic analysis of Omaha was prepared under the dean's direction. This report was requested by the Omaha Chamber of Commerce. In 1940, President Truman appointed John D. Clark to his Council of Economic Advisers.

Earl S. Fullbrook, professor of marketing and a member of the College of Business Administration faculty since 1920, was named by the Board of Regents to succeed Clark. The decision to appoint Fullbrook had actually been made several years earlier. Clark had not intended to remain permanently as dean, but had accepted the post and remained dean longer than he had intended, "because Boucher asked me to come to Nebraska in order to find a permanent dean for him and after I had done so he was good-natured enough to let me stay on in a position which I found so delightful."[30] In 1943, the tentative decision was reached to appoint Fullbrook as dean. Clark explained to Chancellor Gustavson, "Since that provisional decision was made, we gave him leave of absence for two years to serve as executive director of the Chamber of Commerce, where he built up a fine acquaintance with the business men of the state which will be of the greatest value to the university and the college."[31]

The college's contribution to the understanding of business conditions in Nebraska was continued by the Bureau of Business Research, which had been established in 1922. The bureau's publications *Business Review Edition* and *Business in Nebraska Cities* were combined in 1949 into *Business in Nebraska*. These publications made a major contribution to the understanding of the changing business climate in Nebraska. Faculty members of the College of

30. Letter John D. Clark to R. G. Gustavson, July 31, 1946, MSS, University of Nebraska Archives, Gustavson Collection.
31. Ibid.

Business Administration who were recognized for their scholarship during the forties were Professors Karl M. Arndt, George M. Darlington, Clifford M. Hicks, and Charles J. Kennedy.

The decade of the forties, with its years of war and peace, challenged the University of Nebraska as never before. It served more students, and along with this, the quality of the educational program, research, and public service reached new heights of excellence. The colleges and schools of the University had in a sense been revitalized.

This new spirit at the University resulted from the policies and successes of the Gustavson administration. The faculty's morale was restored by the chancellor's forthright administrative style and his strong conviction that the University's reputation depended upon the scholarship of its faculty. Acting out of this conviction, successful efforts were made during the last years of the decade to attract bright, young scholars to the faculty. Although not all remained at the University of Nebraska, those who did laid the foundation for the academic excellence achieved by some departments in the fifties and sixties.

CHAPTER 9

Student Life in War and Peace

No DECADE OF THIS half-century brought more change to student life at the University of Nebraska than that of the forties. Although the campus and the nation hoped for peace and prosperity, the European war clouds had begun to cast their shadows across the United States. Pearl Harbor was a shock to all Americans, although in retrospect the war's coming should not have been a surprise.

When the nation went to war, so did the student body at the University of Nebraska. Men students left school for the military services. Military programs at the University brought thousands of servicemen to the campus. Only the women's enrollment resembled its prewar size. The coeds assumed campus student leadership during the time of national emergency and organized campus activities to contribute to the war effort. Students and faculty worked together to make the University of Nebraska's war projects an outstanding success.

With the end of the war, student life at the University of Nebraska returned to the ways of peace. However, the campus differed in spirit from that of the prewar years. The student body changed with the influx of thousands of veterans. They were older, more serious about their studies, and many were married men with families.

The *Cornhusker* of 1940 listed the possibility of war as the paramount concern of the year. "With the haunting fear of the United States becoming involved in another World War, university students have constantly watched belligerent aggressions of European Countries."[1] The registration of men between the ages of twenty-one and thirty-five for the draft in October 1940 focused student attention on the international situation.

In the spring of 1941, the *Daily Nebraskan* surveyed student opinion on the issue of war. The question, "Do you favor immediate participation of the United States into war," was answered by 75 percent of the students asked with an emphatic "definitely not." Typical student responses were: "No, I think we should stay at home. It didn't get us anyplace last time," or "I think we should wait until we're better prepared. The war's in a deadlock for at least five years anyway." Students agreed that the United States should be militarily prepared to meet any threat to the national safety. This was evident in the 35 percent increase in applications of upperclassmen for admission to the advanced ROTC program in September 1941.

The campus debate over possible American entry into the war was heightened during the last months of peace by the organization of the University America First Committee. The organization received strong support from former Congressman Henry C. Luckey of Lincoln. However, the majority of Nebraska students rejected the America First Committee. An editorial in the *Daily Nebraskan*,

1. *Cornhusker*, 1940, p. 10.

just a month before Pearl Harbor, probably closely expressed the dominant student view that the nation's vital interests were being threatened.

We want to know what's in the name America First, the misnomer adopted by that committee which is telling the people of the United States to have nothing to do with the war in Europe. To us the term America First should mean doing everything in our power to preserve America and the committee by that name is suggesting a course of action which will not preserve the United States or any other part of America for that matter.

The "America First" committee preaches, among other things, that the United States should keep her ships off of the seas and do everything to prepare "at home" against invasion. Those who subscribe to the committee's doctrines are willing to make this brave statement: "I would be the first to fight if the United States were invaded, but I do not want to die in foreign mud." Possibly these people do not realize that to prepare our home defenses we must have products from other countries. For example, we need millions of tons of manganese to be used in making steel which is one of the most vital defense materials if not the most vital. We have to get manganese from other countries and cannot do this without sending our ships to get it.

With such an economic system as ours we cannot say that we can stay at home to prepare our defenses. Aside from the fact that England is fighting our enemy, Germany, and we should help England fight that enemy, we shall also have to fight even to keep building our home defenses. We shall have to fight to keep a real America First.[2]

The debate ended suddenly on Sunday, December 7, 1941, with the Japanese attack on Pearl Harbor. After war was declared those who had previously opposed American entry into the war now rallied to their nation's support.

Although the events leading to the United States involvement in the war overshadowed campus life during the first years of the forties, traditional student activities did continue during the few remaining months of peace. Campus politics still reflected the battle between Greeks and Barbs. In 1940, the Barb candidates were elected Honorary Colonel and Nebraska Sweetheart, but the following year, the Greeks again dominated student elections.

Two student problems troubling Dean of Student Affairs T. J. Thompson during the early forties were TNE (Theta Nu Epsilon), a "sub rosa" drinking fraternity, and the revival of the traditional engineering-law student rivalry. The death of a student at the University of Missouri following a TNE initiation resulted in a strong public reaction against the secret organization. The Lincoln *State Journal* editorialized that "what seems apparent in any discussion of this growth that has fastened itself on American educational institutions is that it is not needed, that it serves no desirable end, and that its elimination would be for the good of all, even its own members."[3]

TNE had been active on the University of Nebraska campus for some fifty years, and it made its presence known by painting the traditional skull and crossbone insignia on campus buildings and walks, by presenting the May queen on Ivy Day a TNE marked bouquet by special messenger, and by projecting its insignia on the wall at a University dance. Dean Thompson announced that the property damage done by painting the insignia on campus walks and buildings would be paid for or the organization would be exposed. Money was received to have the insignia sandblasted from the campus. It is evident that the University administration did not seek to expose the organization. It was rumored, and widely believed, that many prominent business and governmental leaders were alumni members of Theta Nu Epsilon. The following fall, when questioned

2. *Daily Nebraskan,* November 12, 1941.
3. Lincoln, *Nebraska State Journal,* March 16, 1940, p. 8.

about the administration's attitude toward TNE, Dean Thompson replied that he could not make any statement except, "They'd just better behave. . . ."[4] They did behave—that year.

The law-engineer student feud erupted in both 1940 and in 1941. The first incident began with a water fight and ended in a truce after more than a hundred engineers descended upon the Delta Theta Pi fraternity house. The next year, the law students moved a display prepared by the students of the College of Engineering for Engineer's Day. The engineers attacked the Law College building, using rotten eggs as ammunition. In the ensuing confrontation, the lawyers suffered the heaviest casualties. Edward Walla, '41, Leonard Dunker, '43, Robert Gilbert, '41, and Earl Ludlam, '41, were taken to the student infirmary for treatment. The only engineering student who was injured was Maurice Breunsbach, '42. A truce was arranged by Deans O. J. Ferguson, of the College of Engineering, and H. H. Foster, of the College of Law. By this time, the origin of the feud was obscure to the students. "The traditional feud between the two colleges is so old that neither group knows exactly when or why it started. Still, year in and year out, Ivy Day time brought scuffling with the corollary injuries of lessor or greater degree between the groups."[5] The rivalry was largely forgotten during the war years. In the postwar period, veterans enrolled in the Colleges of Law and Engineering had little interest in the pranks which had always renewed the traditional conflict.

Undoubtedly, the most memorable prewar event of campus life was begun by Coach Lawrence "Biff" Jones' announcement of the acceptance of the Rose Bowl invitation. The resulting rally included both town and gown. On December 3, 1940, page one of the Nebraska *State Journal* carried the following story.

A biting cold wind blew from the north, but the nigh hysterical, yelling students took little notice. Most of Monday they raced about, breaking up classes, disrupting business operations and generally making Lincoln the wildest it had been since Nebraska defeated Notre Dame back in 1925.

The rallying began about 15 minutes after the news of Nebraska's acceptance was broadcast. Fraternity and sorority row was packed with hilarious students who refused to go to bed.

The rally grew by leaps and bounds until some 3,000 people surged down R in a huge snake dance. The noisy bunch moved to 14th and O and then back to the campus.

But it didn't stop with that. Some of the craftier youths found a ladder and raised it to the second story window of Carrie Bell Raymond hall, where they found the largest concentration of coeds. They soon emptied a large portion of the building as the rally crowd swelled.

No School Today!

Monday morning school had scarcely begun before a hastily assembled portion of the band started crashing classes. By 9 a.m. more than a thousand students had overpowered most of their academic urges and joined the throng.

Led by Cheerleader Elton Wiley, with his green pork pie hat smashed down on his ears to keep the brisk wind from blowing it away, the wild throng half walked, half ran down 12th to the main business section.

On each corner of O and at nearby intersections, the crowd organized itself enough to roar a cheer for the team, the coach, or the state.

About half an hour later the rally rushed back to the campus for more students. They carried a hastily made sign, "No school today," and sent up impromptu yells varying from "Beat Stanford," "Let's Go West," to old fashioned Indian war cries.

An attempt to break up classes in the Lincoln School of Commerce failed, but they

4. *Daily Nebraskan,* September 19 ,1941.
5. Ibid., May 2, 1940.

were quite successful on their campus. Individual rallies in each building soon joined the main artery until it was all Wiley could do to keep it in hand.

In a few moments they rushed downtown again. Somewhere along the line they picked up a police escort and it wasn't long before good natured Motorcycle Officer LaVerne Campbell and Sgt. L. C. Regler had the youths under perfect control.

The rally moved from its second trip thru the downtown section to the state capitol, where they set up a din with a chant for Gov. Cochran. The governor was in Chicago, so Insurance Director Charles Smrha satisfied the yelling mob with a short talk while state house employees enjoyed a half hour intermission from their work.

Wiley moved from football to politics as he led cheers for Cochran, Governor-elect Dwight Griswold, Quarterback Roy Petsch, Halfback Walt Luther, and anyone else he could remember.

Having thoroly wrecked the routine of the state house, the now slightly hoarse students headed back for the campus and Chancellor C. S. Boucher. They were met between P and Q on 14th by a carload of "strong arm" men with Coach Jones.

There in the center of the street Jones told the rally how much he appreciated their spirit. He wore a broad smile as he said he hadn't slept for two or three nights worrying about bowl games.

Jones Fears Pneumonia

He showed a little good natured concern for any members of his team who might be risking pneumonia by racing up and down the streets and shouting themselves into a sore throat.

Jones' car joined the parade as it headed toward the Administration building to pick up Chancellor Boucher and let him lead the parade in the sidecar of Officer Campbell's motorcycle. The chancellor wasn't there, but the rally moved on just the same.

They picked up Fullback Vike Francis at 12th and P and gave him the chancellor's seat of honor in the motorcycle. And for the third time Monday morning, they moved down P to the Lincoln hotel, where their cheers were broadcast over radio station KFOR.

The rally broke up at noon when luncheon tables beckoned, but professors had few students again for afternoon classes.

The expressions of glee weren't confined to the half-mad students. Business men, clerks, hair dressers, attorneys and pedestrians stood in windows and doorways with ear to ear smiles as the clamor moved by.

Many Nebraskans remember this event and the Rose Bowl game as the last big University event before the war.

A University policy change which greatly affected student life resulted from new housing regulations. In 1941, Dean of Women Helen M. Hosp recommended to the University administration and the Board of Regents that all freshmen women be required to live in University dormitories. The regents approved the new policy with two exceptions; first, those who lived at home, and second, those who could not afford the $270 per year charged for board and room by the University. The dean of women expected that the new policy would result in improved "adjustment to the new college life, in scholarship, and in greater solidarity of the freshman class."[6] Prior to this policy change only 190 women students were living in dormitories with a capacity of 370. The policy resulted in the women's dormitories operating at near capacity and thus substantially increasing the revenue available to the Dormitory Corporation for the retirement of its bonds.

In September 1941, Dean Helen M. Hosp resigned. Vera G. Boyles, a 1913 graduate of the University, was appointed to the position. Mrs. Boyles had been house mother at the Sigma Phi Epsilon fraternity house at the University from

6. *Daily Nebraskan*, February 29, 1940.

1935 to 1940 and was familiar with the Nebraska campus. During the years ahead, because of the war, the dean of women was a very busy person.

In the last year of peace, the staff of the *Cornhusker* identified as major campus events of the year the arrival of a Hollywood movie company on campus to film "Cheers for Miss Bishop," the invasion of Stephen's College "Susies," and the spring Kosmet Klub production which broke tradition by including coeds in the cast. For women students, saddle shoes and anklets were in vogue. For men students, whipcord and tweed sport jackets, sweaters, saddle shoes, and beige gabardine trench coats were the style. Soon these would be changed to olive drab uniforms.

With the beginning of conscription, the influence of women students on the campus increased. The Student Council encouraged women to become more active in campus affairs. Of concern to many coeds was the lack of dates caused by the military draft. In October 1941, Midge Beasley, x'44 and Estella Lennermann, '45, thought that an army camp near Lincoln would solve the problem of weekend dates. Barbara Cook, '42, said that she "cannot understand why any draft board would be so 'mean' as to interfere with a man's college career."[7] However, a male freshman viewed the situation differently, "Conscription has given us lesser lights a chance to shine. It has taken most of the older, smoother Greek gods out of circulation. I certainly cannot complain, for I'm going to take advantage of the situation."[8] But the war came and all was changed!

With the entry of the United States into the global conflict, great changes took place in student life in colleges throughout the nation. The cause of victory mobilized those in the cities, towns, and farms of the nation for the fight against totalitarianism. Students everywhere rallied to their country's support. Many students perceived that the nation's war goals were "to crush dictatorship and exterminate racial prejudices or to squelch totalitarianism."[9] To accomplish these goals, the campus was transformed. Campus politics lost much of its earlier student appeal. Engineer's Week and the rivalry with the Law College were discontinued in 1942. Students collected scrap metal for national defense, and even the 1942 Homecoming featured a scrap metal collection competition, which took the place of the usual decorations.

The Nebraska football team and the Athletic Department supported the scrap metal drive by substituting 100 pounds of scrap iron for part of the admission price to the Nebraska-Minnesota football game at Memorial Stadium. John K. Selleck, athletic business manager, told the fans, "Cornhusker athletes are in action on far-flung battle fronts throughout the world. We hope, that football fans Saturday will build a huge scrap pile. By tossing our scrap into the fight, we can speed the ending of the war and speed the return of those boys."[10]

To keep the University of Nebraska and its work before the public, the Student Council organized the Student Foundation. John J. Douglass, '43, was its first chairman. The purpose of this new campus organization founded by the students was:

To serve as a medium for the promotion of good will toward the University on the part of the public; to promote school spirit among the student body; to relieve the strain of the limited financial budgets; to maintain the present high status of the university, while at the same time, fostering greater progress by it in the field of education.[11]

7. Ibid., October 15, 1941.
8. Ibid.
9. Ibid., March 11, 1942.
10. Lincoln, *Nebraska State Journal,* October 16, 1942, p. 1.
11. *Daily Nebraskan,* February 18, 1942.

This organization was a great success and was incorporated under the laws of the state of Nebraska in 1943 as the Nebraska Student Foundation.

A Student Defense Council was created to organize voluntary student support for the war effort. Patricia Lahr, '39, director of social activities for the Student Union, and Mary Kerrigan, '42, editor of the *Daily Nebraskan*, led the movement to establish this group. Under the auspices of the Student Defense Council, coeds entertained soldiers at dances held at the Student Union, held classes in first aid, and staged a variety show to raise funds to support its morale-building activities. Verna Boyles, the dean of women, approved the project to entertain troops from the neighboring military bases. "Girls should consider as their patriotic duty

Scrap metal collected by students for the war effort.

the entertainment of university boys, but, at the same time, they can give a little of their time to make the out-of-state soldier feel at home."[12] Other activities added by the War Council included selling war bonds and stamps, organizing an air raid warden's school, and arranging blood donation drives.

By the fall of 1942, students at the University of Nebraska clearly recognized and accepted the hardships of the war. A student editorial stated:

We're beginning a new school year. Let's get the most out of college life we can, having a good time as well as studying. But beneath all of this, let's face the facts. We must sit down, have a good talk with ourselves, and realize that we are in school now, preparing for something greater than our own selfish interests, but we are in a college preparing ourselves for a place in the great war program.[13]

The desire to enjoy campus life while contributing to the war effort and waiting to be called into military service is evident in the dramatic increase in the

12. Ibid., November 6, 1942.
13. Ibid., September 17, 1942.

number of fraternity pledges. In the fall of 1941, 272 men pledged fraternities; in 1942, the number had been 470. Fraternity membership not only contributed to the enjoyment of campus life, but also provided psychological support for young men facing the uncertainties of military service.

By 1943, the full impact of the war was felt on the University of Nebraska campus when the army called up the advanced ROTC students to active duty. The activated students were permitted to continue their academic programs until the end of the spring semester, when the seniors left for officer candidate school, and the juniors left for basic training.

The establishment of special military programs at the University, under the command of Colonel J. P. Murphy, also brought the realities of the war closer to the student body. There was a question of whether there would be trouble between the civilian and military students. Some other university campuses had experienced real difficulties. In March 1943, the *Daily Nebraskan* editorially recognized the problem.

The addition of a large number of men on the campus, all in uniform, poses a problem that will have to be faced. It is the problem of several hundred men in uniform living in the same community as a large number of able bodied young men in cords and saddle shoes; of young, red-blooded men living a disciplined, strictly regulated life while at the same time similar men are foot-loose and fancy free. . . . The first step in the process of mutual understanding must be taken by the students. It is up to them to make the air corps men stationed here feel at home. . . . Men on the campus—students and soldiers—are all working for and looking toward the same goal. Starting the first day the air men report here, there should be a recognition that there is much in common between the two groups.[14]

The servicemen assigned to study at the University of Nebraska were welcomed into the student body. The War Council and other campus student organizations made a special effort to help these military students feel that they were "Cornhuskers." Sorority hour dances and membership in the Student Union with two free dances a month helped fill the entertainment bill. Of course the coed line of "we just love soldiers," did much to build soldier-student morale.[15]

By 1943, few civilian men remained on the campus. Women students provided most campus leadership; even the ROTC marching band contained a large number of women students. The Corn Cobs and Kosmet Klub declared themselves inactive while their members went to war. The Innocents scheduled no activities. The University Theatre found itself with predominantly feminine casts. Production of the War Council's variety show, "Red, Hot, Blue," was one of the major student interests.

The death of Henry Frank "Pop" Schulte, the grand old man of University of Nebraska athletics, saddened the campus and Lincoln in October 1944. He came to the University to coach in 1919. The first two years he was head football coach, then he served as line coach and developed some of the most famous lines in Husker history. As track coach, "Pop" Schulte was outstanding. His team won the first league crown for Nebraska in 1921. In the years before his retirement, he produced ten outdoor league titles and nine indoor championships. Most famous of his protégés was Roland "The Gripper" Locke, '27, a world record setter in the dashes. Few members of the University staff received the affection bestowed by the student body and alumni on "Pop" Schulte. His positive influence long remained with those who were members of his teams and those fortunate enough to know him.

In 1945, the success of the D-Day invasion and the island-hopping strategy in

14. Ibid., March 28, 1943.
15. *Cornhusker,* 1944, p. 163.

the Pacific theater caused all Americans to anticipate the successful termination of the war. The Student War Council titled its last review, "Till Johnny Comes Marching Home." It was directed by Lucy Ann Hapeman, '46. In preparation for the postwar world, University of Nebraska students held a mock conference to write a treaty for world peace in March 1945. The idea was suggested by Gerry McKinsey, '46, and was enthusiastically received by the student body. More than 1,500 students participated in the evening sessions held in the Coliseum. Students concluded this experience with the realization that the years ahead would be difficult and the attainment of world peace elusive.

In early May 1945, the nation celebrated V-E Day and the end of the war seemed much closer. In September Japan surrendered, and the world entered the atomic age.

With the opening of the University fall semester in 1945, enrollment expanded rapidly. The era of the veteran had begun. American universities had never experienced such a period of growth nor had a more mature student body. For many veterans the adjustment to student life was not easy. A reporter for the *Daily Nebraskan* found that: "They've discovered it's kind of hard talking 'civilian language' after being in the service so long. And they're a little self-conscious about the difference in their ages and those of the regular under-classmen whom they generally call 'teen-agers.' "[16] A veteran of the battle on the Rhine River in Germany explained his adjustment problem. "When I try to study I find my mind wandering. I tried to study in the library—it was too quiet. I tried the Student Union—it was too noisy. But it's not as hard as I thought it would be."[17] Most veterans met the academic challenge as success-fully as they had met that of the war. During these years the level of student academic performance reached new heights of excellence.

With the return of peace, campus organizations which had been inactive during the war came to life. The first formal Mortar Board Ball after the war was held in December 1945. By the new year, the social season was in full bloom. The 1946 *Cornhusker* reported that: "The social whirl came to life again with the revival of downtown parties—and even now and then an old tuxedo was dragged out of mothballs to make it seem like old times again."[18]

Men's organizations dormant during the war showed new life and vigor during these years. The Kosmet Klub presented its first postwar spring review in 1946. One of the active members of the Klub during these years was Norbert Tiemann, '49. The revival of school football spirit marked the reappearance of the Corn Cobs on the campus. Again, they sold the familiar white mums before the foot-ball games. A card section was an added attraction to the Corn Cobs' organized cheering at football games.

The fraternities' happiness with the return of men to the campus was exceeded only by that of the coeds. It had seemed, in 1943, that fraternities might be doomed as a wartime casualty. Nine had closed and the remaining ten were barely able to remain active. However, by 1946, all but one of the closed fraternities were again represented on the University of Nebraska campus. Nevertheless, they were different; the maturity of many fraternity pledges and returning actives eliminated most of what had been a part of hazing. One house mother commented about her older "boys." "No one has to tell pledges to go to study hall. They're not going to school for fun, they're here for an educa-tion."[19] A returned fraternity active, who had been initiated in 1941, remarked "that for him the 'Rah Rah' stuff is out. When I go to a basketball game now

16. *Daily Nebraskan,* October 3, 1945.
17. Ibid.
18. *Cornhusker,* 1946, p. 154.
19. Omaha *World-Herald,* February 24, 1946, p. 9-A.

. . . it's because I'm interested. I don't go to wave my arms to the strains of 'Dear Old Nebraska U.' "[20]

The N-Club, like the fraternities, had members return to the campus after the interruption of the war. Marvin S. Athey, '46, Gerald J. Kathol, '46, Dean G. Kratz, '46, Gerald Jacupke, '48, Edward Schwartzkopf, '48, and Gould Flagg, '49, were club members who contributed to the rebuilding of school spirit and assisted at the State High School Basketball Tournament and State High School track meets hosted by the University of Nebraska.

Problems inherent in the enrollment explosion at the University caused com-

Prize-winning students at the Beaux Arts Ball, which in 1948 took the theme of satirizing radio.

plaints within the student body. Long lines for registration and for meals caused grievances from students who had anticipated the end of queues with their separation from military service. Registration, in particular, was a major source of student dissatisfaction. The *Daily Nebraskan* editorialized in January 1946.

GET ON THE BALL . . .

The registration situation is inexcusable. Many students have stood in line for three hours in the Temple building, waiting to go through the assignment committee to complete their registration, only to have the door shut in their faces upon progressing that far. Other students have missed classes to fight their way through the lines, only to find that something was neglected and they had to go back to their advisors.

The disregard for organization and efficiency makes us wonder if the administration is capable of taking care of the increased enrollment which they evidently hadn't anticipated. The system of setting up the assignment committee in the YM office at Temple was all right for the war years in which the number of students registering

20. Ibid.

was cut in half. However, now there are some four thousand students trying to register for next semester and by the wildest stretch of imagination they just don't fit into that one room.[21]

The following fall, however, the University postponed the opening of classes several days to complete registering the student body. Throughout most of these postwar years, the registration process was long and difficult for students. Too often students found the needed classes closed and the open classes in conflict with their tentative schedule. Gradually the University community learned to conquer this problem. Substantial improvement was made during the years of Chancellor Gustavson's administration.

Veterans' housing in "Huskerville."

Another source of student discontent was the lack of adequate student housing. Although dormitories had long been provided for women students by the University of Nebraska, men's dormitories were not provided until after the war. At best the dormitories could provide housing for only a small portion of the student population. In response to Chancellor Gustavson's plea for housing in private homes, Lincoln Mayor Lloyd J. Marti proclaimed a "Rooms for Students Week." The favorable response of the people of Lincoln enabled single students to find a room. However, the housing of married students continued to be a difficult problem. The University of Nebraska and other American universities had not generally provided housing for married students before the war. Students who were married veterans believed that the University and the local community had some responsibility for providing housing at a reasonable cost to the nation's defenders who sought to improve themselves by studying under the G.I. Bill. The closing of the Lincoln Army Air Field provided the solution to the problem of married veterans' housing for the University and the Lincoln community. The conversion of the former military hospital area to student apartments relieved much of the critical housing shortage. The Board of Regents established priorities for those eligible for "Huskerville" apartments. Space was assigned first "to Nebraska veterans with children," second, "to Nebraska veterans without children," third, "to non-resident veterans with children," and fourth, "to non-resident veterans without children."[22]

Although married veterans often had difficulty in supporting their families on

21. *Daily Nebraskan,* January 16, 1946.
22. *Minutes,* University of Nebraska Board of Regents, June 22, 1946.

the $90 per month provided by the G.I. Bill, other University students were more prosperous than ever before. There was little demand by students for assistance from the student loan fund and less than 4 percent of the male students sought work through the University employment office. This student prosperity was accompanied by an enormous increase in the number of cars owned by students. The issue of student parking produced the student riot of the decade. The disturbance in early May 1948 involved the city police and Governor Peterson as well as the University community. An eyewitness reported the event in the *Daily Nebraskan:*

When I came out of my 9 o'clock class this morning, I noticed a group of about 500 students around the northwest.side of the Social Science building on 12th and R streets. Upon approaching the crowd, I discovered that the police were attempting to tow away all student automobiles which were double parked.

By 10:30, approximately 2,000 students had gathered around the cars and a force of city police arrived. The police immediately started arguing, and several students were jostled up a bit.

By now about 2,500 students had collected, and the police threw a tear gas bomb into the street, causing the students to withdraw on to the campus lawn.

The students became infuriated at the action of the police, and immediately threw a human chain into the street, blocking all east and west bound traffic.

This human chain had hardly entered the street when fire department trucks arrived, and considered connecting a hose with which to attack the crowd. The alarm may have been false, because they rejected the idea and retired from the scene.

At 11 o'clock I am sure that there were over 3,000 students in the street on their way to the police station, where they were told the mayor was the person to see.

Unfortunately the mayor was out of town. Cobe Venner, director of public safety, said the responsibility for a demonstration by a state institution [was assigned] to the governor or chancellor.

Upon arrival at the capitol, I hurried to be one of the group to talk to the governor. Mr. Peterson was very cordial and gave every one a chance to speak. The requests made by the students were as follows:

1. Release of students who were seized by the police.

2. Release of cars impounded by the police.

3. The name of the person responsible for giving the seizure order, so that a protest could be made.

4. Elimination of the parking problem.

To these requests the governor said: "I am confident that the university officers can and will handle the situation. I will talk to the city police and the chancellor . . . the parking responsibility is that of the chancellor and the Board of Regents. Only when the university requires funds is the governor responsible . . . the city also has a responsibility to provide parking to the students and visitors."

The governor suggested that the representative group he was talking to take the matter to the chancellor.

Chief of Police Carroll said: "The university police ordered the cars to be towed in. The only time the city police go on the campus is when they are called. The university police are deputized by the police department. . . . I am not in a position to say that the cars will be released."

When the student delegation left the governor's office, all of the students had dispersed. The delegation went to Dean Thompson's office, and signed their name stating wether [*sic*] or not they owned automobiles.

Dean Thompson said: "It will take about a week to investigate and find out the exact problem. There are several parking areas, however, that are not being used. . . . There are several universities that do not permit student parking on the campus. I have always been opposed to that, 12th and 13th streets are city streets, so anyone can park on them."

The delegation composed of students left the Dean's office confident that some progress would be made in the parking situation.

The student delegation to see the governor were: Lynnwood Parker, Woody Lange,

Stanley Partsche, Keneth E. Templin, Glenn Gross, Dean Towle, Gladys Jackson, Howard F. Pavelsek, Jim R. Nash, Frank Gorton, Robert Horne, Mick Putney.[23]

As a result of this demonstration, a special committee composed of faculty, student, and administration was appointed to study the campus parking situation. The City Council of Lincoln adopted an ordinance granting the University of Nebraska Board of Regents full authority to establish parking regulations for that portion of the city comprising the campus. In August 1948, the regents accepted the report of the special committee which had studied the parking problem and adopted an extensive parking policy, requiring vehicle registration and parking permits.

During this decade, many Americans believed that a major national goal should be the elimination of racial segregation. Students at the University of Nebraska, in the years following the war, became increasingly critical of the practice of banning participation by black athletes in competition at certain universities within the Big Six. In November 1947, the University of Nebraska Student Council adopted a resolution, on a 17 to 5 vote, requesting the University administration to withdraw from the Big Six Conference unless the clause which prohibited a visiting team playing black athletes in segregated universities be revoked. The offensive conference rule stated:

In each institution of the conference the personnel of athletic squads shall be determined in accordance with the laws of the sovereign state, regulations imposed by said institution's governing body, and the rules and regulations of the conference, and the personnel of visiting squads shall be so selected as to conform with any restrictions imposed upon a host institution by the sovereign authority or the authorities that govern said host institution.[24]

The opposition of the Student Council to this rule was supported by similar action taken by the Corn Cobs, Tassels, and the campus YMCA. A survey taken by the *Daily Nebraskan* of 11 percent of the student body indicated that 89.6 percent of the students questioned believed that black athletes should be permitted to play in all conference competition. However, only 33.2 percent of the students canvassed believed that the University of Nebraska should withdraw from the conference if the discriminatory clause was not removed. Fifty-nine percent interviewed favored the reorganization of the conference to exclude those universities which practiced racial segregation.[25]

The Athletic Council chairman from the University of Oklahoma stated that he believed that the Student Council at the University of Nebraska had been "unfair." "Missouri and Oklahoma are the only schools that do not allow Negroes to play on their athletic teams, and that is something that is out of the hands of both schools' officials—since the states themselves enforce segregation laws."[26]

The University of Nebraska Student Council seized the initiative by calling a conference of student representatives from each university in the conference to discuss the matter of racial discrimination in athletics. The meeting was held at the University of Nebraska Student Union in November 1947. While this did not immediately end racial segregation in conference competition, it was a significant step in the movement to eliminate the injustice from the Mississippi Valley Inter-Collegiate Athletic Association.

There were some University personnel changes which particularly affected student life during the forties. One was the appointment of Marjorie W. Johnson as dean of women in September 1946. She replaced Vera Boyles. The retirement

23. *Daily Nebraskan*, May 8, 1948.
24. Ibid., November 20, 1947.
25. Ibid., November 23, 1947.
26. Lincoln, *Nebraska State Journal*, November 21, 1947, p. 12.

of Florence I. McGahey removed a long-familiar face from the registrar's office. The student health service was reorganized during the Gustavson administration, and Samuel I. Fuenning, M.D., was appointed director.

Awgwan, the University humor magazine, appeared briefly during this decade but was terminated in 1947 because of the lack of student interest and chronic financial losses. A far more successful student undertaking, the Student Foundation, was renamed the University of Nebraska Builders in 1949. The organization, founded in 1942, was a great success and provided real service to the University community. Its name was changed because of confusion between the student group and the University Foundation.

The interest of Chancellor Gustavson in the United Nations was shared by the students and faculty at the University of Nebraska. In 1949, a model UNESCO conference was held on the University campus. Theodore C. Sorensen, '49, was elected student moderator of the conference. He was also elected that spring as permanent chairman of the Constitutional Assembly which was convened to reconstruct student government. Janice Lindquist, '51, served as Constitutional Assembly secretary.

The dedication of the Mueller Carillon Tower, at the 1949 Homecoming, added a new tradition-inspiring symbol to the campus. It was the gift of Ralph S. Mueller, '98, a Cleveland, Ohio, electrical equipment manufacturer. At the time of the dedication, Mueller recalled his student days and remarked that he

took for granted all that was done for me, but in later years I came to realize that it was very generous of the taxpayers of Nebraska to give me my schooling free. I made up my mind that some day I was going to repay those generous taxpayers. Maybe tonight, I can consider the account at least partially balanced.[27]

This was not the first nor would it be the last time that the University of Nebraska would benefit from Ralph S. Mueller's generosity.

VARSITY ATHLETICS

With the advent of the 1940s, the University of Nebraska football program grew to great stature. Even though it was a short-lived glory, the team reached great heights with a Big Six championship and a Rose Bowl appearance in 1940. Then came the steady decline of wartime enrollment and confused, sometimes desperate efforts to recapture the success of previous days.

Few Nebraskans old enough to remember have ever forgotten the Rose Bowl team and a group of young men who captured the hearts of their fans. It would be more than twenty years before they would have anything similar to brag about. Biff Jones had taken a group of sophomores in 1938 and pointed them upward. By 1939 they were a Big Six contender, and in 1940 they were a superb football team ready to challenge the nation. Challenge they did, with men like Ray Prochaska, Bob Kahler, Eddie Schwartzkopf, Forrest Behm, Fred Preston, Warren Alfson, Bob Burruss, Roy Petsch, Harry Hopp, Herman Rohrig, Walter (Butch) Luther, Vike Francis, George (Bus) Knight, and many others, all but one native Nebraskans and proud of their heritage.

They opened against the best team in the nation, Bernie Bierman's Minnesota Gophers at Minneapolis, and almost pulled off the impossible before losing, 13–7. Minnesota rolled on to the national title, while Nebraska bounced back to defeat eight straight opponents, win the Big Six, finish seventh in the nation, and gain an invitation to Pasadena to meet the mighty Stanford Indians on New Year's Day.

27. *Nebraska Alumnus,* November 1949, p. 3.

That season Nebraska whipped Indiana 13–7; Kansas 53–2; Missouri 20–7, with revenge over Paul Christman; Oklahoma 13–0; Iowa 14–6; Pittsburgh 9–7, never before beaten by a Husker team twice in succession; Iowa State 21–12, after trailing 12–0 at halftime; and Kansas State 20–0.

Then came the Rose Bowl bid with classes dismissed, student parades, and the holiday trip to Pasadena. Nebraska acquitted itself in magnificent fashion in Pasadena. Husker fans who trekked west beamed with pride when Professor Donald Lentz's band set a Rose Bowl parade record for most minutes of continuous music while strutting in their new scarlet and cream uniforms. Meanwhile Major Jones and his boys from the Midlands were far from awed by Clark Shaugnessey and his fabulous T-formation whiz kids from Stanford. Nebraska rose to the challenge. The Cornhuskers opened the Rose Bowl classic by marching the length of the field to score, when Vike Francis thundered into the end zone. The Huskers had laughed at the T-formation trickery and thrown down the gauntlet of old-fashioned power. Stanford, however, was everything their admirers had claimed, quick, aggressive, and dangerous. Four times the stubborn Cornhuskers dug in and threw back Standler and Gallerneau inside the Nebraska two-yard line, one of college football's greatest goal-line stands of all times. However, Nebraska was deep in a hole and had to punt three plays later, setting up the most electrifying play of the game. Indian Pete Kmetovic fielded the punt at the Nebraska 43, reversed his field and ran all the way to score the clinching points.

Nebraska had lost the Rose Bowl, but had gained the undying love of her fans and the overwhelming admiration of the nation for a colorful and heroic performance. This inspirational performance in the Rose Bowl would sustain Nebraska fans throughout the dark days of World War II and the remaining years of the decade. Nebraska's football team had reached its zenith, and there would not be another winning season until 1950.

Biff Jones coached one more year, posting a 4–5–0 record with a club that lost several Rose Bowl stars to the military, and at the conclusion of the season the Japanese struck Pearl Harbor. Only the work, devotion, and determination of a handful of men, principally A. J. Lewandowski, enabled Nebraska to keep alive its tradition.

When Jones returned to military life at the start of the war, his backfield coach Glenn Presnell guided the 1942 team to a 3–7–0 mark. Then Lewandowski, who was to serve Nebraska in every possible way, as assistant football coach, head football coach, baseball coach, basketball coach, ticket manager, and athletic director, took over in 1943 and 1944. He recorded a 2–6–0 record both seasons, playing boys too young for military service or physically unable to pass draft examinations. However, Lew promoted his beloved Cornhuskers across the nation and kept them from being entirely forgotten.

In 1945 Nebraska sought out George "Potsy" Clark, a veteran coach and administrator, to be head coach and athletic director. He had a 4–5–0 record, recreated some enthusiasm, and hired former Husker star Bernie Masterson to coach the football team. Masterson had two stormy, faction-riddled seasons at the Husker helm, winning three games in 1946 and two in 1947. Coach Masterson was never able to overcome the confusion of the University athletic program, nor was he able to establish a winning relationship with players. In fairness to Masterson, his was not an easy task. Aside from wanting to win, Nebraska administrators were undecided on what course to take toward that end. Bernie's teams were loaded with war veterans, many with talent, but few willing to subject themselves to vigorous discipline and training after their recent military service. Masterson's contract was canceled after the 1947 season, and Potsy Clark reclaimed the coaching reins while searching for a permanent coach.

Clark's 1948 team did no better, winning only two of eight games. Only the presence of Tom Novak, who had earned All–Big Six honors in 1946 as fullback, and in 1947, as center, gave the fans much to cheer about.

Meanwhile the Athletic Board, torn by the public's demand for a successful football program and the University's refusal to make a total commitment in this direction, went on another search mission. They found the man they wanted at the University of New Hampshire, J. William Glassford, an All-America guard for Jock Sutherland at Pittsburgh in 1936. Glassford was to become one of the most controversial coaches in Nebraska history, but he was to supply some great moments, too. He was a man with charm, charisma, and brilliant coaching ability, but was to be eventually undone by his devotion to the doctrine espoused

Rose Bowl Float in 1941.

by Jock Sutherland in an earlier era and by Nebraska's reluctance to face completely the facts of post–World War II athletic life.

Glassford's foremost contribution to Nebraska football his first year was to bring quarterback Fran Nagle with him from New Hampshire. Nagle was a tall, spindle-legged passer who was to help make the Cornhuskers a Big Seven contender the next year. Along with Tom Novak, who earned All-American honors at center, and a number of Potsy Clark's holdovers, Glassford had a nucleus. He switched from the Single Wing to the Tight-T formation and launched a valiant attempt to bring the Huskers into modern times. The 1949 team managed only four victories, but Glassford's gang was fun to watch. This foundation, plus the fact that Bobby Reynolds was a freshman, made the Cornhusker hopes for the next decade bright indeed.

Cornhusker athletics in other sports fared better than in football during the 1940s. Coach Ed Weir's track teams won conference titles in 1940, 1941, and 1942 and featured such stars as Dean Kratz, Ralph King, Don Cooper, Harry Meginnis, Bobby Ginn, Bill Smutz, Gene (Red) Littler, Harold Hunt, Edsel Wibbels, and others.

Two postwar coaches, Harry Good and Tony Sharpe, arrived from Indiana to rejuvenate the basketball and baseball programs. Good put together a co-championship basketball team in 1948–49 and 1949–50, while Sharpe skippered the baseball team, led by Bob Cerv, to Big Seven excellence.

Basketball stars of the 1940s were led by the postwar contingent of Bus Whitehead, Claude Rutherford, Bob Cerv, Joe Malachek, Dick Srb, Tony Laury, and a number of others.

It was slow going, to be sure, but the 1940s saw Nebraska sink almost to oblivion, climb back up, and then start making athletic progress once again. Then the stormy 1950s descended on the Cornhusker scene.

In the decade of the forties, students at the University of Nebraska had enjoyed the twilight of peace, faced the challenge of a worldwide conflict, and returned to the ways of peace. These events wrought real and permanent changes to student life. Clearly, the enrollment of thousands of veterans was the most significant single factor in the changing campus scene. Student life, although in many ways similar to the past, was quite different at the end of the forties than it had been at the beginning. This was a reflection of the far-reaching changes affecting the nation and the world during the first years of the Atomic Age.

THE FIFTIES

CHAPTER 10

Administration at the Crossroads

UNIVERSITY ADMINISTRATION during the decade of the fifties was challenged by developments and forces emanating from both the national scene and from within the state. During the preceding decade, the major administrative problem was the readjustment to peace and the accompanying boom in enrollment. This involved, oftentimes, questions of quantity more than quality. During the fifties, Gustavson's goal for the University of Nebraska, as it was at most other colleges and universities, was to raise the educational quality of the institution. It became increasingly evident to leaders in American higher education that universities would be called upon to provide increased research and assistance in the solution of national problems. This awareness was also shared by political leaders at the state and national levels.

The desire of universities to improve the quality and research capability of their faculties created a condition of extreme faculty mobility. The supply of talented teachers and dedicated scholars was insufficient to meet the needs of all institutions of higher education. The administration of the University of Nebraska, like all others, faced the problem of acquiring and retaining a quality faculty during a time of intense competition for staff. The retirement of major faculty members during this decade at the University of Nebraska made necessary the search for, and appointment of, young productive scholars and teachers to the faculty. The future of the University of Nebraska largely depended on the ability of the administration to retain the services of its best faculty members as well as to attract a young, promising faculty. Gustavson knew that a university with quality only in its senior faculty had no prospect for the future; whereas one with quality and promise at the assistant and associate professor levels might insure a bright future. The need to maintain and improve the quality of the faculty at the University of Nebraska required more substantial financial support from the state than ever before.

The continuation of the special state institutional mill levy, adopted during the previous decade, was to remain an additional major issue. The inadequacy of University facilities was dramatized by the conditions at the College of Medicine, which nearly resulted in its loss of accreditation. The University of Nebraska was at the crossroads. The low road would lead to the institution being merely a good undergraduate college with a university name, operating somewhere in the eddy currents of American higher education. The high road might well lead the University of Nebraska into the mainstream of American higher education. The University was able, with little to spare, to join the mainstream. Despite the financial problems the faculty, the regents, and the three chancellors of the fifties were able to maintain a steady rate of improvement.

Among the destructive forces operating within American society during the fifties, few matched the effect of McCarthyism on higher education. The issue of national loyalty and academic freedom became an issue on most university campuses, including the University of Nebraska.

This decade also differed from the preceding one in the absence of the extreme enrollment pressures of the postwar years. Although there was an overall enrollment increase in the decade, it was not uniform. However, it was anticipated. The crisis atmosphere following World War II was fortunately absent. September collegiate enrollments for the decade were:

1950	8,031
1951	6,941
1952	6,684
1953	6,770
1954	7,197
1955	7,845
1956	8,425
1957	8,134
1958	8,356
1959	8,411

A CALL TO ACTION

During the opening years of the decade, Chancellor Gustavson clearly articulated his goal for the University. In December 1951, he told the faculty that his administration of the University was guided by four main objectives in a major address reported in the *Daily Nebraskan*, December 21, 1951. The first was that education should teach young people their place in history. For example, "students of agriculture must be taught, not only the skills of agriculture, but also the background of history which will illustrate the value of conserving soil for future generations." Second, education must teach students the value and meaning of freedom. Third, education must allow investigators the freedom to search for truth. This quest must be permitted even though "at times we may find that truth is inconvenient for us to search for or explain." Finally, Gustavson emphasized that this search for truth should be characterized by liberalism. He defined this liberalism as "not a political creed, but a disposition of character. It is the kind of thinking which encourages a restless inquiry into the nature of things about us; which regards very little as absolutely certain; which does not fear witnessing all of the evidence; which scrupulously depends on persuasive reasoning rather than suppression and fear." Any university which could meet these standards would be a leader among the universities of the world. Its graduates would be those who would be guided by reason, discussion, and intellect rather than tradition, fear, and emotion.

To the faculty, Chancellor Gustavson's ideas were an appeal for dedicated and inspirational teaching and productive scholarship. For the Board of Regents, it was a goal worthy of support, but for many legislators and to many citizens, it was another call for increased funds. In their request for the 1951–53 biennium, the regents asked for a $5,300,000 increase in state funds from $8 million to $13.5 million. The regents justified the increase as necessary to adjust salaries for inflation, to pay competitive salaries for new staff, and to strengthen the University's teaching, research, and public service programs. Governor Val Peterson replied to the regents that their request "jars everyone's eye teeth."[1] James Leroy Welsh, president of the Board of Regents, thought that the proper legislative and civic approach to the regents' request should be "not of how little we might spend, but how much we might spend."[2] However, the regents responded to

1. Omaha *World-Herald*, December 19, 1950, p. 1.
2. Ibid.

Governor Peterson's request that they reconsider the University budget request in light of the national emergency resulting from American involvement in Korea. The regents reduced their request by one million dollars to $12.5 million. The Unicameral followed the advice of its Budget Committee by appropriating $12.5 million from state taxes. This was a part of the total University of Nebraska budget of nearly $28 million. This amount included federal support, student fees, endowments, and grants. It must be remembered that during all of these years the budget was voted for two years at a time.

Senator Arthur Carmody, of Trenton, chairman of the Legislative Budget Committee, explained why the group had exceeded the governor's recommendation. "I think the people realize that if they want a better university—and apparently they do—it's going to cost more money."[3] The University of Nebraska had received a significant increase in state support. This resulted from a growing public awareness of, and support for, the University and its work. The activity of the Nebraska State Medical Association in calling public attention to the deficiencies at the University of Nebraska College of Medicine produced widespread public concern regarding the University. At first the Medical Association supported a separate appropriation for the Medical College, but later in the legislative session, the association supported the entire University budget, of which the College of Medicine's budget was a part.

The issue of the 1953–55 budget request was whether progress could be continued. The Board of Regents requested a $3.9 million increase in state tax support for the University. The requested increase would require an increase in state property tax revenues of $1.45 per person annually. This money was needed to adjust salaries of University nonacademic personnel and to meet the rising cost of maintenance and supplies. Forty percent of the increase would be used to meet the spiraling costs of operating the Colleges of Medicine and Agriculture.

Out-going Governor Val Peterson described the increase in budget requests from state institutions as a result of the "drunken inflationary spree in which we have been engaged."[4] The governor further believed that the University of Nebraska had expanded into too many academic areas. "He suggested that the college of liberal arts should come first, the agricultural college second and from there such colleges 'as the state can afford' with elimination if necessary of what he termed 'fringe' colleges and schools."[5] Despite this statement, Governor Peterson recommended an increase of $2 million in state tax support for the University. The incoming governor, Robert B. Crosby, concurred in the recommendation. Ultimately a University of Nebraska budget was adopted that provided for $15 million in state tax support. The total budget was nearly $36 million. The adoption of a special one-quarter mill levy to produce up to $6 million over a period of years for construction and modernization at the College of Medicine was a further indication of legislative willingness to support the University. However, it must be remembered that the College of Medicine was close to losing its accreditation, and the impending crisis was well advertised by the Nebraska State Medical Association. Nevertheless, the special property tax levy was a vital step forward in the improvement of University excellence in medicine.

THE UNIVERSITY OF NEBRASKA FOUNDATION

During the fifties, the University of Nebraska Foundation became a major contributor in the support of the University. The foundation had been established

3. Ibid., March 20, 1951, p. 1.
4. Lincoln *Star*, October 15, 1952, p. 6.
5. Ibid., December 16, 1952, p. 1.

under the direction of Chancellor Edgar A. Burnett during the dark days of the depression and was practically dormant for a decade. With the appointment of Perry W. Branch, '20, as director-secretary of the University of Nebraska Foundation in 1943, a new era of progress began.

The class agent program inaugurated in 1948 was an outstanding success, and foundation assets began a rapid growth. The idea of the program was to use the spirit of competition between graduating classes as the basis for making donations to the foundation. Classes were compared on the number of contributors in relation to the total number of the classes' living graduates whose addresses were known. For ten years, the general chairman of class agents for the campaign was Joe W. Seacrest of Lincoln. At the time of the beginning of the drives in 1948, foundation assets were slightly over half a million dollars; by the end of the fifties the assets exceeded $2.5 million. By 1960 the University of Nebraska Foundation was able to fulfill the expectation of Chancellor Burnett and its incorporators. They had said, "The legislature will provide the necessities, but the Foundation will aim to provide those additional things that will make the University a truly great institution."[6] Between 1948 and 1958, the foundation contributed nearly two million dollars to the University. The funds were used for financial aid of students, to support research projects, and to purchase specialized research instruments and equipment. In his quest for improving the quality of the University, Chancellor Gustavson praised the contributions of the foundation. "In thinking about the future . . . it seems to me that one of our greatest needs is for free and flexible funds. I have been trying to stimulate a research program in the University to [a] greater degree of intensity, and I think with the help of the Foundation I have been successful."[7] This recognition of the foundation's contribution to the improvement of the University of Nebraska has been shared by the faculty, administration, and students of the University.

McCARTHYISM

During the fifties, several American university campuses became the object of searches for all forms of real and imagined disloyalty. Recognizing the political notoriety obtained by the Senator from Wisconsin, many joined the hunt for subversives. For the politically ambitious, the issue of real or imagined subversion appeared as the way to instant public recognition. In many states real havoc was wrought with public institutions and private reputations in the name of patriotism.

In December 1952, a prominent member of American Legion Post No. 1 in Omaha charged that a "certain professor" was using a book in his classes which was partially authored by a person accused of disloyalty. The professor of the history class was not accused by the legionnaire of personal disloyalty. However, his wisdom in selecting instructional materials for the course was questioned.

Within days the Student Council adopted a resolution expressing its confidence in the integrity and loyalty of the teacher involved. The University of Nebraska chapter of the American Association of University Professors recognized the legionnaire's charge as an invitation to full-blown McCarthyism in Nebraska. A resolution was adopted by the AAUP opposing such a course of action.

The American Association of University Professors as a professional body denies the validity of witch-hunts and trials by press, innuendo, pressure groups, or agencies outside the properly constituted legal authorities charged with enforcing the high pro-

6. *Nebraska Alumnus,* December 1958, p. 9.

7. Letter from R. G. Gustavson to Perry Branch, February 4, 1952, MSS, University of Nebraska Archives, Gustavson Collection.

fessional requirements of the privilege of academic freedom and tenure. It also opposes condemnation before charges are proved and adheres to the principle that every teacher because of his oath of office and his professional background is loyal and competent until proven otherwise.[8]

However, this action by a faculty group could only have limited impact on public opinion. Of much greater influence would be the action taken by the leadership of the Nebraska Department of the American Legion. Would the legion lead a witch hunt? An executive committee meeting of the Nebraska legion was scheduled for early February in Grand Island. Surely, the loyalty issue would be raised. In February 1953, Earle W. Wiltse, superintendent of schools at Grand Island and chairman of the legion's state education committee, wrote to Professor Royce H. Knapp of the Teachers College faculty for assistance in developing a program of positive action for the legion, stating in the letter, "please prepare a definite proposal for me to present to the Executive Committee of the American Legion when the group meets in Grand Island."[9] Both Knapp and Wiltse were prominent members of the American Legion. Professor Knapp wrote the following resolution which was edited and introduced by Superintendent Wiltse and approved by the executive committee of the Nebraska Department of the American Legion.

BE IT RESOLVED, by the Department Executive Committee of The American Legion, Department of Nebraska, in regular session convened this 9th day of March, 1953:

1. That the Nebraska Department of the American Legion reaffirms its faith in the effectiveness of the citizenship education carried on in Nebraska's schools, colleges and universities. We believe that training future citizens is one of the major responsibilities of all educational institutions. The Legion commends the educational leadership of Nebraska for the steady and continuing work in the schools and colleges which instills basic loyalties to American ideals by presenting challenging study of the Declaration of Independence and our state and national constitutions, by teaching American history and literature, by teaching our national anthem, by commemorating the lives of our national heroes, by recognizing our national holidays, by presenting the problems and issues of our state and nation by open discussion, and by sponsoring activities that foster individual responsibility, leadership and good sportsmanship.

2. That we condemn the authors of subversive attacks upon the schools, whether they be dissident individuals or groups in the local communities, or inspired by evil forces, financed, directed and operated by agents of subversion against our nation and the American way of life.

3. That we call upon every member of The American Legion to be on the alert in his community to know the schools, and to recognize these attacks when they occur, and to stand ready to support and defend against all enemies.

4. That we do hereby thank the members of the teaching professions and their organizations for the great assistance rendered to the Americanism program of The American Legion.

5. That the Nebraska Department of The American Legion commends the school boards, trustees and regents of our educational system in Nebraska for their careful selection of teachers, faculties, and administrators who are loyal to American premises of liberty. The Legion reaffirms its faith in the academic freedom necessary for stimulating and challenging teaching and research, but emphasizes that such freedom does not constitute license nor does it extend to the privilege of teaching precepts inimical to our American system in our Nebraska schools. The Legion commends those educational institutions which are doing their best, by realistic American teaching, to reveal the truth about communism, socialism, and other undemocratic systems.[10]

8. *Daily Nebraskan,* December 15, 1952.

9. Letter from Earle W. Wiltse to Royce H. Knapp, February 9, 1953, MSS, Knapp Papers.

10. *Daily Nebraskan,* March 11, 1953.

In addition to this reasoned statement, the Nebraska Department of the American Legion funded the establishment of a scholarship for a graduate student to study new programs in citizenship education at the University of Nebraska under the direction of Professor Knapp. Under Knapp's direction, a graduate student in secondary education, Ralph Kellogg, a Korean War veteran, and a group of educational leaders in Nebraska published a manual on citizenship and suggested ideas for schools in *Citizenship Education in Secondary Schools* which the legion published and gave free to all Nebraska schools. Thirteen months after the legionnaire's complaint about a text used in a University class, the legion department adjutant, R. C. Patterson, wrote the chancellor.

As the executive head of the University of Nebraska, you should know that this aid to citizenship education in Nebraska schools would not have been possible had it not been for some outstanding cooperation from Dr. Royce H. Knapp and others at the Teachers College. All credit for the excellence of the published material goes to them. The only part the Legion played was to finance the publishing of the manual and paying a small amount for research expense. . . .

The American Legion appreciates the fact that we can depend on our good friends at the University of Nebraska for cooperation in matters such as this. We are grateful to them and to the University.[11]

The support and confidence given the University of Nebraska by the American Legion was not the usual pattern of legion activity in other states during the McCarthy Era. The publication of the citizenship booklet, combined with the outstanding program of Boy's State by the American Legion, Department of Nebraska, earned the George Washington Honor Medal of the Valley Forge Freedom Foundation. Although some rumors were circulated concerning imagined disloyalty at the University, they were not generally believed. Ruben G. Gustavson recalled a personal event from the early fifties:

Terry Carpenter tried hard to make trouble for me by spreading the rumor that I was a communist. But, good friends in Boulder, at the University of Colorado, and friends in Denver squelched that. He would appear on the radio at North Platte and a stooge would ask him, "Do you really think that Chancellor Gustavson of the University of Nebraska is a communist?" and he would answer, "No, I don't think the Chancellor is a communist, but I can't understand why this rumor keeps on coming up." You see there is no way to get at him for defamation of character because he defended me. What a character![12]

What is remembered with good humor after the passage of nearly twenty years was not considered amusing during the early fifties. In relationship to the difficulties experienced by many institutions of higher education during this era, the University of Nebraska was spared the injustices conducted in the name of patriotism. This was possible, in large part, because the leadership of the Nebraska Department of the American Legion maintained an open-minded position characteristic of true Americanism. They were not swayed by rumor, unsubstantiated charges, a desire to squelch academic freedom, or the temptation to use the issue for publicity. The Nebraska legion actually strengthened programs of Americanism and citizenship education in Nebraska schools and colleges.

THE END OF THE GUSTAVSON ADMINISTRATION

In May 1953, Reuben G. Gustavson announced that he would resign as chancellor of the University of Nebraska to accept the presidency of Resources

11. Letter from R. C. Patterson to John K. Selleck, January 7, 1954, MSS, University of Nebraska Archives, Selleck Collection.
12. Letter from R. G. Gustavson to R. McLaran Sawyer, May 28, 1970, Sawyer Papers.

for the Future, Inc. This organization was founded in 1952 by the Ford Foundation to develop a program and to work in the field of resource development and conservation. On May 16, 1953, the Board of Regents of the University of Nebraska accepted Gustavson's resignation. At his last meeting with the board, Gustavson was presented a letter of recognition by the regents.

All of us have appreciated the candor and integrity which have distinguished the relationship between us and you. This has led to a practice of open and frank discussion in arriving at decisions vitally affecting the character and strength of our University. This has yielded mutual trust and confidence.

Those of us who now take great pride in our part in bringing you to Nebraska recall with deep satisfaction the way in which you met the complex problems which resulted from the influx of World War II veterans on our campus. All of us have been pleased to join with you in a long-range program which is putting our physical plant, our staff, our teaching, our research and service programs on a sound and enduring basis. We want you to know that we are aware that many of the foundation blocks upon which these programs are being built have originated with you.

We have been especially pleased with your continuing efforts, which would have wasted the spirit and strength of ordinary men, to establish a close liaison between our University and the people of Nebraska. We recognize the great service which you have rendered in helping Nebraskans understand the true meaning of a great university—its purposes, its ambitions, its dreams, its morality and its integrity. Surely we have no better gauge of your effectiveness in this endeavor than its remarkable acceptance in our State Legislature. Never has our University been so cordially received, nor so fairly treated, by our lawmakers than in these past seven years.

Finally, we should like to say that we have at all times admired and respected you for your fidelity to the dictates of your own conscience. We recognize you as a man of high principle, complete integrity, courage, deep understanding, humble and warm of heart.[13]

In further recognition of his outstanding service to the University of Nebraska, Reuben G. Gustavson was awarded the honorary Doctor of Humanities degree. The only other former chancellors to receive honorary degrees from the University of Nebraska were Irving J. Mannat and Samuel Avery. E. Benjamin Andrews had been awarded an honorary degree in 1884, sixteen years before becoming chancellor.

The Gustavson administration provided strong leadership. The role of the faculty was strengthened by the reorganization of the committee system. From 1947 to 1952, Carl W. Borgmann was dean of the faculties and contributed substantially to the chancellor's success. University policy was, in the opinion of many faculty members, shaped by a triumvirate composed of Chancellor Gustavson, Dean of Faculties Borgmann, and Graduate Dean Goss. Some faculty wags referred to the triumvirate as "Father, Son and Holy Goss." After Dean Borgmann's acceptance of the presidency of the University of Vermont, Bruce H. Nicoll, assistant director of public relations, was named administrative assistant to the chancellor.

Only in the last months of the Gustavson administration was there any indication that the chancellor might have lost any faculty support. In the critical dispute between the faculties of the Teachers College and the Graduate College, the chancellor opposed the refusal of the Graduate College faculty to approve the establishment of the Doctor of Education degree. In taking the matter to the Board of Regents and ingnoring the wishes of the Graduate faculty, Chancellor Gustavson alienated many senior faculty members. He recognized the seriousness

13. Letter from C. Y. Thompson, J. L. Welsh, E. G. Johnson, J. G. Elliott, and B. N. Greenberg to R. G. Gustavson, June 27, 1953, MSS, University of Nebraska Archives, Gustavson Collection.

of faculty discord and could not have failed to realize the problems for future faculty leadership. After his resignation, Chancellor Gustavson wrote Regent Thompson,

I am somewhat concerned about the split that has taken place in the faculty which I regret more than I can say. Of course the split between the Arts College [who dominated the Graduate College] and the Teachers College has been there for years, but it has come to a head. I sincerely hope that it will disappear.[14]

As an educational leader and internationally recognized scientist, Chancellor Gustavson contributed greatly to the growth of the University of Nebraska, in

Chancellor Gustavson in touch with Nebraska agriculture.

both size and excellence. He was prominent in the movement to reform college athletics, served as a member of the Board of Visitors to the United States Naval Academy, and was president of the National Commission on Accrediting. This organization was established during the fifties by the Association of American Colleges, the Association of Land-Grant Colleges and Universities, the National Association of State Universities, the Association of American Universities, the Association of Urban Universities, the American Association of Junior Colleges, and the Association of Teacher Education Institutions to bring order

14. Letter from R. G. Gustavson to C. Y. Thompson, July 21, 1953, MSS, University of Nebraska Archives, Gustavson Collection.

out of chaos in accreditation. Under Gustavson's leadership the national commission convinced rival accrediting groups to merge or form councils which worked with the long-established six regional accrediting associations. This made possible general institutional evaluation by both regional and professional groups in a single visit. The selection of Chancellor Gustavson for this important task brought credit to both him and the University of Nebraska.

As a citizen of Nebraska, the nation, and the world, Reuben G. Gustavson contributed substantially to the well-being of his fellow man. He was general chairman of the Abraham Lincoln Friendship Train which collected boxcars of grain for starving Europeans. As state campaign chairman, he organized the 1948 Nebraska "March of Dimes." At the second session of the General Conference of the United Nations Educational Scientific and Cultural Organization (UNESCO), held at Mexico City in 1947, Chancellor Gustavson of the University of Nebraska was a voting member of the delegation from the United States of America. Because of his interest in problems of public health, he was appointed a member of the National Advisory Health Council of the United States Public Health Service. Few men could match the service of Reuben G. Gustavson to the state and nation, to higher education, and in the quest for world understanding.

THE CHANCELLORSHIP OF JOHN K. SELLECK

On June 8, 1953, the University of Nebraska Board of Regents appointed John K. Selleck acting chancellor. A native of Lincoln, he received a Bachelor of Science degree in electrical engineering from the University in 1912. After employment with the Illuminating Electric Company in Chicago and service during World War I, he joined the University staff as assistant purchasing agent in 1921. Selleck was appointed business manager for the Department of Intercollegiate Athletics in 1923. Chancellor Boucher named him University comptroller in 1941, and Chancellor Gustavson added the responsibilities of general business manager of the University in 1948. Selleck was also secretary of the University Corporation. On assuming the new assignment as acting chancellor, Selleck said:

My service to the University has always been on the business side of the institution and I am especially pleased, therefore, that I should receive this expression of confidence from our academic staff.

I am sure that I express the sentiments of all of us at the University when I say that I hope that within a very short time an educational leader will be found who can be named Chancellor.[15]

However, the selection of a new chancellor was not made until May 1954. From May to July 1954, after the selection of a permanent chancellor and before his assumption of the office, the Board of Regents appointed John K. Selleck chancellor.

During the brief period of his administration, Chancellor Selleck faced two serious problems, the dispute between the faculties of the Teachers College and the Graduate College and a growing public dissatisfaction with Nebraska intercollegiate athletics. Regent George Liggett thought that the solution of these problems was of major importance in seeking a new chancellor for the University of Nebraska.

What I have in mind is that it appears to me that it would be very wise to go very slow with the [selection of] the new Chancellor. I suspect that any man who is fairly well

15. Omaha *World-Herald,* June 9, 1953, p. 1.

situated is not going to want to come to Nebraska and take over that athletic mess and the fight between the Teachers College and Graduate College.[16]

Statewide dissatisfaction with University of Nebraska athletics resulted from the losses of Husker football teams and from football players' complaints against Coach Glassford. Although many had approved of Chancellor Gustavson's policies toward intercollegiate athletics, Nebraskans yearned for the return of winning football teams. In January 1954, the University of Nebraska Board of Regents began a study of its athletic policies ultimately leading to the abolition of the Board of Intercollegiate Athletics. The athletic director was made directly responsible to the chancellor and the Board of Regents.

John K. Selleck.

During the administration of Acting Chancellor Selleck, the Board of Regents remained firm in their decision to authorize the Teachers College to offer the Doctor of Education degree. Hoping that an acting chancellor might waver on a policy adopted at the end of the Gustavson administration, a group of faculty members attempted to force a reconsideration of the board's policy. In this they failed.

Of major academic importance during the Selleck administration was a clear policy on academic freedom adopted by the Board of Regents. The statement resulted from the widespread controversy concerning the writings and speeches of Professor C. Clyde Mitchell, chairman of the Department of Agricultural Economics. At this time, there was considerable discussion regarding national farm policies, with much disagreement over the desirability of governmental control and national planning. The views of Mitchell were praised by some farm

16. Letter from George Liggett to C. Y. Thompson, February 12, 1954, MSS, University of Nebraska Archives, Hardin Collection.

groups, but strongly opposed by the conservative farm organizations, grain dealers, and most of the business community.

Despite the controversy in which the Board of Regents found itself involved, and despite the personal opposition of some regents to the professor's views, a firm position on academic freedom was adopted. In November 1953, the regents unanimously adopted a resolution introduced by Regent Greenberg defining its policy.

"BE IT RESOLVED by the Board of Regents that the following statement shall be a statement of the official position of the Board of Regents with respect to the rights and privileges of its faculty members."·

Statement of Principles

The foundation of America's strength is diversity. For the diversity of our physical resources under, on and above our varied lands our gratitude belongs to the Almighty. For the diversity of our people and their ideas, beliefs, and thoughts, our thanks belong to the founders of this nation who, by the grace of God, were granted the foresight to appreciate the potential advances that would come from free associations, free exploration, and free expression limited only by responsibility for our general welfare.

Under the philosophy upon which this nation was founded, a great educational system has developed and flourished. At its apex is the realm of higher education where the responsibility for furthering the routes of truth and knowledge rests more heavily than in any other area of the educational system. In the realm of higher education the American right to question, to explore, to express, to examine and re-examine, is of necessity exercised continually. Were it not so, our diverse intellectual resources would become stagnant.

The men and women selected by this University, as a part of the structure of higher education, are chosen for their proficiency, their expertness, in various fields. By virtue of their training and scholarly endowments they must be assured of and are expected to understand both the rights and responsibilities of their positions, including these:

1. The full right to speak as a citizen.
2. The responsibilities of citizenship.
3. The right, as a professional person, to freedom in research and to publication of the results thereof, limited only by the precepts of scholarship and faithful performance of other academic responsibilities.
4. The right, as a professional person, to free and thorough expression in the classroom.

The right to uphold, to discuss and dissent are the moral fiber of America's greatness. They are likewise the strength of a great University.[17]

The unanimity of the Board of Regents is especially significant in spite of the extreme opposition of one regent to the policies advocated by Professor Mitchell.

Despite this policy statement, however, Mitchell was removed as chairman of the Department of Agricultural Economics. He was granted a leave of absence, without salary, and later resigned rather than return to the University of Nebraska. Professor Mitchell's charge that his academic freedom had been abridged by the University administration was investigated by the University Senate Committee on Academic Privilege. The committee reported, in 1957, that in certain respects of the dispute, Professor Mitchell was subjected to administrative pressures which violated his academic freedom.

With the arrival on campus of the new chancellor, the administration of John K. Selleck ended. He had faithfully performed the duties of an acting chancellor. Although the problems of the athletic program and that of the relationship between the Teachers College and the Graduate College remained, action had been taken which eventually led to their solution. Furthermore, the

---

17. *Minutes,* University of Nebraska Board of Regents, November 21, 1953.

policy on academic freedom adopted by the Board of Regents was an important commitment for the future.

In April 1957, John K. Selleck retired from the University of Nebraska. In recognition of his thirty-six years of service, he was awarded the honorary degree of Doctor of Laws. An alumnus wrote of John K. Selleck, "I sincerely believe that there is something great about an institution to which a man will give his life and in turn there is something great about a man who will give his life to an institution."[18]

THE SEARCH FOR A CHANCELLOR

The search for a permanent chancellor to replace Gustavson was a long and difficult process. It raised questions involving freedom of the press and, on one occasion, assumed a certain comic opera quality. When the Board of Regents accepted Gustavson's resignation they invited the faculty to form a committee to suggest names for the positions of acting chancellor and permanent chancellor. However, before a faculty committee could be assembled, a rumor circulated on the campus and in the press that a member of the Board of Regents would attempt to have Dean of Admissions George W. Rosenlof, who had devoted years of dedicated service to the University, immediately appointed as chancellor. Thereupon, a faculty petition containing nearly four hundred names was sent to the board protesting the appointment of Rosenlof or any other person without consultation with the faculty. Consequently, the Rosenlof appointment was not considered officially by the Board of Regents.

By late May, the faculty Liaison and Policy Committees submitted the names of five faculty members to the Board of Regents to advise them on the selection of a chancellor. The regents approved the list and appointed a committed composed of Marvel L. Baker, associate director of the Agricultural Experiment Stations; Niles H. Barnard, chairman and professor in the Department of Mechanical Engineering; Miguel A. Basoco, chairman and professor in the Department of Mathematics; Clifford M. Hicks, chairman and professor in the Department of Business Organization and Management; and Dean A. Worcester, chairman and professor in the Department of Educational Psychology and Measurements. The faculty committee was charged to receive names from the faculty and others and to report to the Board of Regents those whom the group considered qualified for the chancellorship. The committee was also asked to make recommendations for an interim chancellor, but none of the names it recommended for the acting chancellorship was appointed.

On May 29, 1953, the faculty committee reported to the regents "that the faculty has no candidate from its own ranks. The Committee has agreed that it will make no recommendation on any present staff member of the University, except as it may be specifically requested by the Board of Regents."[19] During the ensuing months, the committee reviewed the qualifications of nearly one hundred educators recommended to them for the chancellorship. Fourteen candidates were recommended by the committee to the Board of Regents for their consideration.

In early 1954, the Board of Regents began a series of discussions with those recommended by the Committee for the Chancellorship. Although the regents requested that the names of those being interviewed not be reported in the

18. Letter Eldon Park to John K. Selleck, June 6, 1954, University of Nebraska Archives, Selleck Collection.
19. Letter Faculty Committee to James L. Welsh, May 29, 1953, University of Nebraska Archives, Selleck Collection.

press, the appeal was not honored by the *Lincoln Journal*. The Board of Regents did not make this request to hide their activities from the public, but rather to protect those being considered for the chancellorship from premature publicity. At a meeting of the board, on February 21, 1954, the Board of Regents explained their position.

It is the considered opinion of the Board of Regents that the best interests of the University of Nebraska are not and will not be served by announcing at the time of preliminary discussions the names of men under consideration for the chancellorship.

The Board, therefore, will not authorize any further release of such names until, in its opinion, such release will not be against the best interests of the University.

This decision was reached with full appreciation of the public character of the Board of Regents and in no way alters the Board's own belief that its final actions are matters of public record, deserving the widest possible dissemination by the press, radio, and television.

The decision was deemed necessary to settle a question raised by the Lincoln Journal. The basic question was, Does the responsibility the Board of Regents has to keep the public informed of its actions, both preliminary and final, outweigh the Board's right to solve problems in a manner it deems in the best interests of the University?

The Lincoln Journal raised this question when it refused to abide by a request for anonymity the Board made on behalf of one of the men invited to Nebraska for preliminary talks about the chancellorship. . . .

Applied to the current problem of selecting a chancellor for the University of Nebraska, the Lincoln Journal contention would demand immediate release of the names of all persons the Board plans to consult before reaching a decision.

Such a general announcement, the Board has ample reason to believe, would cause some men whose names are on the list to withdraw from consideration. All of the men on the list hold responsible positions and several of them have already said announcement of their names during the preliminary talks is embarrassing.

None of these men is actively seeking the chancellorship. They are educational leaders who have been recommended for consideration by a special faculty committee of the University. The Board feels that common courtesy, orderly procedure, and the best interests of the University would be abused by refusal to respect their wishes for anonymity during the preliminary phases of a search for a chancellor. Because of this feeling, the Board cannot agree with the philosophy advanced by the Lincoln Journal which would establish as the first prerequisite for the University's chancellor a willingness to have his name made public during the period of prelminary talks. The Board cannot accept such a requirement as having a bearing on any man's ability for the chancellorship. It does not believe the people of Nebraska wish to establish such a requirement. Such a requirement would serve no purpose other than to limit the Board's consideration to those men who have no objection to publicity, regardless of embarrassment to them, during the preliminary phases of a search for a chancellor.

It is the opinion of the Board that its first duty is to perform as it deems best the task for which it was elected; namely, to serve the best interests of the University within the framework provided by Nebraska law. It is also the opinion of the Board that by virtue of its election it is the agency which has the responsibility for determining what is in the best interests of the University if an orderly process of University government is to be maintained.[20]

To respect the requests of those being considered for the chancellorship from premature publicity, the regents decided to conduct future discussions with prospective candidates for the chancellorship outside the state. At this point, the selection process took on some qualities of a comic opera. The press discovered that the regents were to meet with nine candidates for the chancellorship in Chicago. The meetings were held at the Conrad Hilton Hotel on March 19–21, 1954. Chancelor Selleck and the regents attempted to escape the surveillance of

20. *Minutes,* University of Nebraska Board of Regents, February 21, 1954.

the reporters who had followed them to Chicago. The attempts in the elevators and halls of the hotel to avoid the press were unsuccessful. One candidate for the chancellorship, John W. Ashton, vice president of the University of Indiana, asked that his name be withdrawn from consideration because of the publicity. Chancellor Selleck commented:

We were, of course, disappointed to learn that the Lincoln Journal would publish from key-hole sources an account of a part of the discussion with Dr. Ashton. The Journal has caused a very fine man and highly qualified educator to decide he has no interest in heading the University of Nebraska.[21]

Among those who met with the Board of Regents in Chicago was Clifford M. Hardin, dean of the School of Agriculture at Michigan State College. He became the regents' choice for chancellor and visited the campus in early April 1954. However, on April 19, 1954, he wrote Chancellor Selleck,

I can assure you that deciding to remain in East Lansing was the most difficult decision that Mrs. Hardin and I have ever made. The fact that we enjoy our present work so much and combined with the fact that I have so recently assumed my present responsibilities contributed strongly to our decision.[22]

When Hardin's decision was announced to the Board of Regents, it was decided to ask him to reconsider his refusal. After further discussion with the regents, Hardin reversed his earlier decision. On May 7, 1954, the University of Nebraska Board of Regents appointed Clifford Morris Hardin to be the new chancellor of the University of Nebraska.

Clifford Morris Hardin was born on a farm near Knightstown, Indiana, on October 9, 1915. His appointment as chancellor of the University of Nebraska at thirty-eight years of age made him the youngest chancellor in the history of the University and one of the youngest university heads in the nation. He received his education at Purdue University, where he earned the bachelor's degree in 1937, the master's degree in 1939, and the Doctor of Philosophy degree in 1941.

Hardin had launched his professional career as an extension marketing specialist and instructor in agricultural economics at the University of Wisconsin. In 1944, he joined the faculty of Michigan State College at East Lansing, where he became professor and chairman of the Department of Agricultural Economics. In 1948, he was named assistant director of Michigan State's Agricultural Experiment Station, and was appointed director the following year. He became dean of the School of Agriculture in 1953. As an agricultural economist, he was well known for his publications and membership in professional and honorary societies.

Within a short time after his appointment as chancellor, he explained his philosophy of higher education. For a university to fully meet its obligation to society, he explained, it "must have good teachers. I am mentioning teaching as the number one qualification because I believe that it is the heart and soul of a university."[23] Instruction of this quality also required a dedication to research. "It is the well-spring from which new knowledge is born. It gives bloom to our teaching and substance to our total program. I want . . . the University of Nebraska to be a center for research."[24] For those who shared these goals, Chancellor Hardin promised a stimulating atmosphere. "A great university is a

21. Omaha *World-Herald*, March 24, 1954, p. 4.
22. Letter Clifford M. Hardin to John K. Selleck, April 19, 1945, MSS, University of Nebraska Archives, C. Y. Thompson Collection.
23. *Nebraska Alumnus*, June 1954, p. 17.
24. Ibid.

Clifford Morris Hardin.

sounding board for the many voices of free but thoughtful people. It is kindly. It has character and integrity. It respects convention but does not worship it. A great university is optimistic and unafraid."[25]

THE CHALLENGE OF THE LATE FIFTIES

For the University of Nebraska to aspire to the level sought by the chancellor, several serious problems affecting the University had to be solved. A most serious one involved the loss of faculty to other colleges and universities. Higher education enrollments were rapidly increasing across the nation and competition for a high-quality faculty was intense. Chancellor Hardin recognized the need for higher faculty salaries and made this a major administrative goal for the fifties. Faculty losses were substantial. Between 1952 and 1959, some University departments suffered a faculty turnover as high as 45 percent. In 1959, Chancellor Hardin reported that 145 faculty members had resigned within a period of two years and that "money was the most common reason for the resignation."[26]

Another major concern was the continuance of the program of campus construction begun in 1946 and financed by a ten-year special state property tax mill levy. The need for adequate facilities was of special importance because of the anticipated enrollment boom of the sixties. Chancellor Hardin warned, "In education, as in other endeavors, there is a point of saturation . . . a point at which more students cannot be properly served, more research cannot be properly undertaken, and more services properly added without an upward adjustment in revenue."[27]

25. Ibid.
26. *Daily Nebraskan,* June 11, 1959.
27. Ibid., September 26, 1956.

Throughout its history, the University's development and progress largely depended upon public opinion, the recommendation of the governor, and the action of the legislature. In the 1955 legislative session, the University received strong support in the Unicameral. A general fund appropriation of $17.8 million was approved, an increase of nearly 19 percent over the previous biennium. These additional funds permitted the University administration to make adjustments in the salaries of the faculty and nonteaching staff, to provide modest support for research, and to meet general rising costs. However, the factors requiring larger appropriations for the University, competition for faculty, rising wages for all nonacademic workers, and higher prices for everything, continued unabated.

The legislative session of 1957 was pivotal for the University of Nebraska. Not only would increased funds be necessary to meet spiraling costs, but the ten-year special state institutional building levy adopted in 1947 was due to expire. Unfortunately, rainfall in Nebraska had fallen below the normal mean in 1955 and 1956. Strong statements favoring strict economy and even possibly a reduction in the state property tax rate were voiced by the governor, some state senators, and citizens.

The University regents presented a budget request to Governor Victor I. Anderson asking for a $5.5 million increase in state tax funds over the previous biennium. Nearly half of the requested increase was earmarked for faculty salary raises. Chancellor Hardin emphasized that this was required by national conditions in higher education. "We are struggling with the most serious competitive forces in the University's history. . . . These forces do not arise from the main streets of Nebraska, nor from this region, but from all the other sections of the nation."[28]

Governor Anderson, who had intended to recommend a reduction in the state property tax rate to the Unicameral, requested that the University administration and regents reduce their budget request. The chancellor replied, "I don't honestly think I can cut it."[29] The governor then suggested that perhaps the Board of Regents should consider raising tuition fees as a means of increasing University income. Although Governor Anderson later supported most of the budget request, he told University officials, "I know you feel there is a crisis at the University. But there is a crisis out on the farm, too. . . . I feel I have a responsibility to the taxpayer who has had no income for two years."[30] The governor recommended an increase of $3.2 million for the University of Nebraska from state property tax funds. Senator Karl Vogel, of Omaha, chairman of the Budget Committee, thought the recommendation was "pretty liberal. There is a limit to the amount you can tax free people . . . and we're at that level now."[31] Although many recognized the limitations of the state property tax, a proposal by Senator Terry Carpenter for a state sales tax did not win legislative support.

After much discussion, the Budget Committee submitted a majority report which recommended an appropriation of $2.2 million increase for the University from the state mill levy. This was one million dollars less than recommended by the governor. However, an unprecedented minority report by Senators Otto H. Liebers, of Lincoln, and Harry Pizer, of North Platte, supported the $3.2 million recommendation of Governor Anderson.

By late May 1957, when rainfall returned to normal amounts in Nebraska and confidence in the future was restored, the Unicameral approved the state budget,

28. Ibid., November 13, 1956.
29. Lincoln *Star,* November 30, 1956, p. 1.
30. Omaha *World-Herald,* November 30, 1956, p. 1.
31. *Daily Nebraskan,* January 18, 1957.

including a $3.2 million increase for the University from state property tax funds. The regents' action, taken during the legislative session to raise student tuition fees, was an important factor in winning legislative support for the governor's recommendation for the University. The action of the Board of Regents in raising student tuition was in part forced by a bill introduced by Senator Terry Carpenter by which the legislators would have increased tuition. After the regents' action, the bill was indefinitely postponed and became a dead issue at the conclusion of the legislative session.

Another key legislative issue, in this year of decision, was the continuance of the special state mill levy for state institutions. Governor Anderson favored continuing the levy, although he suggested that the rate be reduced from 1.1 mills to .75 of a mill. The legislation was adopted with 45 percent of the funds allocated to the University of Nebraska subject to spending authorization from the governor. The bill was approved by a vote of forty senators. The University of Nebraska had received strong support from the Unicameral.

THE AGE OF SPUTNIK

In October 1957, the Soviet Union launched the first man-made satellite into outer space. In the United States this event produced an unparalleled concern about the quality of American education. This was accompanied by an increasing willingness of the public to provide more funds for educational institutions.

The 1959 session of the Nebraska Unicameral was outstanding in its support of the University. At the request of the state tax commissioner, the regents were asked to submit two budget requests. The first would provide for only continuance of the University's program and a second which would permit some expansion of University programs. The board requested an additional $4.2 million for continuance of the University's work at its present level and an additional $1.6 million for expansion. Governor Ralph G. Brooks, at first, recommended an increase of only $2 million for the University from tax funds. However, after becoming more familiar with University problems, Governor Brooks raised his recommendation from $2 million to $4 million in additional state property tax funds. The chairman of the Unicameral Budget Committee, Senator Otto H. Liebers, strongly supported the governor's revised recommendation, and it received favorable legislative consideration.

The Unicameral also took other action of far-reaching consequences for the University. The adoption of legislation authorizing the Board of Regents to initiate a plan for a contributory faculty retirement program was of major significance. Since the chancellorship of Samuel Avery, the University administration had recognized that the lack of an adequate faculty retirement system was a serious weakness in the University. Few legislative acts would have as beneficial a result as this on the retention of faculty members. Other important legislation included the boosting of the state institutional building levy rate from .75 of a mill to 1.1 mills. This permitted additional construction and provided a needed adjustment to meet rising construction costs. The extension until 1965 of the special .25 of a mill building levy for the University of Nebraska Medical Center in Omaha enabled the University to continue to develop its medical program without sacrificing other University development.

Legislation was adopted authorizing the continuation of the off-campus classes provided under the supervision of the University Extension Division. The state attorney general's ruling that without specific legislative approval the University could not provide off-campus classes made this legislation necessary. In adopting this bill, the Unicameral endorsed the programs of service and instruction to the citizens of Nebraska regardless of their place of residence.

THE NEW ADMINISTRATIVE TEAM

During the last half of the decade, Chancellor Hardin assembled a new administrative group to guide the University of Nebraska through the fifties and into the sixties. In April 1955, Adam C. Breckenridge was appointed as administrative assistant to the chancellor for academic affairs. In October, the title was changed to dean of the faculties. The office of dean of the faculties had been unfilled since the resignation of Carl W. Borgmann in 1953.

Dean Breckenridge was appointed to the University faculty in 1946 and had served as chairman of the Political Science Department. A native of Missouri, he received his Bachelor of Arts degree from Northeast Missouri State College, the Master of Arts degree from the University of Missouri, and the Doctor of Philosophy degree from Princeton University in 1942.

With the retirement of John K. Selleck as University business manager in 1957, a reorganization of the business department was effected. Separate positions of comptroller and business manager were established by the regents. Joseph Soshnik was named University comptroller. A native of Omaha, he received his undergraduate education at Creighton University, the Master of Science degree from the University of Denver, and the Doctor of Philosophy degree, in 1952, from the University of Nebraska. Soshnik had been a member of the Creighton University faculty since 1946, having been named director of the Department of Management in 1952 and associate professor in 1954. He also served as auditor and budget consultant to the Creighton University administration and was assistant to the dean of the College of Administration. The appointment of Soshnik at the University of Nebraska added greatly to the effectiveness of the Hardin administrative team. The Very Rev. Carl M. Reinert, S.J., president of Creighton University expressed his loss:

The University of Nebraska is acquiring a very competent administrator who will certainly be able to handle his difficult assignment with great efficiency. While I'm extremely sorry to see Dr. Soshnik leave Creighton after a very pleasant association, I'm nevertheless happy to know that he has decided to stay in Nebraska and to remain in the field of education at our sister institution.[32]

This was a key appointment in the Hardin administration. Soshnik was later given the additional responsibility of being secretary to the University Board of Regents.

Carl A. Donaldson was appointed University business manager. He received his Bachelor of Science degree in 1928, and his master's in 1931 from the University of Nebraska. At the time of his new assignment, he had been a member of the University staff for nearly thirty years. Donaldson had begun as manager of scientific stores, moved to assistant purchasing agent, and then to director of purchasing and procurement in 1948.

Other significant changes in University administrative personnel included the retirement of George W. Rosenlof as dean of admissions and the appointment of Floyd W. Hoover as registrar. The retirement of Eudora Mallory, in 1957, marked the end of an era in the chancellor's office. As secretary and receptionist, she had served Chancellors Samuel Avery, Edgar A. Burnett, C. S. Boucher, R. G. Gustavson, John K. Selleck, and Clifford M. Hardin. As custodian of the correspondence and records kept in the chancellor's office, she profoundly influenced the research of all future scholars studying the development of the University.

32. Lincoln *Star*, April 3, 1947, p. 3.

In 1958, on the recommendation of Chancellor Hardin, the Board of Regents approved the establishment of a group to undertake a comprehensive self-study of the University. Marvel L. Baker was named coordinator for the study. Separate committees were established in the area of the biological sciences, humanities, physical sciences, and social sciences. The work of these groups provided valuable faculty input regarding University needs and opportunities to the administration and to the Board of Regents. In taking stock of the University, the group under Baker's direction made an important contribution to the Hardin administration.

The fifties was a time of growth and development at the University of Nebraska. During the period the actions of the chancellors and the Board of Regents en-

Nebraska Center for Continuing Education.

couraged those who sought University growth and improvement. The securing of a grant from the W. K. Kellogg Foundation by Chancellor Hardin for the construction of the Nebraska Center for Continuing Education illustrated the new atmosphere at the University of Nebraska. The funds collected by the University from private sources to qualify for acceptance of the Kellogg gift demonstrates that this new feeling of pride and desire for improvement was not confined to the limits of the campus. The generous gifts from combined estates of Frances Sheldon, and her brother, Bromley Sheldon, provided funds for the construction of the Sheldon Memorial Art Gallery during the sixties. This was further evidence of the interest and pride of Nebraskans in their own University.

The establishment of KUON-TV at the University was another illustration of the progressive University administration. Broadcasting, which began in 1954, was a milestone in the development of the concept of service to the people of the state regardless of their residence.

Chancellor Hardin identified the challenge of the coming decade at the Alumni Round-Up in June 1959. The goals of the sixties would be to increase faculty research and graduate training while improving the quality of the faculty and the quality of instruction. The University of Nebraska was prepared to enter the mainstream of American higher education. The era of survival was over; the opportunity to take a part in the nation's affairs and contribute to the national welfare had arrived.

CHAPTER 11

A Decade of Academic Maturity

THE DECADE OF THE fifties was a time of academic maturation at the University of Nebraska. Through the efforts of the chancellors, regents, and the faculty the quality of teaching and research at the University reached new heights of excellence. However, the improvement in quality was not uniform throughout all colleges and schools of the institution, although the commitment for improving the entire University was made. The policy of improvement is especially visible in the actions of the Board of Regents, the administration, and the legislature in dealing with medical education. The concept of service, long a major part of the land-grant university idea, continued to be an important University goal and was even expanded to include assisting the Turkish government to establish a university.

Despite the drop in student enrollment during the first years of the decade, institutional operating costs continued to rise. In addition, the realization that the children born during the "baby boom" of the World War II period would enter college during the last of the fifties and the sixties caused the issue of selective admission to the University to be discussed within and without the academic community. The discussion of University entrance requirements was further complicated by a rising tide of public dissatisfaction with the academic quality of American public education. Many critics of public education urged the return to academically conservative programs in the nation's high schools. At the same time, most professional educators were calling for greater flexibility in the secondary school curriculum. At the University of Nebraska this educational ferment produced conflict over entrance requirements, remedial noncredit classes, the dropout rate, and the role of the Teachers College in the preparation of secondary school teachers and school administrators.

Early in the decade, the Nebraska Association of School Administrators urged the University administration to revise its entrance requirements by abolishing all specific requirements in English, foreign languages, mathematics, science, and social science. The schoolmen recommended instead of specific requirements, fifteen units of "satisfactory work" in an approved secondary school. Those who favored the change argued that the existing entrance requirements caused hardship for graduates of small Nebraska high schools. This was not a new problem. The existence of high schools with only five or fewer teachers and a limited curriculum had long deprived rural Nebraska youth of educational quality. Foreign language instruction in small high schools was becoming increasingly rare. Boyd G. Carter, professor of romance languages, complained in writing for the Modern Language Association of Nebraska that "in 1948–49, for example, only five high schools, excluding Omaha and Lincoln, offered French or German. Spanish is in a somewhat stronger position."[1]

1. Letter, Boyd G. Carter to Carl W. Borgmann, January 18, 1950, MSS, University of Nebraska Archives, Gustavson Collection.

Strong opposition to the elimination of specific subject matter units for entrance into the University of Nebraska was voiced by the Executive Committee of the College of Arts and Sciences. At times, unfortunately, the discussion was characterized by one group accusing the public schools and their administrators of being negligent of their responsibilities and of anti-intellectualism, whereas some schoolmen charged their opponents as being elitist and undemocratic. The intensity of the controversy in Nebraska was heightened by the publication of many books and articles which made the quality and purpose of American public education a national concern. By the last half of the decade, most agreed that quality of instruction on the secondary and collegiate levels should be improved. Nebraska's Education Commissioner, F. B. Decker, stated that teachers in small high schools too often were required to teach subjects for which they were poorly prepared. "I condemn the system which insists that we have so many small high schools. It spreads our teaching talent too thin."[2] The state commissioner also faulted the public for insisting "that the schools offer lots of 'activities' and non-academic training."[3]

The enrollment of students, often from small high schools, with poor preparation for college-level work, necessitated the teaching of remedial courses without college credit at the University. Some capable but poorly prepared students spent as much as an extra semester at the University preparing to begin college-level studies. This practice was not new. During the nineteenth century many Midwestern land-grant universities had a heavier enrollment in their preparatory departments than in the university. However, during this decade with the availability of secondary schools, the assignment of students to remedial courses at the University offended local pride and was occasionally regarded as discrimination.

Some who were critical of the rising state appropriations for the University opposed the concept of remedial instruction at the University. An Omaha *World-Herald* editorial expressed a popular view: "There is no reason why the University should be doing the work of high schools, at double expense to the taxpayers. Until the University refuses to teach high school courses, the under-par high schools will have little incentive to come up to standard."[4] In response to public criticism and legislative concern regarding the cost of remedial instruction, the noncredit courses in physics and chemistry were terminated at the end of the school year in 1957. Chancellor Hardin explained the new policy:

We think that the University should drop all 'remedial' courses. If students cannot read and write properly when they come to college, they should return to high school to learn. So long as the University makes up high school deficiencies, the high schools will continue to turn out inadequately educated graduates.[5]

Nevertheless, the University continued to offer its remedial course in English. With a liberal policy for admitting students to the University, the continuance of remedial work in English could not be discontinued as easily as those in physics and chemistry without greatly lessening the chance of success for marginal or poorly prepared students. Chancellor Hardin defended the open-door admission policy by stating that "the only philosophy that can be followed by a land-grant state university is one allowing the widest possible opportunity to the youth of the state."[6]

The liberal admission policy was tempered by University admissions personnel realistically advising high school principals and counselors of the high risk of

2. Omaha *World-Herald,* May 30, 1956, p. 1.
3. Ibid.
4. Ibid., May 29, 1956, p. 22.
5. Ibid., June 10, 1957, p. 6.
6. Lincoln *Star,* November 4, 1957, p. 1.

failure by academically weak students. Although most marginal students did not complete degree programs, many believed that the time they spent at the University was a valuable educational experience.

By the end of the fifties, the preparation of high school graduates for college work had improved. Between 1955 and 1959, the number of University of Nebraska freshmen enrolled in the remedial English course declined by almost two-thirds. This resulted from improved instruction in the secondary schools and from more realistic counseling of high school seniors by school counselors. Because of the University's increase in the size of many beginning courses, the discouragement of marginal students was proper. Those students who were adequately prepared and motivated for college-level work were not hampered by large classes. However, the poorly prepared or motivated student was usually less likely to succeed in a large class than in a small one.

The University of Nebraska had as a major goal in the fifties improvement in the quality of teaching and faculty research. Also during this period, the academic program improved at a rapidly accelerating rate and the University received increased national and worldwide recognition.

THE COLLEGE OF AGRICULTURE

Throughout the fifties, the College of Agriculture maintained an undergraduate enrollment which varied between nine hundred and one thousand students. William V. Lambert, who was appointed dean in 1948, continued to provide capable leadership throughout the decade. The associate directors of the Agricultural Extension Service were Harry G. Gould and Edward W. Janike. The administration of the Agricultural Experiment Station was ably performed by Marvel L. Baker and Elvin F. Frolik. Both Gould and Baker contributed to the success of the University's project in Turkey after the end of their assignment on the East, or Agricultural, Campus.

As in the past, the efforts of the faculty and staff of the College of Agriculture was directed toward instruction, research, and service to the people of the state and nation. In all three areas of concern, there was outstanding achievement during the fifties. Changes in the instructional departments reflected the increasing complexity of American agriculture. The Department of Rural economics became the Department of Agricultural Economics, early in the decade, to reflect more adequately the work of the department and its increased complexity. Additional courses of instruction were added which were concerned with such topics as land appraisal, agricultural statistics, and market price analysis. Publications by Ernest Feder, Kristjan Kristjanson, and Howard W. Ottoson of the Department of Agricultural Economics concerned the problems of real estate evaluation, property tax structure, and possible forms of farm debtor relief. The Department of Agricultural Engineering, under the chairmanship of Lloyd W. Hurlbut, continued its interest in developing experimental harvesting equipment. Professor George M. Peterson, of the department, served as a consultant to federal agencies concerned with the problem of storing the surplus grain produced by increasingly efficient American agriculture.

The Department of Agronomy, the largest department in the College of Agriculture had a long tradition of outstanding teaching and research. Two of its prominent members during the preceding decades were William W. Burr and Theodore A. Kiesselbach. Franklin D. Keim served as department chairman until 1953, when Elvin F. Frolik was appointed his successor. In 1955, Frolik was appointed associate director of the Experiment Station, and Donald G. Hanway assumed the chairmanship of the Department of Agronomy. Among the active scholars in the department were Professor Frolik, who received research grants from the Atomic Energy Commission and was elected a director of the American Society of Agronomy; Professor Thomas H. Gooding, who received the University of Nebraska Foundation Award for Distinguished Teaching in 1955; Professor John Lonnquist, recognized as a leader in corn research; and Professor Harold F. Rhoades, a researcher in sugar beet production. The large number of technical publications written by members of the Department of Agronomy contributed to an increased productivity on the nation's farms. The dedication of a new agronomy building, in June 1952, provided improved facilities and aided the development of the department. Later, the new quarters were named Keim Hall in honor of Franklin D. Keim, who died in 1956.

The Department of Animal Pathology and Hygiene was administered by Carl Olson, Jr., and G. A. Young during the fifties. Numerous publications testify to the department's dedication to research. The production of specific pathogen free swine was a major research attainment. Because of University financial limitations, requests for expanding the scope of the department into a school of veterinary medicine could not be met. However, the Board of Regents contracted with other universities to provide Nebraska residents instruction in veterinary medicine. In 1959, the regents changed the name of the Department of Animal Pathology and Hygiene to the Department of Veterinary Science.

William J. Loeffel remained as chairman of the Department of Animal Husbandry until his retirement in 1959, when Robert Koch was appointed as his successor. Established research programs with beef cattle, dual-purpose cattle, sheep, and swine were maintained. Professors Marvel L. Baker, Cecil T. Blunn, and Robert M. Koch authored significant research publications. The meat research program, directed by Professor Loeffel, was expanded, and improved facilities were provided. Later, the meat research building was named William J. Loeffel Meat Laboratory.

The Department of Dairy Husbandry faculty published descriptive studies of dairy herds, which reflected desirable management practices. Additional reports concerned feeding studies and dairy products. The Department of Entomology staff studied insect pests which affected agricultural production and developed improved methods of insect control.

Margaret Fedde, chairman of the Department of Home Economics since 1919, retired in 1950. During her years on the University faculty, Professor Fedde had ably provided leadership for the development of the home economics program. She had guided the establishment of the child development laboratory, and helped develop two cooperative residence halls for home economics majors. She was also an outstanding teacher and provided an atmosphere conducive to staff research. Doretta Schlaphoff was appointed Fedde's successor. In 1954, she was followed by Elizabeth F. McKinney as chairman of the Department of Home Economics. The growing importance of this department was reflected in the request of Dean Lambert, in 1954, to the Board of Regents that the work in home economics be elevated from the level of a department to that of a school. The regents approved this change during the next decade. The Department of Horticulture, toward the end of the decade, was redesignated the Department of Horticulture and Forestry. This change mirrored the expanding interests of the departmental staff. Throughout the period, the most noteworthy member of the department was Harvey O. Werner. He continued his valuable research with the potato.

The Departments of Agricultural Chemistry and Chemurgy were combined by the Board of Regents in 1953 to form the Department of Biochemistry and Nutrition. Studies started in the forties on the nutritional value of various feeds continued in the fifties. Rudolph M. Sandstedt received the Thomas Burr Osborne Medal from the American Association of Cereal Chemists as recognition for his basic research in cereal chemistry. Sandstedt was the second member of the University of Nebraska faculty to receive the Osborne Medal. Professor M. J. Blish had received it in 1928.

The research activities of the Agricultural Experiment Station staff continued as a segment of the work of the College of Agriculture. The closing of the Substation at Valentine and the creation of the Fort Robinson Beef Cattle Research Station indicated the desire to adjust the work of the Experiment Station to meet changing agricultural conditions. The new station was established in cooperation with the United States Department of Agriculture and was destined to become a

Professor Rudolph M. Sandstedt of the College of Agriculture.

landmark in the development of beef cattle research in the United States. The other Experimental Substations at North Platte, Scottsbluff, Box Butte, and the Union Fruit farm maintained, as in the past, important facilities for research.

The success of the contracted program between the University and the International Cooperation Administration in Turkey resulted from strong support by the faculty of the College of Agriculture. The first contract provided for agricultural consultation with the Turkish Ministry of Agriculture to develop a program of agricultural education and extension. Harry G. Gould, associate director of the Agricultural Extension Service at the University of Nebraska, accepted the assignment to advise the Turkish Minister of Agriculture in 1950. Additional contracts were negotiated by the Board of Regents in 1954, providing for the assistance of the University of Nebraska in the establishment of a new Turkish university to be patterned after the American land-grant model. The new institution was named Ataturk University and was located at Erzurum in eastern Turkey. Throughout the thirteen years of involvement by the University of Nebraska in the project, Marvel L. Baker provided guidance and counsel for the creation of this Turkish land-grant university. Baker served as dean of the

Ataturk University at Erzurum, Turkey.

University of Nebraska faculty at Erzurum from 1955 to 1957, and again from 1961 to 1962. In addition, forty-five other members of the University of Nebraska staff accepted assignments for varying lengths of time on the faculty of Ataturk University. Members of the Turkish faculty visited the United States and enrolled at the University of Nebraska for further education and training. The contracts were terminated in June 1968. The program was a success and marks a high point in the concept of service by American land-grant universities.

THE COLLEGE OF ARTS AND SCIENCES

Although it was not always the college with the largest student enrollment, the College of Arts and Sciences maintained its leading role in the University instructional program. In 1950, nearly 52 percent of the instruction on the two Lincoln campuses was conducted by the faculty of the College of Arts and Sciences, whereas only 22 percent of the student body matriculated as majors in the college. The largest departments were those of English, chemistry, history, mathematics, political science, and modern languages. No part of the University was more diverse nor more productive in the number of publications than the College of Arts and Sciences. In addition to its departmental structure, the School of Fine Arts and the School of Journalism operated within the framework of the College of Arts and Sciences.

Charles H. Oldfather, dean of the college since 1932, retired in 1952. During his long tenure as dean, the problems associated with depression, war, and the veterans' boom were met and solved. Few University deans could equal his record of service to the institution. After consultation with a faculty committee to advise on the appointment of a new dean, Chancellor Gustavson announced his decision.

In going over the men with whom we have visited from outside the University it is quite clear to me that we have men on our own faculty who are just as competent to fill that place as any of the outsiders we have considered. I have therefore recommended to the Board of Regents the appointment of Dr. Walter E. Militzer.[7]

7. Letter, R. G. Gustavson to C. S. Hamilton, August 1, 1952, MSS, University of Nebraska Archives, Gustavson Collection.

The new dean had been first named to the University of Nebraska faculty in 1936, and appointed professor of chemistry in 1948. Walter F. Wright, professor of English, was appointed assistant dean of the College of Arts and Sciences in 1954.

Despite the heavy instructional load of the faculty of the Arts College, scholarship and publication were not neglected. The goal of the regents and chancellor to raise the quality of the faculty was accomplished in the college. Although there had always been some outstanding scholars on the college faculty, the number who achieved national recognition reached a new mark during the fifties. Among those faculty members who brought distinction to themselves and to the University of Nebraska were: from the Department of Bacteriology Carl E. Georgi and Warren E. Engelhard; from chemistry Henry E. Baumgarten, Norman H. Cromwell, Cliff S. Hamilton, Walter E. Militzer, and E. Roger Washburn; from the Department of English Mamie J. Meredith, James E. Miller, Jr., Karl J. Shapiro, and Walter F. Wright; in geography Leslie Hewes; William K. Pfeiler and Paul Schach from the Department of Germanic Languages; from history Albin T. Anderson, Robert L. Koehl, James C. Olson, Stanley R. Ross, and Robert K. Sakai; in the Department of Physics Robert L. Chasson and Edward J. Zimmerman; Donald M. Pace from physiology; in the Philosophy Department Charles H. Patterson and William H. Werkmeister; from political science Adam C. Breckenridge, Norman L. Hill and Lane W. Lancaster; Paul Meadows and James M. Reinhardt from the Department of Sociology; and from zoology Dwight D. Miller. In addition to these established scholars, the academic departments of the College of Arts and Sciences listed many faculty members at the assistant professor level who would distinguish themselves in the years ahead.

The School of Journalism, attached to the College of Arts and Sciences for administrative purposes, was directed until 1956 by William F. Swindler. He was succeeded by William E. Hall. This school had been cited as an example by Governor Val Peterson of unnecessary University growth. Nevertheless, the school enjoyed the strong support of the University regents, administration, and the Nebraska press. As a result of the increased demand for more broadly educated professional journalists, the curriculum was revised in 1955. To provide for more general education, a "Directed Reading Program" was established. An internship program was initiated in 1957 to fulfill the long recognized need for practical newspaper experience.

The School of Fine Arts was also administratively a part of the College of Arts and Sciences. The school was composed of three departments: art, music and music education, and speech and dramatic art. Arthur E. Westbrook was chairman of the Department of Music until his retirement in 1952. He was succeeded by David Foltz. In 1958, Emanuel Wishnow was appointed chairman of the Department of Music. Wishnow had been a member of the department since the thirties and was conductor of the University Orchestra and String Ensemble. He was strongly supported by the faculty as one who could bring harmony to the department. Leroy T. Lasse, appointed chairman of the Department of Speech and Dramatic Art in 1940, guided this department through the decade. In addition to maintaining the long tradition of excellence in theater production, the department opened a clinic for children with speech problems. John H. Wiley became the first director of the Speech and Hearing Clinic.

The chairmen of the Department of Art during the fifties were Duard W. Laging and Peter Worth. In the early years of the period, the department was reorganized to reduce its operating expenses. Although this produced some faculty discontent and resignations, as well as alumni protests, the Department of Art ended the decade stronger than it had been at the beginning. This favorable result was in large measure the consequence of occurrences outside the academic community. The gifts of Mary Frances Sheldon and Adam Bromley Sheldon for the construction of an art gallery gave new recognition to the importance of art on the Nebraska campus and throughout the state. The gifts, in many respects, complemented the work of the Nebraska Art Association in drawing public attention to the role of art in a civilized society. The Sheldon Memorial Gallery was constructed during the next decade on the site of the old Pharmacy Hall.

The purchase of works of art, by the University of Nebraska, had been made

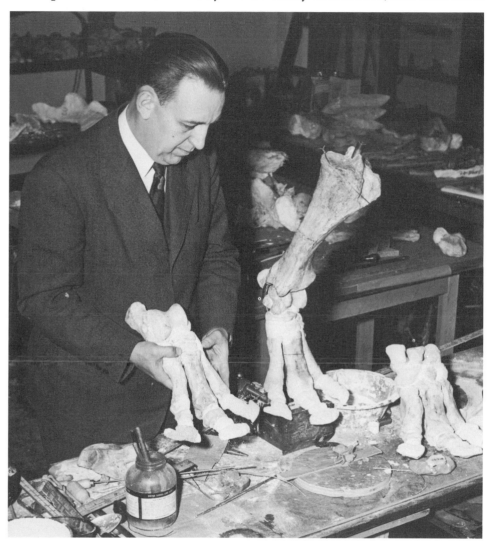

C. Bertrand Schultz, director of the State Museum.

possible by the Frank M. Hall Trust. This was established in 1929, and by 1957 had provided over $160,000 for the purchase of works of art. With the construction of the new gallery, the University of Nebraska would have a suitable place to display its growing art collection.

The program for art instruction received invaluable assistance with a gift from the Woods Charitable Fund, in 1959, for the construction of the Nelle Cochrane Woods Building. This building made possible a long-needed improved facility for art instruction. The development of the Department of Art at the University of Nebraska during the decade of the fifties bears witness to the invaluable role that enlightened private philanthropy can play in the improvement of a state university.

Although not directly a part of the College of Arts and Sciences, the University of Nebraska State Museum furnished instructional facilities for many students, and the museum staff held academic rank in the Arts College. C. Bertrand Schultz, director of the museum, held the rank of professor of geology in the College of Arts and Sciences.

During the decade of the 1950s the museum's research collections assumed major scientific importance. Although the Board of Regents had requested a consolidation of the various departmental collections in 1941, the war and its aftermath delayed the rapid development of an all-University museum. By the fifties, however, the museum collections became a significant part of the systematic biological research program at the University.

The improvement of the State Museum was assisted by the formation of a museum consulting committee composed of the Graduate, Arts and Sciences deans, and the chairmen of the Departments of Sociology and Anthropology, Botany, Entomology, Geology, and Zoology. The museum developed a new display with some sixteen natural habitat groups. These and other exhibits were financed by private gifts, including a sizable grant from the Cooper Foundation through the University of Nebraska Foundation.

By the end of the fifties, the museum's scientific collection exceeded two and one-half million specimens. Unfortunately, the collection was stored at various places throughout the campus. This hampered its efficient use. Furthermore, because of the research of faculty members and graduate students, this valuable scientific collection continued to grow. In 1958, the museum consulting committee recommended that the research collection be consolidated and housed in Nebraska Hall, the former Elgin Watch building. This goal was realized during the sixties.

In the display and educational service activities of the museum, two important additions were made during the fifties, the Division of Health Sciences and the Planetarium. Both of these valuable additions were made possible by gifts from Ralph S. Mueller, '98, of Cleveland, Ohio, through the University of Nebraska Foundation. He also provided permanent endowments for the two new museum activities.

THE TEACHERS COLLEGE

During the fifties, the Teachers College again became a focal point of controversy within the University of Nebraska. The issues were the products of long-standing distrust between the faculties of the Teachers College and the College of Arts and Sciences, the changing enrollment patterns within the University, the evolution of professional education as an academic discipline, and the general public criticism of American education following Sputnik. Despite these problems and disputes of the fifties, the Teachers College maintained a nearly stable enrollment and continued to supply teachers and school administrators to an increasingly concerned society.

The decision of the Board of Regents, in 1953, to authorize the construction of a new University High School building encouraged those who had advocated strengthening the University of Nebraska program in teacher education. The need for this new facility was imperative if the Teachers College was to keep pace with its neighboring institutions. By its action, the Board of Regents made the first of several major commitments to teacher education during the decade of the fifties.

At the mid-century mark, the professional degree of Doctor of Education was granted by more than fifty universities. The degree, which was first instituted at Harvard University some thirty years earlier, was widely accepted by American universities as a professional degree. Attempts at the University of Nebraska during the forties to win approval for this recognized professional degree had been unsuccessful. By the fifties, the lack of such a program at the University of Nebraska branded its Teachers College as unprogressive and disassociated from the mainstream of professional education. Those who denied the legitimacy of professional education as an academic discipline naturally opposed offering the Doctor of Education degree. For them the issue involved a sacrifice of academic standards.

In the spring of 1952, the faculty of the Teachers College took action to bring the issue of establishing the Doctor of Education degree before the University community. The action of the college faculty received the strong support of Nebraska's school administrators. Chancellor Gustavson recognized the growing support for the proposed Doctor of Education program. In a letter to the leading opponent, the Graduate dean, he predicted that:

If the University of Nebraska refuses to give this degree, which does seem to be in high demand by school executives throughout the state, then we will see a petition to have this degree set up at one of the Teachers Colleges, very probably Kearney, and the legislative push will be that this is an area which the University of Nebraska does not wish to cover.[8]

The Graduate dean, Robert Goss, objected to the chancellor's reasoning.

The thing that bothers me the most in this whole proposal is that for the first time in my experience we are being asked to grant a degree solely on the basis of demand for it and with threats of what will happen if we don't do it. I believe that the only basis for granting an advanced degree should be the merits of the proposed program.[9]

Chancellor Gustavson appointed a committee of six members, three of whom were from the faculty of Teachers College, to develop a compromise between the Teachers College faculty and the Graduate Council regarding the proposed Doctor of Education degree. After many meetings, Professor Clifford M. Hicks, chairman of the special committtee, reported to the chancellor that no basis for compromise could be found. The other members of the group were Professors Leslie L. Chisholm, Merle A. Stoneman, Warren R. Baller, William G. Leavitt, and Norman H. Cromwell. The impasse resulted from disagreement over a language requirement and the addition of "cultural courses" for the second language requirement. At this time, a nearly standard language requirement among American graduate colleges for the Doctor of Philosophy degree was a reading knowledge of two foreign languages, usually French and German. Most traditionalists favored the maintenance of the foreign language requirements for doctoral degrees as a guarantee of intellectual rigor and of a broad cultural base. Before the 1960s were over, however, the Graduate faculty voted to approve substitutes for language requirements.

On November 3, 1952, a formal proposal from the Teachers College faculty was presented to the voting members of the Graduate faculty for their consideration and approval. Ignoring the personal appeal by Chancellor Gustavson that the proposal be approved, the voting members of the Graduate faculty present rejected the Teachers College faculty's proposal. The vote was 23 in favor of the motion to approve the establishment of the Doctor of Education degree and 46 opposed. After the meeting, Chancellor Gustavson expressed his dismay to Dean Goss.

8. Letter, R. G. Gustavson to Dean Robert Goss, June 18, 1952, MSS, University of Nebraska Archives, Gustavson Collection.

9. Letter, R. W. Goss to R. G. Gustavson, June 24, 1952, MSS, University of Nebraska Archives, Gustavson Collection.

I have had the opportunity of talking with a number of College Presidents about the status of this degree [Doctor of Education] in their institutions, and I must say that I have yet to find one who does not feel that the degree serves its purpose. . . . I am completely at a loss to understand the attitude of the Graduate Council and Graduate Faculty with respect to this problem.[10]

As he had indicated in his personal appeal to the Graduate faculty, Gustavson overruled the decision of the Graduate faculty on the Doctor of Education degree and recommended the establishment of the degree to the Board of Regents. On April 18, 1953, they formally authorized the Teachers College to grant the professional degree of Doctor of Education. Attempts by those who opposed this action to have the regents reconsider their decision during the Selleck administration were unsuccessful. After considerable discussion the Advanced Professional Division was created within the Teachers College to administer the Master of Education and Doctor of Education degrees. Students pursuing these degrees were technically not graduate students, but were advanced professional students.

The split within the University faculty was unfortunate and demonstrates that within an intellectual community human antagonisms and hostility sometimes are of major significance. However, the controversy at the University of Nebraska was not an isolated event. Throughout American higher education during the decade of the fifties, the legitimacy of professional education as an academic discipline was questioned by liberal arts faculties.

The preparation of secondary school teachers was the basis of an additional conflict between the faculties of the Teachers College and the College of Arts and Sciences. Since the twenties, some members of the academic departments of the Arts College had objected to the enrollment of prospective secondary teachers in the Teachers College. They favored the enrollment of prospective secondary teachers in the Arts College with majors in their respective academic areas. With the general decline in University enrollment during the early fifties, the transference of those preparing for careers as secondary teachers from the Teachers College to the College of Arts and Sciences would maintain or increase enrollment and budget support during a time of anticipated reduction.

The recommendation of University graduates to the State Superintendent of Instruction for teacher certification was solely a function of the Teachers College. In December 1951, the executive committee of the College of Arts and Sciences requested the chancellor and the Board of Regents to make a change allowing the Arts College academic departments to recommend candidates for state certification for secondary school teachers. This change would have required neither matriculation in the Teachers College nor dual matriculation in the Teachers and Arts Colleges for certification by the state as a secondary school teacher. Those proposing this change argued that the established policy was unique and prejudicial to the College of Arts and Sciences. The proposal from the Arts College was studied by Dean of the Faculties Borgmann. He found that the procedures employed at the University of Nebraska for recommending prospective secondary teachers to the State Superintendent of Instruction were not unique nor prejudicial to the College of Arts and Sciences. Moreover, the statutory and constitutional bases for Teachers College control of certifying teachers would have to be fought in the courts. Consequently, no action was taken on the request by either the University administration or the Board of Regents.

After the successful launching of the Russian Sputnik, American public opinion

---

10. Letter, R. G. Gustavson to Dean R. W. Goss, December 15, 1952, MSS, University of Nebraska Archives, Gustavson Collection.

increasingly questioned the quality of the nation's schools. In the debate which followed, some charged that the schools had lost many of their traditional academic values. The alleged lack of emphasis by secondary schools on the time-honored disciplines of science, mathematics, and foreign languages was particularly deplored. For some critics, the villain of the school crisis was the professional educator and the teacher-training institutions.

At the University of Nebraska, the dissatisfaction with the secondary schools was evidenced by the revival of the earlier unsuccessful attempt to transfer control of secondary teacher preparation from the Teachers College to the College of Arts and Sciences. Eleven professors in the Arts College—M. A. Basoco, mathematics; Boyd G. Carter, romance languages; Robert L. Chasson, physics; Norman H. Cromwell, chemistry; William H. Gilliland, geology; Theodore Jorgensen, Jr., physics; James E. Miller, Jr., English; James C. Olson, history; William K. Pfeiler, Germanic languages; Thomas M. Raysor, English; and James L. Sellers, history—called upon the University administration and regents to transfer secondary teacher education to the control of the subject matter departments of the College of Arts and Sciences. This action, the eleven professors believed, would insure "that respect for scholarship and intellectual effort by faculties and students [would] be restored to our education program at the secondary level where it has been lacking."[11] This worthy goal could best be achieved by transferring secondary teacher preparation to the Arts College, since "the able students in the field of the sciences, mathematics, languages and even history and English have frequently been unwilling to submit to the certification procedures imposed upon the prospective teacher."[12]

In November 1957, the Board of Regents approved Chancellor Hardin's proposal that a faculty committee be appointed to study and make recommendations regarding the teacher education program at the University of Nebraska. Chancellor Hardin named a faculty committee of six members, three from the Teachers College, Erwin H. Goldenstein, James A. Rutledge, and Norman F. Thorpe; two from the College of Arts and Sciences, Albin T. Anderson and Cecil E. Vanderzee; and Phillip McVey from the College of Business Administration. This Ad Hoc Committee on Teacher Certification submitted its report to the chancellor and regents in April 1958. The group agreed that all resources of the University should be untilized in the education of prospective teachers and that the teacher education program should be constantly evaluated for improvement. The necessity of cooperation between subject area departments and the Teachers College was recognized and improved communication between the colleges was strongly recommended. However, the Ad Hoc Committee on Teacher Certification split on the issue of dual matriculation of students in the Teachers College and the College of Arts and Sciences. Professors Goldenstein, Rutledge, and Thorpe, from the Teachers College, favored dual matriculation. Professors McVey, Anderson, and Vanderzee opposed it. The deadlock did not concern curriculum or program, but rather whether students preparing for secondary teaching could be counted in the College of Arts and Sciences exclusively. The preparation of secondary teachers was, therefore, not altered by this committee. Students continued to have available the option of being enrolled in Teachers College or that of dual matriculation in Teachers College and the College of Arts and Science. The Teachers College continued its function of recommending prospective teachers to the state for certification. It is unlikely that the budgetary consequences of this issue were not recognized by the members of the committee.

11. Omaha *World-Herald,* November 19, 1957, p. 20.
12. Ibid., November 18, 1957, p. 1.

This consideration of the preparation of secondary teachers coincided with the retirement of Frank W. Henzlik from the deanship of the Teachers College. During the twenty-seven years of his leadership, professional education at the University of Nebraska matured from infancy to adulthood. Walter K. Beggs, professor and chairman of the Department of History and Principles of Education, was appointed to succeed Henzlik by the regents in April 1958. The new dean received his Bachelor of Arts degree from Tarkio College in Missouri. His Master of Arts and Doctor of Philosophy degrees were awarded by the University of Nebraska. After experience as a school superintendent, Beggs joined the University staff as a graduate assistant in 1936. He attained the rank of professor in 1948. In recommending his appointment to the deanship, Chancellor Hardin told the regents:

The recommendation for Dr. Beggs is being made after long and careful consideration of the issues involved in the current unrest concerning the training of teachers and in recognition of the judgments of faculty members and others. I am confident that Professor Beggs, as Dean of Teachers College, will actively seek the full cooperation of the faculties of the several Colleges to the end that maximum use is made of the total resources of the University in the training of teachers.[13]

The reestablishment of a working relationship between the Teachers College and the other colleges of the University, particularly the College of Arts and Sciences, became the first major objective for Dean Walter K. Beggs. A committee was formed composed of Dean Beggs and Assistant Dean Norman F. Thorpe of the Teachers College and Dean Militzer and Professors James C. Olson and Charles W. Colman of the College of Arts and Sciences to reestablish a good rapport between the colleges. The effort was successful. By the end of the decade, Dean Militzer reported to Chancellor Hardin, "We haven't solved all of our problems by any means. In fact, we are just beginning to get at a solution. The prospect, however, looks hopeful. . . ."[14]

With the settlement of this long-standing dispute within the University community, an atmosphere conducive to renewed progress and development was attained.

THE GRADUATE COLLEGE

During the fifties, increased emphasis was given graduate work and research by the regents, chancellor, and the faculty. In the administration of Chancellor Gustavson, a new dedication to research became apparent at the University of Nebraska. Increased research and scholarship were possible during these years because of the growing availability of funding from sources other than state appropriations. Although Nebraskans had long supported their state University, state funds sustained little research. However, increasingly during the fifties, the national government and private business turned to the universities for solutions to their problems. This was most evident in the sciences.

In recognition of the growing role of university research, the regents assigned Graduate Dean Robert W. Goss the additional responsibility of research administrator in 1953. Funding by the federal government and private sources produced an increase in research activity. The progression of this research funding was dramatic.

13. Memo, undated, MSS, University of Nebraska Archives, Hardin Collection.
14. Letter, Walter E. Militzer to Clifford M. Hardin, May 15, 1959, MSS, University of Nebraska Archives, Hardin Collection.

1949–50	$ 131,446
1950–51	302,210
1951–52	423,773
1952–53	343,773
1953–54	403,043
1954–55	542,127
1955–56	709,627
1956–57	838,415
1957–58	1,468,140
1958–59	1,711,000[15]

Accompanying this increased research support, was an increase in the quality and quantity of graduate work at the University of Nebraska. For those who had long recognized the potential of the University for research and scholarship, the fifties was a time of fulfillment.

In 1956, Robert W. Goss, the dean of the Graduate College since 1941, retired. Harold E. Wise, the assistant dean, was named his temporary successor. The following year, the Board of Regents appointed John C. Weaver, a geographer and dean of the School of Arts and Sciences at Kansas State College, to be dean of the Graduate College and university research administrator.

Closely related to the goals of the Graduate College was the University of Nebraska Press. In 1951, the press was ten years old and had published thirty-two books and numerous booklets and brochures. The press, under the direction of Emily Schossberger, was severely hampered in its development by grave lack of working capital. However, with increased support from the chancellor, regents, and private foundation grants, the University of Nebraska Press slowly increased its number of publications. After the resignation of Schossberger in 1958, Bruce H. Nicoll was appointed director of publications and the University of Nebraska Press. With the introduction of a highly successful series of paperback books by the press in 1959, a new era of publication began which ultimately resulted in the University of Nebraska Press attaining national recognition and eminence in its field.

THE COLLEGE OF ENGINEERING AND ARCHITECTURE

The decade of the fifties was a period of unprecedented growth in the College of Engineering. For several years, the enrollment in the college exceeded that of any other part of the University. This was the consequence of the burgeoning demand of industry for engineers and the reputation of the college for a sound engineering program. Evidence of the quality of the curriculum at the University of Nebraska was revealed in a study by Charles J. Baer, of the University of Kansas School of Engineering and Architecture. He reported, in 1955, that over six and one half percent of the graduates of the University of Nebraska College of Engineering were listed in *Who's Who in Engineering*. The only university in the nation which exceeded the University of Nebraska's rating was Dartmouth. Dean Roy Green explained why he believed that his graduates excelled in this rating:

The College's sound judgment in course material; and the adaptability of Nebraska students. . . . it has become a long established fact that boys off the mid-western farms tend to develop into outstanding engineers. The reason . . . is their willingness to accept responsibility. Farm life, with its responsibilities for every member of the family, develops desirable characteristics in the boys from an early age.[16]

15. Lincoln *Star*, May 14, 1958, p. 16.
16. *Daily Nebraskan*, October 26, 1955.

In addition to the problems inherent in rapid growth, the college made adjustment in its instructional programs to better fit the needs of society and a swiftly evolving technology. The two-year technical programs were discontinued in 1950. The programs in Commercial Engineering and Architectural Engineering—not to be confused with the five-year architecture program—were terminated. These changes were adjustments to national trends in engineering and technical education. In 1958, the division of the Department of Chemistry and Chemical Engineering into separate departments of chemistry in the College of Arts and Sciences and chemical engineering in the College of Engineering was brought about by the recommendation of the Engineer's Council for Professional Development. This group serves as the accrediting organization for the nation's engineering schools.

Left to right: Engineering deans Olin J. Ferguson, Roy M. Green, and Merk Hobson.

Until his retirement in 1957, Roy M. Green served as dean of the College of Engineering and Architecture. He had succeeded Dean Ferguson in 1945 and provided able leadership during a time when professional engineering experienced not only a technological revolution but also an expanded expectation of the engineer by society.

The regents appointed Merk Hobson, professor and chairman of the Department of Chemical Engineering as Green's successor. He had received his Bachelor of Science degree from the University of Wisconsin and the Master of Science and the Doctor of Philosophy degrees from Northwestern University. Hobson joined the University of Nebraska faculty as an assistant professor in 1950. At the time of his appointment to the deanship, he was promoted from associate professor to professor. Under his leadership, the College of Engineering and Architecture accelerated its growth and quest for quality into the decade of the sixties.

THE COLLEGE OF LAW

During this decade, the College of Law continued under the able leadership of Dean Edmund O. Belsheim. Law students from Nebraska brought considerable credit to the institution in 1954 by winning the national "Moot Court" competition. Despite the effectiveness of the instructional program, the College of Law became involved in considerable public controversy during the last years of the decade.

This controversy resulted from the involvement of faculty members in the defense of two indigent persons accused of murder and from the participation of one faculty member in drafting a controversial labor bill considered by the legislature. Disregarding the accepted principle that all accused of a crime are entitled to be represented by an attorney, the involvement of members of the Law College faculty in two murder cases was criticized by both the public and

Law students in moot court competition.

by members of the bar. However, in June 1960, a report from the Section of Legal Education and Admissions to the Bar of the American Bar Association asserted that:

An unpopular defendant came to the legal aid clinic in the law school for assistance in the preparation of the defense in a notorious trial. Dean Belsheim, discharged the highest responsibility of a member of the bar, took the steps necessary to prepare a defense. It is alleged that local counsel was secured to represent the defendant, and that Dean Belsheim insisted on continuing to participate in the proceeding, to be assured that the representation was adequate. Members of the local bar felt that Dean Belsheim should have withdrawn as soon as regular counsel was secured.[17]

Another source of dispute related to the drafting of a proposed labor bill by a member of the Law College faculty. In testimony before the Labor and Welfare Committee of the Unicameral, the professor who had drafted the labor bill made a statement which he later corrected in a letter to the committee. The matter involved the professor's membership in Americans for Democratic Ac-

17. Evaluation Report of the University of Nebraska, College of Law, conducted December 2–3, 1959, by Representatives of the Section of Legal Education and Admissions to the Bar of the American Bar Association, p. 14, MSS, University of Nebraska Archives, Hardin Collection.

tion, an organization looked upon by some conservatives with suspicion. A group from the American Bar Association investigated the incident and concluded that "whether this was an unintentional failure of recollection or whether . . . intended to deceive the Committee cannot be answered by us, and it is irrelevant for our purposes. This merely fed the flames of distrust and lent some color of support for hostility already held on other grounds."[18]

This hostility took the form of several resolutions which were introduced into the Unicameral. The attacks against the Law College found little public support and were abandoned. Because of the participation of members of the bar in the criticism of the Law College, representatives of the American Bar Association considered the relationship of the college to the Nebraska bar at the time of an accreditation visit. They concluded that:

If the school expects to recruit the best students in the state who seek a legal education, and if it is to influence the development of the law and lawyers in Nebraska, affirmative steps must be taken to regain the support of the bar. Many members of the bar, and perhaps a majority, strongly support the school and some participate in its programs. This base of support needs to be broadened to the end that the school receive greater financial support, as well as the good will of the bar and the public. Fundamentally, this is a "liberal" faculty, set down in a "conservative" community which has a "conservative" bar.[19]

THE COLLEGES OF MEDICINE, DENTISTRY, AND PHARMACY

This period was a time of crucial importance for medical education at the University of Nebraska. In no part of the institution was the issue of a quality program more acute than in the Medical College. Because of rapidly rising standards in medical education and the inability of the University of Nebraska's Medical College to keep up with the requirements for full-time faculty and improved facilities, several major problems developed. The use of a part-time faculty for clinical instruction caused mounting criticism from medical accrediting groups. Furthermore, the volunteer part-time faculty members were often unable to fulfill their instructional duties. Regent Earle G. Johnson, a Grand Island physician, recognized this problem. "It is my conviction that there are a number of prima donnas in the volunteer faculty of our Medical College. The one thing apparently needs to be done by the Dean is to see that these Professors meet their classes at the appointed hour or they provide a substitute."[20] The use of a part-time unpaid volunteer clinical faculty was necessitated by the limited funds provided for medical education.

Another weakness in the instructional program was the inadequate quantity of clinical material available for study by medical students. Chancellor Gustavson emphasized this need. "Our bed capacity today offers our students not even half of the number which they should have for a good survey of disease. And this cannot help but be reflected, of course, in their fitness to practice medicine for a considerable period of time after they have graduated."[21] Again, the solution required increased financial support.

As a result of the combined efforts of the regents, University administration, and Nebraska State Medical Association, the Unicameral adopted a special state mill levy for the construction of an improved University Medical Center.

18. Ibid.

19. Ibid., p. 15.

20. Letter, Earle G. Johnson, M.D., to R. G. Gustavson, March 19, 1952, MSS, University of Nebraska Archives, Gustavson Collection.

21. Letter, R. G. Gustavson to Governor Robert B. Crosby, March 26, 1953, MSS, University of Nebraska Archives, Gustavson Collection.

However, this improvement in facilities required time and the Medical College's accreditation became tenuous. In 1952, the Liaison Committee on Medical Education, representing the Association of Medical Colleges and the Council on Medical Education and Hospitals of the American Medical Association, placed the University of Nebraska Medical College on "confidential probation." Another survey in 1954 continued the probationary status. Finally in 1956, the accrediting body removed the "confidential probation" and returned the Medical College to fully approved status. The cost of regaining full accreditation was high. In the budget request submitted by the regents for the 1957 legislative session, 17 percent of the University's requested funds were allocated for the Medical Center. The enrollment in the Medical College was 347 and in the School of Nursing 111.

At this time, leadership at the College of Medicine was difficult and often discouraging. The resignation of Dean Harold C. Lueth, in 1952, mirrored the administrative problems resulting from a divided faculty. The University administration sought to reestablish faculty unity by reorganizing the Executive Faculty of the Medical College. The low faculty morale reflected the severe disappointment in the slow progress at the college to improve its facilities and to meet its needs for additional full-time faculty. Certainly, the humiliation of being placed on "confidential probation" was a jolt to faculty confidence.

After consultation with a committee from the faculty of the Medical College, the Board of Regents appointed J. Perry Tollman to be dean of the College of Medicine. He was a native Nebraskan and had been a faculty member at the college since 1931. Tollman had served as chairman of the Department of Pathology, as director of the School of Medical Technologists, and as assistant dean of the college. During the term of his administration, substantial improvements in the programs of the Medical Center were achieved.

The director of the School of Nursing during this decade was Irma M. Kyle, who had been appointed to the post in 1946. Several important changes in the nursing program were approved by the regents during the fifties. A four-year degree program was established, a one-year practical nursing program was instituted in cooperation with the Omaha Public Schools, and a masters degree in psychiatric nursing was approved.

Although the regents considered consolidating the instructional programs in the health-related professions on the Medical Center Campus, the College of Dentistry and Pharmacy were retained on the Lincoln campus. Bert L. Hooper, the dean of dentistry since the thirties, retired and was succeeded by Ralph L. Ireland in 1958. He had been a member of the faculty since 1936 and was chairman of the Department of Pedodontics at the time of his promotion to the deanship. The College of Dentistry still occupied part of Andrews Hall, but a serious problem of crowding developed. In 1955, the Nebraska State Dental Association adopted a resolution which urged improvement in the facilities provided for the College of Dentistry. Chancellor Hardin responded to this plea, "I appreciate particularly the spirit in which it is written, and want to assure you that we are in complete sympathy with its objectives and that we will attempt to attain them just as fast as possible."[22] It was not until 1967, however, that new quarters on the East Campus for the College of Dentistry were dedicated.

The College of Pharmacy, under the direction of Dean Joseph B. Burt, moved into new quarters during the fifties. The new facility was named Lyman Hall in honor of Rufus A. Lyman, the former dean and a pioneer in pharmaceutical

22. Letter, Clifford M. Hardin to Dr. F. A. Pierson, September 8, 1955, MSS, University of Nebraska Archives, Hardin Collection.

education. He wrote the chancellor at the time when the honor was bestowed on him:

The University of Nebraska has done so much for me and for my family in my life time that I did not anticipate this additional honor. Our University has made it possible for me to accomplish some things that have given me great joy and much satisfaction. I only wish I could have more for the University but any man's ability has its limitations.[23]

A major curricular change was approved by the regents for the College of Pharmacy in 1955. The program leading to the Bachelor of Science in Pharmacy degree was changed from a four-year to a five-year program. This change

Professor Harald Holck with a class in the College of Pharmacy.

had been discussed by leaders in pharmaceutical education for nearly twenty-five years. In 1948, a national Pharmaceutical Survey Committee published a report urging the adoption of the five-year curriculum. With this change, it was believed, greater emphasis would be given students' general education.

THE COLLEGE OF BUSINESS ADMINISTRATION

Enrollment in the College of Business Administration was relatively stable throughout the fifties. The college continued to prepare students for business careers, and most graduates hoped to remain in their home state. Additions to the instructional offerings of the college reflected the changing requirements of the business community. Courses in the measurement and indexing of national income emphasized the need to understand the increasingly complex national economy. Faculty publications stressed current business concerns. Among those who contributed to major professional journals were Professors Richard M. Bourne, Dana F. Cole, Raymond C. Dein, Curtis M. Elliott, Clifford M. Hicks, Charles J. Kennedy, Campbell R. McConnell, and Phillip McVey.

23. Letter, Rufus A. Lyman to John K. Selleck, February 11, 1954, MSS, University of Nebraska Archives, Selleck Collection.

The dean of the college until his retirement in 1958 was Earl S. Fullbrook. He was followed by Charles S. Miller. The new dean was a native of Denver, but received his secondary education in Cheyenne, Wyoming. His university work was done at Creighton University and the University of Iowa, where he was awarded the Doctor of Philosophy degree. After a successful career in business, he joined the faculty of the University of Nebraska in 1949. At the time of his promotion to the deanship, Miller was professor of business organization and management.

The decade of the fifties was a time of considerable improvement in the academic programs of the University. Although the rate of improvement was not uniform, the potential inherent in the University of Nebraska faculty for making a substantial contribution to teaching and research was amply demonstrated. It was abundantly clear that with adequate financial support the academic program at the University of Nebraska could rank with that of the nation's leading universities.

CHAPTER 12

Student Life During the "Gray Flannel" Era

THE DECADE OF THE fifties was a complex time for the nation and her people. The Korean conflict and the United States' involvement sent some American youths to the battlefields of Asia, while others remained at home and pursued their own interests. The business community enjoyed, during the early years of the decade, a wartime prosperity. With the termination of the Korean conflict came an economic readjustment to peace and to the continuing cold war. Many Americans sought in the fifties a time of stability and the opportunity to reorder their lives in conformity with their personal goals and ambitions. For many, this meant the acquisition of material prosperity and conformity to the mass culture. However, by the end of the decade, satisfaction with comfortable mediocrity had yielded to a more competitive spirit based on excellence. The launching of the first man-made satellite, Sputnik I, by the Soviet Union heralded the end of national complacency.

Student life at American colleges and universities mirrored the conditions and attitudes of the larger society. During most of the period, the increasing demand for college graduates in business and the professions combined with a seemingly unlimited opportunity for advancement to produce the era of the "gray flannel suit" on the campus and in society. The times suggested to many that the good life was possible for those who conformed to the mass culture and programed their lives successfully. Many young people believed that success resulted from being in the proper place at the proper time and by making a good impression. Ability and individuality were often considered of less importance than superficial appearance. The impulse for conformity was never greater.

Despite the nation's involvement in a war in Asia, students capable of achieving a satisfactory score on the Selective Service deferment examinations were usually granted a draft exemption until after graduation. Other students enrolled in the ROTC programs to insure that their military service would be in a leadership or supervisory capacity that could be valuable later in the business or professional world.

A university degree, to a greater extent than ever before, was considered to be the passport to middle-class status. Some students sought their degrees as middle-class symbols more than for the learning they represented. Enjoying campus social life and making social contacts which would be useful in later life became a major part of many students' curriculum. This emphasis on good times and the belief that with graduation one's future success was assured characterized most of the fifties.

The decade had hardly begun when a scandal regarding student cheating on final examinations was revealed at the University of Nebraska. The extent of campus cheating was discussed by Roswell Howard, '50, Student Council president. "It's unfortunate that from the number of students who cheated on final exams, only seven were caught. Many more are guilty."[1] The *Daily Nebraskan* editorialized that, "We can condemn those who deal in 'hot' exams, pointing out the unfairness and baseness of their actions. . . . But the tradition of stealing exams is pretty well embedded and traditions are hard things to erase."[2] The real culprit, the writer believed, for this deplorable situation was the faculty. "When they stop making such a fetish of their finals, the situation will be greatly relieved."[3] Another student speculated that being supplied with an advance copy of a final examination was perhaps "part of an inter-frat faction that is organized to steal the finals and swear not to tell any information if they are caught. . . . It may be just part of the service a fraternity offers you."[4]

Although the overwhelming majority of students at the University of Nebraska neither cheated nor approved of academic dishonesty, they did criticize the established examination policy. The Student Council recommended to the faculty that less emphasis should be placed on final examinations, that final examinations should not determine more than 25 percent of the semester grade, that instructors should give one test at least every three weeks, and that all testing should emphasize understanding rather than memorization. A student-faculty dialog was initiated, and although it did not result in the elimination of final examinations, it did help to improve teaching efficiency and student evaluation.

Related to the issue of examinations was a growing student concern over the variation in faculty teaching ability and interest. The desirability of instituting a method of rating faculty teaching was urged by the staff of the *Daily Nebraskan* as a practical method to improve University instruction. The idea was accepted by a majority of the faculty, and joint faculty-student committees were formed to consider various methods of evaluating teaching. A scheme for student evaluation of individual instructors was approved by the University Senate. The evaluation procedures adopted had been developed at Purdue University, and faculty participation was voluntary. The results of the evaluation were kept confidential and were reported only to the evaluated faculty member.

The nation's involvement in the Korean conflict during the early fifties returned the issue of possible conscription as a major student concern. Reminiscent of the advice given by Chancellor Boucher in 1940, students were urged by Chancellor Gustavson to "stay in school. Do your best in your studies. When your nation needs you, you will be called."[5] The Selective Service College Qualification Tests, first given in December 1951, often increased student apprehension regarding their draft status. Satisfactory scores on these tests were used by local draft boards as one criterion for granting student draft deferments. Most Nebraska students did not regard educational deferments as an escape from military service, but rather a postponement in the best interest of the student and the nation.

They have been deferred until they finish either the current school year or their education. They will take up their share of the fighting when the current soldiers are discharged. If these men are allowed to get that education the future will not be stripped clean of the necessary college-educated section of our population.[6]

1. *Daily Nebraskan*, February 1, 1950.
2. Ibid.
3. Ibid.
4. Ibid., February 8, 1950.
5. Lincoln *Star*, January 19, 1951, p. 1.
6. *Daily Nebraskan*, March 7, 1952.

Student concern regarding future military service produced a substantial enrollment increase in the University military departments. Colonel James Workman, professor of military science and tactics, reflected on the changing student attitude:

More students . . . are applying for advanced ROTC. There has also been a pronounced improvement in the quality of work done in ROTC courses. This is due in part to the increased interest in the course of study and the incentive provided by the probability of early entry to active service.

Men eligible for ROTC training now see the advantage of such study more than they did before the Korean Conflict.[7]

The national victory of the Republican party in 1952 has often been interpreted as the consequence of the public desire to end the Korean conflict and to return the nation to peace. Students at the University of Nebraska, in a mock election, also overwhelmingly supported Eisenhower over Stevenson. The issues identified by students as most influential in their support of the Eisenhower candidacy were Korea, corruption, and communism.

While the academic community sought tranquility on the international and national scene, student life at the University of Nebraska was not always serene during the fifties. In February 1951, some two hundred male students, chanting the slogan, "male suffrage," crashed the gate at the traditional girls-only production of the Co-ed Follies. Perhaps as a result of the male students' enthusiasm, the popular revue was opened for general student attendance the next year. In early May 1952, male student enthusiasm produced the first "panty raid" of the decade at Nebraska. The commotion began as a water fight at a fraternity house. Swiftly the incident expanded to include both Greeks and Barbs in the disorder. Tiring of the water fight, the men turned their attention to the women's dormitory. Before order was restored, nearly every organized house on campus was entered by the lingerie-seeking mob. In several instances, walls were even scaled to gain entry to upstairs windows.

Public reaction to the campus disturbance, involving both property damage and the invasion of women's housing, was swift and severe. At a time when American young men were being killed on the battlefields of Korea, many Nebraskans were deeply troubled by this campus incident. On May 6, 1952, the members of Selective Service Board No. 30, in Omaha, requested from the chancellor the names "of any male students over eighteen years of age, registrants from this board who took part in the affair which was related by the press as occurring on May 1st and 2nd, involving the invasion of the women's quarters and personal injury to school authorities."[8] Gustavson replied to the Omaha Selective Service Board and emphasized that the press account contained many exaggerations.

This started out as an innocent college prank and then got going into something that was more serious. There was no evidence of insobriety. No women suffered any physical harm. I am sure the whole situation is deeply regretted by the student body, and I am sure that goes for the administration.

I feel that any attempt to use the Selective Service System as a part of the punishment of these boys would be completely out of line. The University, therefore, will not submit any names to the Board.[9]

7. Ibid., November 15, 1951.

8. Letter from Selective Service Local Board No. 30, Omaha to University of Nebraska, May 6, 1952, MSS, University of Nebraska Archives, Gustavson Collection.

9. Letter from R. G. Gustavson to Douglas County Board No. 30, May 13, 1952, MSS, University of Nebraska Archives, Gustavson Collection.

"Panty raid" in 1952. Courtesy of the Lincoln *Journal-Star*.

The local Omaha Selective Service Board, in a later communication, denied that their earlier request had given any

basis for the conclusion that we requested the names "to use the Selective Service System as part of the punishment of these boys." You will note that we requested the names in order that we might "check them against our lists" and in order that the entire matter may be considered properly by our Board in the event any of our registrants were involved.[10]

In a series of meetings with student leaders and after a special University convocation, Chancellor Gustavson felt assured that there would not be a repetition of the disturbances of May 1952. However, after the graduation of these students and during the beginning of the Hardin administration, another "panty

10. Letter from Oscar T. Doerr, Chairman, Douglas County Local Board No. 30 to R. G. Gustavson, May 22, 1952, MSS, University of Nebraska Archives, Gustavson Collection.

raid" shattered campus serenity. The student body at the University of Nebraska was not unique in staging these raids. Many American colleges and universities experienced similar invasions of women's housing by mobs in incidents, which were called during the fifties "panty raids."

Student politics during the early fifties continued to be dominated by those students affiliated with fraternities and sororities. This situation continued because of the inability of Independents or Barbs to agree on political candidates or on issues. Only in several of the professional colleges was there a unified student body. This was especially true in the Colleges of Dentistry and Engineering.

The retirement of Theos J. Thompson as dean of student affairs in June 1952 ended a career of twenty-five years as a friend and disciplinarian of the student body. During his long tenure as dean, many changes had taken place in student life at the University of Nebraska. In the dark days of the depression, Dean Thompson and fraternity alumni formed the Interfraternity Board of Control, which rescued many fraternities from financial bankruptcy and helped maintain the fraternity system at the University. Thompson served twenty-five years on the Athletic Board, spent twenty years as a faculty representative on the Big Six Athletic Council, presided over the University Curriculum Committee for ten years, was a member of the Medical Basic Science Board for fourteen years, and served as a member of a Lincoln Selective Service Board from 1940 to 1947. After his retirement from the University administration, Dean Thompson continued to serve the University in other capacities for several years. Theos J. Thompson died in 1970. To several generations of students at the University of Nebraska, he was a stern disciplinarian but also a respected friend.

Dr. T. J. Thompson is an administrator who tries very hard to understand the students and their problems. His dominant traits are sincerity and loyalty. There is nothing hypocritcal about the man; he is personally convinced that every decision he makes is the very best he can produce. He is loyal not only to his school, but also to his convictions.

The Daily Nebraskan does not agree with every decision Dr. Thompson has made during his career as dean, but it does respect the sincerity which is behind those decisions. It is difficult for any man to control student conduct and still retain his popularity. In this respect, being Dean of Student Affairs could be a discouraging and thankless job. It is hard to remove students from school.[11]

In the fall of 1952, the Division of Student Affairs was created to draw together under one administration most activities concerned with student life. They included registration and records, counseling and testing, orientation, health, remedial services, regulation of student's organizations and activities, discipline, housing, employment, loans, scholarships, placement of nonteaching University graduates, and liaison with fraternities and sororities. To direct this new administrative agency, the Board of Regents appointed J. Phillip Colbert, who had been a member of the College of Engineering faculty since 1925.

Another University personnel change of interest to students was the retirement of Elsie Ford Piper as assistant dean of women in 1950. During her twenty-five years of service at the University, Dean Piper had been a leading campaigner for University-operated residence halls for women students. Helen A. Snyder was appointed by the regents to succeed Dean Piper.

Students at the University of Nebraska maintained their interest in the work of the United Nations during the early fifties. In part this resulted from the interest and activities of Chancellor Gustavson in support of the world organization. The desire of students to be good citizens of their state was clearly demon-

11. *Daily Nebraskan,* April 23, 1952.

strated by their response to the call for volunteers to assist in flood control work in the spring of 1952. The mayor of Omaha complimented the students: "The participation of University students in the flood fight was the 'grandest gesture' he had ever known. He said that it was the 'duty' of the people of Omaha to help in the battle, but citizens from all over the state were represented in the student action."[12]

With the burning of the mortgage on the Student Union in April 1952, an obligation assumed in 1937 was fulfilled. In anticipation of the future enrollment boom and from a desire to provide more adequate recreational facilities, student leaders urged the expansion of the Student Union. Later in the decade, the Board of Regents authorized an expansion of the Union.

During the middle fifties, the quest for fun and excitement by students produced several incidents which caused administrative concern and hostile public criticism. The occurrence of two more "panty raids" and an increase in student violations of state, local, and University liquor regulations affected the public's perception of campus life.

In May 1954, a group of male students conducted a "panty raid" at the Women's Residence Hall. Because of the participation of only a few students in the incident, the absence of serious property damage, and the inability of the University administration to identify the guilty students, decisive disciplinary action was not taken. The dean of student affairs, J. P. Colbert, "pointed out that the mild spring season and the fact that this was a Monday night after house meetings combined to produce a situation encouraging [students] to let off steam."[13] Chancellor Selleck compared the event to the "shirt-tail" raids held on the campus forty years earlier. To be sure, the histories of countless American colleges and universities testify to the frequency of spring brawls on the campuses.

Unfortunately, the "panty raid" of the next spring was not as restrained as that of 1954. The news editor of the *Daily Nebraskan*, Richard Fellman, '56, vividly described the student riot:

Starting with what seemed to be a friendly, innocent water fight, a full-fledged riot gained momentum and grew into a leaderless mob spreading wanton destruction over the entire campus Thursday evening.

By 10:30 p.m., the mob seemed to be heading down 16th Street towards downtown Lincoln. During the three hours of mayhem, all but two sororities had been broken into. In each case, damage had been reported, sometimes reaching estimates of "much over $500."

Reports were given of stolen money and radios, pilfered clothing, broken windows, muddied floors and the inevitable "panties." Exact estimates of specific damage were unavailable, but approximations were given by many sorority leaders and housemothers. Some girls claimed that individual losses of lingerie and cashmere sweaters amounted to more than $50.

The actual riot began by "preliminary horseplay" when the Phi Psis threw water at the Theta and AOPi houses. From there, people were observed entering the crowd from all sources. First-hand reports indicated the crowd "seemed to be getting younger as time went on." Many observers said the mob included large groups of people who seemed like high school students and students from other local colleges. Toward the end of the evening many fraternity pledge groups were helping "stand guard" and cleaned up the disheveled sorority houses.

After the riot had become full-blown, the mob moved in front of the Girls' Dorm. During the next 30 to 45 minutes the Dorm was stormed twice. In each case, the participating members of the mob were encouraged by bystanders and some few occupants of the Dorm.

12. Ibid., April 21, 1952.
13. Ibid., May 12, 1954.

From there, the mob moved to the Kappa House where they broke windows on the second floor and entered, spreading the destruction that, by this time, seemed routine to the uncontrolled group.

After going back to the Dorm and starting a fire in the street, the group moved successively to the Chi Omega, Pi Phi, Gamma Phi, Kappa Delt, Delta Gamma, Alpha Xi, Tri Delt, Theta, AOPi, Alpha Phi, Alpha Chi and finally back over the sorority rounds again. By this time the entire sorority "row" had been invaded.

At 9:15 p.m. a fire was started in the middle of the intersection of 16th and "R" Streets. From this point, the mob assaulted a local city bus and began rocking it and terrorizing the passengers. A woman watching the group snapped a picture. Within seconds the crowd had literally captured the film, breaking into the car and lifting it from the ground.

Moving back to the dorm, a Model A Ford was carried from behind the Lutheran Student House to the front steps of the Dorm. Windows were broken, and the car was tipped on its top. Alcohol and oil was leaking from the engine.

Last night's riot was the third in four years. According to many observers, last year's riot was a street dance compared to what happened Thursday. In previous years, the riots have been towards the middle of May.

An estimated 150 to 250 persons then marched down 16th Street to O Street and then to the intersection of 12th and O Streets. There they turned toward the Lincoln Theater where a display window was broken. The group turned down 13th Street to the Varsity and Stuart Theaters. Both buildings were locked.

Dispersing at 14th and P Streets, the rioters had seemingly lost a leader.[14]

This episode clearly exceeded all limits for student pranks. Condemnation of the mob's actions was swift from student leaders, the University administration, the public, and the state's senators. The University administration, with support from the Board of Regents, took strong disciplinary action. Nineteen students were suspended or dismissed from the University. A few students were convicted of disturbing the peace by Lancaster County courts.

The 1955 spring student riot coincided with a state legislative session. Senator Lester H. Anderson, from Aurora, introduced Legislative Resolution 22, which advocated that "the persons involved in the riotous action and upon [civil] conviction . . . the students found guilty be expelled from the University of Nebraska."[15] Senator Anderson also suggested "that the Legislature take into consideration the appropriation for the University of Nebraska when adopting the budget for the next biennium as to curtailing activities which may attempt to stop such riotous actions in the future."[16] Four days after the introduction of Legislative Resolution 22, a motion by Senator Hal Bridenbaugh to postpone indefinitely was adopted by the Unicameral. The approval of this motion by the senator from Dakota City was a vote of confidence for the regents and the University administration in the supervision of student conduct. Senator Bridenbaugh stated that he had "all the confidence in the world in the Chancellor. Our duty is to make law—not dictate policy."[17] Not until April 1957 did the Board of Regents authorize the dean of student affairs to readmit any of the students dismissed from the University for their misconduct in April 1955.

The other serious malady affecting the student body, during the middle years of the decade, was the increase in liquor violations. In early 1953, the mayor of Lincoln and members of the City Council expressed mounting concern over the increasing number of violations by students of state liquor and beer laws. From the beginning of the 1954 fall semester until mid-October, the Lincoln Municipal Court fined twenty-nine University students for the illegal possession

14. Ibid., April 15, 1955.
15. *Legislative Journal of the State of Nebraska, Sixty-Seventh Session*, p. 988.
16. Ibid.
17. *Daily Nebraskan*, April 19, 1955.

of liquor. Although the number of students fined was a very small number in proportion to the total enrollment, the University administration and regents viewed the possible increase in student illegal drinking with alarm.

To combat this possible trend toward increased campus drinking, the regents approved the University administration's proposal to employ special "security officers." The special officers were authorized to check fraternity social functions and other student activities for possible infractions of the state, local, and University drinking regulations. Although there was some student protest of the appointment of the special University liquor agents, student leaders generally recognized that the action was necessitated by the growing public concern over illegal student drinking. Later, Dean Colbert considered that the University action to control student illegal drinking had been successful.

It is my firm conviction that our special police have been very effective in drying up the indiscriminate drinking on the campus which existed prior to hiring men for special duty. I am under no illusion but that there is drinking by certain members of the student body, but I do believe that for the most part we have driven such drinking off the campus and that such drinking is now done off the campus and under cover. This latter condition will probably always exist among our students just as it exists in society at large. I am also convinced that the hiring of our special police has caused our own University Police to become more diligent in the enforcement of our regulation concerning alcoholic beverages.[18]

For nearly all University students, involvement in either "panty raids" or liquor violations was not a part of their campus experience. Nevertheless, the topics provided much grist for campus discussion. Most students centered their campus life in acceptable and often traditional activities.

Campus politics had long mirrored the favorites of the Greek-letter student social groups. However, the All-University party, also known as the Faction, which was the agency of fraternity political power in campus elections, dissolved itself in 1955. This resulted from the insistence of the Student Council that the Faction be required to submit a constitution for endorsement and be formally approved, as was required of other student organizations. Rather than comply with this requirement the informal alliance dissolved itself. Inasmuch as the goal of the Faction had been to elect candidates to campus offices, its end marked a turning point in student politics. As an unofficial organization, the Faction was efficient in delivering a bloc Greek vote. The "penalty for not voting was a one dollar fine for each person in a house who did not check his name off a list after voting in campus elections."[19]

The construction of additional dormitory facilities for students at the University during the fifties was responsible for changes in housing policy. With the increased availability of dormitory quarters for men students, some of their traditional freedom was lost. The situation was similar to that of the thirties, when to insure occupancy of Carrie Bell Raymond Hall, the regents changed their policies on women's housing. Chancellor Selleck outlined the new direction in policy for men's housing:

In order to insure the filling of the new dormitories for men as well as to start the evolution of our housing policies we expect that the following procedures will be followed by the Housing Office.

All entering men (freshmen and transfer students) not living with parents will be expected to live in dormitories, fraternities, or cooperative houses.

No students will be referred to private rooms until after the dormitories are filled.

18. Letter from J. P. Colbert to John K. Selleck, January 28, 1956, MSS, University of Nebraska Archives, Selleck Collection.
19. *Daily Nebraskan,* March 18, 1955.

Freshmen who go through rush week and who fail to pledge will be placed in the dormitories if possible.

A statement concerning the requirements for freshmen housing will be included in all correspondence to prospective students.

Although a vigorous advertising campaign may fill the dormitories, it is so very important that they be filled I feel we must take a very positive attitude which the above procedures imply.[20]

This change indicates clearly the effect of financial considerations in the shaping of University policy. Many of the policies of educational institutions are the result of noneducational considerations.

International House float.

Among the campus events which caused campus discussion during these years were the banning of the Kosmet Klub's production in 1955 for its "questionable taste," the unsuccessful attempt to restrict men students' extracurricular activities through the adoption of a point system, and a discussion of the relevance of continuing the tradition of freshman beanies. The reestablishment of a campus veterans' organization bore witness to the end of the Korean conflict, although the number of student veterans did not equal that of the previous decade.

During the final years of the decade, student life was perhaps more uneventful than it had been since the twenties. Some have interpreted this as a lack of concern with the problems of society and a general apathy. Others suggest that this was a "cool generation" with no real social or political concern. Students at the University of Nebraska generally regarded their years of study as a period of preparation for a vocation or profession. Their college years were not conceived by most students to be the proper time to effect the reformation of

20. Letter from John K. Selleck to J. P. Colbert and G. W. Rosenlof, May 10, 1954, MSS, University of Nebraska Archives, Selleck Collection.

society. This, most believed, could best be accomplished after graduation and after the graduate had taken his place in the larger society. Furthermore, other factors were also at work to create the illusion of apathy. Many traditional campus activities and events had lost their charm for students. The increased mobility of students resulting from more widespread ownership of automobiles and the growing individualistic spirit of students produced disenchantment with traditional ideas of fun. The proliferation of organized activities and special interest groups jaded many students toward campus organizations. William Hall, director of the School of Journalism, recognized that "the typical college student is engaged in so many activities that he prefers to do something on his own and to get away from the rat race. He may be fed up with organized activities."[21]

Co-ed Follies production "Casey at the Bat."

On the other hand, many students had little time for campus activities because of jobs. An estimated 70 percent of the student body at the University of Nebraska worked to help finance their higher education. Of those students surveyed who worked, approximately 75 percent were employed both during the summer and the school year. Nearly half of the working students earned their University education without parental or outside financial support. Some of what has been regarded as apathy was the limited amount of uncommitted time available to struggling students while trying to meet their educational and economic needs.

There was a change also in the conception of the importance of membership in the Greek-letter organizations. These organizations were losing some of their earlier prominence during the last years of the fifties. The construction of attractive, comfortable, and inexpensive University dormitories eroded the traditional advantage that fraternity membership provided in unequaled accommodations for students. Greek-letter organizations were also being increasingly criti-

21. *Daily Nebraskan,* February 17, 1959.

cized for their racially restrictive membership policies and alleged juvenile initiatory activities.

The editor of the *Daily Nebraskan*, Ernie Hines, '60, who was a member of Beta Theta Pi fraternity, recognized the decline in the number of men going through fraternity rush as symptomatic of a changing student attitude. He called for reforms to revitalize the fraternities.

N-Club initiation.

The IFC should be reminded that a bigger and better package is the only attraction that will sell the fraternity system. This means better scholarship, more constructive pledge programs and sincere efforts to make the fraternity beneficial to both members and the community by stressing help for others instead of raising hell to trouble others.[22]

The acceptance by the entire student body, Greeks and Independents, of a more mature and responsible attitude toward good citizenship in the campus community was evidenced with the creation of the Student Tribunal of the University of Nebraska. The proposal for the system of self-imposed student discipline was originated by the Student Council and endorsed by a student vote. The Board of Regents approved the proposal in the spring of 1958 for

22. Ibid., September 22, 1958.

operation beginning in the fall. Although University authorities retained ultimate control of student discipline, the regents' approval of the Tribunal was a recognition of their belief in the greater maturity of the student body. Not all shared the regents' willingness to increase student power. The *World-Herald* editorialized:

> The University of Nebraska Board of Regents has approved creation of a student tribunal, manned mostly by student "judges," "to serve as a student court on matters of student discipline." The tribunal will hear cases referred to it by the Division of Student Affairs, and will recommend action to the Dean of Student Affairs. Final authority, apparently, will remain with the regular University officials.
>
> We suppose there is no harm in this sort of thing. Some educators set great store by it, and talk sagely of "group integration," "group development," "student democracy," and so on.
>
> However, we saw nothing much wrong with the old system, in which the dean summoned a student who had had too many beers and had socked a policeman, and informed him that he was no longer a student.
>
> After all, it is the duty of the University's duly constituted officers to run the school, and we see no reason why they shouldn't just go ahead and do it.[23]

There has usually been more appreciation of the inherent sense of fair-play, honesty, and untarnished idealism of college students by those who associate with them than from those denied that privilege.

As the decade of the fifties closed on the campus of the University of Nebraska the registrar, Floyd Hoover, noted that "Joe College is rapidly disappearing." The average age of the student body was rising and "about three out of every four of the present entering freshmen came from the upper half of their high school classes, and almost half of this 75 percent came from the upper fourth of their high school classes."[24] In the next decade student life would be profoundly effected by the increased maturity and heightened intellectual ability of the student body.

VARSITY ATHLETICS

Few Nebraska football followers were prepared for the sensational opening of the 1950s, and none could foresee the glory, the tribulations, and the tragedies that were to transpire during a colorful, but stormy, decade.

The record shows that Nebraska's football team achieved 39 victories, 58 defeats, and three ties under three different coaches during the '50s. There were three winning seasons and one .500 year, all under Bill Glassford in the first half of the decade. In order, they were 1950 (6–2–1), 1952 (5–4–1), 1954 (6–5–0), and 1955 (5–5–0).

A gallant and dramatic football player from Grand Island, the incomparable Bobby Reynolds, was to assure two of the winning seasons under Glassford, whose teams had a 27–30–3 record during the first years of the decade.

It was ironic that although the Huskers were to achieve their greatest heights since the Rose Bowl under Glassford, they were also to suffer through their most torturous moment in 1953 when a players' revolt sent shock waves across the state. Glassford refused to surrender his coaching prerogatives, and the Athletic Board and the administration backed the former Pitt All-American.

However, football fans like to remember the good years, and no true Nebraska fan has forgotten 1950. Encouraged by Glassford's recruiting of Fran Nagle and a resulting 4–5–0 year in 1949, the Cornhuskers looked forward to 1950 with enthusiasm. After all, they had a proven quarterback in Nagle and

23. Omaha *World-Herald,* April 4, 1958, p. 38.
24. Ibid., February 15, 1959, p. 2-B.

high hopes for a sophomore from Grand Island named Reynolds. What transpired left Nebraska fans breathless. Reynolds had one of the greatest seasons in college football history, earning All-American honors for himself and national attention for Nebraska.

Sportswriters quickly ran out of adjectives in trying to describe Reynolds, who scored 20 points to tie Indiana in his Husker debut. The next week he led Nebraska to its first win over Minnesota since 1940, and after a loss to Colorado, Nebraska won five straight games to earn a chance to play Oklahoma for the Big Seven title. Although Oklahoma won 49–35, Reynolds scored 21 points in the first half in a sensational game. That almost, but not quite, made fans forget his dazzling run against Missouri during which he reversed his field three times and seemed to run by every player on the field six times. That great performance clinched All-American honors for Reynolds and a place in the hearts of Nebraskans for all time. Reynolds' record was almost unbelievable as he ran wild, earning plaudits as "Mr. Touchdown, U.S.A." What a year this dazzling sophomore had with 22 touchdowns and 25 extra points for 157 points and a national record, 1,342 yards rushing for a Nebraska record. The great 1950 season helped Reynolds launch a career that was to include three records which stood as Nebraska marks—until Jeff Kinney broke two of them in 1971—211 points, 28 touchdowns, and 2,196 yards. After such a great start Nebraska seemed destined for continued football success, but Bobby Reynolds was not superhuman despite his 1950 successes. In fall camp prior to the 1951 season, he suffered a shoulder separation. Glassford could never regroup the Huskers, and the record fell to 2–8–0. Reynolds was also to suffer eye burns from field lime when he finally did return to duty.

The Cornhuskers rallied for a 5–4–1 record in 1952, helped by a healthier Reynolds and an All-American tackle, Jerry Minnick. Reynolds also had his promising baseball career dashed in the spring of 1953 when he broke his leg and underwent surgery. However, his fans never forgot 1950, and in 1969, Cornhusker followers, picking the All-Time Nebraska team in conjunction with the University Centennial, gave the most votes and the captaincy to Bobby Reynolds.

Hard times struck Nebraska football in 1953, limiting Glassford's coaching tenure. In fairness to Glassford, a dedicated coach, although like Sutherland, a tough taskmaster, the odds were stacked against him. Nebraska fans demanded a winning football program, although Gustavson was a leader in the faction that was trying to reform intercollegiate football. Without a scholarship program, Glassford had to recruit players on a job-offer basis, a risky endeavor because some players had to work harder for their stipend than others, thus causing some squad dissension. Glassford drove his squad hard as the 1953 Huskers struggled through a 3–6–1 season. Then one of the darkest chapters of Nebraska football history began to unfold.

Encouraged by disgruntled fans, former players, students, officials, and a news media representative, the dissension-racked football team broke into open revolt. Players called news conferences and threatened to quit unless Glassford was fired. They listed grievances, most of which were vague and dealt with petty, individual likes and dislikes. As the news spread, all sorts of accusations were made, including charges by a Nebraska newspaper that University doctors at Glassford's urging had anesthetized injured players with novacaine and forced them to return to action. These charges were denied by all University parties involved and were never substantiated.

Although a critic of collegiate athletics, Gustavson never wavered in his support of Glassford, and the Athletic Board refused to knuckle under to the players' demands. Glassford, with full backing and with his job secure for the time being, finally met with his players in a soul-searching truce session. Both the coach and the players agreed to let by-gones be by-gones. But while an uneasy truce was established, the player revolt did prove to be the undoing of the problem-plagued Athletic Board. The regents disbanded the board and sought an athletic director who would be responsible only to the chancellor and to the regents. The man chosen was a former Michigan football star who was the athletic director at Toledo University, William "Bill" Orwig.

Orwig tried to mend the wounds while giving complete support to Glassford, but as time and problems progressed, he realized that a change in the football staff was inevitable. In basketball, he hired Toledo coach Jerry Bush to head the Huskers and installed Georgetown's Frank Sevigne as head track coach. One of Orwig's greatest contributions was to establish a solid fund-raising program that got the Huskers out of the under-the-table league. Sevigne raised Nebraska track to a new competitive high and kept the Cornhuskers in the national spotlight.

The football squad approached 1954 outwardly optimistic and united, but under the surface apprehensive and vulnerable. Some unanswered questions at the beginning of the season were whether the players could ever forgive Glassford and pay the price demanded to win, whether Glassford had yielded too much in conceding some points to the players, and if he could rely on his squad when the going got tough. Much to the surprise of many observers, the 1954 team had a great deal more character than could have been expected in view of the winter revolt. The Huskers chalked up their last winning season of the 1950s. The team, however, was inconsistent early as Glassford tried to mold a competitive team. Minnesota, as expected, beat the Huskers, but Nebraska came back to trounce Iowa State before being upset by Kansas State at Lincoln. At that point, there was a suspicion that the old problems were still present, but Glassford found the key, and Nebraska proceeded to reel off four straight wins. With a 5–2 record and a 4–1 Big Seven mark, Nebraska was a title contender. This was a fine comeback, to say the least. However, trouble that was to have far-reaching implications was brewing.

Pittsburgh defeated the Huskers, 21–7, at home, and the stage was set for the championship game at Oklahoma, then in the midst of the Bud Wilkinson hey-day. It was no contest and the Sooners bombed a helpless Nebraska team, 55–7, to sew up the title. Although Nebraska's record was then 5–4 with one game left and a chance for a relatively satisfactory 6–4 record, the fates began moving against Glassford. In 1954, the Big Seven Conference had a contract with the Orange Bowl to supply a team, the Big Seven champion, except that no team could go two years in a row. Since Oklahoma had gone in 1953, the runner-up could go to Miami in 1954. On the day the Sooners plastered Nebraska, 55–7, Kansas upset Missouri to give the Huskers second place. Thus Nebraska, a 6–4 team at best and the victim of a humiliating defeat, was invited to the Orange Bowl. It was plain to all that Nebraska was not a bowl team, but the squad had gotten the trip by virtue of the Big Seven's rules.

Meanwhile, Nebraska had another game—at Hawaii. Already faced with the chore of taking a vulnerable team to the Orange Bowl, Glassford now had to take his team to Hawaii and then get them keyed up all over again for the trip to Miami. There Nebraska was almost certain to be defeated by a fine Duke team, powerful champion of the Atlantic Coast Conference. It was a dilemma from which there could be no escape. Nebraska went to Hawaii; the players and coaches enjoyed in the words of Omaha *World Herald* sportswriter, Gregg McBride, "a whoopee cruise," and easily beat Hawaii, 50–0, for the 6–4 record that would accompany the Huskers to Miami.

By any standards, the Orange Bowl trip to Miami was anticlimatic in the wake of the fun-filled Hawaiian adventure. Glassford then made a strategic error that was to cost him dearly. He was aware that the carefree trip to Hawaii, the easy win, and subsequent lay-off after losses to two good teams, had taken the edge off his team. Discipline and dedication had been lost, and he felt that he had to whip his players back into fighting trim. There was heavy scrimmage, two-a-day drills, as Glassford drove his team vigorously. The Orange Bowl trip should have been a reward for a successful season. Instead, it was a desperate attempt to build a team for an impossible task. As players identified the harsh preparations with spring practice, they began to grumble. Unable to have fun playing football, squad morale collapsed, and some players broke training with regularity. Despite good intentions, Glassford had lost control of his players and his future. The new athletic director, Bill Orwig, sensing the explosive and crisis-laden tenor of the times, looked ahead with a heavy heart as Duke ripped the strife-torn and over-worked Nebraska team, 34–7. It was a pathetic effort by a Cornhusker team that should not have been in Miami.

Glassford, for all his shortcomings, was a fine salesman. He miraculously kept the press with him. Sportswriters accompanying the team gave him a reprieve and called for state support. However, the honeymoon lasted only until the first game of 1955 with Hawaii. Lulled into a false sense of security by the ease of the 50–0 win at Honolulu in 1954, Glassford miscalculated. With mighty Ohio State his second opponent, he gambled that beating Hawaii was a foregone conclusion and elected to spend fall camp getting ready for the Buckeyes. Hawaii, however, was a far different team and had a halfback named Skippy Dyer. The Rainbows came to Lincoln determined and dedicated. Nebraska, on the other hand, viewed the game as a joke, but there was no laughing on Saturday. Dyer slashed through Nebraska's defense, and the Huskers never could solve the Rainbows' valiant defense. While unbelieving Nebraska fans watched in stunned silence, the pesky Hawaiians defeated the Cornhuskers, 6–0. It was, perhaps, the Cornhuskers' most humiliating defeat of all time.

Nothing could save Glassford now. He immediately lost the press, and so violent was the reaction to the loss that the Omaha *World Herald*'s sports editor resigned after a disagreement with his superiors over how to handle the Nebraska football crisis. Nebraska fans, too, turned on Glassford and the team. Once again Nebraska football was embroiled in crisis.

Glassford, even though his days were now numbered, accepted the Hawaii loss as a challenge rather than the catastrophe seen by the fans. He rallied his team and proved again that he was a very capable coach. He whipped the Huskers into a frenzy by convincing them that the press and fans were their mortal enemies, who could only be conquered by winning games.

Stung by defeat and inspired by a hate campaign against the press and fans, Nebraska bounced back to play a great Ohio State team off its feet before losing, 28–20. After beating Kansas State, 16–0, the Huskers lost to Texas A & M and to Pittsburgh. Now Nebraska was 1–4 at the midway point.

As the anti-Glassford campaign continued in the press and the anti-press campaign continued in the football camp, Nebraska finished strong by winning four of their last five games to wind up 5–5 overall and second in the Big Seven with a 5–1 record. It was truly a fine coaching job and a fine effort by the players, but Nebraska had lost again to Oklahoma and to Hawaii.

Glassford had an option in his contract and could have forced a five-year renewal. However, the press openly hoped for a resignation and Director Orwig, feeling a change was Nebraska's only long-range salvation, offered Glassford no pressure to stay. After a brief period of "agonizing reappraisal," Glassford bitterly announced his resignation at a meeting with the press by throwing the media members a written statement and growling with an emotion-choked voice: "Here's what you've all been waiting for!"

Orwig immediately signed a young man he had long wanted to launch on a head coaching career, Oklahoma assistant Pete Elliott, a former Michigan player. However, much to Orwig's disappointment, Elliott stayed only one season, a 4–6 season that ended with a 54–6 lacing at Oklahoma and convinced Elliott that the Sooners were too tough a challenge. He quickly accepted an offer from California, and Orwig promptly hired Elliott's assistant, Bill Jennings, also a former Oklahoma aide under Bud Wilkinson.

Jennings made huge recruiting strides that were to pay large dividends in the 1960s, but he was never to achieve a winning season in five tries. In the final three years of the decade, Nebraska won only eight of thirty games, but the

Assistant basketball coach Tony Sharpe (left, center) and coach Jerry Bush (right, center) with 1958 team.

Huskers kept the fans buzzing with giant upsets such as Penn State (14–7) and Pittsburgh (14–6) in 1958, and Minnesota (36–12) in 1959.

The victory bombshell of the 1950s came in 1959 when underdog Nebraska knocked off Oklahoma, 25–21, in a classic game at Lincoln. It was the first Big Eight loss for Bud Wilkinson and snapped a 74-game streak for the Sooners. Fans went wild, tore down the steel goal post. Classes were dismissed. Jennings was hailed as a genius, and the Huskers were honored as giant-killers. It lasted only a week. The next Saturday Iowa State upset Nebraska, 18–6, and the Huskers were to lead Kansas State, 14–0, before losing 29–14, in the last game.

Many believed that Jennings' team could upset some big teams but were not consistent. Nebraska football went into the 1960s in an optimistic, but apprehensive state of mind. The Huskers were building and getting better, but the feeling began to grow that Bill Jennings and his staff might not be able to achieve the goals.

Thus, the 1950s had featured high moments and deep depression. The reorganization of the Athletic Department helped make possible the success of the '60s. This, and the hiring of a humorous coach from Wyoming, were going to produce the sensational sixties.

In basketball Nebraska tied for the Big Seven title again in 1950, but had to settle for some tremendous upsets under Jerry Bush, such as Nebraska's win over Kansas with Wilt Chamberlin and over Kansas State with Bob Boozer, during the rest of the decade.

Nebraska won the indoor track title in 1951 with two winners, 880 man Hobe Jones and vaulter Leonard Kehl, before surrendering the rest of the decade to Kansas. Outdoors, the Huskers won in 1950 with Harry Meginnis doubling in the sprints and Bob Berkshire winning the highs. Cornhusker track faltered until the arrival of Frank Sevigne and his prize Jamaican import, Keith Gardner, in 1957. Gardner in 1958 won the Schulte Trophy at the Big Eight outdoor and set a standard of excellence that has inspired Nebraska runners to the present time.

In swimming and wrestling, the Huskers were caught up in the Oklahoma domination of those sports and did not challenge.

Nebraska's baseball team under coach Tony Sharpe won the 1950 Big Seven title, led by slugger Bob Cerv, and gained four other runner-up spots in the 1950s.

THE SIXTIES

CHAPTER 13

Administration During the Dynamic Sixties

DURING THE DECADE OF THE sixties, the University of Nebraska completed its first century of service to the people of the state and the nation. This last decade of the first century, compared to Nebraska's past, was characterized by remarkable growth in the University physical plant, student enrollments, and by a higher level of service to the people of the state. It was the era of multiversity: fabulous grants of research and training money poured onto the campuses; intensive research in health, medicine, and physical sciences, massive building programs, and ever-growing budgets characterized American universities in this era. The University of Nebraska joined the big parade, but other universities served as the models. It was the era to emulate Michigan, Illinois, Wisconsin, Ohio State, and Berkeley. The atmosphere on these campuses and the University of Nebraska reached new heights of optimism and confidence for the future during the sixties. Most people believed that the University of Nebraska had entered a period of steady and certain improvement. This belief was sustained by the actions of the Board of Regents, University administration, and by the strong support given the institution by Governors Morrison and Tiemann.

The optimism at the University was shared by most Nebraskans during the sixties. Problems characteristic of an earlier time appeared to be under control. The net out-migration of Nebraskans, in comparison to the fifties, fell by more than a third during the sixties and was reduced to a trickle by the end of the decade. Unemployment remained substantially below the national average while the number of people engaged in agricultural employment decreased. The performance of Nebraska agriculture during the sixties was phenomenal. According to a study by economists at the University, Nebraska's success in

raising its gross income by more than two-thirds in a decade—nearly 70% above the national growth rate—while agricultural employment was dropping by one-third must certainly be recognized. The association of this dramatic change with application of agricultural research and education cannot be ignored.[1]

The general feeling of well-being enjoyed by most Nebraskans resulted in large part from the growth in personal income. In 1959, Nebraska ranked 46th among the 50 states in rate of growth in total personal income. By 1969, the state ranked 32nd. By local benchmarks, the people of Nebraska had made considerable economic progress. However, a recent study by members of the Business College faculty suggests paradoxically that perhaps a different conclusion might be reached.

1. *Business in Nebraska,* June 1971, p. 2.

The picture that emerges . . . of the economic changes in Nebraska during the past decade is one of a state growing more slowly than the nation of which it is a part principally because its economy is made up of largely slow-growth components. In addition, some of its existing sources of income have been growing less rapidly in the state than in the nation.[2]

In higher education, too, the pattern of change was similar to that in the economy. In contrast with its own past, the University of Nebraska enjoyed a period of unprecedented growth and development in the sixties. However, institutional researchers at the University believed that in comparison to the growth that was taking place in other state universities of the nation, the improvements shown at the University of Nebraska could scarcely be characterized as phenomenal. As should be expected, the improvements were often perceived differently by the people of Nebraska than by the public in other parts of the nation.

The problems facing the Board of Regents and the University administration increased in number and complexity. Some citizens failed to understand the role that the University could play in raising the quality of life within the state. State tax support for research was in short supply. A few citizens still believed there was some subversion and political disloyalty at the University, emphasizing again the failure of some to understand the difference between disloyalty and honest questioning.

Although the University regents and administration were always called upon sharply by members of the Budget Committee of the legislature to justify their proposals, they generally received strong governmental support during the decade. The young people of Nebraska indicated their support of the University by enrolling in its schools and colleges in increasing numbers. At no time in its past had enrollment increased at such a pace. The number of full-time September enrollments on the Lincoln campuses expanded markedly. The following data show this growth.

1960	8,711
1961	9,436
1962	10,401
1963	11,466
1964	12,901
1965	15,179
1966	17,054
1967	18,067
1968	19,150
1969	19,618

In addition the number of students served by the summer sessions and the University Extension Division increased by similar percentages.

The most significant event of the decade and perhaps of the half-century, for the future of the institution and the people of the state, was the merger of the municipal University of Omaha with the University of Nebraska. By this action, the mission of the University of Nebraska was directed toward additional goals for which it had not been responsible during nearly a century of existence. What had been a university was now a university system. Shortly after this momentous step, the principal architect of the merger, Chancellor Clifford M. Hardin, was granted a leave of absence by the Board of Regents to accept the post of Secretary of Agriculture in the Cabinet of President Nixon.

2. Ibid., p. 6.

THE STATE OF HIGHER EDUCATION IN NEBRASKA

During the sixty-ninth session of the Nebraska legislature, in 1959, a resolution was adopted which authorized the Legislative Council to make a study of higher education in Nebraska. The project was to encompass public and private institutions, the anticipated public demand for higher education for the next ten years, and the financial resources necessary to meet the anticipated demand. The previous statewide survey of Nebraska's educational institutions by a state agency had been published in 1940.

In recognition of the importance of the study, the legislature authorized the employment of a professional staff. Lyman A. Glenny, a political science professor from Sacramento State College, was appointed to direct the investigation. A large group was brought together to assist him in the survey, including representatives of the public and private institutions of higher education in Nebraska. In addition, Glenny was aided by a number of professional advisory committees and by the Nebraska Citizens Council on Higher Education. The Glenny Report, made public in January 1961, was outstanding in its thoroughness.

At the time he undertook direction of the project, Glenny indicated that his assignment from the Legislative Council's Committee on Higher Education was to determine "how to get the most efficiency out of the dollars spent for higher education in the state."[3] Despite the economy motive for the study, many of its most significant findings recommended additional expenditure for higher education.

The Glenny Report concluded that a relatively high rate of faculty "inbreeding" existed at the University of Nebraska. More than 40 percent of the University faculty had received one or more degrees from Nebraska institutions and 28.5 percent had received their highest degree from a Nebraska institution. The report stated that this problem "is most serious at the State University because of its relatively small graduate enrollment . . . the uneven development of its graduate programs . . . and the fact that it provides education for most faculty members at other institutions in the state."[4] Many Nebraskans who earned their terminal degrees at the University had chosen to remain in their native state, but the public did not consider this necessarily undesirable. The Glenny Report further indicated that the salary levels in all academic ranks at the University of Nebraska were 6 percent below the regional median. These data at least suggest the possibility that the University of Nebraska may have appointed some of its own graduates to the faculty because of their strong desire to remain in the state and also because of the institution's restricted ability to compete in a national market. Although the University of Nebraska graduates were well qualified scholars in their academic disciplines, they probably could rarely bring to the faculty the necessary cross-fertilization of new ideas usually made possible from scholars educated elsewhere. Most educators believe that an institution with an inbred faculty usually lacks sufficient intellectual ferment necessary for excellence.

To improve faculty morale and to increase the University's power to hold faculty and attract new staff for the growing enrollment, the report recommended that "all institutions in the state attempt to effect a salary schedule which will allow a new inexperienced faculty member at least to triple his salary during

3. Omaha *World-Herald*, June 16, 1960, p. 8.
4. Lyman A. Glenny, *Nebraska Study of Higher Education* (Nebraska Legislative Council Committee on Higher Education, January 1961), p. 41.

the course of a life time career at the institution."[5] The reaction of the Legislative Council's Committee to this proposal was to recommend "the removal of the words 'to at least triple his salary' and insertion of 'to have a reasonable salary increase.' "[6]

The legislative group also rejected the recommendation that at least 5 percent of the income of each public institution be spent "on library resources toward the end of making the volume size of its library appropriate to the level and scope of its programs."[7] The legislators substituted a "reasonable amount" for the more specific 5 percent. Because of inadequate support at this time, by the seventies the University of Nebraska faced a library crisis of major proportions.

The Legislative Council's Committee, in general, rejected or advised extreme caution on those recommendations contained in the Glenny Report which called for additional state tax support of public higher education. Nevertheless, the University of Nebraska budget was increased because of the inescapable enrollment pressures and the expanded level of federal funds available to institutions of higher education.

FUNDING A GROWING UNIVERSITY

Between 1960 and 1965, the student enrollment on the Lincoln campuses increased by 6,468 students. Even to the most economy-minded citizen, this growth required major increases in state tax funds for the University. During the 1961, 1963, and 1965 legislative sessions, the University appropriation was a matter of major concern.

In January 1961, out-going Governor Dwight W. Burney recommended a 10 percent increase in tax funds for the University. The new Democratic governor, Frank B. Morrison, called for a greatly expanded role for the state University. "Education means classroom teaching, together with both basic and applied research. If we are to compete in today's world, we must step up the tempo of education. The development of the human mind in its application to research and economic progress is essential to our survival."[8] In his budget message, the governor emphasized that education was the most important function of the state. Governor Morrison stated that progress at the University must be maintained.

By continuing to upgrade the University of Nebraska we are attracting grants of money from outside sources that will enable us to rapidly expand our research programs. We cannot afford, under any circumstances, to curtail our movement in this direction. I cannot emphasize too strongly the necessity of continuing to upgrade the University of Nebraska. . . .

We cannot regard expenditures for education as a normal expense for operation of state government. Wise investment in education is an investment in a capital resource resulting in increased productivity of our people and must, in many respects, be regarded as an investment and not an expense of operation.[9]

The Morrison budget recommendation was nearly equal to the amount requested by the University Board of Regents and was over 2.5 million dollars greater than the amount suggested by Governor Burney.

The legislature, however, did not accept the Morrison figures and preferred the lower Burney budget as the basis for beginning legislative discussion. After

5. Ibid., p. 103.
6. Nebraska Legislative Council Committee Report No. 110, *Report of the Nebraska Legislative Council Committee on Higher Education,* January 1961, p. 6.
7. Ibid., p. 103.
8. Inaugural Message of Frank B. Morrison, January 5, 1961, *Legislative Journal of the State of Nebraska,* Seventy-Second Session, p. 59.
9. Ibid., Budget Message, January 17, 1961, p. 139.

consideration, the Committee on the Budget recommended an appropriation substantially less than that favored by Governor Morrison. In June 1961, the University faculty through its Liaison Committee, made an unusual direct appeal to the state senators for increased University tax support. After the committee called a faculty meeting and received approval of its letter to the legislature it was signed by Dean Robert D. Gibson of the College of Pharmacy, acting as secretary for the faculty, and delivered to each member of the Unicameral. It urged the acceptance of the Morrison budget and suggested that:

The amount to be restored represents a small investment which will yield invaluable dividends in a vital state and national resource.

Because we feel the plight of higher education in the State and in the Nation is so critical we did not believe that we could, in good conscience, remain silent. Hence ths unprecedented action.[10]

Senator Fern Hubbard Orme, of Lincoln, urged the legislature to increase the University tax funds by $4.1 million. Most senators, however, tended to support the lesser recommendation of the Budget Committee. One senator stated that "It's about time the people got a break." A senator from western Nebraska agreed. "We're going to have to start practicing economy or we'll get to the point where people won't be able to pay their taxes."[11]

Ultimately, after the Budget Committee met once more with Chancellor Hardin and the regents, a compromise appropriation was approved which added $610,000 for the operation of the colleges and schools. One reason for the acceptance of this increase was the recognition that legislative action of 1959, which had authorized an improved faculty retirement plan, required funding.

The 1961 legislative session was disappointing to the University community. Adam C. Breckenridge, dean of the faculties, expressed the view:

I hazard the statement that we are just a little less well off than we were a year ago by comparison. . .

We strive for a higher and higher quality of instruction and performance. We hope for a stronger research program than heretofore known, for without it we stagnate to bleed the work of others. We want to give the public the kind of public services they expect us to provide them.[12]

In order for the University to continue to meet its obligation to the public within the limits imposed by the state tax funds provided, the Board of Regents approved the raising of student fees in September 1961. The decade of the sixties witnessed repeated increases in student fees at the University. At many other state universities, similar, but not uniform tuition increases were also ordered by governing boards. A national move had begun to shift more of the cost of higher education to those who were receiving it.

In presenting their budget request for the 1963–65 biennium, the regents asked for an increase of 31 percent in state general tax funds. Governor Frank B. Morrison recommended to the legislature an increase of 20 percent in general tax funds for the University. Morrison again urged the improvement of public higher education in Nebraska and favored a ten-year commitment to obtain this goal.

Spasmodic biennial approaches to budgeting in our long-range educational needs in my opinion is not the proper procedure. A ten-year improvement program for higher education in Nebraska should be set up, realizing that over the next ten years it is

10. Letter, University Faculty to each State Senator, June 8, 1961, MSS, University of Nebraska Archives, Hardin Collection.

11. Omaha *World-Herald,* June 9, 1961, p. 4.

12. *Daily Nebraskan,* December 19, 1961.

going to be necessary to double our budget for higher education. . . . At this time I can see no plateau in the forseeable future of either budgets or programming for higher education, but it is going to be a constant climb. I am prepared to fight for this ten-year program and centralized administration of our higher education complex. We must build this, not competitive with the Big Eight, but as good as anything in America.[13]

Senators Fern Hubbard Orme, Marvin E. Stromer, and Jerome Warner responded by introducing a legislative bill calling for a special .6 mill property tax levy to fund campus development for a decade. The proposal was referred to the Budget Committee and was indefinitely postponed. However, a bill dealing with campus construction, introduced by Senator Terry Carpenter, was adopted. It prohibited spending any of the University of Nebraska College of Dentistry building fund "unless the federal government agrees to furnish money in an amount at least equal to the money to be expended from this fund for the construction or rehabilitation of existing buildings used in the teaching of dentistry at the University of Nebraska."[14] Later in the decade federal funds were made available and a new facility for the College of Dentistry was constructed on the East Campus.

The 1963 legislature also discussed a proposal for a constitutional amendment which would combine into a single board of control the University of Nebraska and the state colleges. However, the proposal was withdrawn by the senator who introduced it, and no action was taken.

As in the previous legislative session, the senators approved an appropriation for the University which was less than that recommended by the governor, but was nevertheless an increase of several million dollars over the previous biennium.

Again in 1965, Governor Morrison strongly supported the University by calling for a 27 percent increase in the budget, an increase amounting to $10.4 million. As in the past, the governor reminded the senators: "This state cannot afford mediocrity. We can and must have excellence. It is our key to a better tomorrow."[15] After the usual hearings and debate, the legislature provided the University with an operating budget of nearly $58 million, of which slightly more than $35 million was from state general funds. The funded operating budget was nearly $4.5 million less than requested by the Board of Regents and $2 million less than the recommendation of the governor.

Although the Unicameral had failed during the first three legislative sessions of the sixties to accept the recommendation of Governor Morrison regarding the operating budget of the University, the funds appropriated had been increased by over $16.5 million. This increase was not, however, the result of a substantially larger state property tax commitment for higher education. From the time of the 1961 appropriation through the 1965 appropriation, that portion of the University of Nebraska operating budget which excluded construction provided from the state general funds remained nearly constant. It is notable that higher education received less support when computed on an ability-to-pay basis. State tax support for all Nebraska public institutions for higher education was $5.25 per $1,000 of personal income in 1959–60 and only $5.14 in the 1966–67 biennium.[16]

13. Budget Message, Frank B. Morrison, January 21, 1963, *Legislative Journal of the State of Nebraska*, Seventy-Third Session, p. 204.

14. *Laws of Nebraska*, 1963, p. 1688.

15. Budget Message, Frank B. Morrison, January 26, 1965, *Nebraska Legislative Journal*, Seventy-Fifth Session, p. 244.

16. *State Tax Support for Public Higher Education in Nebraska During the 1960s* (Office of Institutional Research and Planning, University of Nebraska, September 1970), p. 17.

The authors of one study of state support for public higher education in Nebraska during the first three biennia of the sixties suggest the development of two trends:

—a growth in State appropriations that significantly lagged behind the growth in enrollments in the State-supported Colleges and University; and
—a major *shift* in the distribution of responsibility, for the revenue side of the schools budget *from the State to students and their families.*[17]

By the mid-sixties, the ability of the state's antiquated *ad valorem* property tax structure to support the level of public services demanded by the citizenry had reached its limit. In the area of higher education, growing numbers of Nebraskans were finding acceptable the argument advanced editorially by the Omaha *World-Herald* in 1963.

"Why should taxpayers, most of whom have not had the advantage of college education, continue to subsidize students in state-supported universities who have enrolled, generally, for the frank purpose of eventually earning more than the average citizen?"
   That is a good question.
   Society benefits from its college-trained people, but through the taxpayer and the private donor, society is doing a pretty good job of paying for those benefits.
   The college graduate benefits, too, and handsomely, by having a substantially higher income than the average.
   Why, then, shouldn't tuition cover more of the rising costs? And why shouldn't young people be willing to pay higher tuition fees, and if necessary borrow the money against their expected earnings? And why shouldn't tuition charges have a direct relationship to the prospective earning power—less in the case of the poorer-paid professions and more in the case of those which are most remunerative?
   We doubt if such a system would discourage any young man or woman who really wanted an education. But it might very well weed out in advance many who otherwise would flunk out. At any rate, some such plan may have to be tried as college costs go higher and higher.[18]

Would the public turn from the long-accepted tradition of the land-grant university characterized by low student fees and liberal entrance requirements? Had this concept, born a century earlier, become too expensive for the twentieth century? As Nebraskans become more remote in time from their frontier heritage and experience would they tend to lose that willingness to provide opportunities for self-improvement? These questions remained unanswered at the end of the sixties.

THE ETERNAL ISSUE

Throughout the history of American higher education, the role of universities as sources of information on controversial subjects has led to controversy. The expression of divergent or unpopular beliefs by members of an academic community has constantly been an issue in both public and private colleges and universities. Many taxpayers have objected to faculty and students in publicly supported institutions questioning the status quo. To question the accepted beliefs of the majority of those in a society that provide the financial support for an institution to many has been considered extreme ingratitude if not blatant disloyalty. The academic community has, on the other hand, since before the founding of our Republic invited free discussion as a basic protection of freedom and progress. This is an eternal issue in education. Concern regarding freedom of discussion and the expression of minority opinion will continue as a major

17. Ibid., p. 20.
18. Omaha *World-Herald,* July 15, 1963, p. 4.

theme in higher education so long as truth and reason are the objectives of higher education.

At the University the issue of freedom of opinion and research reappeared during the decade of the sixties with reference to the tax system of Nebraska. It had long been recognized by informed citizens that the state tax structure of Nebraska with its heavy reliance on the property tax was inadequate for the twentieth century. Economists at the University of Nebraska had concerned themselves with problems of property taxation and with the alternate methods of raising state revenue. Should the University of Nebraska, as an educational institution dedicated to the service of the people, provide the citizenry with information or evaluation of the various tax systems used by state governments to yield tax revenues? Many believed that this type of information was no different from that provided to the state's farmers and ranchers regarding various agricultural practices. The College of Agriculture and the Agricultural Experiment Station had provided the facts which enabled many Nebraskans to make intelligent economic choices. After considerable thought, the University of Nebraska Extension Division announced a series of two-day workshops in 1961 to discuss the topic, "Let's Talk About Nebraska Taxes." Despite the organized opposition of one citizens' group to the project, the Board of Regents and many leading state senators approved the educational program. J. G. Elliott, president of the Board of Regents, endorsed the program. "We discussed the tax workshops informally and felt that they reflected the philosophy of Universities and especially land-grant colleges to provide education to the people of the state."[19] Senator Richard Marvel, chairman of the Legislative Budget Committee, announced that he did not consider the tax institute "a new activity, but one conducted through the framework of the University's regular educational approach."[20]

Another controversy in American higher education has resulted from certain opinions expressed in student publications. At the University of Nebraska, during the early sixties, the issue of student opinions on public issues became a topic of controversy. In 1961, the editor of the *Daily Nebraskan* urged the abolition of the United States House of Representatives Un-American Activities Committee. The student editorial immediately produced a call by an Omaha American Legion post for a legislative investigation of the University and its School of Journalism for possible Communist influence. The inclusion of the School of Journalism specifically by the legion was based on the false assumption that it, rather than the Publication Board, was responsible for the *Daily Nebraskan*.

The state's press rallied to defend the student editor's right to express his opinion, although most believed that his position was unsound. The editor of the Norfolk *Daily News* expressed a widely held view:

Certainly, unless the American Legion Post is opposed to the fundamental principle of free speech, the young man should be allowed the right to express an opinion. We disagree wholly with his opinion, but we would consider ourselves most un-American if we should deny him his right to say what he thinks. We can see no logic or sense in the Legion Post's conclusion that because one student takes a position against the committee there must be a nest of subversiveness at the University.[21]

Comments by other Nebraska editors were similar.

On July 18, 1961, the University of Nebraska Board of Regents issued a public statement of policy and information in which they reaffirmed their loyalty to

19. *Daily Nebraskan,* April 18, 1962.
20. Ibid., November 17, 1961.
21. Norfolk *Daily News,* January 21, 1961.

"American principles." Furthermore, the regents defended the loyalty of the administrative officers, faculty, and employees of the University and pledged their determination to deal firmly with any disloyalty if it should ever appear. Regarding the student body, the regents exhibited a perceptive understanding of youth and the meaning of education.

The doors of the University are open to all students who have demonstrated scholastic ability and the desire to participate in higher education. It must be expected that some of those who enter will demonstrate the usual manifestations of immaturity and inexperience, as did their forebears at similar points of personal development. This, inevitably, involves outcroppings of the natural impatience most young people have to correct immediately the inequities and ills of the world as they see them. It also occasionally involves an exercise of the inclination some young people have to disturb the *status quo* and the minds of those who would prescribe their thoughts and utterances. These, however, are factors which the University has learned to take into account as it has continued, for almost a century now, to develop teaching programs designed to promote maturity, responsibility, understanding, and the fullest possible utilization of individual ability.[22]

The president of the Nebraska AFL-CIO Council complimented the regents' statement by writing that "we are delighted that our faith in the University of Nebraska is reaffirmed; that our boys and girls can find there the American freedoms of inquiry, responsible expression and the unhampered pursuit of learning."[23]

In the fall of 1961, Governor Frank B. Morrison also supported the concepts of freedom of expression and inquiry in an address to the student members of Phi Delta Phi, a law fraternity: "Our tendency not to disagree because we might lose business or favor creates a uniformity of thought and action . . . and this uniformity—really conformity—is the greatest danger today to our democratic process, for democracy advances through conflict."[24]

Freedom of expression and the open exchange of conflicting ideas had never had greater encouragement than during these years. Once again, the attempt of a few to make the University, its administration, faculty, and students an issue in the continuing struggle between divergent political and economic philosophies failed.

REORGANIZATION

Since the early years of the Gustavson administration, the basic administrative structure of the University had remained unchanged. By the sixties the growth in enrollment, research, and service programs indicated the necessity of reorganizing the University's administrative structure. Administrative reform was recommended in the 1961 Glenny Report and by the legislature in 1965.

In August 1962, Chancellor Clifford M. Hardin presented to the Board of Regents a proposal for the reorganization of the University administration. The regents approved the plan, which included the creation of three vice chancellorships. Adam C. Breckenridge was given the title of vice chancellor in addition to that of dean of the faculties. Joseph Soshnik was designated as vice chancellor for business and finances. Roy G. Holly, the Graduate dean, was additionally appointed vice chancellor for graduate and professional education and research. Following Holly's resignation in 1965, Dean Merk Hobson, of the College of Engineering and Architecture, was appointed vice chancellor for

22. *Minutes,* University of Nebraska, Board of Regents, July 18, 1961.

23. Letter, Richard W. Nisley to Chancellor Clifford M. Hardin, July 19, 1961, MSS, University of Nebraska Archives, Hardin Collection.

24. *Daily Nebraskan,* September 22, 1961.

research and dean of the Graduate College. In June 1966, Hobson's appointment was changed to that of vice chancellor and dean of the faculties.

In addition to the creation of the three vice chancellorships, the 1962 reorganization effected other personnel changes. G. Robert Ross, dean of student affairs, was assigned the responsibility for registration and records, admissions, housing, the Nebraska Student Union, and the Student Health Service.

The goal of the 1962 reorganization was to have all units of the University, except Public Relations and Intercollegiate Athletics, report to a vice chancellor or to the dean of student affairs rather than directly to the chancellor. Hardin explained, "The prime purpose of the adjustment is to serve better the current needs of the university and to relieve the Chancellor's office of much routine and detail work."[25] In addition to the new vice chancellors, Hardin was aided by an assistant to the chancellor. James S. Pittenger had occupied the post until 1962 when he was succeeded by Michael Shugrue. In 1966, Gene A. Budig, former administrative assistant to Governor Frank B. Morrison, was named assistant to the chancellor.

During the 1965 legislative session, a resolution was adopted providing that, "The Board of Regents of the University of Nebraska be instructed to establish a Bureau of Institutional Research as an arm of the office of the Chancellor, to promote administrative efficiency and educational planning."[26] In August 1965, the regents established the Office of Institutional Research. Harry S. Allen was appointed its first director. By these changes undertaken during the first half of the decade, the University administration was better prepared for the challenge of the last years of the sixties.

A NEW ERA

Beginning during the 1967 legislative session and concluding with the merger with Omaha's municipal university in 1968, higher education in Nebraska was profoundly changed. The alteration of the state's tax structure caused by the elimination of the state property tax and the adoption of a sales-income tax produced a less regressive and more productive revenue base for the state.

In their request for funds for the 1967-69 biennium, the regents requested a near doubling of the budget. Dr. B. N. Greenberg, chairman of the Board of Regents Finance Committee, described the request as one which "incorporates the idea of both catch-up and keeping up."[27] Governor Norbert T. Tiemann reduced the regents' request in his budget message but still favored an increase of over 40 percent in the University budget. The governor told the legislators:

We are justifiably proud of the athletic accomplishments of Nebraska's Cornhuskers. But is it not equally as important that we be able to continue to take pride in the University's academic accomplishments? The educational world is as competitive as the business world, and in recent years Nebraska has not kept pace.[28]

With an improved state tax base, the support of Governor Tiemann, and the consent of the legislature, the level of state support for higher education was dramatically improved in 1967 and 1969. However, as these favorable changes were taking place in Nebraska, the other states of the region—Colorado, Iowa, Kansas, Minnesota, Missouri, North and South Dakota, and Wyoming also en-

25. Omaha *World-Herald*, August 21, 1962, p. 2.

26. *Legislative Journal of the State of Nebraska*, Seventy-Fifth Session, p. 1538.

27. *Daily Nebraskan*, September 15, 1966.

28. Budget Message, Norbert T. Tiemann, March 13, 1967, *Nebraska Legislative Journal*, Seventy-Seventh Session, Vol. I, p. 944.

joyed substantial increases in state tax support. The director of institutional research at the University reported that:

On a personal income basis, Nebraska appropriations of State funds for public higher education were $9.15 in 1969–70, an increase of $3.49 and 61.7 percent from the 1965–66 level of $5.66. Both the absolute dollar and percentage increases were in excess of the similar statistics for all eight adjacent states and the nation as a whole. Yet, . . . this left Nebraska in seventh place among the group of nine Midland states, and represents, for Nebraska, no improvement in comparative rank from 1959–60 and only a one notch move from 1965–66![29]

Still, during the last years of the decade, faculty morale at the University of Nebraska greatly improved as it appeared that the public now recognized the ability and willingness of the University community to contribute to the improvement of the quality of life in Nebraska. The new tax structure could provide the University with the state funds necessary to develop the full potential for teaching, service, and research.

The merger of the University of Omaha with the University of Nebraska was a major turning point in public higher education in Nebraska. Although the merger of other state institutions of higher education with the University of Nebraska had been discussed from time to time and had even been authorized, no action had been taken. In 1965, the Unicameral legislature authorized the University of Nebraska Board of Regents to incorporate into the system junior colleges when it could be mutually agreed upon by the regents and the junior college's board. Discussions were held by the regents and the board of McCook Junior College, but it was mutually agreed to maintain the status quo.

The merger with Omaha University, however, was encouraged by Chancellor Hardin and was accomplished after a short courtship which was largely conducted in the legislature. A bill was introduced in the Unicameral providing for the merger of the two institutions if the voters of Omaha would approve. The legislation, L.B. 736, was adopted by the Unicameral without the emergency clause on a vote of 31 to 18 and was signed by Governor Norbet T. Tiemann. In a December 1967 election the voters of Omaha approved the merger by a vote of 4 to 1. Whether the Omaha vote primarily indicated the desire for improved quality in state-supported higher education or merely a desire for tax relief will be a major determination for a future historian to resolve. The long-range effects and wisdom of the merger must also await the judgment of time. Certainly, the future historian will evaluate the event in light of the ability and willingness of Nebraskans and their government to follow through on the commitment for an enlarged system of higher education.

In October 1968, the Board of Regents reorganized the University's structure to reflect the merger. A systems administration was established, composed of principally: Chancellor Clifford M. Hardin as the chief administrative officer of the University, Joseph Soshnik as vice chancellor for administration, and Merk Hobson as vice chancellor for academic affairs. The position of executive dean for graduate studies was also approved. Norman H. Cromwell was later appointed to this post. To administer the operational units of the University system, the regents subsequently created three presidencies. Cecil L. Wittson was named president of the University Medical Center, Kirk E. Naylor was appointed president of the University of Nebraska at Omaha, and Joseph Soshnik was designated president of the Lincoln campuses and outstate activities. In 1969, C. Peter Magrath, dean of the College of Arts and Sciences, was appointed dean of faculties for the Lincoln campuses and outstate activities.

29. *State Tax Support for Public Higher Education in Nebraska During the Sixties* (italics omitted), p. 22.

Merger ceremony at the University of Nebraska at Omaha.

THE END OF THE HARDIN ADMINISTRATION

In December 1968, President-elect of the United States Richard M. Nixon announced the appointment of Chancellor Clifford Morris Hardin as his Secretary of Agriculture. The acceptance of this assignment from the President ended the second longest chancellorship in the history of the University of Nebraska. Only Samuel Avery's tenure exceeded that of Hardin.

During the fifties and sixties, Chancellor Hardin had sought to convince the people of Nebraska that their state University held the key to the improvement of both the standard of living and the quality of life in Nebraska. His success in this effort was apparent in the budget increases made possible by the strong support given the University by Governors Morrison and Tiemann, and by the state legislature.

For Hardin, the greatest responsibility of the University was to provide the young people of Nebraska the opportunity for self-improvement. "The first responsibility of the University is to its students. We are convinced that the people of Nebraska want us to accept for admission all students who come to us with proper preparation and intentions."[30] The phenomenal enrollment spiral during the years of the Hardin administration bears witness to the success of the University to provide this opportunity to the state's youth. However, the repeated necessity of increasing the level of student fees restricted the opportunity for higher education among disadvantaged youth, particularly among those from minority groups.

The University of Nebraska benefited from a period of unprecedented con-

Merk Hobson.

struction during the Hardin administration, and many recall this time as primarily one of building. However, the chancellor never tired of telling of the institution's most valuable asset—the faculty. "It is axiomatic—but so important that frequent repetition appears justified—that high quality stems primarily from the presence of an outstanding faculty. The dollars required to attract and retain such a faculty remain our greatest need."[31] Statements made by the regents and other University administrators at legislative budget hearings affirm their belief that they too give first priority to the acquisition and retention of a quality faculty. The implementation by the regents, with legislative approval, of a Teachers Insurance and Annuity Association of America and College Retirement Equities Fund of New York retirement plan improved the ability of the

30. Clifford M. Hardin, "Alumni Round Up Speech," June 8, 1963, MSS, University of Nebraska Archives, Hardin Collection.
31. Ibid.

University of Nebraska to attract and retain faculty members. This was combined with an extension in other fringe benefits. The exodus of a number of key faculty members during the early sixties represented a greater dissatisfaction with the legislature than with the policies of the regents or University administration.

On December 13, 1968, the Board of Regents took action to provide for the continuing administration of the University of Nebraska. Clifford M. Hardin, as chancellor and professor of agricultural economics with tenure, was granted a leave of absence without salary until January 20, 1970. In June 1969, Hardin resigned the chancellorship but was granted an indefinite leave as a professor of agricultural economics by the Board of Regents.

Durward B. Varner.

To continue administrative leadership at the University, the regents appointed Vice Chancellor Merk Hobson to be acting chancellor. At the same meeting G. Robert Ross was named corporation secretary, and Gene A. Budig was appointed assistant corporation secretary.

Acting Chancellor Hobson made it clear that he considered the appointment temporary and that he did not aspire to the permanent chancellorship.

I accepted the job . . . because I feel a great sense of loyalty to the University of Nebraska. . . . I want to do what will best serve the organization, and the Regents are the judge of that. But if Chancellor Hardin decides not to return, it becomes an entirely different situation.[32]

The Board of Regents formed a committee composed of faculty, students, and administrative representatives to advise them in the selection of a permanent chancellor for the University of Nebraska. In December 1969, the regents ap-

32. Omaha *World-Herald,* December 15, 1968, p. 18-B.

pointed Durward B. Varner to the chancellorship effective February 1, 1970. During the period between the announcement of Varner's appointment and his assumption of duties, Acting Chancellor Hobson was appointed chancellor.

Durward B. Varner, the new chancellor, brought to Nebraska the experience and background for the job of developing a University system. For ten years previously he had served as chancellor of Oakland University at Rochester, Michigan, which had been built as a new institution under his direction. His earlier background also prepared him for his assignment at Nebraska. A native Texan, Varner was graduated from Texas A & M in 1940. He later earned a master's degree in political science and economics at the University of Chicago.

His professional career began when he was named assistant to the president of the Federal Land Bank of Houston, Texas. He served in the armed forces during World War II and attained the rank of lieutenant colonel. After the war he returned to Texas A & M, where he served as assistant dean of students. From 1949 to 1959 he was a faculty member at Michigan State University, first serving as assistant professor of agricultural economics, then director of the Cooperative Extension Service, and finally as vice president of Michigan State University in charge of off-campus instruction and continuing education.

THE FOUNDATION

Although it is a separate corporation, the University of Nebraska Foundation continued to supply important financial support to the institution. The foundation had been organized in 1936 by thirty prominent Nebraska business and professional men called together for this purpose by Chancellor Edgar A. Burnett. In 1942 when Perry W. Branch, '20, became full-time secretary of the foundation, its assets were $42,000; when he retired in 1962, they were over $4,500,000. By the sixties the foundation was able to provide the level of assistance to the University envisioned by Chancellor Burnett and its founders during the bleak days of the depression. Perry W. Branch was succeeded at the foundation by Harry R. Haynie, '38, who reported to the trustees in April 1969 that the assets exceeded $13,500,000. The growth in the foundation's resources was a tribute to all those who supported the University's goal of service. President Haynie reported in 1969:

The progress continued slow but steady. It took the Foundation 16 years—or to 1952 —to reach the first million dollars in assets; it took another four years to obtain the second million; another three years for the third million; two years for the fourth million bringing us to 1961. From 1961 to 1964, the Foundation added about a million dollars a year. During the past two years, we have added two million dollars during each of these years.[33]

With its growing assets the foundation was able to provide increasing assistance to the University. In 1960, $359,875 was made available to the University. By 1969 the amount had risen to $3.1 million. Among the most significant new programs funded by the foundation were those providing the chancellor with an unrestricted account for the institution's needs and the distinguished professorship program. Under the former, the chancellor was provided with $30,000 in 1964 for his discretionary use for the University. This allocation, by 1969, was increased to $175,000.

The Endowment Fund for Distinguished Teaching was established as a separate entity under the aegis of the University of Nebraska Foundation in

33. Speech by Harry R. Haynie to Trustees of the University of Nebraska Foundation, April 30, 1969, MSS, University of Nebraska Foundation.

June 1963. However, the Board of Regents had adopted a policy in May 1960 providing for the creation of Regents' Professorships in cases where an outside donor would provide the funds. The expansion of the idea by the foundation made it possible for interested persons to join with others in the establishment of a distinguished professorship. It is significant that this program was initiated at a time when the University was experiencing difficulty in meeting the salary levels at the full professor level. However, the charter of the Endowment Fund for Distinguished Teaching states that: "It shall be expressly understood that no part of these funds is to be considered as a substitute for funds received from the State of Nebraska in the form of tax support for the University."[34] Despite this disclaimer, the foundation did assume the burden of providing the additional funds for faculty salaries necessary to attract and retain key members of the faculty.

THE BEGINNING OF A SECOND CENTURY

On Friday, February 14, 1969, a special University of Nebraska Centennial Convocation was held at the Coliseum to mark the end of a century of service to the people of Nebraska. For one hundred years the University had sought to fulfill the command of its charter, to "afford to the inhabitants of this state the means of acquiring a thorough knowledge of the various branches of literature, science, and the arts."

By all Nebraska benchmarks, the decade of the sixties had been the most dynamic in the history of the University. The increased interest of the public in higher education and the expanded role of the federal government in providing financial assistance for campus construction and research had made this possible. In addition, the support given to the University by Governors Morrison and Tiemann enabled the regents, administration, and faculty to meet the needs of the people of Nebraska, the nation, and the world.

The University began its second century a stronger academic institution than at any time in its past. The teaching program served more students than ever before, with instructional programs in Lincoln and at both the Medical Center and the University of Nebraska at Omaha. In addition, the University Extension Division served students throughout the world. Research work by the faculty, at the beginning of the second century, had attained eminence in many fields. Never before had the University contributed more to man's quest for knowledge. In areas of public service, too, the accomplishments fulfilled the land-grant university ideal.

However, the attainment of the University of Nebraska's full potential for teaching, research, and service during its second century will depend on factors from both within and without the institution. Much will depend on the success of the regents, administration, and faculty to develop an integrated system following the merger with Omaha University. The obtaining of state financial support adequate to sustain the enlarged University will be a key factor. Moreover, it seems doubtful that many Nebraskans fully realized either the financial consequences or educational promise inherent in the merger. The reduction of federal funding of construction, research, and student development also greatly affected all universities by the seventies. Much of the construction, research, and program development achieved at the University of Nebraska from the mid-fifties to the end of the sixties was made possible by federal funds. As the second century of the University began, the continued catalytic role of federal

34. "Endowment Fund For Distinguished Teaching," MSS, University of Nebraska Foundation.

funding in higher education was in doubt. This, combined with a business decline and the apparent temporary over-supply of college graduates for the job
market, produced some public questioning of the continuation of higher education at its current level. Perhaps, what is needed is the belief in the future that
sustained the Burnett administration during the thirties. There can be no doubt
that during the University's second century, it will be expected to minister to a
wide variety of societal needs, and it is certain that the problems of the future
will be understood and solved by the educated.

CHAPTER 14

A Decade of Academic Growth and Promise

ACADEMIC LIFE AT THE University of Nebraska during the decade of the sixties was characterized by many changes and developments even though spiraling enrollments produced a host of problems for those concerned with both instructional programs and admission policy. While struggling to cope with the ever-increasing size of the student body, the faculty endeavored to improve the level of its public service and to expand its productive scholarship. Few periods in the University's past can equal the intellectual activity and production of the sixties. Although the University had in its past listed great scholars and teachers among its faculty, during the sixties many faculty members' research and publications exceeded that of all past decades. The phenomenal growth in the size of the Graduate College faculty demonstrates this rising level of productive scholarship.

As the number of applications for admission to the University increased, the administration and regents sought ways to improve counseling and advising services for the wide range of individual talents and abilities of its students. The University recognized its responsibility to advise those students whose academic performance in high school was limited of their prospects of scholastic achievement or failure at the University. To provide additional data for counseling prospective students, the Board of Regents required that beginning in the fall of 1963, all prospective nonresident students submit their scores from the College Entrance Board Examination, or a score from a similarly recognized test, with their application for admission to the University. In the fall of 1967, the Board of Regents further altered their admissions policy by requiring that all undergraduate applications for admission include college aptitude test scores. This change was not, however, an abandonment of the traditional "open door" admissions policy of the University. The regents stated that the test "results are to be used in advising, course placement, and financial determinations."[1] A University spokesman further explained the policy to the press. "The Regents long have held the position that selective admission cannot be considered until there is adequate alternate public education available to Nebraska collegians. . . . This alternative has not developed rapidly in Nebraska."[2]

The University's program of student advisement, which discouraged the attendance of those with little hope of academic success, began to show its effectiveness. This, along with the rising quality of the state's high school graduates, ended the need for remedial courses. The last remedial course,

1. *Minutes,* Board of Regents, September 12, 1967.
2. Omaha *World-Herald,* September 13, 1967, p. 1.

English A, which had been offered since 1925 for those students who lacked sufficient preparation for regular freshman English, was discontinued in February 1961.

In addition to the concerns arising from the increasing number of applications for admission to the University, the faculty turned its attention to the grading system. Prior to the 1960s, the University had used only three grading systems. Before 1910, the system used the letters E, G, M, P, and F to evaluate student classwork. The scheme was later changed to percentage grades by which grades were stated from 50 to 100. A student might get 83 in English, 69 in history, or 87 in mathematics. In September 1941, the cut-off for failure was raised from 50 to 60. In 1947, following action by the University Senate, a nine-point scale was adopted for purposes of grading. University transcripts advised that the 1 to 9 scale could be converted to letter grades as follows: 9,8 equal A; 7,6 equal B; 5,4 equal C; 3,2 equal D; and 1 equals F.

Sheldon Memorial Art Gallery.

In March 1965, a resolution was introduced in the University Senate by Dean Walter E. Militzer, of the College of Arts and Science, to change to a grading system using five grades, A, B, C, D, and F, instead of the nine-point scale. After a wide discussion in the University the proposal was adopted and became effective in September 1965. The change was approved largely because the University of Nebraska was the only major university to use a nine-point scale, and the evaluation of student transcripts by other institutions often caused difficulties for the Nebraska graduate. Furthermore, many faculty members were critical of a grading system which attempted to classify student accomplishment into nine categories.

By the spring of 1968, it was clearly apparent to the faculty and the administration that the five-letter grading system was not functioning properly. A sudden increase in the number of students on academic probation signaled the trouble. Apparently, some faculty members had adjusted to the new grading scheme by a general lowering of all student grades. A special faculty committee composed of Professors Royce H. Knapp, Frank J. Dudek, and Lyle E. Young was appointed by Chancellor Hardin to study the dilemma. Following the committee's report the University Senate, after a long debate and much emotion, approved the creation of four additional grades: A plus, B plus, C plus, and D plus. Some students, especially the leaders of ASUN objected to the change because they were not consulted during the study. The grading system was now back where it had been before the 1965 change. The only difference was that it now used nine letter grades instead of the 1 to 9 scale. However, the later authorization of a limited pass-fail grading system provided a degree of flexibility in the University's grading system.

In addition to the regular programs of teaching, research, and service conducted by the colleges and schools of the University, some special programs were established or expanded during the sixties. University participation in a program for educational television, which had begun in 1951, culminated in the creation of the Nebraska Educational Television Commission by the Unicameral in 1963. By the end of the decade, the Nebraska educational television network covered the state and was recognized as a leader in the nation. The University also became involved in a variety of special projects during the decade. In 1963, Peace

Professor Wesley C. Meierhenry on television.

Corps volunteers were prepared for service in Latin America. Later, in combination with the Northern Natural Gas Company, an Urban Job Corps Center was located in Lincoln at the site of the former Lincoln Air Base. Other innovative instructional programs approved by the regents included the creation of a Teaching Council in 1968 to encourage, support, and coordinate innovative teaching at the University. The establishment of the Centennial Education Program in the fall of 1969 again reflected a willingness to try new methods of organizing the instructional program. Although these innovations became perhaps the advance agents of educational change, the principal responsibility for teaching remained in the colleges and schools which constituted the traditional University.

THE COLLEGE OF AGRICULTURE AND HOME ECONOMICS

Following permissive legislation in 1963, the Board of Regents redesignated the College of Agriculture as the College of Agriculture and Home Economics. In

October 1964, the traditional College of Agriculture Campus, or Ag Campus, was renamed by the regents the East Campus. This change reflected the expanded use of the area, which now included the Nebraska Center and would soon include the College of Dentistry.

Student enrollment in the College of Agriculture and Home Economics more than doubled during the decade. The agricultural enrollment grew from 606 in 1960 to 1,367 in 1969, while that in home economics expanded from 332 to 877. These enrollment changes advanced the college in size nationally from nineteenth to eleventh place.

Following the resignation of Dean William V. Lambert, the regents named Elvin F. Frolik to be his successor in April 1960. Chancellor Hardin explained at the time of the appointment, "Normally we would probably have waited a little longer to make a selection, but in this case the faculty enthusiasm for Dr. Frolik was so overwhelming that there seemed to be no point in waiting."[3] The new dean, a native Nebraskan, earned his B.S. and M.S. degrees at the University of Nebraska and the Ph.D. from the University of Minnesota in 1948. After experience as a county agent in Nemaha County during the thirties, he joined the staff of the Department of Agronomy, where he served as chairman from 1952 to 1955. Prior to his appointment as dean, Frolik had been associate dean and director of the Experiment Station. Dean Frolik was followed at the Experiment Station by Herbert H. Kramer. In 1966, Howard W. Ottoson, chairman of the Department of Agricultural Economics, was named associate dean of the college and director of the Experiment Station.

By action of the Board of Regents, following authorization by the Unicameral, the Department of Home Economics was raised to the status of a school in 1962. Florence E. McKinney, chairman of the Department of Home Economics since the mid-fifties, and her staff had long favored this change because of the broadened scope of home economics as an academic discipline and because of its rising student enrollment. Hazel Fox was appointed acting director of the school during its first year and was succeeded by Virginia Trotter as director and associate dean of the College of Agriculture and Home Economics. To facilitate the work of the school, five departments were established: Food and Nutrition; Family Economics and Management; Human Development and the Family; Textiles, Clothing and Design; and Home Economics Education.

Another program change of the College of Agriculture and Home Economics affected the facility at Curtis, Nebraska. The Nebraska School of Agriculture had been opened by the regents in 1913 following specific legislative direction. The school operated as an agriculturally oriented high school. In 1965 following a legislative resolution, the regents changed the mission of the school to that of a two-year post–high school institution specializing in technical education in agriculture. To reflect the new objectives at the facility, the name was changed to the University of Nebraska School of Technical Agriculture.

For the academic departments of the college, on the Lincoln campus, Franklin E. Eldridge, who served as director of resident instruction, continued to improve the quality of the instructional program while meeting the demands imposed by the rising enrollment. The Department of Agronomy remained the largest in the college under the chairmanship of Donald G. Hanway. Research in wheat and corn breeding attracted national attention. Among those making major research contributions were Professors C. O. Grander, Francis A. Haskins, Virgil A. Johnson, John H. Lonnquist, and John Schmidt.

Programs in the Department of Animal Science were strengthened by the new facilities of Marvel Baker Hall, completed in 1969. The building was named in

3. Letter, Clifford M. Hardin to M. K. Douthit, April 14, 1960, MSS, University of Nebraska Archives, Hardin Collection.

honor of Professor Marvel Baker, a distinguished animal scientist and former dean at the college. In 1968 the dairy production programs were incorporated in the Department of Animal Science. During the sixties leadership was provided in the Department of Biochemistry and Nutrition by John Pazur and Raymond Borchers. The Department of Agricultural Economics emphasized marketing and rural development under the chairmanship of Howard W. Ottoson and Glen J. Vollmar. The Department of Vocational Education became the Department of Agricultural Education in 1965, and James T. Horner succeeded Howard Deems as chairman the same year.

Substantial changes were made in the Department of Agricultural Engineering. Graduate offerings were increased and a program in mechanized agriculture was reestablished. Departmental leadership was provided by Lloyd W. Hurlbut, until his death in 1965, and then by John R. Davis, the new chairman. After Davis was named dean of the College of Engineering and Architecture in 1966, Robert W. Kleis was appointed chairman. Kleis became associate director of the Agricultural Experiment Station in 1967, and William E. Splinter was selected to fill the chairmanship of the Department of Agricultural Engineering in 1968. In cooperation with the Department of Agronomy, the Department of Agricultural Engineering developed a strong research program in livestock waste management for pollution control.

The Entomology Department continued research in corn rootworm control and definition of wheat streak mosaic transmission mechanism. Roscoe Hill was succeeded as chairman of the department by Earle S. Raun in 1966. In 1969, the latter was appointed associate director of the Agricultural Extension Service and was followed as chairman of the Department of Entomology by Elvis A. Dickason. The Department of Food Science and Technology was established in 1968 with a nucleus of staff from the processing component of the discontinued Dairy Science Department. Under the leadership of the departmental chairman, T. E. Hartung, research contributions were made in the areas of food enzymology and sanitation.

The Department of Horticulture and Forestry emphasized research in vegetable crop production in Nebraska. The long-established program in potato breeding was continued and a new one begun in bean breeding. In addition, significant studies were initiated in agricultural climatology. The program of the Department of Plant Pathology related closely to the research needs of the state. J. M. Daly was followed as chairman of the department in 1965 by Michael G. Boosalis. The Poultry Science Department, with John L. Adams as chairman, occupied new facilities during the decade and continued their productive research program.

In 1965, George A. Young was succeeded as chairman of the Department of Veterinary Science by Marvin J. Twiehaus. Significant research accomplishments were made in the development of a rapid diagnosis technique for hog cholera by fluorescent antibody tissue staining and in the isolation of a virus causing calf scours.

A key factor in all the research programs was the Agricultural Experiment Station and the Substations located throughout the state. The acquisition of a former United States Army munitions plant, near Mead, provided a site of approximately 9,000 acres for research work. With the exception of the poultry flocks, all livestock research was transferred from the East Campus to the Mead Field Laboratory. Only thirty-five miles from Lincoln, this facility provided expanded research opportunities.

The North Platte Station remained the principal out-state research facility during the decade, and expanded its studies in irrigation systems and pasture irrigation. The role of the facility was enlarged in 1967 when the Unicameral provided for the establishment of an animal disease diagnostic laboratory at North Platte. The station at Concord, the Northeast Station, served the needs of that region, emphasizing programs relating to crops of the area, beef cattle nutrition, swine housing and management, and soil and water conservation.

The High Plains Agricultural Laboratory was established in 1965 on 2,300 acres of federal land transferred to the University. It had been the site of the Sioux Ordinance Depot north of Sidney in Cheyenne County. The laboratory was organized as a satellite of the station at Scottsbluff. Staff members from Scottsbluff and Lincoln used the site for research related to crop production in a high plains environment. In 1967, the former Box Butte Station's land was transferred by Box Butte County to the University and was redesignated as the Northwest Agricultural Laboratory. This too was administered as a second satellite of the Scottsbluff Station. Research there emphasized sugar beet, bean, and potato production.

A landmark advance in animal research was made possible through the co-operation of the college and the United States Department of Agriculture during the sixties. The location of the United States Meat Animal Research Center near Clay Center, Nebraska, and the establishment of the South Central Station of the University of Nebraska's Agricultural Station at the same location marked the beginning of a new era in cooperative animal research. The location of this facility, which consolidated Department of Agriculture research in beef cattle, sheep, and swine in Nebraska, is a tribute to the efforts of Dean Frolik and the University's long tradition for quality research in animal science. Because of the superior facilities at Clay Center, the beef cattle research work at Fort Robinson, near Crawford, was phased out as the new station developed.

Organizational changes which brought closer coordination between the experiment program and the other activities of the College of Agriculture and Home Economics furthered the work at the experiment stations. Four primary out-state stations were designated as "campus type" centers for extension and research. The Scottsbluff, North Platte, Northeast, and Southeast Stations were assigned an expanded role during the sixties. Also, to strengthen the Experiment Station program, the chairmen of the college's academic departments were given the responsibility for their subject area programs of research and instruction at the Experiment Station and its branches. Consistent with this change, the staff members at all out-state stations were made academic members of a parent department on the Lincoln campus.

In addition to the many programs operated in Nebraska, the College of Agriculture and Home Economics offered technical assistance to developing countries of the world. By 1968, the program begun the previous decade in Turkey was concluded, but a new program had been established in Colombia, South America. In this new effort, the University of Nebraska served as the prime contractor for the Agency for International Development, the Kellogg and Ford Foundation. The Rockefeller Foundation also provided some support for the Colombia project, as did the Mid-American State Universities Association. As it had throughout the past fifty years, the College of Agriculture and Home Economics successfully worked to fulfill the land-grant college ideal—to improve man's quality of life.

THE COLLEGE OF ARTS AND SCIENCES

In addition to providing programs leading to degrees in liberal arts, the College of Arts and Sciences continued to provide instruction in a variety of general education courses for the increasing number of students enrolled in the other colleges and schools of the University. Although the Arts College enrollment expanded, its greatest increase resulted from this service function to the other colleges of the University. During most of these years, the college was administered by Dean Walter E. Militzer. Following his retirement from administration and return to teaching and research in the Department of Chemistry in 1967, Professor Robert L. Hough, from the Department of English, became dean of the College of Arts and Sciences. In June 1968, C. Peter Magrath, professor and chairman of the Department of Political Science at Brown University, was appointed dean by the regents. This appointment had followed a nationwide search by a faculty-administrator committee created to advise the board. At the time of this selection Chancellor Hardin expressed his optimism in the appointment. "We are looking forward to aggressive and imaginative leadership from a man at the age of 35 who already has an outstanding record as teacher, scholar, and administrator."[4]

To assist the dean in the administration of the college, which encompassed over twenty departments and two schools, an administrative staff developed. For varying periods during the decade, Professors Walter F. Wright, Robert L. Hough, and Gene B. Hardy of the Department of English served as assistant or associate deans. The science areas were represented in the college's administration by Professors Harry L. Weaver, from the Botany Department, and Walter H. Bruning, from the Department of Chemistry.

A major administrative problem for the Arts College was that of providing a high quality instructional program, on both the undergraduate and graduate levels, which would be innovative within the limitations of a lean budget. With enrollment pressures in both the undergraduate and graduate areas, new problems developed at the departmental level. In April 1961, the chairman of the English Department reported his plight to Dean Militzer.

Four years ago Freshman English accounted for 9,960 credit hours, this year 11,006—a rise of 1,046 or 10%. Intermediate courses (sophomore level) during this period rose from 6,442 credit hours to 7,037—an increase of 595 credit hours or about 9%. Most dramatic have been increases in courses at the 200- and 300-level. Four years ago, 2447 credit hours were taught at the 200-level, this year 3,114—an increase of 667 hours or 27%. And at the 300-level credit hours rose from 152 to 447, or a total of 295 or 195%. . . .

Generally speaking, the higher the level of a course, the more demands made on the professor; that is, the 27% and 195% increase in the upper-level credit hours taught by the Department of English represents a remarkable increase in staff hours and energies put into the major and graduate programs. This extraordinary increase in departmental responsibility and commitment at the upper levels of its program must be taken into account when examining the needs of the freshman level.[5]

Similar staffing problems affected several departments of the Arts College.

The need for additional Arts and Science faculty positions was complicated by the same pressures in most of the nation's colleges and universities. By 1963, Dean Militzer believed that the college's low budget made both the retention of able faculty members and the recruiting of new staff very difficult.

Amounts allocated for salary increases are not enough to meet the competition we face with other universities. . . . we received about half the amount necessary to play in the same stadium with our sister institutions. The amount allocated for new positions does not begin to cover what we need for the increases in enrollment. If we finance new staff out of the funds allocated and from the fees from new students, we will be forced to have pre-doctorate instructors and graduate teaching assistants. This practice will

4. *Daily Nebraskan,* December 13, 1967.

5. Letter, James E. Miller, Jr., to Walter E. Militzer, April 27, 1961, MSS, University of Nebraska Archives, Hardin Collection.

hardly ensure us a balanced staff and could lead to a serious weakening of our standing.[6]

By the end of the decade, the financial situation was improved, partly because of the state tax reform of 1967. Nevertheless, it is seldom that an educational institution can ever completely catch up with those universities which enjoy unwavering state support.

Despite the strictures of the budget, the decade was one of accomplishment by the faculty of the College of Arts and Sciences. In research and publication many faculty members made recognized contributions to their disciplines. Changes in curricular offerings reflected the faculty's desire to meet student needs and to introduce innovative and experimental teaching methods into the classroom. Program development was, however, limited by enrollment pressures and the budget. In activities where outside financial support became available, educational experimentation and innovation were accomplished. The construction of the Behlen Laboratory of Physics and the Nelle Cochrane Woods Art building were improvements in academic programming made possible by private philanthropy. The development of innovative and experimental instructional programs by Professor Paul A. Olson, and others, was made possible by federal grants. The growing national reputation achieved in this era by the University's science departments was, in part, the result of grants from agencies of the federal government. This was not unique to the University of Nebraska, since federal support of universities during the sixties was a principal factor in determining which institutions achieved national recognition for research or educational innovation.

Reflective of the University of Nebraska's growing interest in Latin America, the Latin-American Institute was established in 1966 to prepare undergraduate students for possible employment in Latin America and to strengthen the academic programs concerned with the area. The curriculum of the institute was enriched by the establishment of an exchange program with El Colegio de Mexico and by the addition of instruction in Portuguese. A Far Eastern Institute was also founded, but the resignation of its director terminated the program.

In addition to the regular academic departments, the College of Arts and Sciences included for administrative purposes several schools. In 1967, the Board of Regents dissolved the School of Fine Arts and reconstituted it as a department, whereas the Department of Music was raised to the status of the School of Music. These changes reflected the policy of the regents and administration to give greater emphasis to the performing arts. To administer the School of Music, the regents named Professor Emanuel Wishnow to be director and Professor David Fowler as vice director. Under their leadership, the music programs grew in both enrollment and in the variety of course offerings. Student participation was stimulated by the elimination of additional fees for students enrolled for lessons in all branches of applied music. The University of Nebraska School of Music was a Midwestern pioneer in the elimination of additional fees for music students.

With the opening of the Westbrook Music Building in 1967 and the completion of the Kimball Recital Hall in 1971, there was a steady growth in the presentation of opera and other large-ensemble student group performances by the orchestra, band, University Singers, Madrigals, and the Glee Club. With the improved facilities, there was also an increase in the number of performances by individual soloists and small ensembles of faculty and students. By the end of the decade, in excess of one hundred concerts were being presented annually by the students and faculty of the School of Music. The success achieved at the University of

6. *Daily Nebraskan*, October 2, 1963.

Nebraska in music education was due to the dedication of the faculty members involved and the determination of the administration and regents, particularly during the sixties, to develop an outstanding program. This accomplishment is especially noteworthy when one recalls that the University had only operated its own music program since the early thirties.

The School of Journalism, also a part of the College of Arts and Sciences, expanded in both enrollment and curriculum during the sixties. Until his resignation in 1966, William E. Hall served as director of the school. When he departed for Ohio State, he was succeeded by Neale Copple, a 1947 graduate of the University of Nebraska, who achieved national recognition as a journalist while associated with the Lincoln *Journal.* Copple had first joined the faculty of the School of Journalism in 1957 to develop courses in public affairs reporting. The success of the program in journalism was facilitated by the recognition by both

Professor Donald A. Lentz and the University Band.

faculty and director that two distinct types of preparation were required for faculty members. Because of this duality, that of theory and practical experience, a dual hiring and promotion policy was formulated. Two distinct routes of professional preparation were recognized. One required the Ph.D. with some professional experience, the other the master's degree and a minimum of ten years of significant experience as a journalist. This blending of theory and practice within the faculty was a significant factor in the development of the Nebraska curriculum.

During the decade, the traditional summer internship program was expanded and a new program of summer editing internships established. The strong ties of the School of Journalism with the state's press were tested in the early sixties when the school was falsely accused of political disloyalty by several publicity-seeking citizens. The unquestioned support given the school and its staff demonstrated clearly the high esteem in which it was held by the state's working journalists.

In 1963, radio broadcasting courses were transferred from the Speech Department to the School of Journalism, and a new curriculum was developed. Other new or expanded courses included work in advertising, depth reporting, creative editing, and photography. An improved cooperative program was developed with the Teachers College for the preparation of secondary school teachers of journalism. These improvements were possible because of faculty and administrative concern which was aided by philanthropic encouragement. Among those who provided financial help were the *Reader's Digest* Foundation and the Newspaper Fund Incorporated of the *Wall Street Journal*. In 1963, the School of Journalism moved from Burnett Hall to Nebraska Hall. By the end of the decade, it had already outgrown these quarters.

The State Museum, under the direction of Professor C. Bertrand Schultz, enjoyed its greatest period of growth during the sixties. Although the regents had favored a consolidation of the University's scientific collections as early as 1941, it was not accomplished until this decade. Early in this period the scientific collections were stored in seven buildings on the City and East campuses, and at Mead. In the late sixties it was decided to have the exhibits of the museum restricted to the lower three floors of Morrill Hall, and to provide space in Nebraska Hall for the systematic biological and anthropological collections and associated research facilities.

A grant was made to the University of Nebraska in 1968 by the National Science Foundation and additional funds were provided by the Nebraska state legislature to construct a new storage and research facility on the fourth and fifth floors of Nebraska Hall. Some 65,000 square feet of air-conditioned and well lighted space were provided to house the approximately 2,760,000 scientific specimens from the museum's division of anthropology, botany-herbarium, entomology, parasitology, zoology, invertebrate paleontology, and vertebrate paleontology. Although construction work was well under way in 1969, the actual moving of the specimens did not commence until early 1970. Ample space was provided in the storage areas for research projects by faculty members, graduate students, museum staff members, and visiting scientists from other educational institutions throughout the world.

Funds for exhibits and research continued to be provided by interested citizens. The largest single gift-endowment ever made to the museum was provided by the estate of Professor E. F. Schramm, who had been on the staffs of the museum and Department of Geology for more than forty years. Other substantial gifts were provided by Mr. and Mrs. Walter Behlen of Columbus, Nebraska, Ralph Mueller of Cleveland, Ohio, and the Cooper Foundation. The displays of anthropology and geology were moved to the third floor of Morrill Hall during the late 1960s, and became important in rounding out the educational exhibit program of the museum. A sound system also was provided to make the exhibits more educational and meaningful.

THE COLLEGE OF BUSINESS ADMINISTRATION

The dean of the College of Business Administration throughout the sixties was Charles S. Miller. During these years the undergraduate enrollment in the college increased from 960 to 2,069; and the number of graduate students expanded from 78 to 179. Partially because of this rapid expansion, the Board of Regents approved a reorganization of the College of Business Administration in 1968. The Department of Business Organization and Management was divided into four new Departments of Accounting, Finance, Management, and Marketing. These and the Department of Economics composed the teaching areas of the college.

Graduate programs had long been offered in the area of business and economics. In June 1962, the Board of Regents authorized the college to grant a new graduate degree, that of Master of Business Administration. This new graduate-level program differed from the earlier programs in that it accepted students with undergraduate degrees from other than the business areas. The Master of Business Administration program was immediately accredited by the American Association of Collegiate Schools of Business, of which the University of Nebraska had been a founding member in 1919.

In addition to its instructional activities, the college provided useful service to Nebraskans. The Bureau of Business Research provided valuable information and analysis of the state's economic condition. In 1963, in response to the request of a group of state business leaders, a program was instituted to assist elementary and secondary teachers in presenting economic instruction. This effort was formalized in the creation of the Nebraska Council for Economic Education, which operates on a budget raised from private sources. By the end of the decade, over one thousand teachers had benefited from either the special work-

Left to right: College of Business Administration deans Charles S. Miller, Earl S. Fullbrook, John Clark, and James E. LeRossignol.

shops or from classes provided by the college through the Nebraska Council for Economic Education.

The success of the College of Business Administration was the result of the dedicated work of its faculty. Among those who made major contributions to the development of the program were: Curtis M. Elliott, professor of economics and insurance; Professors Charles J. Kennedy, Campbell R. McConnell, and Wallace C. Peterson of the Department of Economics; and Professor of Accounting Raymond C. Dein. With the retirement in 1968 of Professor Edward B. Schmidt, specialist in taxation, who had been a faculty member since 1932, and Professor Clifford M. Hicks, specialist in business law, a faculty member whose service spanned forty-two years, the college lost two outstanding teachers. During the 1960s four staff members became Regents' Professors. They were Campbell R. McConnell, Wallace C. Peterson, Curtis M. Elliott, and William D. Torrence.

THE COLLEGE OF ENGINEERING AND ARCHITECTURE

Beginning in the fifties and throughout the decade of the sixties, engineering education in the United States shifted its emphasis from one of primary professional practice to one of a more mathematically and scientifically oriented course of study with greater emphasis on graduate study and research. These national trends in engineering education were responsible for major curricular revisions and the reactivation of the Engineering Experiment Station by the College of Engineering and Architecture.

As part of the University self-study project at the end of the fifties, the faculty of the college defined two major areas for development. The first area was the expansion of the college's graduate programs in all engineering departments to the doctorate level as quickly as financial resources would permit. This decision was in response to developing national trends in engineering education, a greater demand by students for graduate work, and the increasing research interest and activity by the college faculty.

The second priority for development was an expansion of the college's efforts in extension activities which would benefit practicing professional engineers and architects of the state as well as those industries within Nebraska oriented toward science and engineering. To accomplish these objectives, the college initiated graduate-level instruction for practicing engineers in Omaha in the fall of 1960. Technical and economic feasibility of a two-way television communication system was established for use in the program of instruction, but the necessary financial resources for implementation were not available. The request for funding the proposed communication system was not only denied by the legislature, there was also sufficient criticism of the plan by the senators to terminate the program after two years despite its attractiveness to practicing professionals in the Omaha area.

The establishment of doctoral programs in engineering was rapid during the sixties. The first doctoral program was approved by the regents for the Department of Engineering Mechanics in 1960. The Department of Chemical Engineering gained approval for a doctoral program in 1963, followed by the Department of Electrical Engineering in 1964 and the Department of Mechanical Engineering in 1968. Graduate study and research profited from the work of the Engineering Experiment Station, the establishment of an Engineering Research Center in 1967, and by the acquisition of the former ordnance facility at Mead. Development of the Field Laboratory supplied a needed site for research by the Departments of Agricultural Engineering and Civil Engineering. In cooperation with the United States Army Corps of Engineers, the Civil Engineering Department developed a well equipped hydraulics laboratory, at Mead, designed to model sections of the Missouri River permitting significant studies in erosion control.

In response to national trends, the faculty of the Department of Architecture proposed college status for architecture. Since the creation of a new college would require legislative approval, alternative action was taken, and the faculty unanimously approved redesignating the Department of Architecture as the School of Architecture. Acting upon this faculty recommendation, the Board of Regents established the school in 1964. Under the aegis of the school, a new program leading to the degree Bachelor of Science in Construction Science was installed by the regents in 1966.

During the decade of the sixties, leadership in the College of Engineering and Architecture was provided by two deans. Until his appointment as vice chancellor for research and dean of the Graduate College in 1965, Merk Hobson guided the development of the college. He was succeeded by John R. Davis, who had been chairman of the Department of Agricultural Engineering. Throughout the decade, Professor James S. Blackman served as assistant and associate dean. James H. Weber, Luh C. Tao and Turgut Sarpkaya were appointed Regents' Professors.

By the end of the decade, the College of Engineering and Architecture was developing plans for an expanded program in the area of Industrial and Management Systems Engineering and was making rapid progress in the development of its Institute of Computational Science.

THE GRADUATE COLLEGE

During the sixties, the scope of the Graduate College at the University steadily expanded. This was the result of strong national concern with graduate programs in American universities and of the increasing research interest of the Nebraska faculty. The qualification of 451 staff for membership in the Graduate College faculty attests to the rising level of scholarship at the University. To qualify for membership on the Graduate faculty, it was necessary to submit evidence of recognition by one's professional peers outside the University of Nebraska. This evidence was usually in the form of publications in professional journals.

Enrollment in the various advanced degree programs administered by the Graduate College increased markedly during the decade. A major factor at the University of Nebraska as well as at the other major universities of the nation was the support given by the federal government to increase the production of earned doctorates. In September 1960, there were 935 students enrolled in the Graduate College. By the fall of 1969, the number had increased to 2,688. A significant factor in this phenomenal growth was the dissolution of the Advanced Professional Division of Teachers College and the registration of all students working toward advanced degrees or six-year certificates in education with the Graduate College. This change marked the closing of the rift between the faculty of the Teachers College and that of the Graduate College. The Advanced Professional Division had been created during the Gustavson administration by the Board of Regents when the graduate faculty would not approve the inclusion of professional degrees in education within the structure of the Graduate College. By 1967-68, nearly 20 percent of the doctorates awarded by the Graduate College were in education.

Following the resignation of Dean John C. Weaver, in 1961, the Board of Regents named Roy G. Holly, chairman of the Department of Obstetrics and Gynecology at the Medical College, to be dean of the Graduate College and University Research Administrator. After Holly's resignation to return to teaching at another institution, Merk Hobson, the dean of the College of Engineering and Architecture, was named Graduate dean and vice chancellor for research. When Vice Chancellor Hobson was assigned other duties by the regents, the associate dean of the Graduate College, James C. Olson, was appointed dean. Olson was given the additional title of vice chancellor for graduate studies by the regents in March 1968. He left this post in July of the same year to accept the chancellorship of the University of Missouri at Kansas City. Because of the growing importance of seeking federal and private funds to support faculty research, the regents separated this function from that of the dean of the Graduate College and created a new full-time position of Research Administrator in 1967. Francis C. Schmehl, a chemist active in cancer research and an administrator with the Division of Research Facilities and Resources of the National Institute of Health, was appointed by the regents to the new position.

THE COLLEGE OF LAW

The first year of this decade was the last year that Edmund O. Belsheim served as dean of the College of Law. During the years of his administration, the college made substantial advances in the evolution of its curriculum toward goals which enabled students to meet more effectively the changing public expectancy of members of the bar. In July 1960, the regents appointed Professor David Dow to be dean of the College of Law. He had joined the faculty following World War II and had participated in the reactivation of the college in 1946. When Dow returned to full-time teaching in 1966, Professor Henry M. Grether, Jr., was named dean.

During the sixties, enrollment in the College of Law increased dramatically. In June 1960, when the college held its ninetieth commencement, 31 students were graduated from a total enrollment of 109. In 1969, the college graduated 83 seniors from a student body of 265. To prepare its graduates for the practice of law, the faculty was constantly aware of those changes which altered the work of the practicing attorney. Today, he is not only concerned with legal relations of a private nature, but also with the relation of government to business, labor, and agriculture, as well as the social, economic, and political consequences of these relationships. Alert to these changes, the faculty adjusted its curriculum. Between 1967 and 1970, 33 credit hours of new law courses were added, while 21 hours of courses were eliminated from the college offerings. The curriculum was broadened to give additional emphasis to such areas as legislation, administrative procedure, taxation, labor law, and international law. Improvements in teaching methods were adopted which more effectively aided in the development of basic skills and techniques used by lawyers in the courts and in the legislative and quasi-judicial bodies.

In 1964, the six-year program established with the College of Arts and Sciences and the College of Business Administration was expanded to include the College of Agriculture. These combined programs allow a student to enter the Law College after three years of academic work and to earn a degree from both the College of Law and the other participating college. To conform to a changing practice in American law colleges, the Board of Regents authorized the College of Law to grant the degree of Juris Doctor in 1964. This new degree replaced the traditional Bachelor of Laws degree. By further action of the regents, all past graduates of the college were granted the Juris Doctor degree in lieu of the bachelor's degree originally conferred upon them.

In cooperation with the Nebraska State Bar Association, the college continued to publish the quarterly *Nebraska Law Review*, and thus gave invaluable experience to those students involved. The Allen Moot Court Competition, named in honor of the first graduate of the college, Thomas Stinson Allen, '89, remained a highlight of the academic year. It gave students experiences designed to help them in the fields of legal research, oral argument, brief writing, and teaching. National Moot Court Competition provided Nebraska students further opportunities to compete with those from the nation's finest law schools. Students from the University of Nebraska compiled an enviable record. In 1961, Nebraska was the national runner-up, winning the national Best Team Oral Argument Award and the outstanding individual speaker. In 1962, Nebraska had to be content with the regional trophy and two rounds of national competition. The 1964, 1965, and 1967 teams, runners-up in the regional, participated in the national competition. In 1965 and 1967, the team was eliminated in the national quarter-finals, and received outstanding speaker in the 1967 regional competition. In 1966 and 1967, the team won the Regional Best Brief Award. In 1968, the college entered two teams in the regional competition for the first time. One team won the Best Respondent Brief Award. The other team won the Regional Championship, with the runner-up Petitioner's Brief, and a member of the team won the regional best individual argument award.

To provide students additional experience, the Legal Aid Bureau, a cooperative undertaking of the student Barrister's Club and the Lincoln Bar Association, supplied legal advice and assistance to those persons who were not able to pay an attorney's fee or to those whose cases were unremunerative on a contingent fee basis for the private practitioner. The Legal Aid Bureau was discontinued in 1967. However, in June 1969, the Nebraska Supreme Court promulgated a rule which allowed third-year students, certified as competent by the dean of the Law College, to practice law in certain circumstances under the direct supervision of an attorney. This improved clinical approach allowed many Nebraska students to receive invaluable experience.

In other activities, the faculty of the College of Law also arranged for experiences which would better prepare students for legal practice. A Legislative Seminar drafted bills for the Unicameral and testified before various committees considering them. Other students worked during the summer as plainclothesmen with the Lincoln Police Department and several more worked as guards at the Nebraska Penal Complex. Students were placed as clerks in law offices, outside the larger cities, to gain insight into the private practice of law in a small community. Because of these additional educational experiences, the Nebraska law student was well prepared for his professional life.

THE COLLEGES OF MEDICINE, DENTISTRY, AND PHARMACY

During the sixties the commitment made by the legislature in 1953 to upgrade the facilities at the medical campus in Omaha realized many of its objectives. During the ten years, 1953–63, that the special mill levy was collected, about $7.5 million was spent for improvement at the medical campus. Some major improvements which were made possible by the levy were the renovation of the South Laboratory Building, the construction of new research facilities, enlargement of the University Hospital by construction of Unit III, a new School of Nursing facility, a service building, and the modernization of the power plant.

Despite these improvements, the College of Medicine had not reached the quality level desired by the faculty, regents, and the public. A continuing problem was the lack of sufficient beds in the University Hospital. In 1962, the hospital's bed capacity was only 145, the lowest in any medical college hospital in the nation. To solve this and other pressing problems, Dean J. Perry Tollman and the regents announced a long-term plan for improvement at the college in November 1962. Besides enlarging the capacity of the University Hospital, the strengthening of all departments through the addition of more full-time faculty members became a major goal.

In June 1964, Tollman announced his resignation as dean, and after a leave of absence, returned to his teaching career in the Department of Pathology. Following consultation with the faculty and representatives of the Nebraska Medical Society, the Board of Regents appointed Cecil L. Wittson as dean. He had joined the medical faculty in 1950 as director of the Nebraska Psychiatric Institute and as professor and chairman of the Department of Neurology and Psychiatry. In accepting the assignment, the new dean won strong public support when he said: "I feel strongly that the area of general practice must be given special support."[7] By the late 1960s the College of Medicine included a Department of Family Practice which was regarded by many medical educators as a model.

The steady improvement at the Medical College was the result not only of state financial support but also of private philanthropy and substantial grants from the federal government. The Eugene C. Eppley Institute for Research in Cancer and Allied Diseases was funded with a $2.5 million gift from the Eugene

7. Omaha *World-Herald,* August 10, 1964, p. 4.

C. Eppley Foundation, a $800,000 grant from the United States Public Health Service, and $350,000 in state funds. In 1966 a grant from the federal government of $8,079,924 was given to match a state appropriation of $7,650,000. These funds made possible nearly 200 additional University Hospital beds, a two-floor addition to the clinic wing, a new Basic Science Building, and a revamping of older portions of the University Hospital. This federal-state partnership also provided needed financing for research and student development programs. Without the massive assistance of federal funds, it is very unlikely that these improvements in medical education at the University of Nebraska could have been accomplished. By the end of the decade, most American educational leaders and members of boards of control anticipated increased federal support of medical education. By the early seventies, these hopes were not fulfilled.

Under the leadership of Dean Rena Boyle, the School of Nursing received important national recognition. Graduates of the school consistently ranked first in the nation on their scores on national nursing examinations. In addition to the baccalaureate program, a master's degree program and a two-year associate degree curriculum were added during the decade.

At the Lincoln campus, substantial progress was made in education for the health professions, especially by the College of Dentistry. It had long been recognized that the facilities for dental education at the University were not adequate. In 1960, the report from the Council on Dental Education of the American Dental Association stated that:

The physical facilities cannot be described categorically as either good, average, or poor. The amount of available space is not adequate for even the relatively small classes that are accommodated in this program, and it is generally recognized by the administrators of both the dental school and the University that more space must be made available. From another standpoint, one must commend the school on the excellent utilization of space and the excellent planning to make the space available serve in the best manner possible.

The chairs and units in the clinic are of an adequate vintage and are essentially all made for left-handed students. Replacement parts are no longer available and while the students appear to learn their operative procedures well, this equipment is undoubtedly quite a handicap and it would certainly be a shock to the students from other schools who are examined in these facilities by the state board.[8]

Through the combined efforts of the state legislature, University administration, dental faculty, and the federal government, improvement in the college's facilities were accomplished. In 1963, the Unicameral passed L.B. 26, introduced by Senators Terry Carpenter and Marvin E. Stromer, which established the University of Nebraska College of Dentistry Building Fund, consisting of revenue raised by a .25 mill property tax levied from 1953 through 1964. The federal government supplied matching funds for the construction of the new facility on the East Campus. However, to qualify for the federal grant, the college was required to increase the size of its entering freshman class by twenty students or by 10 percent of the previous entering classes. The freshman class was increased from thirty-six to sixty students. With the dedication of the new College of Dentistry Building on the East Campus on November 10, 1967, a new era in dental education began at the University.

Major curricular changes in the college during the sixties included the creation of a Department of Periodontics in 1960, a program for training dental hygenists in 1964, and the combining of the Departments of Operative Dentistry and Fixed Denture Prosthesis into the Department of Restorative Dentistry in

8. Letter, Secretary, Council on Dental Education to Clifford M. Hardin, July 21, 1960, MSS, University of Nebraska Archives, Hardin Collection.

1969. Graduate programs were offered in the fields of orthodontics, periodontics, and oral surgery. Dean Ralph L. Ireland led the College of Dentistry during this time of development. He had first joined the staff in 1936 and was chairman of the Department of Pedodontics at the time of his appointment to the deanship in 1958. The improvements in the facilities and curriculum at the College of Dentistry during the sixties bear witness to his abilities as a dental educator. Following Dean Ireland's retirement in 1968, the Board of Regents named Richard E. Bradley as dean. Dean Bradley had been a member of the faculty since 1959 in the Department of Periodontics and had been named associate dean in 1967.

During this decade enrollment in the College of Pharmacy increased from a low of only 32 in 1960 to 238 in 1969. This phenomenal growth reflected the rising demand for pharmacists as well as the high national reputation of the college. Following the retirement of Dean Joseph B. Burt in 1961, after forty-one years of service, the Board of Regents appointed Robert D. Gibson as the dean.

TEACHERS COLLEGE

Under the guidance of Dean Walter K. Beggs, the Teachers College reached new heights of national recognition during the sixties. Because of the successful efforts of the dean to ameliorate the almost traditional feud between the Teachers College and the College of Arts and Sciences, the faculty was able to direct more of its energies to research and educational leadership. Out of the cooperative efforts of Dean Beggs and Dean Walter E. Militzer, of the College of Arts and Sciences, a new era of mutually beneficial participation was achieved. The success of the meetings between these two deans prompted other University deans to ask to join the informal discussions. Soon the unofficial group included all those deans representing undergraduate instruction on the Lincoln campuses. Although it never achieved an official status during the sixties, the Undergraduate Council contributed much to successful coordination and cooperation among all the undergraduate college programs on the Lincoln campuses. Furthermore, the wholesome spirit which developed within the group lessened the misunderstandings and suspicion which had too often marred the relationship between the colleges and offered the hope that the disruptive feuds of the past would not be repeated.

To assist in the administration of the Teachers College, Professors Wesley C. Meierhenry and Norman F. Thorpe served under various titles during the sixties as key personnel in the dean's office. The role of the department chairman was greatly expanded by Dean Beggs, who believed that each department should develop primarily under the direction of its chairman. This contrasts with the earlier Henzlik period, when the dean exercised personal direction over the smallest detail and additionally held one departmental chairmanship throughout his administration. To facilitate the work of the college, Dean Beggs established a Chairmen's Council to advise him and coordinate departmental efforts. This administrative arrangement functioned well throughout the decade, a time when the college experienced rapid growth. Enrollment expanded from 1,406 in 1960 to 4,065 in 1969. Facilities for the college were inadequate throughout the decade, but makeshift arrangements enabled the instructional program to continue.

During this decade the campus schools which provided elementary and secondary instruction were closed. Bancroft School was closed early in the decade and the University High School at the end of the summer session in 1967. To provide for the educational laboratories lost by these changes, contractual arrangements were made with the Lincoln School Board. Clare McPhee School was constructed jointly by the University and the Lincoln School Board in 1963 to provide an elementary laboratory school. A similar arrangement was made for use by the University of the East High School complex.

The rising national stature of the Teachers College resulted from the increasing levels of faculty scholarship and the participation of the staff in national professional organizations. The large number of Teachers College faculty members admitted to voting membership in the Graduate Faculty attests to the level of productive scholarship, as well as to Dean Beggs's emphasis on his faculty being fully represented in that body. The national image of the Teachers College was also improved by the recognition given members of the

Left to right: Teachers College deans Frank W. Henzlik and Walter K. Beggs, with Mrs. Henzlik.

faculty by professional organizations. At one time, five national presidencies were held by professors in the college: Galen Saylor led the Association for Supervision and Curriculum Development, Rosalie W. Farley was president of the Department of Rural Education of the National Education Association, Merle A. Stoneman was president of the National Association for School House Construction, Warren R. Baller was president of the National Association of College Teachers of Education, and Dean Beggs was president of the Association of Land-Grant Deans of Education. Other faculty members recognized with presidencies of national professional organizations during the sixties included: Sue Arbuthnot by the Association of Childhood Education International, Erwin H. Goldenstein by the National Association of College Teachers of Education, Knute O. Broady by the National University Extension Association, James M. May by the Department of Elementary School Principals, and Wesley C. Meierhenry by the Department of Audio Visual Instruction, the latter two being important sections of the National Education Association.

During the sixties the summer session, under the directorship of Frank E.

Sorenson, continued to serve a growing number of students. In 1968, the Board of Regents changed the summer program from an eight-week session to two five and one-half week sessions. In addition to the regular instructional program, Professor Sorenson instituted a number of special short courses, forums, and workshops centered on school problems as a regular part of the summer offerings.

During the last decade of the University's first century, a new high standard of academic excellence had been attained. The institution continued, as in the past, to be particularly concerned with problems unique to the state, but also made contributions of national and international significance. While state financial support had enabled the University of Nebraska to remain a respected member of the national academic community, national prominence could not have been achieved in some areas without federal support or private philanthropy.

The University of Nebraska's academic programs served the people of the state in a far more comprehensive way in 1969 than in 1920. Much more was expected of a university, and the University of Nebraska fulfilled this expectation. To many it seemed that the people of the state had finally accepted the statements by Chancellors Gustavson and Hardin that if given sufficient financial support the University could improve the quality of life in the state. This belief, coupled with more adequate state appropriations and the successful competition for federal funds, produced a feeling of optimism among the faculty which was unmatched in this half-century. During the administrations of Reuben G. Gustavson and Clifford M. Hardin, the University had prepared itself to enter that part of the mainstream of higher education dominated by prestige institutions. By the end of the sixties, the University of Nebraska was ready to make its move to become a major national center of higher education. The faculty was able and willing. However, it remained in doubt whether the favorable public attitude would continue and the support of the federal government would be maintained. At the end of the University of Nebraska's first century, it was at the crossroads. Whether it could achieve national excellence or would see the opportunity slip away would be decided in its second century.

CHAPTER 15

The Growth of Student Power
in the Sixties

FROM 1920 UNTIL THE sixties, the patterns in student life during each decade at the University of Nebraska were remarkably similar. Students were concerned about the traditional Greek-Barbarian conflict, rivalry between students enrolled in different colleges, the public's criticism of student conduct, the desire to prepare for a life's vocation, and the hope that perhaps some lifelong friendships and associations would be formed. Although during the sixties these recurring themes were still present, student life was additionally affected by events outside the University to an extent unmatched at any time since World War II. National events which influenced campus life throughout the land during this decade were the civil rights movement, the trend toward lowering the voting age, the new politics of confrontation, the recognition of what has been termed the "Counter-culture," the war in Vietnam, and the women's liberation movement. At the University of Nebraska, the consequence of these developments was tempered by the basic conservatism of the academic community and of the state. However, despite this cautious stance, by the end of the decade some fundamental changes had taken place in student attitudes and in the ways that students were perceived by the regents, administration, and faculty.

During the first years of the decade many believed that the students of this era would be little different from those of the past. Professor Dudley Bailey, director of the freshman English program, wrote that:

> We in the Department of English have no reason to despair of youth. Of course, we might allow ourselves to become preoccupied with the irrelevancies of university life. If we should let ourselves share in some students' temporary concern over last spring's beer bust, last week's football game, last night's fraternity initiation, today's editorial in the student paper, or next month's Kosmet Klub revue, we might be led to lugubrious statements about the younger generation. But in our wiser moments we realize that these are matters that do not count for much. As I stated at the outset, I believe our years give us some advantage over our students. For we have come to realize some differences that we were not certain of when we were students. We have become increasingly aware, for instance, that many student complaints do not matter greatly, even to the students themselves, who may register them with some degree of passion. Students quite properly retain the right to "gripe" about their class schedules, parking regulations, the hours and food at the dormitory, tough courses, low-grading professors, prerequisites for courses they want to take, and requirements for the degree; and most of them do gripe about these things in proper form. They likewise have the right to complain about their elders and the mess they've made of the world; this has been the child's right since Cain's and Abel's day. But anybody who takes such complaints seriously mistakes students. The fact is that they are comparatively indifferent to schedules and parking places, they like life at the dorm, they want tough courses and

high standards above all else, and they work hard to find things which will allow their respect to equal their very considerable love for parents and teachers.

On the other hand, when we hear students complain against mediocrity—in our programs, our teaching, our administration, our library, our physical facilities—we had better sit up and take notice, for such complaints strike at the heart of the University, quite as complaints against mediocrity in all aspects of a society strike at the heart of that society.[1]

Frank M. Hallgren, the associate dean of student affairs, believed that the students of the sixties were better prepared to meet the challenges of an uncertain future than those attending the University during the years before World War II. He also believed that they shared the popular societal concept of success.

College students are concerned with their material well-being and security. This need not be the cause for condemnation. College students are the products of a society where material well-being and security are acceptable goals. In addition our society makes these goals possible without demanding the sacrifice of even more important goals. There is no evidence that they do not have ideals, in fact noble ideals, which they would not sacrifice for materialism.[2]

Many national student movements of the late sixties were to involve protests against the sacrifice of these noble ideals on the altar of materialism. Issues involving civil rights or the Vietnam war became matters of conscience and morality for many American college and university students.

During the first years of the decade the perennial issues of campus drinking and the existence of sub-rosa fraternities again attracted administrative attention. Campus drinking was not a new issue at the University of Nebraska, and had long been a point of dispute on most collegiate campuses. The tacit approval of many alumni of discreet drinking in Greek houses and the apparent inconsistent enforcement of anti-drinking regulations by University authorities perpetuated the liquor issue. Student confusion regarding University drinking policy is apparent from events reported in the *Daily Nebraskan,* on December 9, 1963, following the Cornhusker victory over Oklahoma on the gridiron. Captain Eugene Masters of the University police was reported to have said, "There can be no liquor in organized houses at any time. This is an Administrative policy and we can do nothing about it." Despite this clear statement, there was apparently a deliberate lack of enforcement of the policy to allow students to celebrate the football victory. Several co-eds reported that the University police had come to their sorority house during the dinner hour and told them, "Our eyes are closed to everything except fights and property damage." A fraternity housemother told the *Daily Nebraskan* reporter that she was given the impression that for one night "the lid was off." She also recalled that the officers said, "that they didn't want anyone driving around, or having woodsies and that they could have a good time and be safe if they stayed on campus." Following the night's celebration, J. Winston Martin, dean of men, told members of the Inter-Fraternity Council that no disciplinary action would be taken against the houses which took advantage of the "open campus" following the victory over Oklahoma. Martin disclaimed any approval of the happenings by the University administration and suggested that any violation of policy or law was the responsibility of the University police. It is not surprising that students were uncertain about University drinking policies and perhaps believed that if regulations were ignored by a sufficient number, they would be immune from disciplinary action.

1. *Nebraska Alumnus,* May 1961, p. 10.
2. Ibid., p. 11.

The apparent action of the University police suggests that they too accepted the concept of immunity by mass violation of regulations.

The existence of sub-rosa fraternities again became a topic on the campus during the 1960s. Despite the attempt of Chancellor Gustavson to rid the campus of secret fraternities, they survived and again became a factor of campus life. With the suppression of Theta Nu Epsilon in 1951, it went underground and was replaced by other secret groups, Pi Xi, Red Dot, and Rho Delta. According to a *Daily Nebraskan* reporter, "with the aid of a prominent TNE Lincoln alum, the organization was re-established in 1957."[3] By the early 1960s at least two and perhaps as many as four secret fraternities existed on the University of Nebraska campus. The reawakening of student interest in these clandestine organizations stemmed largely from the immaturity of a few fraternity men and the misguided encouragement given them by alumni who as perennial sophomores sought perhaps to regain their youth by associating with students in a secret group. The role of alumni in the subrosas was acknowledged editorially by the *Daily Nebraskan* on April 6, 1962.

One of the biggest questions in our mind is, why do the prominent men of Lincoln, some quite prominent in University affairs and those of their own fraternity activity— and those of our alumni groups, seem to find it so important to keep TNE alive? We really question whether or not they really are interested in their University and a strong Greek system at all.

To counteract this negative sub-rosa influence, the University administration sought the support of the Inter-Fraternity Council and the alumni of the recognized fraternities. Professor C. Bertrand Schultz, an alumnus and Greek, was especially helpful to the administration in the elimination of the sub rosas from the campus. By 1962, the secret organizations had either gone underground again or had been dissolved. The success of the program of suppression can, however, be questioned. At the Homecoming game in 1965, a plane flew over the stadium pulling a banner which read, "Welcome TNE alums." By the last half of the decade sub-rosa fraternities had become archaic. With liberalized University housing regulations which permitted many students to live off-campus, the thrill of illegally drinking with other students in some basement had lost its imagined prestige. Also, the lowering of the legal age for drinking made membership in such organizations unnecessary.

The expansion of University efforts to provide more adequate campus housing additionally changed the patterns of campus life. In September 1960, Burr Hall on the East Campus became the University's first co-ed dormitory. Men and women students shared a common lounge with separate wings for the living areas. Because of the increasing demand for University-operated housing and the prediction for the continued expansion of the student body, the Board of Regents embarked on a major program of dormitory construction in January 1962. To fund these dormitories, revenue bonds were issued which would be retired from funds generated from the housing operation. By the end of the decade over 5,000 students resided in dormitories operated by the University, while the number living in fraternities or sororities remained nearly constant.

In the sixties the Student Council considered, a second time, affiliating with the United States National Student Association. In 1962, the issue was debated by the council and a decision was reached in April. Those who had favored affiliation with the national organization believed that it would increase campus concern with international events. Steve Gage, '62, Student Council president, favored the view that, "Without NSA, the Student Council will continue to blunder into areas

3. *Daily Nebraskan,* November 5, 1962.

which the Council has had no experience in and possesses no background material on."[4] Other students, however, did not believe that sufficient information was available about the organization to warrant affiliating with it, and the campus Young Republican group voted unanimously to oppose affiliating with the NSA. On a 19 to 10 vote the Nebraska Student Council voted against affiliation. This again reaffirmed the traditional conservative orientation of the Nebraska student body. This conservatism was also shared by most of the students at other Universities of the Big Eight Conference. Toward the end of this decade, it was revealed that the National Student Association had been subsidized by the Central Intelligence Agency as part of its information-gathering apparatus.

Student preference in national politics also continued to be conservative. In 1960 a student mock election supported the Nixon-Lodge Republican candidacy by nearly 2 to 1 over the Kennedy-Johnson Democratic ticket. By 1962, however, Nebraska students favored President Kennedy over all proposed Republican rivals, but the support for Kennedy was still less than the total of the four leading Republican hopefuls.

Again during these years, the matter of compulsory ROTC became a topic of campus discussion. This issue was not a new one to the University of Nebraska campus, having appeared periodically since the 1920s. While students did not object to an ROTC program on the campus, they had long opposed the required enrollment of all able-bodied men for two years of military training. The Board of Regents traditionally had supported the policy of compulsory ROTC training for freshmen and sophomores. Although federal law permitted land-grant universities to abolish the mandatory two-year requirement for male students, the regents had repeatedly stated their belief that the spirit of the Morrill Act called for the continuation of the two-year compulsory program. In May 1964, the regents reevaluated their ROTC policy and joined the majority of universities which made participation in military training optional. At the time of this change in policy by the Nebraska regents only 16 percent of the institutions offering army ROTC still required two years participation. Certainly the regents were influenced in this decision by the action of some forty colleges and universities which eliminated the compulsory feature between 1959 and 1964 and by specific action from the United States Department of Defense, in 1961, advising institutions of their right to determine whether ROTC programs should be compulsory or elective. The continuation of military training at land-grant universities on a voluntary basis was a major factor in preserving the basic civilian orientation of the nation's officer corps. Had military training been continued on a compulsory basis, it is obvious that faculties throughout the nation would have strongly opposed the continuation of all ROTC programs. On some prestigious campuses the reserve officer programs were terminated.

In mid-summer 1962, the retirement of J. Phillip Colbert as dean of students was announced. He had joined the faculty of the College of Engineering in 1925 and was named dean of student affairs in 1952 following Theos J. Thompson. At the time of his retirement as an administrator and return to the classroom, Dean Colbert commented on the changes which had taken place within the student body during the years of his association with it:

They are much more serious now, they have become more serious about the problems confronting the University and the country. . . . The students still have enthusiasm for activities and good fun . . . they still enjoy their social life and athletics as much as ever, but on top of this, they are more serious.[5]

4. Ibid., April 19, 1962.
5. Ibid., April 6, 1962.

To guide student life at the University, the regents appointed G. Robert Ross as dean of the Division of Student Affairs. The new dean, a native of Texas, earned his Bachelor of Science in Agricultural Economics and his master's degree in sociology from Texas A & M. He was awarded the Ph.D. in psychology in 1955 from the University of Denver. Prior to his acceptance of the Nebraska appointment he was dean of students at Ball State Teachers College at Muncie, Indiana. To assist Dean Ross, the regents appointed Lee W. Chatfield as associate dean of student affairs in 1963. A native of Ord, Nebraska, and a graduate of the University, Chatfield first joined the faculty as an assistant professor in the Department of Military Science in 1940. Following service in World War II, he returned to the University as an assistant to Dean Theos J. Thompson.

By the mid-sixties students were acutely aware of national issues involving racism and civil rights, the Vietnam war, and equality for women. Although students had been concerned about the equal rights of racial minority groups since World War II, this concern had often been superficial or temporary. Following the example set by the Kennedy administration, the movement led by Martin Luther King, and the adoption of civil rights legislation by Congress in 1963, many campus leaders throughout the nation urged their fellow students to actively support campaigns for social justice. During the 1964 spring vacation, a small group of students from the University of Nebraska joined with other students in a voter registration campaign in North Carolina under the sponsorship of the National Young Women's Christian Association. That same semester the *Daily Nebraskan* featured a series of articles on the status of black students at the University of Nebraska. The articles concluded that many black students were subjected to racial discrimination. It was suggested that this discrimination often resulted from the public's conservatism and resistance to change rather than a recognized or conscious racial bias. As a University student, an article stated that:

. . . the Negro at the University achieves equality. He labors through the same assignments, discusses the same issues, turns in similar papers, and ultimately gets the grade he deserves.

Negroes at the University are much the same as their white counterparts in academic endeavors.[6]

Campus discussions of social justice continued. In early 1965, the Student Council adopted a resolution urging all campus organizations to delete any racial restrictions from their constitutions. By spring the Panhellenic Council and the Inter-Fraternity Council had adopted policies opposing any racial discrimination by their affiliated groups. At its meeting on April 16, 1965, the Board of Regents approved these student-formulated statements and instructed the vice chancellor for student affairs to gather information from national fraternities regarding their racial policies, to work with students to eliminate any "discriminatory practices and attitudes," and to report progress on these matters to the regents as soon as possible. On June 11, 1965, the Board of Regents again stated their opposition to discrimination and on August 6, 1965, adopted a comprehensive statement of their policy.

To ensure a uniformity of understanding, the Board of Regents directs that the following resumé of University policy on discrimination be distributed to members of the faculty, the administrative, and professional-managerial staffs.

Pertaining to Students

University policy prohibits denial of University privileges to students on grounds of race, color, nationality, or religion. In this context "University privileges" include Uni-

6. Ibid., March 26, 1964.

versity housing, dining, and recreational facilities, as well as admission to the University, assignment to classes, the awarding of scholarships, fellowships, assistantship, and financial aid.

It is further the policy of the University that student organizations at the University of Nebraska must base their selection of students for membership on criteria which will not include race or color. Membership selection for student groups based on reasonable criteria shall remain the responsibility of individual groups.

Pertaining to Staff

University policy forbids discrimination against any employee or applicant for employment, because of his race, sex, color, religion, or national origin. This policy includes hiring, placement, upgrading, transfer, demotion, recruitment, training and pay.

It was moved by Regent Greenberg, seconded by Regent Elliott, motion put to vote and carried, that the following resolution be adopted.

To some civil rights activists, the policy of the regents was not completely satisfactory. Their criticism reflected a basic philosophical difference in the role that a university should play in society. They believed that it should be a major instrument for social change. Most Nebraskans, however, believed that a university should only assist the forces in society which would bring about changes desired by the majority.

By the fall of 1965, the Vietnam war was a major topic of campus discussion. Attempts to organize opposition to the war were made by a new campus student organization, Students for a Democratic Society. This group described itself as "an association of young people on the left who seek alternatives to poverty, racism, corporate or military rule in public affairs and governments which people no longer control. . . ."[7] Although the SDS became an important fact of campus life on some American campuses, it failed, despite minor faculty support, to attract a significant student membership at the University of Nebraska. Consequently, its duration on the campus was short. Its admitted leftist orientation was unacceptable to most Nebraskans, who preferred a middle-of-the-road position. While growing numbers of students, faculty, and citizens gradually adopted views in opposition to the Vietnam war, organized opposition to the national policy attracted few and was not very successful during the last years of the University's first century. After the Centennial in February 1969, opposition to the war became more widespread, more vocal, and more successful.

Regulation of student housing by the University developed over the years out of a feeling of paternalism and from the practical necessity of collecting sufficient revenue from student housing to retire the bonds issued to fund the projects. Because of administrative paternalism, the regulation of women's housing by American universities had always been more restrictive than for men students. During this period at the University of Nebraska, policy changes were made which gradually eliminated the dual standard in housing. A significant change was made in 1964 when senior women who were twenty-one years old or older were permitted to live off-campus. For those co-eds who lived on campus, the policy establishing the hour by which they must be in the dormitory or sorority house had always been unpopular. The remarks of several co-eds reported in the *Daily Nebraskan* on December 9, 1965, differ little from similar comments made by women students thirty years earlier. "I feel like I'm being locked up. . . . I was trusted at home to come in when I wished and I should be here." A sophomore student added:

They're trying to enforce morality . . . and it simply can't be done. We're supposed to be at college for academic and social advancement and are not given the opportunity

7. Omaha *World-Herald,* October 16, 1965, p. 1.

to do either. We're bossed around like grade school children and that is no preparation for society. . . . They don't admit we have minds of our own that are perfectly able to distinguish right from wrong.

Certainly it was an anachronism that during a period characterized by discussion of equal civil rights for blacks and the passage of federal anti-discrimination legislation that women students would still be paternalized by discriminatory housing regulations. The dual housing regulations were vigorously opposed by women students, and changes were effected. In October 1966, a system was established by which senior women were allowed keys to the dormitories. By early 1969 this scheme had been expanded to include sophomore women. By the end of the University's centennial year, housing regulations for men and women students were identical, with only single freshmen under eighteen years of age being required to live in on-campus housing, including University residence halls, cooperatives, fraternities, and sororities.

Because of the tremendous growth in enrollment and the increased availability of University operated on-campus housing, the influence of fraternities and sororities on campus life was reduced. During the twenties, thirties, and forties, Greek letter organizations had dominated organized campus life. The fifties was a time of transition and by the sixties, Greek dominance was a thing of the past. The reorganization of student government at the University in 1965 marks a major student political realignment. The Student Council's constitution had permitted some students double or triple representation in student government because the council was composed of college representatives as well as those from several student organizations. The proposed new agency for student government, the Association of the Students of the University of Nebraska (ASUN) would include in its legislative branch only representatives chosen from the colleges by direct apportionment. Furthermore, the president and vice president would be elected directly by the student body rather than from the student representatives as had been the practice with the Student Council. The ratification by the student body of the new constitution for student government at the University by a 1,333 to 335 vote suggests strong support among those students concerned with student government for reform. Of greater significance, however, is that less than 10 percent of the student body exercised their franchise. Clearly student government interested only a minor portion of those enrolled at the University, and it represented the views of an almost insignificant number. By the late sixties, few traditional campus issues remained that could stir students. Liberalized University housing regulations, lowering the voting age, and the greater public acceptance of young people by society made most campus politics seem irrelevant and more appropriate to the past than the present.

Issues which, however, concerned students at the University and throughout the nation were those of personal freedom and participation in the decision-making processes within the academic community. During the 1966–67 academic year, students expressed an interest in having a written statement of student responsibilities and rights at the University of Nebraska. As a result of this concern, the ASUN developed a statement termed the "Student Bill of Rights" which was adopted by the Student Senate and endorsed by the student body in a referendum in the spring of 1967. Following this action, representatives of student government discussed the "Student Bill of Rights" informally with the Board of Regents. It was agreed by the regents, chancellor, and students that a committee representing all parts of the academic community be formed to study the document and to redraft it in the form of a policy statement. The ad hoc committee of six, which included the president and first vice president of the student body, deliberated through the 1967–68 academic year and prepared a proposed policy statement entitled, "The Student in the Academic Community." The proposed policy was approved by the ASUN Senate on April 7, by referendum of the student body on April 10, by the University Faculty Senate on May 14, and by the Board of Regents on May 19, 1968. The swift approval given this policy by the academic community proves that rapid action is possible when based on mutual trust and consensus or perhaps on the fear of serious student disorders.

"The Student in the Academic Community" policy statement reaffirmed the rights of students as citizens and as members of an academic community. It was recognized that regulations affecting students were necessary but that they should "seek the best possible reconciliation between personal freedom and necessary order." It was also acknowledged that students should participate in the formulation of rules for conduct. Off-campus student rights were recognized as well as the special status of students as members of the University community.

. . . Students are subject, however, to the special obligations which accrue to them as members of the academic community. Institutional effort should be exerted to develop, not inhibit, intellectual and personal development of students by the exercise of the rights of citizenship both on and off campus.

The enforcement of obligations of students to the larger society is the responsibility of the legal and judicial authorities duly established for that purpose. If students are alleged violators of the law, they should proceed through legal channels and institutional authority should never be used merely to duplicate those functions.

When the interests of the academic community are clearly involved, the authority of the institution should be asserted. The fact that a violation occurs off campus does not preclude the interest and involvement of the University.

When participating in off-campus activities, students should make it clear that in their public expression or demonstrations they speak and act only for themselves as individuals.

This policy was a departure from the traditional concept that an educational institution should act in *loco parentis*. At a time when federal courts were upholding the rights of high school students to wear long hair and to defy school boards' dress codes, it was time for universities to stop attempting to regulate the personal lives of students. Seldom had parents been successful in, or desirous of, enforcing rules for their eighteen- to twenty-one-year-old offspring of the nature attempted by the University for many years. Now except for their special obligations to the academic community, the students' rights to the same degree of personal freedom and responsibility as exercised by all other young adults in society was acknowledged.

The policy recognized the student's right to freedom of expression in the classroom and the obligation of the faculty to establish clearly understood standards of academic performance. Procedures for student appeals of course grades were recommended and established by all University departments. In all matters affecting the student body, their right to consultation was respected. "The Student in the Academic Community" policy statement reads:

. . . The students should have clearly defined means to participate equitably in the formulation of institutional policies and procedures which affect student life. Student government is the principal agency for student participation in the decision-making process of the University.

Students were now, as never before, recognized by the faculty, administration, and regents as full partners in the academic community. To implement the policies contained in "The Student in the Academic Community," the regents created the University Council on Student Life. The council was granted general policy-making power and supervision of student life subject to the approval of those charged by law with the governance of the University—the Board of Regents. The University Council on Student Life was composed of thirteen members, six representing the faculty and administration and seven students, including the president of ASUN and six students selected by the ASUN. By allowing students to comprise the majority of the council, the regents had recognized the maturity of the student body to a degree unknown in the past.

As the University of Nebraska began its second century, the success of these new policies and plans to allow students an expanded role in the decision-making process would depend on the acceptance by students of their responsibilities as citizens of the University community. Judged by the events of a half century, most students would give little attention or concern to matters of student government and would regard their years at the University as a temporary and transient time of life. With the decline of relatively conservative fraternity and sorority campus political power, there emerged on all campuses of the nation small groups of politically oriented students who viewed the university as the lever by which they could move the world. Because of the apathy of most students and the carnival atmosphere of confrontation situations for the immature, these activist students often came to be disproportionately represented in student organizations and government. The future of student participation in American campus decision-making will depend on the greatly expanded involvement of the student body in campus affairs. If, however, student activities are dominated by small activist groups—from either the extreme right or left—the pendulum will swing back away from the trend to involve students more deeply as partners in the academic society.

VARSITY ATHLETICS

Nebraska once again moved into a decade with high expectations in the wake of the mixed season of 1959. There were signs that the Cornhuskers had turned the corner in their post–World War II building drive when the 1960 season opened with a sensational 14–13 upset of mighty Texas at Austin. However, as so often had happened in the past, Coach Bill Jennings' teams lacked consistency, with great moments and sad moments, optimism and pessimism. Although the Huskers wound up with another lackluster 4–6–0 record, Jennings was again able to forestall an all-out assault on his regime by whipping Oklahoma 17–14 at Norman in the finale. After four years, Jennings still lacked a winning season, but he had beaten Texas and Oklahoma for the second straight year. In the wake of a Sooner recruiting scandal that saw him play a leading role, dating back to his days as an Oklahoma coach under Bud Wilkinson, Jennings dreaded the trip to Norman. Yet, ironically, he won, and Nebraska fans would grant him one more season.

Things never went quite right for Jennings in 1961, but the recruiting ground work was laid for a sensational final eight years of the decade. When the Huskers managed only a 3–6–1 season, with wins over North Dakota, Kansas State, and Iowa State, it became evident that Jennings would not have his contract renewed. Earlier in 1961, Athletic Director Bill Orwig had resigned to take a similar position at his alma mater, Michigan. After his resignation, the Nebraska program was administered by a makeshift arrangement—Comptroller Joseph Soshnik and faculty representative Charles Miller, dean of the College of Business Administration, as co-athletic directors, with A. J. Lewandowski as business manager and ticket director.

On the morning of the Colorado game, which Nebraska lost 7–0 in the mud and never made a first down, Lewandowski died of a heart attack. Tippy Dye was recruited as the new athletic director. Dye, former basketball coach at

Washington and at Ohio State, was the athletic director at Wichita University and had the reputation of getting things rolling. Ironically, he almost chose the wrong man for the football job, but fate intervened, and the Cornhuskers started on the road to national prominence that was to culminate with two national championships in the next decade. While Dye was wooing Wichita coach Hank Foldberg, Nebraska Chancellor Clifford Hardin and Regent Clarence Swanson were checking with Biggie Munn and Duffy Daugherty at Michigan State. A fellow named Bob Devaney, coaching at the University of Wyoming, was recommended. Eventually, Devaney slipped into Lincoln under an assumed name to be interviewed. It was agreed that he would be Bill Jennings' successor, if he could get a release from his lifetime contract at Wyoming. Wyoming did not want Devaney to leave, but finally he was released, and in February 1962, Devaney and assistants Jim Ross, John Melton, Mike Corgan, and Carl Selmer took over the Cornhusker reins. It was a providential event for Nebraska's football program and for the Cornhuskers' victory-starved fans.

No one expected Devaney to perform miracles, but he did. During the next eight years of the 1960s, his teams would win 68, lose only 18, and tie none, while winning five Big Eight Championships and playing in six post-season games. No coach ever made such an impact on the state.

While Devaney took over the football fortunes with gusto, Dye set about to totally revise the image of the Athletic Department. Jerry Bush resigned as basketball coach after the 1963 season, and Tippy hired his former star player, Joe Cipriano, from Idaho, a move that would lead to the best seasons in Nebraska history and a National Invitational Tournament appearance in the mid-1960s.

However, it was football that the 1960s will be remembered for by Cornhusker fans. Devaney noted upon his arrival that Jennings had, indeed, done a masterful job of recruiting. The sophomores of 1961 had the potential to be the stars of 1962, with organization and inspiration. Devaney and his staff, which also included holdovers Cletus Fischer and George Kelly from the Jennings era, put it all together in unbelievable fashion. Nebraska, coming off a 3–6–1 season, stunned the nation by winning its first six games, defeating Michigan at Ann Arbor, Kansas State at Manhattan, and Colorado at Boulder, before bowing to Missouri at Columbia. But the Cornhuskers bounced back to obliterate Kansas and Gale Sayers at Lawrence 40–16 in an unforgettable contest. After blanking Oklahoma State, Nebraska found itself in a strange, unfamiliar situation, that of playing Oklahoma at Norman for the Big Eight title. Disappointingly, the Sooners defeated the awestruck Cornhuskers, 34–7.

However, Nebraska had an exciting and proud 8–2–0 record, the first winning season since 1954 and the best record since the Rose Bowl year of 1940. Shortly after the Oklahoma game, Nebraska was contacted by the Gotham Bowl director, Bob Curran of New York City, and offered a chance to play Miami of Florida in Yankee Stadium on December 15. Financially, it was not a bonanza, but Devaney recognized that it was a chance to get further exposure for his football program and wanted to accept. So did the players. University officials, Chancellor Hardin, and the regents were somewhat apprehensive, as was Devaney, about the financial assurances from the Gotham Bowl. However, Nebraska accepted the bid and made ready to fly to New York, subject to Curran providing a certified cashier's check for $35,000 before the Cornhuskers took off from the Lincoln airport. The day before the game, which was ill-fated from the outset after running into all sorts of promotional and financial setbacks, including a newspaper strike that prevented most New Yorkers from even knowing there would be a game, the Nebraska team gathered at Lincoln's Municipal Airport and waited for word from New York. Would Curran get the guarantee money certified so there could be a Gotham Bowl game, or would Nebraska stay home?

Action was hot and heavy in New York, where Nebraska Ticket Manager Jim Pittenger, Publicity Director John Bentley, Lincoln *Journal* sports editor Dick Becker, and Lincoln *Star* sports editor Don Bryant kept in constant contact with Curran, who was racing around Manhattan trying to line up the advance guarantee. After a couple of misfires, Curran finally arranged the advance, presented Pittenger with the certified check, and a call was made to the Lincoln airport. Nebraska's team took off for New York and a memorable, if bitter cold adventure. There were only some 6,000 fans in Yankee Stadium the next day, and the temperature was a frigid 14 degrees at kickoff time. Players wore tennis shoes and ice-skated over the frozen turf of Yankee Stadium. In one of college football's most exciting games, Miami's George Mira threw for more than 300 yards, Nebraska's Willie Ross had a 92-yard kickoff return, Cornhusker Dennis Claridge out-quarterbacked Mira, and the Cornhuskers won their first bowl game by a score of 36–34.

Thus, Nebraska wound up with a 9–2–0 record, but more important was the fact that Devaney had instilled a winning pride into a group of juniors who would be a devastating force the coming fall, Claridge, Ross, Johnson, Kirby, Brown, and Voss. Devaney's Cornhuskers slipped only once in 1963, a 17–13 loss to Air Force at Lincoln on a last-quarter touchdown pass. After piling up eight wins in nine outings, some easily and some sensationally, it was again showdown time with Oklahoma. The two teams met in Lincoln for the Big Eight title on November 23, with the Orange Bowl waiting to give the winner a bid.

Again, however, fate affected Nebraska's football history. While Nebraska fans were awaiting the championship contest on Friday afternoon, the news flashed across the nation in dramatic and horrifying suddenness that President John F. Kennedy had been assassinated in Dallas. Nebraskans were just as stunned as the rest of the nation, and as the awful truth sunk in on Americans everywhere, University of Nebraska officials put in a long night. Should the game be played, or should it be canceled in a gesture of mourning? There was sentiment both ways, as many college games were canceled. But a much more intricate drama was unfolding in Lincoln.

The Nebraska-Oklahoma game was a sellout and fans had traveled from all parts of the nation. It was imperative for the Orange Bowl to select a participant. Nobody had much enthusiasm for the game in the wake of President Kennedy's death, but it should be played if at all possible. The Big Eight Conference urged that the contest be held. Oklahoma Coach Bud Wilkinson, a close personal friend of the Kennedy family, was in telephone contact with Attorney General Kennedy, who urged that the game be played, expressing the Kennedy family's belief that the late President would have wanted the nation to proceed with its activities. On through the night went the agonizing debate, and it was not until noon of the following day, two hours before the kickoff, that it was finally decided to play the game. Nebraska "played its best defensive game in 50 years," according to Omaha *World Herald* sports writer Gregg McBride, and ripped Oklahoma for a 29–7 lead after three quarters. Devaney turned the game over to his subs in the final portion of the game, but Nebraska emerged the Big Eight champion and the Orange Bowl selectee with a dramatic and convincing 29–20 thrashing of Oklahoma in Bud Wilkinson's final game as coach of the Sooners.

In Miami on New Years afternoon, the Cornhuskers, with a 68-yard run by Claridge, some great blocking by All-America guard Bob Brown, and two field goals by Dave Theisen, whipped Auburn, 13–7. Devaney had done it again, two bowl wins, a 19–3–0 record in two years, and the Big Eight championship. With that foundation, Nebraska was on its way to a decade of football excellence. In 1964 the Cornhuskers won nine straight before losing to Oklahoma, but won the Big Eight title. Invited to the Cotton Bowl, they led Arkansas until the final minutes before losing, 10–7, as the Razorbacks won the national title.

The Cornhuskers won their third straight Big Eight title in 1965, this time going undefeated through a ten-game schedule before losing the national championship to Alabama, 39–28, in the Orange Bowl. Undaunted, Devaney continued in 1966 as the Huskers won nine straight before again bowing to Oklahoma in the finale. However, Nebraska had another Big Eight crown and another bowl bid, this time to the Sugar Bowl and another crack at Alabama. But Alabama won again, 34–7, and there were signs that Nebraska might have trouble continuing its lofty status.

Among the stars of those championship years were, in 1964, Bobby Churchich, who took over at quarterback when Fred Duda broke a leg, Kent McCloughan, Lyle Sittler, and All-America Larry Kramer; in 1965, All-Americans Tony Jeter, Freeman White, and Walt Barnes, Churchich, and Duda; in 1966, All-Americans Wayne Meylan, Larry Wachholtz, and LaVerne Allers, Harry Wilson, and Churchich.

Nebraska based its 1967 hopes on a 6-7 rookie quarterback named Frank Patrick, and he proceeded to smash all the Husker passing records. However, the Cornhuskers were not consistent and dipped to a 6–4 record, dismal by the standards established by Devaney. When the same thing occurred in 1968, this time with quarterback Ernie Sigler, an unsung veteran squadman, there were rumblings that Devaney had passed his prime, lost his touch, and could not win the big ones. Bob Devaney and his staff fooled them all. They rolled up their sleeves, intensified teaching and recruiting and launched in 1969 what was to become one of the greatest teams in college football history, the 1971 national champions.

Taking two brilliant, but sophomore, quarterbacks, Van Brownson and Jerry Tagge, a great sophomore running back, Jeff Kinney, and a host of big, strong, quick, and aggressive linemen, Devaney fashioned the nucleus of a super team. It did not start in sensational fashion as Nebraska lost the opening game of 1969 to Southern California, 31–21, at Lincoln. But the Huskers gained a great deal of confidence, and fans saw promise as Texas A & M and Minnesota were defeated. The next week was a memorable one for Devaney and Cornhusker followers when they reflect back from 1972. Nebraska lost to Missouri at Columbia, 17–7, but they were not to lose again in 1969, in 1970, or in 1971. Starting the next week against Kansas, the Huskers won six straight Big Eight games and tied for the championship, then bombed Georgia, 45–6, in the Sun Bowl. It all added up to a 9–2–0 season, a Bob Devaney season the fans had come to expect in the earlier years of the 1960s.

Nebraska went on to undefeated seasons in 1970 and 1971, winning the Big Eight titles both years and emerging with back-to-back national championships, the coveted number one ranking. However, it was the colorful 1960s and the Bob Devaney legend that set the stage for national supremacy. Devaney's eight-year record during the 1960s boosted the decade's football mark to 75–30–1, second only to the 1900–09 era in Nebraska history.

Meanwhile, other Nebraska sports were growing and prospering. Under Dye's direction, the total athletic program grew. The football stadium was expanded from 31,000 to 67,000 seating capacity, and thanks to Devaney's football, Memorial Stadium was sold out for every game.

Nebraska's basketball team, sparked by Stuart Lantz, Tom Baack, and by Coach Cipriano's drive, developed into a consistent winner. The Husker track team, coached by Frank Sevigne, won the Big Eight indoor title in 1963, the outdoor title in 1966, and finished in the first division seven times during the decade. Track featured such stars as world champion sprinter Charlie Greene and NCAA champion Peter Scott. Greene won the Big Eight Schulte Award three straight years, an unmatched accomplishment. In 1967 when Dye moved to Northwestern University, Devaney became athletic director, as well as football coach.

During the 1960s, Orval Borgialli was Nebraska's wrestling coach, and led the development of that sport to an all-time high. He also developed the state high school wrestling tournament into one of the top sports events in Nebraska. John Reta took over as the Nebraska swimming coach, while Francis Allen became the Husker gymnastics coach.

Recipients of Honorary Degrees Granted by the University of Nebraska 1919–1969

1919
William L. Seibert — Doctor of Engineering

1920
Charles R. Richards — Doctor of Engineering
Roscoe W. Thatcher — Doctor of Agriculture
Raymond Eli Benedict — Master of Forestry
Clarence Curtis Culver — Electrical Engineer

1921
David Kinley — Doctor of Laws
John Holland Rose — Doctor of Laws
Harold Gifford — Doctor of Laws

1922
Sergei V. Rachmaninoff — Doctor of Music
Charles W. Pugsley — Doctor of Agriculture

1923
Albert Watkins — Doctor of Laws
William Granger Hastings — Doctor of Laws

1924
William Edwin Hardy — Master of Arts

1925
Francis David Farrell — Doctor of Agriculture
Irving Samuel Cutter — Doctor of Science
Anson Marsten — Doctor of Engineering
John Eschelman Miller — Master of Arts
John Henry Weller — Civil Engineer

1926
Francis La Flesche — Doctor of Letters

1927
Frederick Blackmar Mumford — Doctor of Agriculture
Lucius S. Storrs — Doctor of Engineering
Cassius Asa Fisher — Doctor of Science
Robert Harshe — Doctor of Fine Arts

Leila Mechlin	Doctor of Fine Arts
Sven Birger Sandzen	Doctor of Fine Arts
John Edward Summers	Doctor of Laws
August Frederick Jonas	Doctor of Laws
Willson Orton Bridges	Doctor of Laws

1928

Charles Newton Gould	Doctor of Science
Holmes Smith	Doctor of Fine Arts
Herbert Silas Evans	Doctor of Engineering
Warren Abner Seavey	Doctor of Laws

1929

Frederick Kenelm Nielsen	Doctor of Laws
Henry H. Wilson	Doctor of Laws

1930

Francis Samuel Philbrick	Doctor of Laws

1931

Malcolm Glen Wyer	Doctor of Library Science
Jay Brownlee Davidson	Doctor of Engineering
Harold VanBuren Magonigle	Doctor of Architecture
Grace Abbott	Doctor of Laws
Willford Isbell King	Doctor of Laws

1932

Derrick Norman Lehmer	Doctor of Science
Gustaf Waldemar Elmen	Doctor of Engineering
Oscar VanPelt Stout	Doctor of Engineering

1934

James Stuart Dales	Doctor of Laws
Bess Streeter Aldrich	Doctor of Letters
E. Parmelee Prentice	Doctor of Agriculture
Walter Bowers Pillsbury	Doctor of Laws
Owen D. Young	Doctor of Laws

1935

George William Norris	Doctor of Laws
James William Crabtree	Doctor of Laws
Samuel Avery	Doctor of Laws
Charles Henry Purcell	Doctor of Engineering
Howard Hanson	Doctor of Music
Jesse Perry Rowe	Doctor of Science
Madison Bentley	Doctor of Laws
Henry Baldwin Ward	Doctor of Laws
Robert Gordon Sproul	Doctor of Laws

1936

Edward Charles Elliott	Doctor of Laws
Willets Herbert Sawyer	Doctor of Engineering

1937

Christian Lauriths Christensen	Doctor of Agriculture
Robert Anderson Gantt	Doctor of Engineering
Walter Jacob Wohlenberg	Doctor of Engineering

1938
John Davidson Clark   Doctor of Laws
Harry Levi Hollingworth   Doctor of Laws
Leta Stetter Hollingworth   Doctor of Laws
William Linn Westermann   Doctor of Laws
John Torrence Tate   Doctor of Science

1939
Orien Wesley Fifer   Doctor of Laws
Frederic Benjamin Garver   Doctor of Laws
Frederick Maurice Hunter   Doctor of Laws
Hartley Burr Alexander   Doctor of Letters
LaMonte Judson Belnap   Doctor of Engineering
Ernest Emmanuel Howard   Doctor of Engineering

1940
Frederic Edward Clements   Doctor of Laws
Gladys Henry Dick   Doctor of Laws
Alvin Saunders Johnson   Doctor of Laws
Joel Stebbins   Doctor of Laws
Alexander Jerry Stoddard   Doctor of Laws

1941
Viola Florence Barnes   Doctor of Laws
Thomas Jean Hargrave   Doctor of Laws
Arthur Sperry Pearse   Doctor of Laws
Mark Morton   Doctor of Agriculture
John Chatfield Page   Doctor of Engineering
Karl Chandler Randall   Doctor of Engineering

1942
Charles Michael Bracelen   Doctor of Laws

1943
Frederick James Kelly   Doctor of Laws
John Todd Zimmer   Doctor of Science
Ralph Scott Mueller   Doctor of Engineering

1944
Stanley Bracken   Doctor of Engineering
Eugene Edward Lundquist   Doctor of Engineering
Howard Remus Smith   Doctor of Agriculture

1945
Edgar Franklin Howe   Master of Agriculture
Edwin Harrison Brown   Doctor of Engineering
Harry Clyde Ingles   Doctor of Engineering
Edwin Ray Guthrie   Doctor of Laws
Frank Henry Woods   Doctor of Laws
Ruth Frances Woodsmall   Doctor of Laws

1946
Ernst Athern Bessey   Doctor of Laws
Ben Mark Cherrington   Doctor of Laws

1947
Gilmour Byers MacDonald   Doctor of Agriculture
Frederick Carl Holtz   Doctor of Engineering
John Cyprian Stevens   Doctor of Engineering

1948

Ned Culbertson Abbott	Doctor of Laws
Guy Thomas Buswell	Doctor of Laws
John Wayne Delehant	Doctor of Laws
Harold Eugene Edgerton	Doctor of Engineering

1949

Milton Stover Eisenhower	Doctor of Humane Letters
George Wells Beadle	Doctor of Science
Randolph T. Major	Doctor of Science
James P. Growdon	Doctor of Engineering

1950

Mari Susette Sandoz	Doctor of Literature
Ewald T. Grether	Doctor of Laws
Arthur Bessey Smith	Doctor of Engineering

1951

Samuel Roy McKelvie	Doctor of Agriculture
Cornelius B. Philip	Doctor of Science
Harold Claf Peterson	Doctor of Engineering
Warren S. Thompson	Doctor of Laws
Harvey M. Johnsen	Doctor of Laws

1952

Henry Albert Jones	Doctor of Science
Ruth O'Brien	Doctor of Science
George Paul Luckey	Doctor of Engineering
Joy Paul Guilford	Doctor of Laws
Trygve Halvdan Lie	Doctor of Laws

1953

Charles Mitchell Candy	Doctor of Engineering
Jane Margueretta Hoey	Doctor of Humanities
Hazel Gertrude Kinscella	Doctor of Music
Harry Scott Smith	Doctor of Science
Herbert Brownell, Jr.	Doctor of Laws
Reuben Gilbert Gustavson	Doctor of Humanities

1954

Kenneth Fisher Warner	Doctor of Agriculture
Ivan Daley Wood	Doctor of Agriculture
Jay Wright Forrester	Doctor of Engineering
Frederick Adam Figi	Doctor of Science
Louis Christian Zopf	Doctor of Science

1955

Arthur William Farrall	Doctor of Engineering
Elmer Clark Bratt	Doctor of Laws
Hollis Leland Caswell	Doctor of Laws
Homer Leroy Shantz	Doctor of Laws
Leslie Lewis Zook	Doctor of Science
John Clare Whitehorn	Doctor of Science

1956

Lee Alton Kilgore	Doctor of Engineering
Darryl Francis Zanuck	Doctor of Humanities
Benjamin Albert Botkin	Doctor of Letters

1957
William Jay Turnbull   Doctor of Engineering
Clarence A. Davis   Doctor of Laws
Paul Bigelow Sears   Doctor of Laws
John Kent Selleck   Doctor of Laws
Henry Margenau   Doctor of Science

1958
George Fred Sprague   Doctor of Science
Franklin D. Murphy   Doctor of Science

1959
Charles Yoder Thompson   Doctor of Agriculture
Walter Dietrich Behlen   Doctor of Engineering
John Moore Allison   Doctor of Laws

1960
William Arthur McConnell   Doctor of Engineering
Earl O. Heady   Doctor of Science
Gerald Lloyd Phillippe   Doctor of Laws
Loren Corey Eiseley   Doctor of Letters

1961
J. Lee Rankin   Doctor of Laws
Ruth M. Leverton   Doctor of Science

1962
Louis Carl Lundstrom   Doctor of Engineering
Glenn Willard Burton   Doctor of Science
Donald Frederick Othmer   Doctor of Engineering
Arthur Thomas Jersild   Doctor of Laws
Carl M. Reinert   Doctor of Laws
Milan James Kopac   Doctor of Science

1963
Samuel Miller Brownell   Doctor of Laws
Hazel Pearl Abel   Doctor of Laws
Anatole G. Mazour   Doctor of Laws
G. Robert Coatney   Doctor of Science
Otto H. Liebers   Doctor of Laws

1964
Wayne Otis Reed   Doctor of Laws
Percy Craig Spencer   Doctor of Laws
Wayne H. Worthington   Doctor of Engineering
Peter Kiewit   Doctor of Laws
Georgian Adams   Doctor of Science
William Charles Norris   Doctor of Science
Theos Jardin Thompson   Doctor of Science
Arthur C. Bryan   Doctor of Laws
Samuel C. Waugh   Doctor of Laws

1965
John Robert Brown   Doctor of Laws
Albert Henry Moseman   Doctor of Science
William O. Jones   Doctor of Science
Elmo B. Roper   Doctor of Science
Forrest Edwin Behm   Doctor of Laws

Ihsan Dogramaci   Doctor of Laws
Arjay Ray Miller   Doctor of Laws

1966
Earl Meloy Cline   Doctor of Laws
David Fellman   Doctor of Laws
Harold Frank Robinson   Doctor of Science
James Herbert Jensen   Doctor of Laws
Edward Stanley   Doctor of Laws
Doretta Schlaphoff Hoffman   Doctor of Science

1967
Joseph Grant Knapp   Doctor of Science
J. Martin Klotsche   Doctor of Laws
Hart Perry   Doctor of Laws
Merle Eugene Curti   Doctor of Letters
Robert Arnold Alberty   Doctor of Science
Robert Henry Dietz   Doctor of Science
Joseph McVicker Hunt   Doctor of Science
Aileene Simpson Lockhart   Doctor of Science

1968
Joyce Clyde Hall   Doctor of Humanities
Ralph Johnson Bunche   Doctor of Humane Letters
Donald Theodore Meier   Doctor of Laws
Lee C. White   Doctor of Laws
Laurens Williams   Doctor of Laws
Wright Morris   Doctor of Letters
Henry Arnold Karo   Doctor of Science
Vance D. Rogers   Doctor of Humane Letters
John B. Dawson   Doctor of Laws
William H. Kearns   Doctor of Laws

1969 (Midyear Commencement and Centennial Convocation)
Virgil Edward Boyd   Doctor of Laws
Adrian Morris Srb   Doctor of Science
Robert F. Goheen   Doctor of Laws
Whitney M. Young, Jr.   Doctor of Humane Letters
Olga Nielsen Sheldon
  (Mrs. A. Bromley Sheldon)   Doctor of Humane Letters
Edwin John Wellhausen   Doctor of Science
Sarah Ladd Woods
  (Mrs. Thomas H. Woods)   Doctor of Humane Letters
J. George Harrar   Doctor of Laws

1969 (Summer Commencement)
Reuben Nakian   Doctor of Fine Arts
Martha Groves McKelvie   Doctor of Humane Letters
Theodore C. Sorensen   Doctor of Laws
C. Dwight Waldo   Doctor of Letters
Francis P. Schmitt   Doctor of Music
Margaret I. Liston   Doctor of Science

Recipients of Distinguished Service Awards and Nebraska Builder Awards 1940–1960

A certificate and a medal awarded jointly by the Executive Committee of the University of Nebraska Alumni Association and the Board of Regents of the University of Nebraska.

1940
Emory R. Buckner, A.B. 1904, New York City
Richard C. Patterson, Jr., x09, New York City
Guy E. Reed, A.B. 1911, Chicago
George W. Holmes, x03, Lincoln

1941
Paul T. Babson, B.A. 1917, Boston
Herbert Brownell, Jr., B.A. 1924, New York
Alvin E. Evans, M.A. 1898, Lexington, Kentucky
John H. Agee, LL.B. 1910, Lincoln
R. E. Campbell, B.Sc. in E.E. 1910, Lincoln

1942
Alfred H. Luncin, A.B. 1906, LL.B. 1906, Seattle
R. A. Van Orsdel, A.B. 1906, Washington, D.C.
Alice von Bergen, A.B. 1919, Omaha
Wendell Berge, A.B. 1925, Washington, D.C.
Arthur A. Dobson, B.Sc. 1911, Lincoln

1943
William G. Altstadt, B.Sc. in Bus. Adm. 1924, Los Angeles, Calif.
Edward Provost Brown, B.L. 1892, Davey, Nebraska
Guy C. Chambers, LL.B. 1916, Lincoln
Admiral Emory D. Stanley, A.B. 1904, Washington D.C.

1944
Frank H. Woods, 1890, Lincoln
Vincent C. Hascall, 1912, Omaha
Howard S. Wilson, 1917, Lincoln
Merril V. Reed, 1914, New York

1945
Dr. Walter H. Judd, 1920, Washington, D.C.
Mrs. Donald W. Miller, 1910, Lincoln
Evert L. Stancliff, 1913, Mexico City, Mexico
Thurl B. Strain, 1914, Lincoln

1946
Charles Abel Bennett, 1911, Leland, Mississippi
Earl Cline, 1913, Lincoln
Nathan J. Gold, 1913, Lincoln
Joe W. Seacrest, 1919, Lincoln

Nebraska Builder Award
Robert Henry Willis

1947
Marion A. Shaw, 1917, David City
Andrew F. Schoeppel, 1922, Wichita, Kansas
C. Petrus Peterson, 1909, Lincoln
Drs. Francis F. and Enna Boose Tucker, 1894 and 1896, Daytona Beach, Florida
Mr. and Mrs. Fred C. (Adelloyd Whiting) Williams, 1900, Lincoln

Nebraska Builder Award
Paul Henry Grummann

1948
Louise Pound, 1892, Lincoln
Bertha Luckey, 1910, Cleveland, Ohio
Clarence E. Swanson, 1922, Lincoln
John L. Riddell, 1920, York
Kenneth S. Wherry, 1914, Pawnee City

Nebraska Builder Award
Asa Thomas Hill

1949
Willard J. Turnbull, 1925, Vicksburg, Mississippi
Dr. John D. Clark, 1905, Washington, D.C.
Max Meyer, 1906, Lincoln
Mrs. Ruth Bryan Rohde, x05, Ossining, New York
Maud Wilson, 1913, Corvallis, Oregon

1950
Clyde B. Dempster, 1917, Beatrice
Mrs. Gladyce Weil Simmons and Robert Glenmore Simmons, 1915, Lincoln
Dr. E. L. MacQuiddy, 1921, Omaha
Eugene Holland, 1913, Chicago

1951
Mary Ann Rokahr, 1914, Washington, D.C.
Samuel C. Waugh, 1915, Lincoln
Percy C. Spencer, 1916, New York City
L. R. Blanchard, 1911, Rochester, New York
Daniel Gutleben, 1900, San Francisco, California

Nebraska Builder Award
John Hyde Sweet

1952
Don E. Ahrens, 1914, Detroit, Michigan

John M. Allison, 1927, Washington, D.C.
Judge John C. Pickett, 1922, Cheyenne, Wyoming
Oliver B. Thorgrimson, 1901, Seattle, Washington
Judge Adolph E. Wenke, 1923, Stanton and Lincoln

1953
Dwight P. Griswold, 1914, Scottsbluff
Rear Admiral Alfred R. Harris, 1923, Great Lakes, Illinois
John F. Lawlor, 1922, Lincoln
Ruth Sheldon, 1920, Washington, D.C.
Charles L. Stone, 1898, Cleveland Heights, Ohio

1954
Spencer V. Cortelyou, 1902, Los Angeles, California
Mrs. Mortimer J. Brown (Mary Beth Wallace), x05, Niagara Falls, New York
James E. Lawrence, 1911, Lincoln
Orval L. Brace, 1916, Houston, Texas
Glenn Stearns Everts, 1920, Philadelphia, Pennsylvania

Nebraska Builder Award
Charles J. Warner, 1899, Waverly

1955
Harold (Tim) Corey, x17, Austin, Minnesota
Robert W. Devoe, 1909, Lincoln
Mrs. Roscoe Hill (Ruth Elizabeth Davis), 1929, Lincoln
Otto H. Liebers, 1913, Lincoln
Ralph E. Weaverling, 1911, Kansas City, Missouri

Nebraska Builder Award
Dr. George E. Condra, 1897, Lincoln

1956
Mrs. Haven N. Smith (Virginia Dodd), 1936, Chappell
Edwin J. Faulkner, 1932, Lincoln
John Kenneth Cozier, 1924, Shaker Heights, Ohio
Dr. George Nakagawa, 1924, Honolulu, T.H.
Eugene C. Dinsmore, 1921, Omaha

Nebraska Builder Award
Harry B. Coffee, 1913, Omaha

1957
Mrs. Harold P. Stebbins (Hazel Struble), 1930, Lincoln
J. Stewart Elliott, 1910, Beatrice
Ellsworth Moser, 1918, Omaha
J. Lee Rankin, 1928 (A.B.), 1930 (LL.B.), Washington, D.C.

Nebraska Builder Award
George W. Holmes, ex 1903, Lincoln

1958
Robert A. Hardt, 1922, Montclair, New Jersey
Dr. Earle G. Johnson, 1910, Grand Island
Allen J. Sutherland, 1918, San Diego, California

Nebraska Builder Award
Otto Kotouc, Sr., 1908, Humboldt

1959
Norman C. Carlson, Lincoln

Matthew G. Herold, New York, New York
Arthur W. Sampson, Berkeley, California

1960
Mr. and Mrs. Roy M. Green (Norma Kidd), Lincoln
Dr. Elizabeth Mason-Hohl, Hollywood, California
Charles W. Steadman, Cleveland, Ohio

Nebraska Builder Award
Morris E. Jacobs, Omaha

1961
David L. Erickson, Lincoln
William R. (Link) Lyman, San Marino, California
Floyd S. Oldt, Dallas, Texas
James Stuart, Lincoln

Nebraska Builder Awards
Byron Dunn, Lincoln
George E. Johnson, Hastings

1962
George B. Cook, Lincoln
James R. Lineburg, Los Angeles, California
Edward W. Lyman, Omaha
Anan Raymond, Chicago, Illinois

Nebraska Builder Award
Willis A. Strauss, Omaha

1963
Perry W. Branch, Lincoln
Mrs. Perry W. Branch, Lincoln
Ralph E. Kiplinger, Omaha
Carl W. Olson, Lincoln
Mrs. Howard R. Peterson, Chicago
Leslie A. Welch, Kansas City, Missouri

Nebraska Builder Awards
Essie E. Davis, Hyannis
Bennett S. Martin, Lincoln

1964
Jessie Stearns Buscher, Washington, D.C.
Leo Hill, Lincoln
Fay Smith, Imperial

Nebraska Builder Awards
George B. Cook, Lincoln
Sterling H. McCaw, Norfolk
Henry F. Klosterman, David City

1965
Herbert Cameron, Los Angeles, California
Robert A. Dobson, Lincoln
Maurice S. Hevelone, Beatrice
Mrs. J. Merton Kuhr, Blair

Nebraska Builder Awards
Gilbert Carl Swanson, Omaha
Joseph W. Seacrest, Lincoln

1966
Margaret Fedde, 1914, Lincoln
Felber Maasdam, 1934, Burbank, California
Dr. Merritt C. Pedersen, 1922, Lincoln
Grace L. Spacht, 1924, Portland, Oregon

Nebraska Builder Awards
William W. Cooks, Sr.
Nathan Jules Gold, Lincoln

1967
Dr. Paul O. Bare, 1934, Wilmington, Delaware
Harry P. Letton, Jr., 1935, Los Angeles, California
Howard E. Miller, x03, Cleveland, Ohio
Edmund Steeves, 1939, Detroit, Michigan
Milton I. Wick, 1922, Scottsdale, Arizona

Nebraska Builder Awards
Robert Erle Campbell, Lincoln
George C. Gerdes, Alliance
A. V. Sorensen, Omaha

1968
Ford Bates, 1915, Omaha
Milton C. Ebers, x34, Fremont
D. A. Forsberg, 1928, Madison, Wisconsin
Frederick E. Lange, 1928, Minneapolis, Minnesota
Alan C. McIntosh, 1928, Luverne, Minnesota

Nebraska Builder Awards
William Eugene Galbraith, Beemer
Forrest Stetson Lee, Brownlee
Elijah A. Levitt, York
H. C. Filley, Lincoln

1969
Dr. Paul M. Bancroft, Lincoln
Ernest C. Hodder, Scottsdale, Arizona
John S. McDermott, Kansas City, Missouri
Walter L. Meyer, Littleton, Colorado
Winslow M. Van Brunt, Bellevue

Nebraska Builder Awards
Clarence E. Swanson, Lincoln
Elwood N. Thompson, Lincoln
J. Leroy Welsh, Omaha

A NOTE ON SOURCES

NEARLY ALL OF THIS *History of the University of Nebraska* has been written from primary source materials in the custody of the University Archives. The manuscript collection of each chancellor and acting chancellor of the period—Samuel Avery, 1908–28; Edgar A. Burnett, 1927–38; Chauncey S. Boucher, 1938–46; Reuben G. Gustavson, 1946–53; John K. Selleck, 1953–54; and Clifford M. Hardin, 1954–69—contains a wealth of information. Included in these files are correspondence with members of the Board of Regents, governors, legislators, University staff members, students, parents, citizens, and nationally recognized leaders in higher education, business, and politics. These collections also include manuscripts of public speeches and a wide variety of University committee reports.

The *Minutes* of the University of Nebraska Board of Regents contain the official record of all action taken by the governing board. The incidental papers of the Board of Regents contain much of the material used by the board in the formulation of its policies. Additional material in the custody of the Archives includes a wide variety of reports prepared by members of the institution's administrative staff and faculty for either the chancellor or the board.

Sources pertinent to the institution's academic development include the minutes of the faculty meetings of the various colleges, the correspondence files of several deans and the separate colleges' catalogs. Additionally, the chancellors' files contain considerable correspondence regarding the development of academic programing.

Archival sources relative to student life include the minutes of student organizations, scrapbooks of campus groups, and the correspondence of University officials regarding campus activities. The student newspaper, the *Daily Nebraskan;* the annual, *Cornhusker;* and the *Nebraska Alumnus* also provided valuable information.

Useful published materials which were extensively used included the Legislative Journals of the State of Nebraska for each regular and special session of the half-century. The Lincoln, *Nebraska State Journal* (which published under several changes in title during the period) and the Omaha *World-Herald* are newspapers which provided good coverage of University affairs and often included direct quotations from University officials, political leaders, and citizens unavailable in any other source. Some other published sources used which provided insight into the development of the University and the state include: Addison E. Sheldon, *Nebraska, The Land and the People* (Chicago: Lewis Publishing Co., 1931); John D. Hicks, *My Life with History* (Lincoln; University of Nebraska Press, 1968); John Andrew Rice, *I Came Out of the Eighteenth Century* (New York: Harpers, 1942); Frederick Ware with Gregg McBride, *Fifty Years of Football* (Omaha: World Publishing Co., 1940); James C. Olson, *History of Nebraska* (Lincoln: University of Nebraska Press, 1966); and Robert N. Manley, *Centennial History of the University of Nebraska,* Vol. I (Lincoln: University of Nebraska Press, 1969).

Except for those credited to other sources, all photographs used to illustrate this book were furnished by the University of Nebraska.

AFTERWORD

FEW INSTITUTIONS have more resiliency than a university. This narration of the first one hundred years of existence of the University of Nebraska underscores this point with eloquence!

Born in a period of great uncertainty, this pioneer land-grant institution has withstood the threats of war, of drought, of depression, of legislative assault, of questionable governance, of meager financial resources—and seems to have grown stronger with each victory. These pages have recorded the periods of adversity but also moments of triumph for this pioneering institution—and there have been proud accomplishments. Internationally recognized names like Pound and Cather and Sandoz serve as permanent testimony to the contributions of the University. Throughout this recorded history runs a spirit far more important than the names and dates and events—a guiding spirit which is both symbolic and characteristic of the University of Nebraska. Perhaps it can be described best with a single word—*partnership*—because more than any other single descriptive quality, this notion emerges. Joint survival, joint development, joint achievement through partnership between a university and a state and the people of a state.

To be sure, there have been scholars of distinction—but they rarely served in the abstract sense of scholarship for the sake of scholarship.

There have been distinguished scientists—but their science seemed not so much for the sake of pure science as for service to the state and its people.

Even the athletic teams have been far more than campus activities—they have served as symbols for all the people of Nebraska.

No single quality emerges with the force of this sense of being a part of, and a party to, the development of a state—a true *state* university.

And now we turn to the tasks of the second century.

No one can doubt that the second century of the University of Nebraska will bring new problems, new threats, new challenges. We can only speculate as to their precise nature, but that they will come can be forecast with certainty.

Survival—in a new sense—will be a recurring concern. Evidence grows to suggest that institutions of higher learning will be expected to explore new techniques, new approaches, even new institutional forms in the decades immediately ahead. Committed to helping individuals and society to avoid obsolescence, strong suggestions continue to surface that colleges and universities may themselves be suffering from this very malady!

Collective bargaining is already emerging as a central issue on many campuses in America. If it becomes a national phenomenon, as is forecast by many educational leaders, then a new set of problems will evolve. What of the traditional pattern of governance within the university? What of the role of the faculty as partners in the internal policy determinations? Will students then unionize as a protective move? What will be the resulting role of legislative bodies, governing boards, administrators?

Coordination is a rapidly emerging concern for all those involved in the broader view of higher education. This notion is currently directed to statewide coordination, but many educational analysts predict that coordination will extent to multi-state compacts, especially at the graduate and professional levels. If this development occurs, new administrative arrangements—often complex—must be developed.

No listing of the probable new concerns for public universities in the next century—however tentative and limited—could omit identification of a new partner in the enterprise. During the first hundred years, the relationship between the land-grant institutions and the federal government was developed around the concept of federal funds for agricultural research and extension. For the most part, the federal government was a silent and congenial partner, a provider of funds for these programs with few strings attached. Late in the century other forms of federal aid came into the picture, and with each passing year the role of the federal government became more vigorous. As the second century of this University dawns, there is no longer a question about the involvement of the federal government. It is a strong and muscular third party, and those who have been involved in the past ten years have little if any doubt about the permanence of this third party in the enterprise. Federal funds will play an increasingly important role, and the voice of the federal establishment will be heard with frequency and with clarity.

These problems, and others, confront this University as it moves into the second century of service to Nebraska. But no problem, no concern, no priority— no challenge—is greater for the University of Nebraska at this moment in its history than the task of improving the academic quality of the institution. This is imperative if it is to make its maximum contribution to the development of a state possessing extraordinary potential. It is no accident that the University of Nebraska was included among the first four public universities in America elected to join that group of distinguished American universities known as the Association of American Universities. That high standing among universities had been reached because the citizens of this state developed an expectation that their state university was to rank among the best, and they were willing to provide the resources to make this possible.

Now the mission must be to regain that standing among universities. This can be achieved but it can be done only if the citizens of this state join together, as they have done historically, with their government, with the regents, with the administration, and with the faculty to make this happen. It will call for a deliberate new commitment.

It will mean a new emphasis on the quality of instruction.

It will mean a new concern for graduate education that is recognized for its quality throughout America.

It will involve a new understanding of the entire learning process—the fundamental business of the University.

It will require a new appreciation for the role of the faculty and a new sense of dedication on the part of that faculty in bringing distinction to this University.

It means a renewed commitment to serving the people of Nebraska through research, through extension, and through new concepts of delivering education to the citizens of this state—a reinforcement of its historic role.

Above all, it calls for a renewed sense of pride in the University of Nebraska— on all its campuses.

The beginning of the second century signals what may well be a new era for higher education in general and for this University in particular. Precisely the form this "new era" will take is not yet known. Yet, for those involved in key management roles—trying to maintain a sense of perspective—some salient facts and factors emerge which have a special significance:

—Our society is increasingly complex and interrelated, and answers are demanded for questions which were unknown two decades ago.

—Our fund of knowledge is expanding at a rate unprecedented in the history of mankind—at a rate beyond the comprehension of most of us—and in the intricate interrelationship of this knowledge resides many of the solutions we so desperately seek.

—Our worldwide network of instantaneous communications—a development of the last decade—has opened a range of opportunities and responsibilities never imagined possible a quarter century ago.

—Change is so rapid in our newly discovered world community—political, economic, social change—that even our most informed and perceptive observers are overwhelmed by the events of a single day.

It is against this background—this recognition of the realities of our times—that we develop a sense of direction for this University—for all of higher education.

The only hope—the only conceivable hope—for coping with the dynamics of our society—for maintaining an orderly structure—is through the improved and accelerated development of our human resources. There simply is no other way. If we are to achieve an ordered and orderly society—if we stubbornly cling to the hope of peace and understanding among men—if we genuinely aspire to a fellowship of man where true freedom is understood and protected, where the goals of truth and justice and human dignity are cherished—if these are priority objectives of our society—then there is no alternative to higher education—improved, expanded, enriched higher education—available to all our citizens as a public investment.

It is an imperative of the second half of the twentieth century.

As we make ready for the responsibilities of the second hundred years of the University of Nebraska, it would be well to remind ourselves that this University was created more than one hundred years ago by a group of hardy pioneer citizens fighting for their very existence and uncertain always about the future. Even under these difficult and trying circumstances they made a fundamental decision—they concluded that the well-being of this state dictated that a public university of high quality be created. They wanted their sons and daughters to have an educational opportunity comparable to that anywhere in this nation. They had the vision to create this, the first public university west of the Missouri River. Beyond this, they had the courage to provide from their meager resources the funds to make it possible. For them this was an enormous sacrifice—far beyond that which we know today—but they did so with pride and enthusiasm.

They viewed it as an investment in tomorrow for Nebraska. It was their best bet for insuring the tomorrow which we enjoy today.

We, too, have a stake in tomorrow.

DURWARD B. VARNER

INDEX